PRIMARY SOURCES

The Great Works of Ancient Greece,

the Roman Empire and

the Middle Ages

4th edition

M. B. McLatchey

D1511429

DEDICATION

To our warriors

TABLE OF CONTENTS

PREFACE VI

PART I: GREECE.. 1

THE ILIAD (HOMER) 2
    BOOK I – QUARREL BETWEEN AGAMEMNON & ACHILLES 4
    BOOK XXII – ACHILLES AVENGES HIS COUSIN'S DEATH 13
    BOOK XXIV – PRIAM RANSOMS THE BODY OF HECTOR 20

THE ODYSSEY (HOMER) 32
    BOOK I – ULYSSES, THAT INGENIUS HERO 34
    BOOK II – TELEMACHUS EMBARKS TO FIND HIS FATHER 40
    BOOK IX – ULYSSES TELLS STORY OF HIS STRUGGLES................. 45
    BOOK X – AEOLUS, THE LAESTRYGONES, CIRCE 53
    BOOK XI – THE VISIT TO THE DEAD 61
    BOOK XII – THE SIRENS, SCYLLA AND CHARYBDIS 66
    BOOK XIII – ULYSSES RETURNS TO ITHACA 73
    BOOK XVI – FATHER-SON REUNION 77
    BOOK XVII – TELEMACHUS AND HIS MOTHER MEET 82
    BOOK XIX – ULYSSES INTERVIEWS PENELOPE 85
    BOOK XX – ULYSSES CANNOT SLEEP, SIGNS FROM HEAVEN 90
    BOOK XXI – TRIAL OF AXES, ULYSSES REVEALS HIMSELF 92
    BOOK XXII – THE KILLING OF THE SUITORS 95
    BOOK XXIII – PENELOPE RECOGNISES HER HUSBAND 100
    BOOK XXIV – MINERVA CALLS FOR PEACE 105

SAPPHO'S LYRICS 109
    LYRIC XXX 109
    LYRIC XXXVI 110
    LYRIC XLII 110
    LYRIC LV 110
    LYRIC LX 111

PLATO'S READINGS 112
    APOLOGY 114
    CRITO 132
    PHÆDO 143
    REPUBLIC – ALLEGORY OF THE CAVE 149

NICOMACHEAN ETHICS (ARISTOTLE).. 153
    THE ETHICS OF HAPPINESS... 153

PART II: THE ROMAN REPUBLIC AND EMPIRE **157**

TREATISE ON FRIENDSHIP (CICERO) 158

THE CARMINA OF CATULLUS 163
    LESBIA'S SPARROW...164
    TO LESBIA 165
    HOW THE LOVER LOVES 165

THE AENEID (VIRGIL) 166
    BOOK FIRST - THE COMING OF AENEAS TO CARTHAGE....................168
    BOOK FOURTH – THE LOVE OF DIDO, AND HER END 179
    BOOK SIXTH – THE VISION OF THE UNDERWORLD 189
    BOOK TWELFTH – THE SLAYING OF TURNUS 202

PART III: THE MIDDLE AGES...**209**

DIVINE COMEDY (DANTE)..210
    CANTO I 211
    CANTO II 214
    CANTO III..217

THE CANTERBURY TALES (CHAUCER) 222
    THE CANTERBURY TALES PROLOGUE 222
    THE PARDONER'S PROLOGUE 223

EVERYMAN (ANONYMOUS)..225

PART IV: ADDITIONAL READINGS..**249**

THE EMPEROR'S NEW CLOTHES (H.C. ANDERSON)..251
THE DECLARATION OF INDEPENDENCE (JEFFERSON) 255
FEDERALIST NO. 10 (MADISON)..258
FEDERALIST NO. 47 (MADISON)..262
THE CONSTITUTION OF THE UNITED STATES...266
THE BILL OF RIGHTS..274
DEMOCRACY IN AMERICA (DE TOCQUEVILLE) 276
BEN FRANKLIN READINGS (FRANKLIN) 281
    AUTOBIOGRAPHY 282
    THE WAY TO WEALTH: INDUSTRY PLUS FRUGALITY 286
    CONSTITUTIONAL CONVENTION ADDRESS ON PRAYER 289
A VINDICATION OF THE RIGHTS OF WOMAN (WOLLSTONECRAFT)....................290

True knowledge exists in knowing that you know nothing.

- Socrates 469 BC–399 BC

In defense of the man who searches for the truth in life, the Greek philosopher Socrates maintained that knowledge was not revealed by reciting a litany of accepted facts, but rather by uncovering what remained unknown. That is, the wise man is the one who knows what he does not know. Take nothing for granted. Question accepted wisdom. Pursue the question until it reveals another question. The methods that Socrates recommended to his students describe the modus operandi of scholars throughout history: know the accepted interpretations of the past and, in a noble pursuit of the truth, question them.

In their pursuit of the truth, scholars make use of two types of sources: primary and secondary. Briefly defined, whereas secondary sources provide scholarly interpretations of the past, primary sources provide first-hand testimony of the past. Unlike the historian who summarizes Cicero's "Lecture on Friendship," the primary source gives us Cicero himself – his exact words as they appeared in a letter that he sent to a friend in the 1st century B.C.

As a supplement to any survey text that students might use in an introductory-level humanities course, this collection of primary sources is intended to expose students to the original voices of the past. Primary sources can appear in many forms. They may include letters, manuscripts, diaries, journals, newspapers, speeches, interviews, memoirs, documents produced by government agencies such as Congress or the Office of the President, photographs, audio recordings, film or video recordings, research data, and objects or artifacts such as works of art or ancient roads, buildings, tools, and weapons.

While there will always be a history of scholarly commentary that students of the humanities should become acquainted with, the primary source offers a rare and unfiltered look at figures and events from the past. As such, the primary source invites a fresh look into the past that may ultimately cast doubt on accepted scholarship – and that may even alter accepted interpretations of the past. Simply put, in our search for the truth, the primary source is of primary importance. It serves as the raw material to interpret the past that scholars often trust most.

The primary sources compiled herein present merely a sampling of the most representative works from the Ancient Period through the Middle Ages, plus an additional selection of more modern voices. These works are representative in that they feature ideas and values that characterized their historical periods. In cases where the length of a work prohibited reproduction in total, excerpts are presented.

Because a reading proficiency in the ancient languages is not typically expected of undergraduate students in the humanities, ancient texts presented here have been translated into English. Hence, to the extent that students are not exposed to the nuances of the original Greek or Latin texts, they remain one step removed from the true primary sources.

For this fourth edition, new texts from the ancient period have been added in order to provide a fuller understanding of foundational literary works that have defined western culture. New to this edition, Homer's *Odyssey* broadens our scope on questions begun in its companion epic, *The Iliad*. Excerpts from *The Odyssey* were carefully selected with an interest in exposing students to the evolution of ancient Greece from a time that honored the military warrior to a time that honored the citizen warrior.

Also in this edition, more selections have been added to the *Additional Readings* section to invite students to explore more extensively the imprint of early political and social ideas on later thinkers. When, for example, Thomas Jefferson imports Aristotle's definition of *happiness* for his Declaration of Independence, he also imports ancient Greek ideals. When Ben Franklin calls on Socrates or Cicero in his 18th-century speeches, he recommends to his peers that they use the ancients for their models. In reading across historical lines, students have the opportunity here to examine cultural connections – or differences – regarding a variety of topics.

For their recommendations on how to improve this new edition for their practical use, I especially thank my students. As a result of their suggestions, I have provided in this edition more historical backdrop to the readings and more frequent annotations for guidance in the readings.

I have also kept the students' best interests in mind when selecting new translations for this edition. I have favored translations that offer relative ease in reading, but that also invite students to explore the complex cultural and literary questions in these works. In addition, the translations presented here offer us a lens on literary history. Samuel Butler's use of Roman names throughout his translations of Homer's *Iliad* and *Odyssey*, for example, recalls a long tradition of translations of Homer up to the 1950's. Whereas the Greeks relied heavily on an oral tradition and left us virtually nothing in writing, the Romans were great recorders of ancient history and literature. As such, when translating works such as Homer's great epics, the Romans passed on – and, for centuries, scholars adopted – the Romans' Latinized names for Greek gods and heroes. Butler is one of those scholars. In his translations of Homer's epics, *The Iliad* and *The Odyssey*, Butler employs Roman names for ancient gods and the Latin variant, Ulysses, rather than the Greek name, Odysseus. For the purposes of most scholarship, the names Odysseus and Ulysses refer to the same mythic warrior and should be regarded as interchangeable.

It is worth noting that Butler's translation of Homer's *Odyssey* is likely to have been the text that influenced later literary works well into the 21st century A.D . Some examples are Dante Alighieri's 14th-century *Inferno*, Miguel de Cervantes' *Don Quixote* (1605), Joseph Conrad's *Heart of Darkness* (1902), James Joyce's *Ulysses* (1922), and even L. Frank Baum's *The Wonderful Wizard of Oz* (1900) and *"Sinbad the Sailor"* from Arabian Nights.

The readings in this text are divided into four parts. Parts I through III move chronologically from the Greek Heroic Age to the periods of the Roman Republic and the Late Middle Ages. In Part IV, *Additional Readings*, a selection of 18th-century works invites students to explore links between ancient and modern ideas and to consider the larger social and political questions that have defined the western world for generations. In particular, students may examine the degree to which the shapers of America's Republic consciously inherited the values of the world's first Democracy in Greece and first Republic in Rome.

Throughout the book, I offer both introductory commentaries and side notes. The introductions are intended to help students see the historical contexts for the literary works. In cases where I am not the author of these introductions, I have indicated as much. The marginal annotations throughout the text serve two purposes: some notes simply summarize the narratives; others highlight key themes that the works explore. My hope is that these notes will help students to not only understand the texts, but to also see how they fit into a history of ideas and events.

I encourage students in the humanities to explore these core texts as well as related primary documents in their entirety. Widely available today on the internet, these primary sources offer today's students in the humanities an exceptional opportunity to hear from the voices of the past, and to discover – just as Socrates had hoped – what they do not know.

M.B. McLatchey

July 2015

Fourth Edition

Let me not then die ingloriously and without a struggle,

but let me first do some great thing

that shall be told among men hereafter.

— Homer, *The Iliad*

PART I: GREECE

ANCIENT AND CLASSICAL PERIODS

THE ILIAD

BY HOMER

TRANSLATED FROM THE GREEK BY SAMUEL BUTLER

Introduction by M. B. McLatchey

The Iliad is among the oldest works of Western literature and its written version is usually dated around 750 B.C. Traditionally attributed to the Greek poet, Homer, *The Iliad* is an epic poem that contains over 15,000 lines. It is written in what is now called Homeric Greek, a literary amalgam of Ionic Greek with other dialects.

In the epic's opening lines the poet calls on the muses of poetry to inspire his poetic performance. He also introduces us to the main character, Achilles, through whom the epic will explore its central question of what it means to live a heroic life.

The story is set during the final few weeks in the final year of the Trojan war – a war that has wearied both the Greeks and the Trojans for a decade, and that has involved a ten-year siege of the city of Troy (Ilium) by a coalition of Greek states. The poem's mythic and historic values lie in the fact that many passages refer to Greek legends about the cause of the war and to prophesies of its hero's death and his heroic place in history.

Fig. 1: Shield of Achilles

The poem opens with a quarrel between the Greek King Agamemnon and his warrior general, Achilles. Their quarrel establishes the themes that loom throughout the epic. There is the theme of hubris – an excessive pride that misdirects the hero, Achilles; there is the ancient Greek concept of a universal order; and lastly, there is the struggle that the ancient Greeks saw between a man's fate and his free will.

Students often ask, *How did Achilles actually die?* What will define Achilles as hero in this epic is his readiness in the final scene to die gloriously – to finally embrace the prized Greek concept of *kleos*. This means, first and foremost, that he must die in the field that defines him, celebrating his unique talent. Ironically, Homer does not actually depict this final dying scene. Achilles' death will be revealed to us through later legends and through passages from Homer's companion epic, *The Odyssey*. At the end of *The Iliad*, Achilles emerges as the best of the Achaeans, not because he dies in the field that defines him, but because he proves himself capable of *metamorphosis* – in particular, a growth in character that aligns his talents to his country's ideals.

COMPLETE LIST OF BOOKS FROM THE ILIAD

BOOK I *   The quarrel between Agamemnon and Achilles & Achilles withdraws from the war

BOOK II   Jove sends a lying dream to Agamemnon; the Achaeans and Trojans war

BOOK III   Paris and Menelaus fight, and Paris is worsted and Venus saves him

BOOK IV   A quarrel in Olympus

BOOK V   Venus rescues Aeneas

BOOK VI   Hector and Andromache

BOOK VII   Hector and Ajax fight

BOOK VIII   Hector's triumph is stayed by nightfall

BOOK IX   The Embassy to Achilles

BOOK X   Ulysses and Diomed go out as spies

BOOK XI   Hector is wounded by Diomed and Paris wounds Diomed

BOOK XII   The Trojans and their allies break the wall, led on by Hector

BOOK XIII   Neptune helps the Achaeans

BOOK XIV   Hector is wounded

BOOK XV   The Trojans again become victorious

BOOK XVI   Patroclus fights in the armor of Achilles and is killed Hector

BOOK XVII   The fight around the body of Patroclus

BOOK XVIII   The grief of Achilles over Patroclus

BOOK XIX   Achilles is reconciled with Agamemnon

BOOK XX   A fight between Achilles and Aeneas and Achilles kills many Trojans

BOOK XXI   Achilles drives the Trojans within their gates

BOOK XXII *   The death of Hector

BOOK XXIII   The funeral of Patroclus and the funeral games

BOOK XXIV *   Priam ransoms the body of Hector; Hector's funeral

---

* Books included in this edittion of *Primary Sources.*

BOOK I – QUARREL BETWEEN AGAMEMNON & ACHILLES

The quarrel between Agamemnon and Achilles opens the poem and establishes Achilles' character. Achilles withdraws from the war, and sends his mother Thetis to ask Jove to help the Trojans win, thus causing Agamemnon to realize Achilles' military worth.

Sing, O goddess, the anger of Achilles son of Peleus, that brought countless ills upon the Achaeans. Many a brave soul did it send hurrying down to Hades, and many a hero did it yield a prey to dogs and vultures, for so were the counsels of Jove fulfilled from the day on which the son of Atreus, king of men, and great Achilles, first fell out with
5   one another.

And which of the gods was it that set them on to quarrel? It was the son of Jove and Leto; for he was angry with the king and sent a pestilence upon the host to plague the people, because the son of Atreus had dishonored Chryses his priest.

Achilles' arrogance and temper create disastrous consequences in this epic. Because King Agamemnon dishonored a priest, the gods delivered a plague upon the Greeks.

Now Chryses had come to the ships of the Achaeans to free his daughter, and had
10   brought with him a great ransom: moreover he bore in his hand the scepter of Apollo wreathed with a suppliant's wreath, and he besought the Achaeans, but most of all the two sons of Atreus, who were their chiefs.

"Sons of Atreus," he cried, "and all other Achaeans, may the gods who dwell in Olympus grant you to sack the city of Priam, and to reach your homes in safety; but
15   free my daughter, and accept a ransom for her, in reverence to Apollo, son of Jove."

On this the rest of the Achaeans with one voice were for respecting the priest and taking the ransom that he offered; but not so Agamemnon, who spoke fiercely to him and sent him roughly away. "Old man," said he, "let me not find you tarrying about our ships, nor yet coming hereafter. Your scepter of the god and your wreath shall profit you
20   nothing. I will not free her. She shall grow old in my house at Argos far from her own home, busying herself with her loom and visiting my couch; so go, and do not provoke me or it shall be the worse for you."

Priest asks gods for their help.

The old man feared him and obeyed. Not a word he spoke, but went by the shore of the sounding sea and prayed apart to King Apollo whom lovely Leto had borne. "Hear
25   me," he cried, "O god of the silver bow, that protectest Chryse and holy Cilla and rulest Tenedos with thy might, hear me oh thou of Sminthe. If I have ever decked your temple with garlands, or burned your thigh-bones in fat of bulls or goats, grant my prayer, and let your arrows avenge these my tears upon the Danaans."

Gods grant priest his wishes: 10 days of disease to Greek people and cattle.

Thus did he pray, and Apollo heard his prayer. He came down furious from the summits
30   of Olympus, with his bow and his quiver upon his shoulder, and the arrows rattled on his back with the rage that trembled within him. He sat himself down away from the ships with a face as dark as night, and his silver bow rang death as he shot his arrow in the midst of them. First he smote their mules and their hounds, but presently he aimed his shafts at the people themselves, and all day long the pyres of the dead were burning.

For nine whole days he shot his arrows among the people, but upon the tenth day Achilles called them in assembly—moved thereto by Juno, who saw the Achaeans in their death-throes and had compassion upon them. Then, when they were got together, he rose and spoke among them.

Achilles convenes Achaeans and inquires why the gods are angry. How do the Greeks seem to understand their relationship to their gods?

5 "Son of Atreus," said he, "I deem that we should now turn roving home if we would escape destruction, for we are being cut down by war and pestilence at once. Let us ask some priest or prophet, or some reader of dreams (for dreams, too, are of Jove) who can tell us why Phoebus Apollo is so angry, and say whether it is for some vow that we have broken, or hecatomb that we have not offered, and whether he will accept the
10 savour of lambs and goats without blemish, so as to take away the plague from us."

With these words he sat down, and Calchas son of Thestor, wisest of augurs, who knew things past present and to come, rose to speak. He it was who had guided the Achaeans with their fleet to Ilius, through the prophesyings with which Phoebus Apollo had inspired him. With all sincerity and goodwill he addressed them thus:—

Prophet Calchas exposes Agamemnon as cause for the gods' anger.

15 "Achilles, loved of heaven, you bid me tell you about the anger of King Apollo, I will therefore do so; but consider first and swear that you will stand by me heartily in word and deed, for I know that I shall offend one who rules the Argives with might, to whom all the Achaeans are in subjection. A plain man cannot stand against the anger of a king, who if he swallow his displeasure now, will yet nurse revenge till he has wreaked it.
20 Consider, therefore, whether or no you will protect me."

And Achilles answered, "Fear not, but speak as it is borne in upon you from heaven, for by Apollo, Calchas, to whom you pray, and whose oracles you reveal to us, not a Danaan at our ships shall lay his hand upon you, while I yet live to look upon the face of the earth—no, not though you name Agamemnon himself, who is by far the
25 foremost of the Achaeans."

Thereon the seer spoke boldly. "The god," he said, "is angry neither about vow nor hecatomb, but for his priest's sake, whom Agamemnon has dishonored, in that he would not free his daughter nor take a ransom for her; therefore has he sent these evils upon us, and will yet send others. He will not deliver the Danaans from this pestilence
30 till Agamemnon has restored the girl without fee or ransom to her father, and has sent a holy hecatomb to Chryse. Thus we may perhaps appease him."

With these words he sat down, and Agamemnon rose in anger. His heart was black with rage, and his eyes flashed fire as he scowled on Calchas and said, "Seer of evil, you never yet prophesied smooth things concerning me, but have ever loved to foretell that which
35 was evil. You have brought me neither comfort nor performance; and now you come seeing among Danaans, and saying that Apollo has plagued us because I would not take a ransom for this girl, the daughter of Chryses. I have set my heart on keeping her in my own house, for I love her better even than my own wife Clytemnestra, whose peer she is alike in form and feature, in understanding and accomplishments. Still I will give
40 her up if I must, for I would have the people live, not die; but you must find me a prize

Agamemnon responds angrily to Calchas's report that the king is the cause of the gods' anger. What character traits does the king reveal in the following speech?

instead, or I alone among the Argives shall be without one. This is not well; for you behold, all of you, that my prize is to go else whither."

Achilles advises Agamemnon to return priest's daughter and appease the gods.

And Achilles answered, "Most noble son of Atreus, covetous beyond all mankind, how shall the Achaeans find you another prize? We have no common store from which to
5   take one. Those we took from the cities have been awarded; we cannot disallow the awards that have been made already. Give this girl, therefore, to the god, and if ever Jove grants us to sack the city of Troy we will requite you three and fourfold."

How does Agamemnon disrespect Achilles in front of his troops?

Then Agamemnon said, "Achilles, valiant though you be, you shall not thus outwit me. You shall not overreach and you shall not persuade me. Are you to keep your own prize,
10 while I sit tamely under my loss and give up the girl at your bidding? Let the Achaeans find me a prize in fair exchange to my liking, or I will come and take your own, or that of Ajax or of Ulysses; and he to whomsoever I may come shall rue my coming. But of this we will take thought hereafter; for the present, let us draw a ship into the sea, and find a crew for her expressly; let us put a hecatomb on board, and let us send Chryseis
15 also; further, let some chief man among us be in command, either Ajax, or Idomeneus, or yourself, son of Peleus, mighty warrior that you are, that we may offer sacrifice and appease the anger of the god."

How does Achilles disrespect his king, Agamemnon? What cultural/military codes does Achilles say Agamemnon violated?

Achilles scowled at him and answered, "You are steeped in insolence and lust of gain. With what heart can any of the Achaeans do your bidding, either on foray or in open
20 fighting? I came not warring here for any ill the Trojans had done me. I have no quarrel with them. They have not raided my cattle nor my horses, nor cut down my harvests on the rich plains of Phthia; for between me and them there is a great space, both mountain and sounding sea. We have followed you, Sir Insolence! for your pleasure, not ours—to gain satisfaction from the Trojans for your shameless self and for
25 Menelaus. You forget this, and threaten to rob me of the prize for which I have toiled, and which the sons of the Achaeans have given me. Never when the Achaeans sack any rich city of the Trojans do I receive so good a prize as you do, though it is my hands that do the better part of the fighting. When the sharing comes, your share is far the largest, and I, forsooth, must go back to my ships, take what I can get and be thankful,
30 when my labor of fighting is done. Now, therefore, I shall go back to Phthia; it will be much better for me to return home with my ships, for I will not stay here dishonored to gather gold and substance for you."

Agamemnon angrily dismisses Achilles.

And Agamemnon answered, "Fly if you will, I shall make you no prayers to stay you. I have others here who will do me honor, and above all Jove, the lord of counsel. There
35 is no king here so hateful to me as you are, for you are ever quarrelsome and ill-affected. What though you be brave? Was it not heaven that made you so? Go home, then, with your ships and comrades to lord it over the Myrmidons. I care neither for you nor for your anger; and thus will I do: since Phoebus Apollo is taking Chryseis from me, I shall send her with my ship and my followers, but I shall come to your tent and take your
40 own prize Briseis, that you may learn how much stronger I am than you are, and that another may fear to set himself up as equal or comparable with me."

The son of Peleus was furious, and his heart within his shaggy breast was divided whether to draw his sword, push the others aside, and kill the son of Atreus, or to restrain himself and check his anger. While he was thus in two minds, and was drawing
45 his mighty sword from its scabbard, Minerva came down from heaven (for Juno had sent her in the love she bore to them both), and seized the son of Peleus by his yellow hair, visible to him alone, for of the others no man could see her. Achilles turned in

amaze, and by the fire that flashed from her eyes at once knew that she was Minerva. "Why are you here," said he, "daughter of aegis-bearing Jove? To see the pride of Agamemnon, son of Atreus? Let me tell you—and it shall surely be—he shall pay for this insolence with his life."

5 And Minerva said, "I come from heaven, if you will hear me, to bid you stay your anger. Juno has sent me, who cares for both of you alike. Cease, then, this brawling, and do not draw your sword; rail at him if you will, and your railing will not be vain, for I tell you—and it shall surely be—that you shall hereafter receive gifts three times as splendid by reason of this present insult. Hold, therefore, and obey."

God intervenes. Achilles decides not to kill his king. What conflicts are examined here?

10 "Goddess," answered Achilles, "however angry a man may be, he must do as you two command him. This will be best, for the gods ever hear the prayers of him who has obeyed them."

He stayed his hand on the silver hilt of his sword, and thrust it back into the scabbard as Minerva bade him. Then she went back to Olympus among the other gods, and to
15 the house of aegis-bearing Jove.

But the son of Peleus again began railing at the son of Atreus, for he was still in a rage. "Wine-bibber," he cried, "with the face of a dog and the heart of a hind, you never dare to go out with the host in fight, nor yet with our chosen men in ambuscade. You shun this as you do death itself. You had rather go round and rob his prizes from any man
20 who contradicts you. You devour your people, for you are king over a feeble folk; otherwise, son of Atreus, henceforward you would insult no man. Therefore I say, and swear it with a great oath—nay, by this my scepter which shalt sprout neither leaf nor shoot, nor bud anew from the day on which it left its parent stem upon the mountains— for the axe stripped it of leaf and bark, and now the sons of the Achaeans bear it as
25 judges and guardians of the decrees of heaven—so surely and solemnly do I swear that hereafter they shall look fondly for Achilles and shall not find him. In the day of your distress, when your men fall dying by the murderous hand of Hector, you shall not know how to help them, and shall rend your heart with rage for the hour when you offered insult to the bravest of the Achaeans."

Achilles angrily addresses Agamemnon. What characterization of his king does Achilles present? What does this speech reveal about Achilles' character?

30 With this the son of Peleus dashed his gold-bestudded scepter on the ground and took his seat, while the son of Atreus was beginning fiercely from his place upon the other side. Then uprose smooth-tongued Nestor, the facile speaker of the Pylians, and the words fell from his lips sweeter than honey. Two generations of men born and bred in Pylos had passed away under his rule, and he was now reigning over the third. With all
35 sincerity and goodwill, therefore, he addressed them thus:—

"Of a truth," he said, "a great sorrow has befallen the Achaean land. Surely Priam with his sons would rejoice, and the Trojans be glad at heart if they could hear this quarrel between you two, who are so excellent in fight and counsel. I am older than either of you; therefore be guided by me. Moreover I have been the familiar friend of men even
40 greater than you are, and they did not disregard my counsels. Never again can I behold such men as Pirithous and Dryas shepherd of his people, or as Caeneus, Exadius, godlike Polyphemus, and Theseus son of Aegeus, peer of the immortals. These were the mightiest men ever born upon this earth: mightiest were they, and when they fought the fiercest tribes of mountain savages they utterly overthrew them. I came from distant
45 Pylos, and went about among them, for they would have me come, and I fought as it was in me to do. Not a man now living could withstand them, but they heard my words,

What advice does the elder Nestor give to Agamemnon and Achilles?

and were persuaded by them. So be it also with yourselves, for this is the more excellent way. Therefore, Agamemnon, though you be strong, take not this girl away, for the sons of the Achaeans have already given her to Achilles; and you, Achilles, strive not further with the king, for no man who by the grace of Jove wields a scepter has like honor with
5 Agamemnon. You are strong, and have a goddess for your mother; but Agamemnon is stronger than you, for he has more people under him. Son of Atreus, check your anger, I implore you; end this quarrel with Achilles, who in the day of battle is a tower of strength to the Achaeans."

Agamemnon complains that Achilles is not a fit general. Would you agree?

And Agamemnon answered, "Sir, all that you have said is true, but this fellow must
10 needs become our lord and master: he must be lord of all, king of all, and captain of all, and this shall hardly be. Granted that the gods have made him a great warrior, have they also given him the right to speak with railing?"

Achilles threatens his king, then abandons him.

Achilles interrupted him. "I should be a mean coward," he cried, "were I to give in to you in all things. Order other people about, not me, for I shall obey no longer.
15 Furthermore I say—and lay my saying to your heart—I shall fight neither you nor any man about this girl, for those that take were those also that gave. But of all else that is at my ship you shall carry away nothing by force. Try, that others may see; if you do, my spear shall be reddened with your blood."

When they had quarreled thus angrily, they rose, and broke up the assembly at the ships
20 of the Achaeans. The son of Peleus went back to his tents and ships with the son of Menoetius and his company, while Agamemnon drew a vessel into the water and chose a crew of twenty oarsmen. He escorted Chryseis on board and sent moreover a hecatomb for the god. And Ulysses went as captain.

These, then, went on board and sailed their ways over the sea. But the son of Atreus
25 bade the people purify themselves; so they purified themselves and cast their filth into the sea. Then they offered hecatombs of bulls and goats without blemish on the sea-shore, and the smoke with the savour of their sacrifice rose curling up towards heaven.

Thus did they busy themselves throughout the host. But Agamemnon did not forget the threat that he had made Achilles, and called his trusty messengers and squires
30 Talthybius and Eurybates. "Go," said he, "to the tent of Achilles, son of Peleus; take Briseis by the hand and bring her hither; if he will not give her I shall come with others and take her—which will press him harder."

He charged them straightly further and dismissed them, whereon they went their way sorrowfully by the seaside, till they came to the tents and ships of the Myrmidons. They
35 found Achilles sitting by his tent and his ships, and ill-pleased he was when he beheld them. They stood fearfully and reverently before him, and never a word did they speak, but he knew them and said, "Welcome, heralds, messengers of gods and men; draw near; my quarrel is not with you but with Agamemnon who has sent you for the girl Briseis. Therefore, Patroclus, bring her and give her to them, but let them be witnesses
40 by the blessed gods, by mortal men, and by the fierceness of Agamemnon's anger, that if ever again there be need of me to save the people from ruin, they shall seek and they

shall not find. Agamemnon is mad with rage and knows not how to look before and after that the Achaeans may fight by their ships in safety."

Patroclus did as his dear comrade had bidden him. He brought Briseis from the tent and gave her over to the heralds, who took her with them to the ships of the Achaeans—and the woman was loth to go. Then Achilles went all alone by the side of the hoar sea, weeping and looking out upon the boundless waste of waters. He raised his hands in prayer to his immortal mother, "Mother," he cried, "you bore me doomed to live but for a little season; surely Jove, who thunders from Olympus, might have made that little glorious. It is not so. Agamemnon, son of Atreus, has done me dishonor, and has robbed me of my prize by force."

Achilles returns war prize, Briseis, to the king. He then calls on his immortal mother, Thetis, for aid. What loyalty issues are addressed here?

As he spoke he wept aloud, and his mother heard him where she was sitting in the depths of the sea hard by the old man her father. Forthwith she rose as it were a grey mist out of the waves, sat down before him as he stood weeping, caressed him with her hand, and said, "My son, why are you weeping? What is it that grieves you? Keep it not from me, but tell me, that we may know it together."

Achilles drew a deep sigh and said, "You know it; why tell you what you know well already? We went to Thebe the strong city of Eetion, sacked it, and brought hither the spoil. The sons of the Achaeans shared it duly among themselves, and chose lovely Chryseis as the mead of Agamemnon; but Chryses, priest of Apollo, came to the ships of the Achaeans to free his daughter, and brought with him a great ransom: moreover he bore in his hand the scepter of Apollo, wreathed with a suppliant's wreath, and he besought the Achaeans, but most of all the two sons of Atreus who were their chiefs.

Achilles relates his conflict with his king to his mother. Assess Achilles' version of reality. What character traits emerge?

"On this the rest of the Achaeans with one voice were for respecting the priest and taking the ransom that he offered; but not so Agamemnon, who spoke fiercely to him and sent him roughly away. So he went back in anger, and Apollo, who loved him dearly, heard his prayer. Then the god sent a deadly dart upon the Argives, and the people died thick on one another, for the arrows went every whither among the wide host of the Achaeans. At last a seer in the fullness of his knowledge declared to us the oracles of Apollo, and I was myself first to say that we should appease him. Whereon the son of Atreus rose in anger, and threatened that which he has since done. The Achaeans are now taking the girl in a ship to Chryse, and sending gifts of sacrifice to the god; but the heralds have just taken from my tent the daughter of Briseus, whom the Achaeans had awarded to myself.

"Help your brave son, therefore, if you are able. Go to Olympus, and if you have ever done him service in word or deed, implore the aid of Jove. Ofttimes in my father's house have I heard you glory in that you alone of the immortals saved the son of Saturn from ruin, when the others, with Juno, Neptune, and Pallas Minerva would have put him in bonds. It was you, goddess, who delivered him by calling to Olympus the hundred-handed monster whom gods call Briareus, but men Aegaeon, for he is stronger even than his father; when therefore he took his seat all-glorious beside the son of Saturn, the other gods were afraid, and did not bind him. Go, then, to him, remind him of all this, clasp his knees, and bid him give succor to the Trojans. Let the Achaeans be hemmed in at the sterns of their ships, and perish on the sea-shore, that they may reap

Achilles asks his mother to help him conspire against his king and his troops. How might we define Achilles' scheme?

what joy they may of their king, and that Agamemnon may rue his blindness in offering insult to the foremost of the Achaeans."

Achilles' mother agrees to conspire with him against his king and troops.

Thetis wept and answered, "My son, woe is me that I should have borne or suckled you. Would indeed that you had lived your span free from all sorrow at your ships, for it is all too brief; alas, that you should be at once short of life and long of sorrow above your peers: woe, therefore, was the hour in which I bore you; nevertheless I will go to the snowy heights of Olympus, and tell this tale to Jove, if he will hear our prayer: meanwhile stay where you are with your ships, nurse your anger against the Achaeans, and hold aloof from fight. For Jove went yesterday to Oceanus, to a feast among the Ethiopians, and the other gods went with him. He will return to Olympus twelve days hence; I will then go to his mansion paved with bronze and will beseech him; nor do I doubt that I shall be able to persuade him."

On this she left him, still furious at the loss of her that had been taken from him. Meanwhile Ulysses reached Chryse with the hecatomb. When they had come inside the harbor they furled the sails and laid them in the ship's hold; they slackened the forestays, lowered the mast into its place, and rowed the ship to the place where they would have her lie; there they cast out their mooring-stones and made fast the hawsers. They then got out upon the sea-shore and landed the hecatomb for Apollo; Chryseis also left the ship, and Ulysses led her to the altar to deliver her into the hands of her father. "Chryses," said he, "King Agamemnon has sent me to bring you back your child, and to offer sacrifice to Apollo on behalf of the Danaans, that we may propitiate the god, who has now brought sorrow upon the Argives."

Achaeans return daughter, Chryseis, to priest. Gods end plague.

So saying he gave the girl over to her father, who received her gladly, and they ranged the holy hecatomb all orderly round the altar of the god. They washed their hands and took up the barley-meal to sprinkle over the victims, while Chryses lifted up his hands and prayed aloud on their behalf. "Hear me," he cried, "O god of the silver bow, that protectest Chryse and holy Cilla, and rulest Tenedos with thy might. Even as thou didst hear me aforetime when I prayed, and didst press hardly upon the Achaeans, so hear me yet again, and stay this fearful pestilence from the Danaans."

Thus did he pray, and Apollo heard his prayer. When they had done praying and sprinkling the barley-meal, they drew back the heads of the victims and killed and flayed them. They cut out the thigh-bones, wrapped them round in two layers of fat, set some pieces of raw meat on the top of them, and then Chryses laid them on the wood fire and poured wine over them, while the young men stood near him with five-pronged spits in their hands. When the thigh-bones were burned and they had tasted the inward meats, they cut the rest up small, put the pieces upon the spits, roasted them till they were done, and drew them off: then, when they had finished their work and the feast was ready, they ate it, and every man had his full share, so that all were satisfied. As soon as they had had enough to eat and drink, pages filled the mixing-bowl with wine and water and handed it round, after giving every man his drink-offering.

What attitude toward their gods do ancient Greeks reveal in this scene?

Thus all day long the young men worshipped the god with song, hymning him and chanting the joyous paean, and the god took pleasure in their voices; but when the sun went down, and it came on dark, they laid themselves down to sleep by the stern cables of the ship, and when the child of morning, rosy-fingered Dawn, appeared they again set sail for the host of the Achaeans. Apollo sent them a fair wind, so they raised their mast and hoisted their white sails aloft. As the sail bellied with the wind the ship flew through the deep blue water, and the foam hissed against her bows as she sped onward. When they reached the wide-stretching host of the Achaeans, they drew the vessel ashore, high and dry upon the sands, set her strong props beneath her, and went their ways to their own tents and ships.

But Achilles abode at his ships and nursed his anger. He went not to the honorable assembly, and sallied not forth to fight, but gnawed at his own heart, pining for battle
5 and the war-cry.

Now after twelve days the immortal gods came back in a body to Olympus, and Jove led the way. Thetis was not unmindful of the charge her son had laid upon her, so she rose from under the sea and went through great heaven with early morning to Olympus, where she found the mighty son of Saturn sitting all alone upon its topmost ridges. She
10 sat herself down before him, and with her left hand seized his knees, while with her right she caught him under the chin, and besought him, saying:—

"Father Jove, if I ever did you service in word or deed among the immortals, hear my prayer, and do honor to my son, whose life is to be cut short so early. King Agamemnon has dishonored him by taking his prize and keeping her. Honor him then yourself,
15 Olympian lord of counsel, and grant victory to the Trojans, till the Achaeans give my son his due and load him with riches in requital."

Jove sat for a while silent, and without a word, but Thetis still kept firm hold of his knees, and besought him a second time. "Incline your head," said she, "and promise me surely, or else deny me—for you have nothing to fear—that I may learn how greatly
20 you disdain me."

At this Jove was much troubled and answered, "I shall have trouble if you set me quarrelling with Juno, for she will provoke me with her taunting speeches; even now she is always railing at me before the other gods and accusing me of giving aid to the Trojans. Go back now, lest she should find out. I will consider the matter, and will bring
25 it about as you wish. See, I incline my head that you may believe me. This is the most solemn promise that I can give to any god. I never recall my word, or deceive, or fail to do what I say, when I have nodded my head."

As he spoke the son of Saturn bowed his dark brows, and the ambrosial locks swayed on his immortal head, till vast Olympus reeled.

30 When the pair had thus laid their plans, they parted—Jove to his house, while the goddess quitted the splendor of Olympus, and plunged into the depths of the sea. The gods rose from their seats, before the coming of their sire. Not one of them dared to remain sitting, but all stood up as he came among them. There, then, he took his seat. But Juno, when she saw him, knew that he and the old merman's daughter, silver-footed
35 Thetis, had been hatching mischief, so she at once began to upbraid him. "Trickster," she cried, "which of the gods have you been taking into your counsels now? You are always settling matters in secret behind my back, and have never yet told me, if you could help it, one word of your intentions."

"Juno," replied the sire of gods and men, "you must not expect to be informed of all
40 my counsels. You are my wife, but you would find it hard to understand them. When it is proper for you to hear, there is no one, god or man, who will be told sooner, but when I mean to keep a matter to myself, you must not pry nor ask questions."

The ancient Greeks incorporated the mathematical concept of the "golden mean" into their profile of the ideal Greek warrior, who would model a sound body and a sound mind. What imbalance in Achilles' profile is emerging?

Achilles' mother asks Zeus and the gods to agree to her son's plan. Note that Butler's translation interchanges Greek and Roman names for gods. For example, Jove here should be Zeus, the Greek name for the supreme sky god.

Jove agrees to answer the prayers and wishes of Achilles' mother. However, what interesting dynamic among male and female gods is revealed through Jove's concern about Juno?

Juno rages against Jove, and they argue.

"Dread son of Saturn," answered Juno, "what are you talking about? I? Pry and ask questions? Never. I let you have your own way in everything. Still, I have a strong misgiving that the old merman's daughter Thetis has been talking you over, for she was with you and had hold of your knees this self-same morning. I believe, therefore, that you have been promising her to give glory to Achilles, and to kill much people at the ships of the Achaeans."

"Wife," said Jove, "I can do nothing but you suspect me and find it out. You will take nothing by it, for I shall only dislike you the more, and it will go harder with you. Granted that it is as you say; I mean to have it so; sit down and hold your tongue as I bid you for if I once begin to lay my hands about you, though all heaven were on your side it would profit you nothing."

On this Juno was frightened, so she curbed her stubborn will and sat down in silence. But the heavenly beings were disquieted throughout the house of Jove, till the cunning workman Vulcan began to try and pacify his mother Juno. "It will be intolerable," said he, "if you two fall to wrangling and setting heaven in an uproar about a pack of mortals. If such ill counsels are to prevail, we shall have no pleasure at our banquet. Let me then advise my mother—and she must herself know that it will be better—to make friends with my dear father Jove, lest he again scold her and disturb our feast. If the Olympian Thunderer wants to hurl us all from our seats, he can do so, for he is far the strongest, so give him fair words, and he will then soon be in a good humor with us."

Juno's children console her. The gods feast, then sleep.

As he spoke, he took a double cup of nectar, and placed it in his mother's hand. "Cheer up, my dear mother," said he, "and make the best of it. I love you dearly, and should be very sorry to see you get a thrashing; however grieved I might be, I could not help, for there is no standing against Jove. Once before when I was trying to help you, he caught me by the foot and flung me from the heavenly threshold. All day long from morn till eve, was I falling, till at sunset I came to ground in the island of Lemnos, and there I lay, with very little life left in me, till the Sintians came and tended me."

Juno smiled at this, and as she smiled she took the cup from her son's hands. Then Vulcan drew sweet nectar from the mixing-bowl, and served it round among the gods, going from left to right; and the blessed gods laughed out a loud applause as they saw him bustling about the heavenly mansion.

Thus through the livelong day to the going down of the sun they feasted, and every one had his full share, so that all were satisfied. Apollo struck his lyre, and the Muses lifted up their sweet voices, calling and answering one another. But when the sun's glorious light had faded, they went home to bed, each in his own abode, which lame Vulcan with his consummate skill had fashioned for them. So Jove, the Olympian Lord of Thunder, hied him to the bed in which he always slept; and when he had got on to it he went to sleep, with Juno of the golden throne by his side.

BOOK XXII – ACHILLES AVENGES HIS COUSIN'S DEATH

Achilles avenges the death of his cousin, Patroclus, when he kills the Trojan general, Hector in battle. Afterwards, he desecrates the body of Hector by attaching his dead body to his chariot and dragging it back to the Greeks' camp.

Thus the Trojans in the city, scared like fawns, wiped the sweat from off them and drank to quench their thirst, leaning against the goodly battlements, while the Achaeans with their shields laid upon their shoulders drew close up to the walls. But stern fate bade Hector stay where he was before Ilius and the Scaean gates. Then Phoebus Apollo
5 spoke to the son of Peleus saying, "Why, son of Peleus, do you, who are but man, give chase to me who am immortal? Have you not yet found out that it is a god whom you pursue so furiously? You did not harass the Trojans whom you had routed, and now they are within their walls, while you have been decoyed hither away from them. Me you cannot kill, for death can take no hold upon me."

10 Achilles was greatly angered and said, "You have baulked me, Far-Darter, most malicious of all gods, and have drawn me away from the wall, where many another man would have bitten the dust ere he got within Ilius; you have robbed me of great glory and have saved the Trojans at no risk to yourself, for you have nothing to fear, but I would indeed have my revenge if it were in my power to do so."

15 On this, with fell intent he made towards the city, and as the winning horse in a chariot race strains every nerve when he is flying over the plain, even so fast and furiously did the limbs of Achilles bear him onwards. King Priam was first to note him as he scoured the plain, all radiant as the star which men call Orion's Hound, and whose beams blaze forth in time of harvest more brilliantly than those of any other that shines by night;
20 brightest of them all though he be, he yet bodes ill for mortals, for he brings fire and fever in his train—even so did Achilles' armor gleam on his breast as he sped onwards. Priam raised a cry and beat his head with his hands as he lifted them up and shouted out to his dear son, imploring him to return; but Hector still stayed before the gates, for his heart was set upon doing battle with Achilles. The old man reached out his arms
25 towards him and bade him for pity's sake come within the walls. "Hector," he cried, "my son, stay not to face this man alone and unsupported, or you will meet death at the hands of the son of Peleus, for he is mightier than you. Monster that he is; would indeed that the gods loved him no better than I do, for so, dogs and vultures would soon devour him as he lay stretched on earth, and a load of grief would be lifted from my
30 heart, for many a brave son has he reft from me, either by killing them or selling them away in the islands that are beyond the sea: even now I miss two sons from among the Trojans who have thronged within the city, Lycaon and Polydorus, whom Laothoe peeress among women bore me. Should they be still alive and in the hands of the Achaeans, we will ransom them with gold and bronze, of which we have store, for the
35 old man Altes endowed his daughter richly; but if they are already dead and in the house of Hades, sorrow will it be to us two who were their parents; albeit the grief of others will be more short-lived unless you too perish at the hands of Achilles. Come, then, my son, within the city, to be the guardian of Trojan men and Trojan women, or you will both lose your own life and afford a mighty triumph to the son of Peleus. Have pity
40 also on your unhappy father while life yet remains to him—on me, whom the son of Saturn will destroy by a terrible doom on the threshold of old age, after I have seen my sons slain and my daughters hauled away as captives, my bridal chambers pillaged, little

King Priam begs his son, Hector, to retreat and spare himself the wrath of Achilles.

children dashed to earth amid the rage of battle, and my sons' wives dragged away by the cruel hands of the Achaeans; in the end fierce hounds will tear me in pieces at my own gates after someone has beaten the life out of my body with sword or spear-hounds that I myself reared and fed at my own table to guard my gates, but who will yet lap my

5 blood and then lie all distraught at my doors. When a young man falls by the sword in battle, he may lie where he is and there is nothing unseemly; let what will be seen, all is honorable in death, but when an old man is slain there is nothing in this world more pitiable than that dogs should defile his grey hair and beard and all that men hide for shame."

Hector's mother also begs him to retreat from Achilles and his troops.

10 The old man tore his grey hair as he spoke, but he moved not the heart of Hector. His mother hard by wept and moaned aloud as she bared her bosom and pointed to the breast which had suckled him. "Hector," she cried, weeping bitterly the while, "Hector, my son, spurn not this breast, but have pity upon me too: if I have ever given you comfort from my own bosom, think on it now, dear son, and come within the wall to

15 protect us from this man; stand not without to meet him. Should the wretch kill you, neither I nor your richly dowered wife shall ever weep, dear offshoot of myself, over the bed on which you lie, for dogs will devour you at the ships of the Achaeans."

Thus did the two with many tears implore their son, but they moved not the heart of Hector, and he stood his ground awaiting huge Achilles as he drew nearer towards him.

20 As a serpent in its den upon the mountains, full fed with deadly poisons, waits for the approach of man—he is filled with fury and his eyes glare terribly as he goes writhing round his den—even so Hector leaned his shield against a tower that jutted out from the wall and stood where he was, undaunted.

Hector decides he must fight Achilles. Identify the different reasons that Hector and Achilles go to war. Of the two military generals, which one seems to fight for the right cause?

"Alas," said he to himself in the heaviness of his heart, "if I go within the gates,

25 Polydamas will be the first to heap reproach upon me, for it was he that urged me to lead the Trojans back to the city on that awful night when Achilles again came forth against us. I would not listen, but it would have been indeed better if I had done so. Now that my folly has destroyed the host, I dare not look Trojan men and Trojan women in the face, lest a worse man should say, 'Hector has ruined us by his self-

30 confidence.' Surely it would be better for me to return after having fought Achilles and slain him, or to die gloriously here before the city. What, again, if I were to lay down my shield and helmet, lean my spear against the wall and go straight up to noble Achilles? What if I were to promise to give up Helen, who was the fountainhead of all this war, and all the treasure that Alexandrus brought with him in his ships to Troy, aye,

35 and to let the Achaeans divide the half of everything that the city contains among themselves? I might make the Trojans, by the mouths of their princes, take a solemn oath that they would hide nothing, but would divide into two shares all that is within the city—but why argue with myself in this way? Were I to go up to him he would show me no kind of mercy; he would kill me then and there as easily as though I were a

40 woman, when I had off my armor. There is no parleying with him from some rock or oak tree as young men and maidens prattle with one another. Better fight him at once, and learn to which of us Jove will vouchsafe victory."

Enter Achilles. Hector flees.

Thus did he stand and ponder, but Achilles came up to him as it were Mars himself, plumed lord of battle. From his right shoulder he brandished his terrible spear of Pelian

45 ash, and the bronze gleamed around him like flashing fire or the rays of the rising sun. Fear fell upon Hector as he beheld him, and he dared not stay longer where he was but fled in dismay from before the gates, while Achilles darted after him at his utmost speed. As a mountain falcon, swiftest of all birds, swoops down upon some cowering dove— the dove flies before him but the falcon with a shrill scream follows close after, resolved

to have her—even so did Achilles make straight for Hector with all his might, while Hector fled under the Trojan wall as fast as his limbs could take him.

On they flew along the wagon-road that ran hard by under the wall, past the lookout station, and past the weather-beaten wild fig-tree, till they came to two fair springs which
5   feed the river Scamander. One of these two springs is warm, and steam rises from it as smoke from a burning fire, but the other even in summer is as cold as hail or snow, or the ice that forms on water. Here, hard by the springs, are the goodly washing-troughs of stone, where in the time of peace before the coming of the Achaeans the wives and fair daughters of the Trojans used to wash their clothes. Past these did they fly, the one
10 in front and the other giving chase behind him: good was the man that fled, but better far was he that followed after, and swiftly indeed did they run, for the prize was no mere beast for sacrifice or bullock's hide, as it might be for a common foot-race, but they ran for the life of Hector. As horses in a chariot race speed round the turning-posts when they are running for some great prize—a tripod or woman—at the games in honor of
15 some dead hero, so did these two run full speed three times round the city of Priam. All the gods watched them, and the sire of gods and men was the first to speak.

"Alas," said he, "my eyes behold a man who is dear to me being pursued round the walls of Troy; my heart is full of pity for Hector, who has burned the thigh-bones of many a heifer in my honor, one while on the crests of many-valleyed Ida, and again on the
20 citadel of Troy; and now I see noble Achilles in full pursuit of him round the city of Priam. What say you? Consider among yourselves and decide whether we shall now save him or let him fall, valiant though he be, before Achilles, son of Peleus."

Then Minerva said, "Father, wielder of the lightning, lord of cloud and storm, what mean you? Would you pluck this mortal whose doom has long been decreed out of the
25 jaws of death? Do as you will, but we others shall not be of a mind with you."

And Jove answered, "My child, Trito-born, take heart. I did not speak in full earnest, and I will let you have your way. Do without let or hindrance as you are minded."

Thus did he urge Minerva who was already eager, and down she darted from the topmost summits of Olympus.

30 Achilles was still in full pursuit of Hector, as a hound chasing a fawn which he has started from its covert on the mountains, and hunts through glade and thicket. The fawn may try to elude him by crouching under cover of a bush, but he will scent her out and follow her up until he gets her—even so there was no escape for Hector from the fleet son of Peleus. Whenever he made a set to get near the Dardanian gates and
35 under the walls, that his people might help him by showering down weapons from above, Achilles would gain on him and head him back towards the plain, keeping himself always on the city side. As a man in a dream who fails to lay hands upon another whom he is pursuing—the one cannot escape nor the other overtake—even so neither could Achilles come up with Hector, nor Hector break away from Achilles; nevertheless
40 he might even yet have escaped death had not the time come when Apollo, who thus far had sustained his strength and nerved his running, was now no longer to stay by him. Achilles made signs to the Achaean host, and shook his head to show that no man was to aim a dart at Hector, lest another might win the glory of having hit him and he might himself come in second. Then, at last, as they were nearing the fountains for the
45 fourth time, the father of all balanced his golden scales and placed a doom in each of them, one for Achilles and the other for Hector. As he held the scales by the middle,

Gods observe the contest and discuss the conflict between Achilles and Hector. What concept of the role of gods in ancient Greek lives is revealed here?

Achilles signals to his men: spare Hector so that I may kill him myself. Why does Achilles want this glory?

the doom of Hector fell down deep into the house of Hades—and then Phoebus Apollo left him. Thereon Minerva went close up to the son of Peleus and said, "Noble Achilles, favored of heaven, we two shall surely take back to the ships a triumph for the Achaeans by slaying Hector, for all his lust of battle. Do what Apollo may as he lies groveling
5   before his father, aegis-bearing Jove, Hector cannot escape us longer. Stay here and take breath, while I go up to him and persuade him to make a stand and fight you."

Gods intervene: Minerva tricks Hector by advising him to fight Achilles.

Thus spoke Minerva. Achilles obeyed her gladly, and stood still, leaning on his bronze-pointed ashen spear, while Minerva left him and went after Hector in the form and with the voice of Deiphobus. She came close up to him and said, "Dear brother, I see you
10   are hard pressed by Achilles who is chasing you at full speed round the city of Priam, let us await his onset and stand on our defense."

And Hector answered, "Deiphobus, you have always been dearest to me of all my brothers, children of Hecuba and Priam, but henceforth I shall rate you yet more highly, inasmuch as you have ventured outside the wall for my sake when all the others remain
15   inside."

Then Minerva said, "Dear brother, my father and mother went down on their knees and implored me, as did all my comrades, to remain inside, so great a fear has fallen upon them all; but I was in an agony of grief when I beheld you; now, therefore, let us two make a stand and fight, and let there be no keeping our spears in reserve, that we
20   may learn whether Achilles shall kill us and bear off our spoils to the ships, or whether he shall fall before you."

Hector asks Achilles to abide by codes of warfare.

Thus did Minerva inveigle him by her cunning, and when the two were now close to one another great Hector was first to speak. "I will no longer fly you, son of Peleus," said he, "as I have been doing hitherto. Three times have I fled round the mighty city
25   of Priam, without daring to withstand you, but now, let me either slay or be slain, for I am in the mind to face you. Let us, then, give pledges to one another by our gods, who are the fittest witnesses and guardians of all covenants; let it be agreed between us that if Jove vouchsafes me the longer stay and I take your life, I am not to treat your dead body in any unseemly fashion, but when I have stripped you of your armor, I am to
30   give up your body to the Achaeans. And do you likewise."

Achilles rejects Hector's plea to honor his codes of war. What ideas about rules of warfare are examined here?

Achilles glared at him and answered, "Fool, prate not to me about covenants. There can be no covenants between men and lions, wolves and lambs can never be of one mind, but hate each other out and out all through. Therefore there can be no understanding between you and me, nor may there be any covenants between us, till one or other shall
35   fall and glut grim Mars with his life's blood. Put forth all your strength; you have need now to prove yourself indeed a bold soldier and man of war. You have no more chance, and Pallas Minerva will forthwith vanquish you by my spear: you shall now pay me in full for the grief you have caused me on account of my comrades whom you have killed in battle."

Achilles and Hector battle.

40   He poised his spear as he spoke and hurled it. Hector saw it coming and avoided it; he watched it and crouched down so that it flew over his head and stuck in the ground beyond; Minerva then snatched it up and gave it back to Achilles without Hector's seeing her; Hector thereon said to the son of Peleus, "You have missed your aim, Achilles, peer of the gods, and Jove has not yet revealed to you the hour of my doom,
45   though you made sure that he had done so. You were a false-tongued liar when you deemed that I should forget my valor and quail before you. You shall not drive your

spear into the back of a runaway—drive it, should heaven so grant you power, drive it into me as I make straight towards you; and now for your own part avoid my spear if you can—would that you might receive the whole of it into your body; if you were once dead the Trojans would find the war an easier matter, for it is you who have harmed

5 them most."

He poised his spear as he spoke and hurled it. His aim was true for he hit the middle of Achilles' shield, but the spear rebounded from it, and did not pierce it. Hector was angry when he saw that the weapon had sped from his hand in vain, and stood there in dismay for he had no second spear. With a loud cry he called Deiphobus and asked him for

10 one, but there was no man; then he saw the truth and said to himself, "Alas! the gods have lured me on to my destruction. I deemed that the hero Deiphobus was by my side, but he is within the wall, and Minerva has inveigled me; death is now indeed exceedingly near at hand and there is no way out of it—for so Jove and his son Apollo the far-darter have willed it, though heretofore they have been ever ready to protect me. My doom

15 has come upon me; let me not then die ingloriously and without a struggle, but let me first do some great thing that shall be told among men hereafter."

As he spoke he drew the keen blade that hung so great and strong by his side, and gathering himself together be sprang on Achilles like a soaring eagle which swoops down from the clouds on to some lamb or timid hare—even so did Hector brandish

20 his sword and spring upon Achilles. Achilles mad with rage darted towards him, with his wondrous shield before his breast, and his gleaming helmet, made with four layers of metal, nodding fiercely forward. The thick tresses of gold with which Vulcan had crested the helmet floated round it, and as the evening star that shines brighter than all others through the stillness of night, even such was the gleam of the spear which

25 Achilles poised in his right hand, fraught with the death of noble Hector. He eyed his fair flesh over and over to see where he could best wound it, but all was protected by the goodly armor of which Hector had spoiled Patroclus after he had slain him, save only the throat where the collar-bones divide the neck from the shoulders, and this is a most deadly place: here then did Achilles strike him as he was coming on towards him,

30 and the point of his spear went right through the fleshy part of the neck, but it did not sever his windpipe so that he could still speak. Hector fell headlong, and Achilles vaunted over him saying, "Hector, you deemed that you should come off scatheless when you were spoiling Patroclus, and recked not of myself who was not with him. Fool that you were: for I, his comrade, mightier far than he, was still left behind him at

35 the ships, and now I have laid you low. The Achaeans shall give him all due funeral rites, while dogs and vultures shall work their will upon yourself."

Achilles delivers a fatal strike against Hector and then taunts him.

Then Hector said, as the life ebbed out of him, "I pray you by your life and knees, and by your parents, let not dogs devour me at the ships of the Achaeans, but accept the rich treasure of gold and bronze which my father and mother will offer you, and send

40 my body home, that the Trojans and their wives may give me my dues of fire when I am dead."

Hector begs Achilles for a proper mourning of his death among the Trojans, but Achilles rebukes him.

Achilles glared at him and answered, "Dog, talk not to me neither of knees nor parents; would that I could be as sure of being able to cut your flesh into pieces and eat it raw, for the ill you have done me, as I am that nothing shall save you from the dogs—it shall

45 not be, though they bring ten or twenty-fold ransom and weigh it out for me on the spot, with promise of yet more hereafter. Though Priam son of Dardanus should bid them offer me your weight in gold, even so your mother shall never lay you out and make lament over the son she bore, but dogs and vultures shall eat you utterly up."

Hector sees Achilles' iron
heart.

Hector with his dying breath then said, "I know you what you are, and was sure that I should not move you, for your heart is hard as iron; look to it that I bring not heaven's anger upon you on the day when Paris and Phoebus Apollo, valiant though you be, shall slay you at the Scaean gates."

5 When he had thus said the shrouds of death enfolded him, whereon his soul went out of him and flew down to the house of Hades, lamenting its sad fate that it should enjoy youth and strength no longer. But Achilles said, speaking to the dead body, "Die; for my part I will accept my fate whensoever Jove and the other gods see fit to send it."

Achilles' troops take turns
driving their swords into
Hector's dead body.

As he spoke he drew his spear from the body and set it on one side; then he stripped 10 the blood-stained armor from Hector's shoulders while the other Achaeans came running up to view his wondrous strength and beauty; and no one came near him without giving him a fresh wound. Then would one turn to his neighbor and say, "It is easier to handle Hector now than when he was flinging fire on to our ships"—and as he spoke he would thrust his spear into him anew.

What does Achilles' speech
here reveal about his reason to
fight Hector?

15 When Achilles had done spoiling Hector of his armor, he stood among the Argives and said, "My friends, princes and counselors of the Argives, now that heaven has vouchsafed us to overcome this man, who has done us more hurt than all the others together, consider whether we should not attack the city in force, and discover in what mind the Trojans may be. We should thus learn whether they will desert their city now 20 that Hector has fallen, or will still hold out even though he is no longer living. But why argue with myself in this way, while Patroclus is still lying at the ships unburied, and unmourned—he whom I can never forget so long as I am alive and my strength fails not? Though men forget their dead when once they are within the house of Hades, yet not even there will I forget the comrade whom I have lost. Now, therefore, Achaean 25 youths, let us raise the song of victory and go back to the ships taking this man along with us; for we have achieved a mighty triumph and have slain noble Hector to whom the Trojans prayed throughout their city as though he were a god."

Achilles drags Hector's body
back to the Achaean camp. Is
Achilles' desecration of
Hector's body justified?

On this he treated the body of Hector with contumely: he pierced the sinews at the back of both his feet from heel to ankle and passed thongs of ox-hide through the slits he 30 had made: thus he made the body fast to his chariot, letting the head trail upon the ground. Then when he had put the goodly armor on the chariot and had himself mounted, he lashed his horses on and they flew forward nothing loth. The dust rose from Hector as he was being dragged along, his dark hair flew all abroad, and his head once so comely was laid low on earth, for Jove had now delivered him into the hands 35 of his foes to do him outrage in his own land.

Trojans mourn the death of
their general, Hector. King
Priam plans to retrieve his
son's dead body.

Thus was the head of Hector being dishonored in the dust. His mother tore her hair, and flung her veil from her with a loud cry as she looked upon her son. His father made piteous moan, and throughout the city the people fell to weeping and wailing. It was as though the whole of frowning Ilius was being smirched with fire. Hardly could the 40 people hold Priam back in his hot haste to rush without the gates of the city. He groveled in the mire and besought them, calling each one of them by his name. "Let be, my friends," he cried, "and for all your sorrow, suffer me to go single-handed to the ships of the Achaeans. Let me beseech this cruel and terrible man, if maybe he will respect the feeling of his fellow-men, and have compassion on my old age. His own 45 father is even such another as myself—Peleus, who bred him and reared him to be the bane of us Trojans, and of myself more than of all others. Many a son of mine has he slain in the flower of his youth, and yet, grieve for these as I may, I do so for one— Hector—more than for them all, and the bitterness of my sorrow will bring me down to the house of Hades. Would that he had died in my arms, for so both his ill-starred mother who bore him, and myself, should have had the comfort of weeping and mourning over him."

Hector's wife had as yet heard nothing, for no one had come to tell her that her husband
5 had remained without the gates. She was at her loom in an inner part of the house, weaving a double purple web, and embroidering it with many flowers. She heard the cry coming as from the wall, and trembled in every limb; the shuttle fell from her hands, and again she spoke to her waiting-women. "Two of you," she said, "come with me that I may learn what it is that has befallen; I heard the voice of my husband's honored
10 mother; my own heart beats as though it would come into my mouth and my limbs refuse to carry me; some great misfortune for Priam's children must be at hand. May I never live to hear it, but I greatly fear that Achilles has cut off the retreat of brave Hector and has chased him on to the plain where he was singlehanded; I fear he may have put an end to the reckless daring which possessed my husband, who would never remain
15 with the body of his men, but would dash on far in front, foremost of them all in valor."

Her heart beat fast, and as she spoke she flew from the house like a maniac, with her waiting-women following after. When she reached the battlements and the crowd of people, she stood looking out upon the wall, and saw Hector being borne away in front of the city—the horses dragging him without heed or care over the ground towards the
20 ships of the Achaeans. Her eyes were then shrouded as with the darkness of night and she fell fainting backwards. Her husband's sisters and the wives of his brothers crowded round her and supported her, for she was fain to die in her distraction; when she again presently breathed and came to herself, she sobbed and made lament among the Trojans saying, "Woe is me, O Hector; woe, indeed, that to share a common lot we were born,
25 you at Troy in the house of Priam, and I at Thebes under the wooded mountain of Placus in the house of Eetion who brought me up when I was a child—ill-starred sire of an ill-starred daughter—would that he had never begotten me. You are now going into the house of Hades under the secret places of the earth, and you leave me a sorrowing widow in your house. The child, of whom you and I are the unhappy parents,
30 is as yet a mere infant. Now that you are gone, O Hector, you can do nothing for him nor he for you. Even though he escape the horrors of this woeful war with the Achaeans, yet shall his life henceforth be one of labor and sorrow, for others will seize his lands. The day that robs a child of his parents severs him from his own kind; his head is bowed, his cheeks are wet with tears, and he will go about destitute among the
35 friends of his father, plucking one by the cloak and another by the shirt. Someone or other of these may so far pity him as to hold the cup for a moment towards him and let him moisten his lips, but he must not drink enough to wet the roof of his mouth; then one whose parents are alive will drive him from the table with blows and angry words. 'Out with you,' he will say, 'you have no father here,' and the child will go crying back
40 to his widowed mother—he, Astyanax, who erewhile would sit upon his father's knees, and have none but the daintiest and choicest morsels set before him. When he had played till he was tired and went to sleep, he would lie in a bed, in the arms of his nurse, on a soft couch, knowing neither want nor care, whereas now that he has lost his father his lot will be full of hardship—he, whom the Trojans name Astyanax, because you, O
45 Hector, were the only defense of their gates and battlements. The wriggling writhing worms will now eat you at the ships, far from your parents, when the dogs have glutted themselves upon you. You will lie naked, although in your house you have fine and goodly raiment made by hands of women. This will I now burn; it is of no use to you, for you can never again wear it, and thus you will have respect shown you by the Trojans
50 both men and women." In such wise did she cry aloud amid her tears, and the women joined in her lament.

Hector's wife grieves his death. How does Hector's wife's speech illuminate the traits of two different warriors?

BOOK XXIV – PRIAM RANSOMS THE BODY OF HECTOR

Priam ransoms the body of Hector. Achilles recognizes in Priam a king whom he can respect. Achilles undergoes a clarifying transformation. Hector's funeral occurs.

Achilles mourns death of Patroclus and continues to desecrate Hector's body.

Gods discuss Achilles' behavior and pity Hector.

The assembly now broke up and the people went their ways each to his own ship. There they made ready their supper, and then bethought them of the blessed boon of sleep; but Achilles still wept for thinking of his dear comrade, and sleep, before whom all things bow, could take no hold upon him. This way and that did he turn as he yearned
5 after the might and manfulness of Patroclus; he thought of all they had done together, and all they had gone through both on the field of battle and on the waves of the weary sea. As he dwelt on these things he wept bitterly and lay now on his side, now on his back, and now face downwards, till at last he rose and went out as one distraught to wander upon the seashore. Then, when he saw dawn breaking over beach and sea, he
10 yoked his horses to his chariot, and bound the body of Hector behind it that he might drag it about. Thrice did he drag it round the tomb of the son of Menoetius, and then went back into his tent, leaving the body on the ground full length and with its face downwards. But Apollo would not suffer it to be disfigured, for he pitied the man, dead though he now was; therefore he shielded him with his golden aegis continually, that he
15 might take no hurt while Achilles was dragging him.

Thus shamefully did Achilles in his fury dishonor Hector; but the blessed gods looked down in pity from heaven, and urged Mercury, slayer of Argus, to steal the body. All were of this mind save only Juno, Neptune, and Jove's grey-eyed daughter, who persisted in the hate which they had ever borne towards Ilius with Priam and his people;
20 for they forgave not the wrong done them by Alexandrus in disdaining the goddesses who came to him when he was in his sheep yards, and preferring her who had offered him a wanton to his ruin.

When, therefore, the morning of the twelfth day had now come, Phoebus Apollo spoke among the immortals saying, "You gods ought to be ashamed of yourselves; you are
25 cruel and hard– hearted. Did not Hector burn you thigh-bones of heifers and of unblemished goats? And now dare you not rescue even his dead body, for his wife to look upon, with his mother and child, his father Priam, and his people, who would forthwith commit him to the flames, and give him his due funeral rites? So, then, you would all be on the side of mad Achilles, who knows neither right nor ruth? He is like
30 some savage lion that in the pride of his great strength and daring springs upon men's flocks and gorges on them. Even so has Achilles flung aside all pity, and all that conscience which at once so greatly banes yet greatly boons him that will heed it. A man may lose one far dearer than Achilles has lost—a son, it may be, or a brother born from his own mother's womb; yet when he has mourned him and wept over him he will let
35 him bide, for it takes much sorrow to kill a man; whereas Achilles, now that he has slain noble Hector, drags him behind his chariot round the tomb of his comrade. It were better of him, and for him, that he should not do so, for brave though he be we gods may take it ill that he should vent his fury upon dead clay."

Juno spoke up in a rage. "This were well," she cried, "O lord of the silver bow, if you would give like honor to Hector and to Achilles; but Hector was mortal and suckled at a woman's breast, whereas Achilles is the offspring of a goddess whom I myself reared and brought up. I married her to Peleus, who is above measure dear to the immortals;
5   you gods came all of you to her wedding; you feasted along with them yourself and brought your lyre—false, and fond of low company, that you have ever been."

Then said Jove, "Juno, be not so bitter. Their honor shall not be equal, but of all that dwell in Ilius, Hector was dearest to the gods, as also to myself, for his offerings never failed me. Never was my altar stinted of its dues, nor of the drink-offerings and savour
10   of sacrifice which we claim of right. I shall therefore permit the body of mighty Hector to be stolen; and yet this may hardly be without Achilles coming to know it, for his mother keeps night and day beside him. Let some one of you, therefore, send Thetis to me, and I will impart my counsel to her, namely that Achilles is to accept a ransom from Priam, and give up the body."

15   On this Iris fleet as the wind went forth to carry his message. Down she plunged into the dark sea midway between Samos and rocky Imbrus; the waters hissed as they closed over her, and she sank into the bottom as the lead at the end of an ox-horn, that is sped to carry death to fishes. She found Thetis sitting in a great cave with the other sea-goddesses gathered round her; there she sat in the midst of them weeping for her noble
20   son who was to fall far from his own land, on the rich plains of Troy. Iris went up to her and said, "Rise Thetis; Jove, whose counsels fail not, bids you come to him." And Thetis answered, "Why does the mighty god so bid me? I am in great grief, and shrink from going in and out among the immortals. Still, I will go, and the word that he may speak shall not be spoken in vain."

25   The goddess took her dark veil, than which there can be no robe more somber, and went forth with fleet Iris leading the way before her. The waves of the sea opened them a path, and when they reached the shore they flew up into the heavens, where they found the all-seeing son of Saturn with the blessed gods that live for ever assembled near him. Minerva gave up her seat to her, and she sat down by the side of father Jove.
30   Juno then placed a fair golden cup in her hand, and spoke to her in words of comfort, whereon Thetis drank and gave her back the cup; and the sire of gods and men was the first to speak.

"So, goddess," said he, "for all your sorrow, and the grief that I well know reigns ever in your heart, you have come hither to Olympus, and I will tell you why I have sent for
35   you. This nine days past the immortals have been quarrelling about Achilles waster of cities and the body of Hector. The gods would have Mercury slayer of Argus steal the body, but in furtherance of our peace and amity henceforward, I will concede such honor to your son as I will now tell you. Go, then, to the host and lay these commands upon him; say that the gods are angry with him, and that I am myself more angry than
40   them all, in that he keeps Hector at the ships and will not give him up. He may thus fear me and let the body go. At the same time I will send Iris to great Priam to bid him go to the ships of the Achaeans, and ransom his son, taking with him such gifts for Achilles as may give him satisfaction."

Silver-footed Thetis did as the god had told her, and forthwith down she darted from
45   the topmost summits of Olympus. She went to her son's tents where she found him grieving bitterly, while his trusty comrades round him were busy preparing their morning meal, for which they had killed a great woolly sheep. His mother sat down beside him and caressed him with her hand saying, "My son, how long will you keep on

Juno defends Achilles' behavior. What attribute of the gods is revealed here?

Gods conspire to free Hector because he respected them.

Gods command Achilles' mother to inform Achilles of their anger at him.

thus grieving and making moan? You are gnawing at your own heart, and think neither of food nor of woman's embraces; and yet these too were well, for you have no long time to live, and death with the strong hand of fate are already close beside you. Now, therefore, heed what I say, for I come as a messenger from Jove; he says that the gods

5 are angry with you, and himself more angry than them all, in that you keep Hector at the ships and will not give him up. Therefore let him go, and accept a ransom for his body."

And Achilles answered, "So be it. If Olympian Jove of his own motion thus commands me, let him that brings the ransom bear the body away."

Gods command King Priam to retrieve Hector's body. What do these divine interventions reveal about Greek concepts of the gods?

10 Thus did mother and son talk together at the ships in long discourse with one another. Meanwhile the son of Saturn sent Iris to the strong city of Ilius. "Go," said he, "fleet Iris, from the mansions of Olympus, and tell King Priam in Ilius, that he is to go to the ships of the Achaeans and free the body of his dear son. He is to take such gifts with him as shall give satisfaction to Achilles, and he is to go alone, with no other Trojan,

15 save only some honored servant who may drive his mules and wagon, and bring back the body of him whom noble Achilles has slain. Let him have no thought nor fear of death in his heart, for we will send the slayer of Argus to escort him, and bring him within the tent of Achilles. Achilles will not kill him nor let another do so, for he will take heed to his ways and sin not, and he will entreat a suppliant with all honorable

20 courtesy."

On this Iris, fleet as the wind, sped forth to deliver her message. She went to Priam's house, and found weeping and lamentation therein. His sons were seated round their father in the outer courtyard, and their raiment was wet with tears: the old man sat in the midst of them with his mantle wrapped close about his body, and his head and neck

25 all covered with the filth which he had clutched as he lay groveling in the mire. His daughters and his sons' wives went wailing about the house, as they thought of the many and brave men who lay dead, slain by the Argives. The messenger of Jove stood by Priam and spoke softly to him, but fear fell upon him as she did so. "Take heart," she said, "Priam offspring of Dardanus, take heart and fear not. I bring no evil tidings, but

30 am minded well towards you. I come as a messenger from Jove, who though he be not near, takes thought for you and pities you. The lord of Olympus bids you go and ransom noble Hector, and take with you such gifts as shall give satisfaction to Achilles. You are to go alone, with no Trojan, save only some honored servant who may drive your mules and wagon, and bring back to the city the body of him whom noble Achilles has slain.

35 You are to have no thought, nor fear of death, for Jove will send the slayer of Argus to escort you. When he has brought you within Achilles' tent, Achilles will not kill you nor let another do so, for he will take heed to his ways and sin not, and he will entreat a suppliant with all honorable courtesy."

Priam plans to depart for Achilles' camp.

Iris went her way when she had thus spoken, and Priam told his sons to get a mule-

40 wagon ready, and to make the body of the wagon fast upon the top of its bed. Then he went down into his fragrant store-room, high-vaulted, and made of cedar-wood, where his many treasures were kept, and he called Hecuba his wife. "Wife," said he, "a messenger has come to me from Olympus, and has told me to go to the ships of the Achaeans to ransom my dear son, taking with me such gifts as shall give satisfaction to

45 Achilles. What think you of this matter? for my own part I am greatly moved to pass through the camps of the Achaeans and go to their ships."

His wife cried aloud as she heard him, and said, "Alas, what has become of that judgment for which you have been ever famous both among strangers and your own people? How can you venture alone to the ships of the Achaeans, and look into the face of him who has slain so many of your brave sons? You must have iron courage, for if
5 the cruel savage sees you and lays hold on you, he will know neither respect nor pity. Let us then weep Hector from afar here in our own house, for when I gave him birth the threads of overruling fate were spun for him that dogs should eat his flesh far from his parents, in the house of that terrible man on whose liver I would fain fasten and devour it. Thus would I avenge my son, who showed no cowardice when Achilles slew
10 him, and thought neither of flight nor of avoiding battle as he stood in defense of Trojan men and Trojan women."

Priam's wife questions Priam's judgment.

Then Priam said, "I would go, do not therefore stay me nor be as a bird of ill omen in my house, for you will not move me. Had it been some mortal man who had sent me some prophet or priest who divines from sacrifice—I should have deemed him false
15 and have given him no heed; but now I have heard the goddess and seen her face to face, therefore I will go and her saying shall not be in vain. If it be my fate to die at the ships of the Achaeans even so would I have it; let Achilles slay me, if I may but first have taken my son in my arms and mourned him to my heart's comforting."

So saying he lifted the lids of his chests, and took out twelve goodly vestments. He took
20 also twelve cloaks of single fold, twelve rugs, twelve fair mantles, and an equal number of shirts. He weighed out ten talents of gold, and brought moreover two burnished tripods, four cauldrons, and a very beautiful cup which the Thracians had given him when he had gone to them on an embassy; it was very precious, but he grudged not even this, so eager was he to ransom the body of his son. Then he chased all the Trojans
25 from the court and rebuked them with words of anger. "Out," he cried, "shame and disgrace to me that you are. Have you no grief in your own homes that you are come to plague me here? Is it a small thing, think you, that the son of Saturn has sent this sorrow upon me, to lose the bravest of my sons? Nay, you shall prove it in person, for now he is gone the Achaeans will have easier work in killing you. As for me, let me go
30 down within the house of Hades, ere mine eyes behold the sacking and wasting of the city."

Priam will not be persuaded to stay.

He drove the men away with his staff, and they went forth as the old man sped them. Then he called to his sons, upbraiding Helenus, Paris, noble Agathon, Pammon, Antiphonus, Polites of the loud battle-cry, Deiphobus, Hippothous, and Dius. These
35 nine did the old man call near him. "Come to me at once," he cried, "worthless sons who do me shame; would that you had all been killed at the ships rather than Hector. Miserable man that I am, I have had the bravest sons in all Troy—noble Nestor, Troilus the dauntless charioteer, and Hector who was a god among men, so that one would have thought he was son to an immortal—yet there is not one of them left. Mars has
40 slain them and those of whom I am ashamed are alone left me. Liars, and light of foot, heroes of the dance, robbers of lambs and kids from your own people, why do you not get a wagon ready for me at once, and put all these things upon it that I may set out on my way?"

Thus did he speak, and they feared the rebuke of their father. They brought out a strong
45 mule-wagon, newly made, and set the body of the wagon fast on its bed. They took the mule-yoke from the peg on which it hung, a yoke of boxwood with a knob on the top of it and rings for the reins to go through. Then they brought a yoke-band eleven cubits long, to bind the yoke to the pole; they bound it on at the far end of the pole, and put the ring over the upright pin making it fast with three turns of the band on either side

the knob, and bending the thong of the yoke beneath it. This done, they brought from the store-chamber the rich ransom that was to purchase the body of Hector, and they set it all orderly on the wagon; then they yoked the strong harness-mules which the Mysians had on a time given as a goodly present to Priam; but for Priam himself they
5 yoked horses which the old king had bred, and kept for his own use.

Thus heedfully did Priam and his servant see to the yolking of their cars at the palace. Then Hecuba came to them all sorrowful, with a golden goblet of wine in her right hand, that they might make a drink-offering before they set out. She stood in front of the horses and said, "Take this, make a drink-offering to father Jove, and since you are
10 minded to go to the ships in spite of me, pray that you may come safely back from the hands of your enemies. Pray to the son of Saturn lord of the whirlwind, who sits on Ida and looks down over all Troy, pray him to send his swift messenger on your right hand, the bird of omen which is strongest and most dear to him of all birds, that you may see it with your own eyes and trust it as you go forth to the ships of the Danaans. If all-
15 seeing Jove will not send you this messenger, however set upon it you may be, I would not have you go to the ships of the Argives."

And Priam answered, "Wife, I will do as you desire me; it is well to lift hands in prayer to Jove, if so be he may have mercy upon me."

Priam asks gods for safe passage into Achilles' enemy camp.

With this the old man bade the serving-woman pour pure water over his hands, and the
20 woman came, bearing the water in a bowl. He washed his hands and took the cup from his wife; then he made the drink-offering and prayed, standing in the middle of the courtyard and turning his eyes to heaven. "Father Jove," he said, "that rulest from Ida, most glorious and most great, grant that I may be received kindly and compassionately in the tents of Achilles; and send your swift messenger upon my right hand, the bird of
25 omen which is strongest and most dear to you of all birds, that I may see it with my own eyes and trust it as I go forth to the ships of the Danaans."

So did he pray, and Jove the lord of counsel heard his prayer. Forthwith he sent an eagle, the most unerring portent of all birds that fly, the dusky hunter that men also call the Black Eagle. His wings were spread abroad on either side as wide as the well-made
30 and well-bolted door of a rich man's chamber. He came to them flying over the city upon their right hands, and when they saw him they were glad and their hearts took comfort within them. The old man made haste to mount his chariot, and drove out through the inner gateway and under the echoing gatehouse of the outer court. Before him went the mules drawing the four-wheeled wagon, and driven by wise Idaeus; behind
35 these were the horses, which the old man lashed with his whip and drove swiftly through the city, while his friends followed after, wailing and lamenting for him as though he were on his road to death. As soon as they had come down from the city and had reached the plain, his sons and sons-in-law who had followed him went back to Ilius.

But Priam and Idaeus as they showed out upon the plain did not escape the ken of all-
40 seeing Jove, who looked down upon the old man and pitied him; then he spoke to his son Mercury and said, "Mercury, for it is you who are the most disposed to escort men on their way, and to hear those whom you will hear, go, and so conduct Priam to the ships of the Achaeans that no other of the Danaans shall see him nor take note of him until he reach the son of Peleus."

Thus he spoke and Mercury, guide and guardian, slayer of Argus, did as he was told. Forthwith he bound on his glittering golden sandals with which he could fly like the wind over land and sea; he took the wand with which he seals men's eyes in sleep, or wakes them just as he pleases, and flew holding it in his hand till he came to Troy and to the Hellespont. To look at, he was like a young man of noble birth in the hey-day of his youth and beauty with the down just coming upon his face.

Mercury escorts Priam into the enemy camp.

Now when Priam and Idaeus had driven past the great tomb of Ilius, they stayed their mules and horses that they might drink in the river, for the shades of night were falling, when, therefore, Idaeus saw Mercury standing near them he said to Priam, "Take heed, descendant of Dardanus; here is matter which demands consideration. I see a man who I think will presently fall upon us; let us fly with our horses, or at least embrace his knees and implore him to take compassion upon us?"

When he heard this the old man's heart failed him, and he was in great fear; he stayed where he was as one dazed, and the hair stood on end over his whole body; but the bringer of good luck came up to him and took him by the hand, saying, "Whither, father, are you thus driving your mules and horses in the dead of night when other men are asleep? Are you not afraid of the fierce Achaeans who are hard by you, so cruel and relentless? Should some one of them see you bearing so much treasure through the darkness of the flying night, what would not your state then be? You are no longer young, and he who is with you is too old to protect you from those who would attack you. For myself, I will do you no harm, and I will defend you from anyone else, for you remind me of my own father."

And Priam answered, "It is indeed as you say, my dear son; nevertheless some god has held his hand over me, in that he has sent such a wayfarer as yourself to meet me so opportunely; you are so comely in mien and figure, and your judgment is so excellent that you must come of blessed parents."

Then said the slayer of Argus, guide and guardian, "Sir, all that you have said is right; but tell me and tell me true, are you taking this rich treasure to send it to a foreign people where it may be safe, or are you all leaving strong Ilius in dismay now that your son has fallen who was the bravest man among you and was never lacking in battle with the Achaeans?"

And Priam said, "Who are you, my friend, and who are your parents, that you speak so truly about the fate of my unhappy son?"

The slayer of Argus, guide and guardian, answered him, "Sir, you would prove me, that you question me about noble Hector. Many a time have I set eyes upon him in battle when he was driving the Argives to their ships and putting them to the sword. We stood still and marvelled, for Achilles in his anger with the son of Atreus suffered us not to fight. I am his squire, and came with him in the same ship. I am a Myrmidon, and my father's name is Polyctor: he is a rich man and about as old as you are; he has six sons besides myself, and I am the seventh. We cast lots, and it fell upon me to sail hither with Achilles. I am now come from the ships on to the plain, for with daybreak the Achaeans will set battle in array about the city. They chafe at doing nothing, and are so eager that their princes cannot hold them back."

Then answered Priam, "If you are indeed the squire of Achilles son of Peleus, tell me now the whole truth. Is my son still at the ships, or has Achilles hewn him limb from limb, and given him to his hounds?"

"Sir," replied the slayer of Argus, guide and guardian, "neither hounds nor vultures have
5 yet devoured him; he is still just lying at the tents by the ship of Achilles, and though it is now twelve days that he has lain there, his flesh is not wasted nor have the worms eaten him although they feed on warriors. At daybreak Achilles drags him cruelly round the sepulcher of his dear comrade, but it does him no hurt. You should come yourself and see how he lies fresh as dew, with the blood all washed away, and his wounds every
10 one of them closed though many pierced him with their spears. Such care have the blessed gods taken of your brave son, for he was dear to them beyond all measure."

The old man was comforted as he heard him and said, "My son, see what a good thing it is to have made due offerings to the immortals; for as sure as that he was born my son never forgot the gods that hold Olympus, and now they requite it to him even in
15 death. Accept therefore at my hands this goodly chalice; guard me and with heaven's help guide me till I come to the tent of the son of Peleus."

Then answered the slayer of Argus, guide and guardian, "Sir, you are tempting me and playing upon my youth, but you shall not move me, for you are offering me presents without the knowledge of Achilles whom I fear and hold it great guilt to defraud, lest
20 some evil presently befall me; but as your guide I would go with you even to Argos itself, and would guard you so carefully whether by sea or land, that no one should attack you through making light of him who was with you."

The bringer of good luck then sprang on to the chariot, and seizing the whip and reins he breathed fresh spirit into the mules and horses. When they reached the trench and
25 the wall that was before the ships, those who were on guard had just been getting their suppers, and the slayer of Argus threw them all into a deep sleep. Then he drew back the bolts to open the gates, and took Priam inside with the treasure he had upon his wagon. Ere long they came to the lofty dwelling of the son of Peleus for which the Myrmidons had cut pine and which they had built for their king; when they had built it
30 they thatched it with coarse tussock-grass which they had mown out on the plain, and all round it they made a large courtyard, which was fenced with stakes set close together. The gate was barred with a single bolt of pine which it took three men to force into its place, and three to draw back so as to open the gate, but Achilles could draw it by himself. Mercury opened the gate for the old man, and brought in the treasure that he
35 was taking with him for the son of Peleus. Then he sprang from the chariot on to the ground and said, "Sir, it is I, immortal Mercury, that am come with you, for my father sent me to escort you. I will now leave you, and will not enter into the presence of Achilles, for it might anger him that a god should befriend mortal men thus openly. Go you within, and embrace the knees of the son of Peleus: beseech him by his father, his
40 lovely mother, and his son; thus you may move him."

Priam enters Achilles' tent and begs for mercy. Note the appeal to the concept of *pathos* here. *Pathos*: pity, as for one's enemy, that renders respect.

With these words Mercury went back to high Olympus. Priam sprang from his chariot to the ground, leaving Idaeus where he was, in charge of the mules and horses. The old man went straight into the house where Achilles, loved of the gods, was sitting. There he found him with his men seated at a distance from him: only two, the hero
45 Automedon, and Alcimus of the race of Mars, were busy in attendance about his person, for he had but just done eating and drinking, and the table was still there. King Priam entered without their seeing him, and going right up to Achilles he clasped his knees and kissed the dread murderous hands that had slain so many of his sons.

As when some cruel spite has befallen a man that he should have killed someone in his own country, and must fly to a great man's protection in a land of strangers, and all marvel who see him, even so did Achilles marvel as he beheld Priam. The others looked one to another and marvelled also, but Priam besought Achilles saying, "Think of your
5   father, O Achilles like unto the gods, who is such even as I am, on the sad threshold of old age. It may be that those who dwell near him harass him, and there is none to keep war and ruin from him. Yet when he hears of you being still alive, he is glad, and his days are full of hope that he shall see his dear son come home to him from Troy; but I, wretched man that I am, had the bravest in all Troy for my sons, and there is not one
10 of them left. I had fifty sons when the Achaeans came here; nineteen of them were from a single womb, and the others were borne to me by the women of my household. The greater part of them has fierce Mars laid low, and Hector, him who was alone left, him who was the guardian of the city and ourselves, him have you lately slain; therefore I am now come to the ships of the Achaeans to ransom his body from you with a great
15 ransom. Fear, O Achilles, the wrath of heaven; think on your own father and have compassion upon me, who am the more pitiable, for I have steeled myself as no man yet has ever steeled himself before me, and have raised to my lips the hand of him who slew my son."

Thus spoke Priam, and the heart of Achilles yearned as he bethought him of his father.
20 He took the old man's hand and moved him gently away. The two wept bitterly—Priam, as he lay at Achilles' feet, weeping for Hector, and Achilles now for his father and now for Patroclus, till the house was filled with their lamentation.

But when Achilles was now sated with grief and had unburdened the bitterness of his sorrow, he left his seat and raised the old man by the hand, in pity for his white hair and
25 beard; then he said, "Unhappy man, you have indeed been greatly daring; how could you venture to come alone to the ships of the Achaeans, and enter the presence of him who has slain so many of your brave sons? You must have iron courage: sit now upon this seat, and for all our grief we will hide our sorrows in our hearts, for weeping will not avail us. The immortals know no care, yet the lot they spin for man is full of sorrow;
30 on the floor of Jove's palace there stand two urns, the one filled with evil gifts, and the other with good ones. He for whom Jove the lord of thunder mixes the gifts he sends, will meet now with good and now with evil fortune; but he to whom Jove sends none but evil gifts will be pointed at by the finger of scorn, the hand of famine will pursue him to the ends of the world, and he will go up and down the face of the earth, respected
35 neither by gods nor men. Even so did it befall Peleus; the gods endowed him with all good things from his birth upwards, for he reigned over the Myrmidons excelling all men in prosperity and wealth, and mortal though he was they gave him a goddess for his bride. But even on him too did heaven send misfortune, for there is no race of royal children born to him in his house, save one son who is doomed to die all untimely; nor
40 may I take care of him now that he is growing old, for I must stay here at Troy to be the bane of you and your children. And you too, O Priam, I have heard that you were aforetime happy. They say that in wealth and plenitude of offspring you surpassed all that is in Lesbos, the realm of Makar to the northward, Phrygia that is more inland, and those that dwell upon the great Hellespont; but from the day when the dwellers in
45 heaven sent this evil upon you, war and slaughter have been about your city continually. Bear up against it, and let there be some intervals in your sorrow. Mourn as you may for your brave son, you will take nothing by it. You cannot raise him from the dead, ere you do so yet another sorrow shall befall you."

Achilles and Priam weep. Achilles delivers his speech about men and gods. Note the appeal to the concept of *catharsis*. *Catharsis*: the purging of emotions that results in a clear mind.

How does Achilles demonstrate character growth in this final and seminal speech that he delivers to Priam?

Priam asks Achilles to not bid him to dine, while his son's dead body lies nearby, but Achilles insists that they eat together. Priam agrees.

And Priam answered, "O king, bid me not be seated, while Hector is still lying uncared for in your tents, but accept the great ransom which I have brought you, and give him to me at once that I may look upon him. May you prosper with the ransom and reach your own land in safety, seeing that you have suffered me to live and to look upon the
5 light of the sun."

Achilles looked at him sternly and said, "Vex me, sir, no longer; I am of myself minded to give up the body of Hector. My mother, daughter of the old man of the sea, came to me from Jove to bid me deliver it to you. Moreover I know well, O Priam, and you cannot hide it, that some god has brought you to the ships of the Achaeans, for else, no
10 man however strong and in his prime would dare to come to our host; he could neither pass our guard unseen, nor draw the bolt of my gates thus easily; therefore, provoke me no further, lest I sin against the word of Jove, and suffer you not, suppliant though you are, within my tents."

The old man feared him and obeyed. Then the son of Peleus sprang like a lion through
15 the door of his house, not alone, but with him went his two squires Automedon and Alcimus who were closer to him than any others of his comrades now that Patroclus was no more. These unyoked the horses and mules, and bade Priam's herald and attendant be seated within the house. They lifted the ransom for Hector's body from the wagon, but they left two mantles and a goodly shirt, that Achilles might wrap the
20 body in them when he gave it to be taken home. Then he called to his servants and ordered them to wash the body and anoint it, but he first took it to a place where Priam should not see it, lest if he did so, he should break out in the bitterness of his grief, and enrage Achilles, who might then kill him and sin against the word of Jove. When the servants had washed the body and anointed it, and had wrapped it in a fair shirt and
25 mantle, Achilles himself lifted it on to a bier, and he and his men then laid it on the wagon. He cried aloud as he did so and called on the name of his dear comrade, "Be not angry with me, Patroclus," he said, "if you hear even in the house of Hades that I have given Hector to his father for a ransom. It has been no unworthy one, and I will share it equitably with you."

30 Achilles then went back into the tent and took his place on the richly inlaid seat from which he had risen, by the wall that was at right angles to the one against which Priam was sitting. "Sir," he said, "your son is now laid upon his bier and is ransomed according to desire; you shall look upon him when you take him away at daybreak; for the present let us prepare our supper. Even lovely Niobe had to think about eating, though her
35 twelve children—six daughters and six lusty sons—had been all slain in her house. Apollo killed the sons with arrows from his silver bow, to punish Niobe, and Diana slew the daughters, because Niobe had vaunted herself against Leto; she said Leto had borne two children only, whereas she had herself borne many—whereon the two killed the many. Nine days did they lie weltering, and there was none to bury them, for the
40 son of Saturn turned the people into stone; but on the tenth day the gods in heaven themselves buried them, and Niobe then took food, being worn out with weeping. They say that somewhere among the rocks on the mountain pastures of Sipylus, where the nymphs live that haunt the river Achelous, there, they say, she lives in stone and still nurses the sorrows sent upon her by the hand of heaven. Therefore, noble sir, let us
45 two now take food; you can weep for your dear son hereafter as you are bearing him back to Ilius—and many a tear will he cost you."

With this Achilles sprang from his seat and killed a sheep of silvery whiteness, which his followers skinned and made ready all in due order. They cut the meat carefully up into smaller pieces, spitted them, and drew them off again when they were well roasted. Automedon brought bread in fair baskets and served it round the table, while Achilles
5 dealt out the meat, and they laid their hands on the good things that were before them. As soon as they had had enough to eat and drink, Priam, descendant of Dardanus, marvelled at the strength and beauty of Achilles for he was as a god to see, and Achilles marvelled at Priam as he listened to him and looked upon his noble presence. When they had gazed their fill Priam spoke first. "And now, O king," he said, "take me to my
10 couch that we may lie down and enjoy the blessed boon of sleep. Never once have my eyes been closed from the day your hands took the life of my son; I have groveled without ceasing in the mire of my stable-yard, making moan and brooding over my countless sorrows. Now, moreover, I have eaten bread and drunk wine; hitherto I have tasted nothing."

Priam and Achilles dine, then prepare for sleep.

15 As he spoke Achilles told his men and the women-servants to set beds in the room that was in the gatehouse, and make them with good red rugs, and spread coverlets on the top of them with woolen cloaks for Priam and Idaeus to wear. So the maids went out carrying a torch and got the two beds ready in all haste. Then Achilles said laughingly to Priam, "Dear sir, you shall lie outside, lest some counselor of those who in due course
20 keep coming to advise with me should see you here in the darkness of the flying night, and tell it to Agamemnon. This might cause delay in the delivery of the body. And now tell me and tell me true, for how many days would you celebrate the funeral rites of noble Hector? Tell me, that I may hold aloof from war and restrain the host."

And Priam answered, "Since, then, you suffer me to bury my noble son with all due
25 rites, do thus, Achilles, and I shall be grateful. You know how we are pent up within our city; it is far for us to fetch wood from the mountain, and the people live in fear. Nine days, therefore, will we mourn Hector in my house; on the tenth day we will bury him and there shall be a public feast in his honor; on the eleventh we will build a mound over his ashes, and on the twelfth, if there be need, we will fight."

Achilles and Priam agree to a truce to allow a proper mourning ceremony for Hector.

30 And Achilles answered, "All, King Priam, shall be as you have said. I will stay our fighting for as long a time as you have named."

As he spoke he laid his hand on the old man's right wrist, in token that he should have no fear; thus then did Priam and his attendant sleep there in the forecourt, full of thought, while Achilles lay in an inner room of the house, with fair Briseis by his side.

35 And now both gods and mortals were fast asleep through the livelong night, but upon Mercury alone, the bringer of good luck, sleep could take no hold for he was thinking all the time how to get King Priam away from the ships without his being seen by the strong force of sentinels. He hovered therefore over Priam's head and said, "Sir, now that Achilles has spared your life, you seem to have no fear about sleeping in the thick
40 of your foes. You have paid a great ransom, and have received the body of your son; were you still alive and a prisoner the sons whom you have left at home would have to give three times as much to free you; and so it would be if Agamemnon and the other Achaeans were to know of your being here."

Gods rouse Priam to return to his own camp.

When he heard this the old man was afraid and roused his servant. Mercury then yoked their horses and mules, and drove them quickly through the host so that no man perceived them. When they came to the ford of eddying Xanthus, begotten of immortal Jove, Mercury went back to high Olympus, and dawn in robe of saffron began to break
5 over all the land. Priam and Idaeus then drove on toward the city lamenting and making moan, and the mules drew the body of Hector. No one neither man nor woman saw them, till Cassandra, fair as golden Venus standing on Pergamus, caught sight of her dear father in his chariot, and his servant that was the city's herald with him. Then she saw him that was lying upon the bier, drawn by the mules, and with a loud cry she went
10 about the city saying, "Come hither Trojans, men and women, and look on Hector; if ever you rejoiced to see him coming from battle when he was alive, look now on him that was the glory of our city and all our people."

At this there was not man nor woman left in the city, so great a sorrow had possessed them. Hard by the gates they met Priam as he was bringing in the body. Hector's wife
15 and his mother were the first to mourn him: they flew towards the wagon and laid their hands upon his head, while the crowd stood weeping round them. They would have stayed before the gates, weeping and lamenting the livelong day to the going down of the sun, had not Priam spoken to them from the chariot and said, "Make way for the mules to pass you. Afterwards when I have taken the body home you shall have your
20 fill of weeping."

On this the people stood asunder, and made a way for the wagon. When they had borne the body within the house they laid it upon a bed and seated minstrels round it to lead the dirge, whereon the women joined in the sad music of their lament. Foremost among them all Andromache led their wailing as she clasped the head of mighty Hector in her
25 embrace. "Husband," she cried, "you have died young, and leave me in your house a widow; he of whom we are the ill-starred parents is still a mere child, and I fear he may not reach manhood. Ere he can do so our city will be razed and overthrown, for you who watched over it are no more—you who were its savior, the guardian of our wives and children. Our women will be carried away captives to the ships, and I among them;
30 while you, my child, who will be with me will be put to some unseemly tasks, working for a cruel master. Or, may be, some Achaean will hurl you (O miserable death) from our walls, to avenge some brother, son, or father whom Hector slew; many of them have indeed bitten the dust at his hands, for your father's hand in battle was no light one. Therefore do the people mourn him. You have left, O Hector, sorrow unutterable
35 to your parents, and my own grief is greatest of all, for you did not stretch forth your arms and embrace me as you lay dying, nor say to me any words that might have lived with me in my tears night and day for evermore."

Bitterly did she weep the while, and the women joined in her lament. Hecuba in her turn took up the strains of woe. "Hector," she cried, "dearest to me of all my children.
40 So long as you were alive the gods loved you well, and even in death they have not been utterly unmindful of you; for when Achilles took any other of my sons, he would sell him beyond the seas, to Samos Imbrus or rugged Lemnos; and when he had slain you too with his sword, many a time did he drag you round the sepulcher of his comrade— though this could not give him life—yet here you lie all fresh as dew, and comely as one
45 whom Apollo has slain with his painless shafts."

Thus did she too speak through her tears with bitter moan, and then Helen for a third time took up the strain of lamentation. "Hector," said she, "dearest of all my brothers-in-law—for I am wife to Alexandrus who brought me hither to Troy—would that I had died ere he did so—twenty years are come and gone since I left my home and came

Trojans greet Priam and dead Hector at their city gates.

Proper mourning ceremony for Hector begins. In what ways did enemies show respect for one another ultimately?

from over the sea, but I have never heard one word of insult or unkindness from you. When another would chide with me, as it might be one of your brothers or sisters or of your brothers' wives, or my mother-in-law—for Priam was as kind to me as though he were my own father—you would rebuke and check them with words of gentleness and
5 goodwill. Therefore my tears flow both for you and for my unhappy self, for there is no one else in Troy who is kind to me, but all shrink and shudder as they go by me."

She wept as she spoke and the vast crowd that was gathered round her joined in her lament. Then King Priam spoke to them saying, "Bring wood, O Trojans, to the city, and fear no cunning ambush of the Argives, for Achilles when he dismissed me from
10 the ships gave me his word that they should not attack us until the morning of the twelfth day."

Forthwith they yoked their oxen and mules and gathered together before the city. Nine days long did they bring in great heaps of wood, and on the morning of the tenth day with many tears they took brave Hector forth, laid his dead body upon the summit of
15 the pile, and set the fire thereto. Then when the child of morning, rosy-fingered dawn, appeared on the eleventh day, the people again assembled, round the pyre of mighty Hector. When they were got together, they first quenched the fire with wine wherever it was burning, and then his brothers and comrades with many a bitter tear gathered his white bones, wrapped them in soft robes of purple, and laid them in a golden urn, which
20 they placed in a grave and covered over with large stones set close together. Then they built a barrow hurriedly over it keeping guard on every side lest the Achaeans should attack them before they had finished. When they had heaped up the barrow they went back again into the city, and being well assembled they held high feast in the house of Priam their king. Thus, then, did they celebrate the funeral of Hector tamer of horses.

THE ODYSSEY

BY HOMER

TRANSLATED FROM THE GREEK BY SAMUEL BUTLER

Introduction by M.B. McLatchey

The Odyssey is our earliest of epic homecoming stories in Western literature. After sacking Troy by masterfully gaining entrance to the city with a wooden Trojan Horse and proving his military genius in a ten-year war with the Trojans, the Greek commander, Ulysses finds himself engaged in yet another ten-year war: namely, his struggle to find his way home again. In the ten years it takes Ulysses to return to his homeland of Ithaca, he fights a series of battles against one-eyed monsters, seductive sirens, and duplicitous sorcerers. These are battles that test him physically, psychologically, and spiritually – and that ultimately test his commitment to his troops, to his country, to his family, and to his own core values.

Fig. 2: Trojan Horse

For modern-day readers, as for the ancient Greeks, Homer's *Odyssey* is about *going home* in both the material sense and the spiritual sense. Indeed, scholars have pointed to the degree to which *The Iliad* and *The Odyssey* function as cultural companions to one another. Together these epics capture two competing human desires equally valued by the ancient Greeks: the desire to die gloriously in battle (*kleos*) and the desire to die peacefully at home, loved and respected by one's fellow citizens (*nostos*). What ultimately defines Ulysses as a hero in *The Odyssey* is his capacity to return from war and learn how to live among his fellow citizens – thus, answering to these two competing and highly-prized ambitions. In effect, he must make the transition that history requires of him: from *military warrior* to *citizen warrior*.

The Odyssey is also a story of a homeland that has changed in the warrior's 20-year absence. There is Ulysses's son, Telemachus, who has grown from infancy to adulthood in his father's absence, but who yearns to know his father; Ulysses's wife, Penelope, who has remained loyal to her husband against the advances of rival suitors; and lastly, there is Ulysses's country that has lost sight of its guiding ideals. Hence, what the war hero, Ulysses, discovers when he arrives home is that he must fight yet another war: that of reconciling his past with the present; of adapting the ideals he fought for in battle to the ideals of his new life as a civilian.

Of the twenty-four books in *The Odyssey*, the ones included here are intended to capture the questions and cultural concepts central to this epic: What will the ancient Greeks call a heroic and complete life? What virtues must the hero embody? What will the ideal husband, wife, father, son, and citizen look like?

COMPLETE LIST OF BOOKS FROM THE ODYSSEY

BOOK I*   SETTING THE STAGE – ULYSSES, THAT INGENIUS HERO

BOOK II*   TELEMACHUS EMBARKS UPON HIS JOURNEY TO FIND HIS FATHER

BOOK III   TELEMACHUS VISITS NESTOR AT PYLOS

BOOK IV   SUITORS IN ITHACA PLOT TO MURDER TELEMACHUS

BOOK V   CALYPSO – ULYSSES REACHES SCHERIA ON A RAFT

BOOK VI   THE MEETING BETWEEN NAUSICAA AND ULYSSES

BOOK VII   RECEPTION OF ULYSSES AT THE PALACE OF KING ALCINOUS

BOOK VIII   BANQUET IN THE HOUSE OF ALCINOUS – THE GAMES

BOOK IX *   ULYSSES TELLS HIS STORY TO PHAIKIANS: STRUGGLES TO GET HOME

BOOK X *   AEOLUS, THE LAESTRYGONES, CIRCE

BOOK XI *   THE VISIT TO THE DEAD

BOOK XII *   THE SIRENS, SCYLLA AND CHARYBDIS, THE CATTLE OF THE SUN

BOOK XIII *   ULYSSES LEAVES SCHERIA AND RETURNS TO ITHACA

BOOK XIV   ULYSSES IN THE HUT WITH EUMAEUS

BOOK XV   MINERVA SUMMONS TELEMACHUS FROM LACEDAEMON

BOOK XVI *   FATHER-SON REUNION: ULYSSES REVEALS HIMSELF TO TELEMACHUS

BOOK XVII *   ULYSSES COMES TO ITHAKA

BOOK XVIII   PENELOPE GETS PRESENTS FROM THE SUITORS

BOOK XIX *   ULYSSES INTERVIEWS PENELOPE

BOOK XX *   ULYSSES CANNOT SLEEP AND SIGNS FROM HEAVEN

BOOK XXI *   THE TRIAL OF THE AXES AND ULYSSES REVEALS HIMSELF

BOOK XXII *   THE KILLING OF THE SUITORS

BOOK XXIII *   PENELOPE RECOGNISES HER HUSBAND

BOOK XXIV *   MINERVA CALLS FOR PEACE

---

* Books included in this editition of *Primary Sources*.

BOOK I – ULYSSES, THAT INGENIUS HERO

SETTING THE STAGE – ULYSSES, THAT INGENIUS HERO – THE GODS IN COUNCIL – MINERVA'S VISIT TO ITHACA – THE CHALLENGE FROM TELEMACHUS TO THE SUITORS.

Tell me, O Muse, of that ingenious hero who travelled far and wide after he had sacked the famous town of Troy. Many cities did he visit, and many were the nations with whose manners and customs he was acquainted; moreover he suffered much by sea while trying to save his own life and bring his men safely home.

5 But do what he might he could not save his men, for they perished through their own sheer folly in eating the cattle of the Sun-god Hyperion; so the god prevented them from ever reaching home. Tell me, too, about all these things, oh daughter of Jove, from whatsoever source you may know them.

So now all who escaped death in battle or by shipwreck had got safely home except 10 Ulysses, and he, though he was longing to return to his wife and country, was detained by the goddess Calypso, who had got him into a large cave and wanted to marry him.

But as years went by, there came a time when the gods settled that he should go back to Ithaca; even then, however, when he was among his own people, his troubles were not yet over; nevertheless all the gods had now begun to pity him except Neptune, who 15 still persecuted him without ceasing and would not let him get home.

Now Neptune had gone off to the Ethiopians, who are at the world's end, and lie in two halves, the one looking West and the other East. He had gone there to accept a hecatomb of sheep and oxen, and was enjoying himself at his festival; but the other gods met in the house of Olympian Jove, and the sire of gods and men spoke first. At 20 that moment he was thinking of Aegisthus, who had been killed by Agamemnon's son Orestes; so he said to the other gods:

"See now, how men lay blame upon us gods for what is after all nothing but their own folly. Look at Aegisthus; he must needs make love to Agamemnon's wife unrighteously and then kill Agamemnon, though he knew it would be the death of him; for I sent 25 Mercury to warn him not to do either of these things, inasmuch as Orestes would be sure to take his revenge when he grew up and wanted to return home. Mercury told him this in all good will but he would not listen, and now he has paid for everything in full."

When Minerva said, "Father, son of Saturn, King of kings, it served Aegisthus right, and so it would anyone else who does as he did; but Aegisthus is neither here nor there; 30 it is for Ulysses that my heart bleeds, when I think of his sufferings in that lonely sea-girt island, far away, poor man, from all his friends. It is an island covered with forest, in the very middle of the sea, and a goddess lives there, daughter of the magician Atlas, who looks after the bottom of the ocean, and carries the great columns that keep heaven and earth asunder.

Note the accent on actions and consequences. Also, note the distinction between Ulysses and his men. How would you characterize this difference?

Note the involvement of ancient Greek gods in human lives that points to the tension between *fate* (will of the gods) and *free will* (will of human beings).

Note the ancient Greek theological principle drawn here – that men must not blame the gods for how their lives turn out.

Ancient Greek gods favor and facilitate some human beings and haunt and harness others.

This daughter of Atlas has got hold of poor unhappy Ulysses, and keeps trying by every kind of blandishment to make him forget his home, so that he is tired of life, and thinks of nothing but how he may once more see the smoke of his own chimneys. You, sir, take no heed of this, and yet when Ulysses was before Troy did he not propitiate you
5 with many a burnt sacrifice? Why then should you keep on being so angry with him?"

And Jove said, "My child, what are you talking about? How can I forget Ulysses than whom there is no more capable man on earth, nor more liberal in his offerings to the immortal gods that live in heaven? Bear in mind, however, that Neptune is still furious with Ulysses for having blinded an eye of Polyphemus king of the Cyclopes.
10 Polyphemus is son to Neptune by the nymph Thoosa, daughter to the sea-king Phorcys; therefore though he will not kill Ulysses outright, he torments him by preventing him from getting home. Still, let us lay our heads together and see how we can help him to return; Neptune will then be pacified, for if we are all of a mind he can hardly stand out against us."

15 And Minerva said, "Father, son of Saturn, King of kings, if, then, the gods now mean that Ulysses should get home, we should first send Mercury to the Ogygian island to tell Calypso that we have made up our minds and that he is to return. In the meantime I will go to Ithaca, to put heart into Ulysses' son Telemachus; I will embolden him to call the Achaeans in assembly, and speak out to the suitors of his mother Penelope, who
20 persist in eating up any number of his sheep and oxen; I will also conduct him to Sparta and to Pylos, to see if he can hear anything about the return of his dear father--for this will make people speak well of him."

So saying she bound on her glittering golden sandals, imperishable, with which she can fly like the wind over land or sea; she grasped the redoubtable bronze-shod spear, so
25 stout and sturdy and strong, wherewith she quells the ranks of heroes who have displeased her, and down she darted from the topmost summits of Olympus, whereon forthwith she was in Ithaca, at the gateway of Ulysses' house, disguised as a visitor, Mentes, chief of the Taphians, and she held a bronze spear in her hand. There she found the lordly suitors seated on hides of the oxen which they had killed and eaten, and
30 playing draughts in front of the house. Men-servants and pages were bustling about to wait upon them, some mixing wine with water in the mixing-bowls, some cleaning down the tables with wet sponges and laying them out again, and some cutting up great quantities of meat.

Telemachus saw her long before anyone else did. He was sitting moodily among the
35 suitors thinking about his brave father, and how he would send them flying out of the house, if he were to come to his own again and be honored as in days gone by. Thus brooding as he sat among them, he caught sight of Minerva and went straight to the gate, for he was vexed that a stranger should be kept waiting for admittance. He took her right hand in his own, and bade her give him her spear. "Welcome," said he, "to our
40 house, and when you have partaken of food you shall tell us what you have come for."

He led the way as he spoke, and Minerva followed him. When they were within he took her spear and set it in the spear-stand against a strong bearing-post along with the many other spears of his unhappy father, and he conducted her to a richly decorated seat under which he threw a cloth of damask. There was a footstool also for her feet,and he
45 set another seat near her for himself, away from the suitors, that she might not be annoyed while eating by their noise and insolence, and that he might ask her more freely about his father.

What are the characteristics of an enemy to Ulysses, as drawn by Minerva?

Note the lively interaction between gods and humans. How might this be explained in terms of psychological or religious ideas?

What guidance can Telemachus gain from the gods?

A maid servant then brought them water in a beautiful golden ewer and poured it into a silver basin for them to wash their hands, and she drew a clean table beside them. An upper servant brought them bread, and offered them many good things of what there was in the house, the carver fetched them plates of all manner of meats and set cups of
5 gold by their side, and a manservant brought them wine and poured it out for them.

What irregularities and improprieties do the suitors seem to demonstrate?

Then the suitors came in and took their places on the benches and seats. Forthwith men servants poured water over their hands, maids went round with the bread-baskets, pages filled the mixing-bowls with wine and water, and they laid their hands upon the good things that were before them. As soon as they had had enough to eat and drink they
10 wanted music and dancing, which are the crowning embellishments of a banquet, so a servant brought a lyre to Phemius, whom they compelled perforce to sing to them. As soon as he touched his lyre and began to sing Telemachus spoke low to Minerva, with his head close to hers that no man might hear.

"I hope, sir," said he, "that you will not be offended with what I am going to say. Singing
15 comes cheap to those who do not pay for it, and all this is done at the cost of one whose bones lie rotting in some wilderness or grinding to powder in the surf. If these men were to see my father come back to Ithaca they would pray for longer legs rather than a longer purse, for money would not serve them; but he, alas, has fallen on an ill fate, and even when people do sometimes say that he is coming, we no longer heed them;
20 we shall never see him again. And now, sir, tell me and tell me true, who you are and where you come from. Tell me of your town and parents, what manner of ship you came in, how your crew brought you to Ithaca, and of what nation they declared themselves to be--for you cannot have come by land. Tell me also truly, for I want to know, are you a stranger to this house, or have you been here in my father's time? In
25 the old days we had many visitors for my father went about much himself."

And Minerva answered, "I will tell you truly and particularly all about it. I am Mentes, son of Anchialus, and I am King of the Taphians. I have come here with my ship and crew, on a voyage to men of a foreign tongue being bound for Temesa with a cargo of iron, and I shall bring back copper. As for my ship, it lies over yonder off the open
30 country away from the town, in the harbour Rheithron under the wooded mountain Neritum. Our fathers were friends before us, as old Laertes will tell you, if you will go and ask him. They say, however, that he never comes to town now, and lives by himself in the country, faring hardly, with an old woman to look after him and get his dinner for him, when he comes in tired from pottering about his vineyard. They told me your
35 father was at home again, and that was why I came, but it seems the gods are still keeping him back, for he is not dead yet not on the mainland. It is more likely he is on some sea-girt island in mid ocean, or a prisoner among savages who are detaining him against his will. I am no prophet, and know very little about omens, but I speak as it is borne in upon me from heaven, and assure you that he will not be away much longer; for he
40 is a man of such resource that even though he were in chains of iron he would find some means of getting home again. But tell me, and tell me true, can Ulysses really have such a fine looking fellow for a son? You are indeed wonderfully like him about the head and eyes, for we were close friends before he set sail for Troy where the flower of all the Argives went also. Since that time we have never either of us seen the other."

45 "My mother," answered Telemachus, "tells me I am son to Ulysses, but it is a wise child that knows his own father. Would that I were son to one who had grown old upon his own estates, for, since you ask me, there is no more ill-starred man under heaven than he who they tell me is my father."

And Minerva said, "There is no fear of your race dying out yet, while Penelope has such a fine son as you are. But tell me, and tell me true, what is the meaning of all this feasting, and who are these people? What is it all about? Have you some banquet, or is there a wedding in the family--for no one seems to be bringing any provisions of his own? And 5 the guests--how atrociously they are behaving; what riot they make over the whole house; it is enough to disgust any respectable person who comes near them."

"Sir," said Telemachus, "as regards your question, so long as my father was here it was well with us and with the house, but the gods in their displeasure have willed it otherwise, and have hidden him away more closely than mortal man was ever yet 10 hidden. I could have borne it better even though he were dead, if he had fallen with his men before Troy, or had died with friends around him when the days of his fighting were done; for then the Achaeans would have built a mound over his ashes, and I should myself have been heir to his renown; but now the storm-winds have spirited him away we know not whither; he is gone without leaving so much as a trace behind him, and I 15 inherit nothing but dismay. Nor does the matter end simply with grief for the loss of my father; heaven has laid sorrows upon me of yet another kind; for the chiefs from all our islands, Dulichium, Same, and the woodland island of Zacynthus, as also all the principal men of Ithaca itself, are eating up my house under the pretext of paying their court to my mother, who will neither point blank say that she will not marry, nor yet 20 bring matters to an end; so they are making havoc of my estate, and before long will do so also with myself."

What ancient Greek values do the suitors challenge?

"Is that so?" exclaimed Minerva, "then you do indeed want Ulysses home again. Give him his helmet, shield, and a couple of lances, and if he is the man he was when I first knew him in our house, drinking and making merry, he would soon lay his hands about 25 these rascally suitors, were he to stand once more upon his own threshold. He was then coming from Ephyra, where he had been to beg poison for his arrows from Ilus, son of Mermerus. Ilus feared the ever-living gods and would not give him any, but my father let him have some, for he was very fond of him. If Ulysses is the man he then was these suitors will have a short shrift and a sorry wedding.

30 "But there! It rests with heaven to determine whether he is to return, and take his revenge in his own house or no; I would, however, urge you to set about trying to get rid of these suitors at once. Take my advice, call the Achaean heroes in assembly to-morrow morning--lay your case before them, and call heaven to bear you witness. Bid the suitors take themselves off, each to his own place, and if your mother's mind is set 35 on marrying again, let her go back to her father, who will find her a husband and provide her with all the marriage gifts that so dear a daughter may expect. As for yourself, let me prevail upon you to take the best ship you can get, with a crew of twenty men, and go in quest of your father who has so long been missing. Someone may tell you something, or (and people often hear things in this way) some heaven-sent message may 40 direct you. First go to Pylos and ask Nestor; thence go on to Sparta and visit Menelaus, for he got home last of all the Achaeans; if you hear that your father is alive and on his way home, you can put up with the waste these suitors will make for yet another twelve months. If on the other hand you hear of his death, come home at once, celebrate his funeral rites with all due pomp, build a barrow to his memory, and make your mother 45 marry again. Then, having done all this, think it well over in your mind how, by fair means or foul, you may kill these suitors in your own house. You are too old to plead infancy any longer; have you not heard how people are singing Orestes' praises for having killed his father's murderer Aegisthus? You are a fine, smart looking fellow; show your mettle, then, and make yourself a name in story. Now, however, I must go back to

What does Minerva mean when she says "It rests with heaven…"?

my ship and to my crew, who will be impatient if I keep them waiting longer; think the matter over for yourself, and remember what I have said to you."

"Sir," answered Telemachus, "it has been very kind of you to talk to me in this way, as though I were your own son, and I will do all you tell me; I know you want to be getting
5 on with your voyage, but stay a little longer till you have taken a bath and refreshed yourself. I will then give you a present, and you shall go on your way rejoicing; I will give you one of great beauty and value--a keepsake such as only dear friends give to one another."

Minerva answered, "Do not try to keep me, for I would be on my way at once. As for
10 any present you may be disposed to make me, keep it till I come again, and I will take it home with me. You shall give me a very good one, and I will give you one of no less value in return."

With these words she flew away like a bird into the air, but she had given Telemachus courage, and had made him think more than ever about his father. He felt the change,
15 wondered at it, and knew that the stranger had been a god, so he went straight to where the suitors were sitting.

Phemius was still singing, and his hearers sat rapt in silence as he told the sad tale of the return from Troy, and the ills Minerva had laid upon the Achaeans. Penelope, daughter of Icarius, heard his song from her room upstairs, and came down by the great staircase,
20 not alone, but attended by two of her handmaids. When she reached the suitors she stood by one of the bearing posts that supported the roof of the cloisters with a staid maiden on either side of her. She held a veil, moreover, before her face, and was weeping bitterly.

"Phemius," she cried, "you know many another feat of gods and heroes, such as poets
25 love to celebrate. Sing the suitors some one of these, and let them drink their wine in silence, but cease this sad tale, for it breaks my sorrowful heart, and reminds me of my lost husband whom I mourn ever without ceasing, and whose name was great over all Hellas and middle Argos."

Note the ancient Greek mother-son relationship.

"Mother," answered Telemachus, "let the bard sing what he has a mind to; bards do not
30 make the ills they sing of; it is Jove, not they, who makes them, and who sends weal or woe upon mankind according to his own good pleasure. This fellow means no harm by singing the ill-fated return of the Danaans, for people always applaud the latest songs most warmly. Make up your mind to it and bear it; Ulysses is not the only man who never came back from Troy, but many another went down as well as he. Go, then,
35 within the house and busy yourself with your daily duties, your loom, your distaff, and the ordering of your servants; for speech is man's matter, and mine above all others -- for it is I who am master here."

She went wondering back into the house, and laid her son's saying in her heart. Then, going upstairs with her handmaids into her room, she mourned her dear husband till
40 Minerva shed sweet sleep over her eyes. But the suitors were clamorous throughout the covered cloisters, and prayed each one that he might be her bed fellow.

Then Telemachus spoke, "Shameless," he cried, "and insolent suitors, let us feast at our pleasure now, and let there be no brawling, for it is a rare thing to hear a man with such a divine voice as Phemius has; but in the morning meet me in full assembly that I may give you formal notice to depart, and feast at one another's houses, turn and turn about, at your own cost. If on the other hand you choose to persist in spunging upon one man, heaven help me, but Jove shall reckon with you in full, and when you fall in my father's house there shall be no man to avenge you."

5   The suitors bit their lips as they heard him, and marvelled at the boldness of his speech. Then, Antinous, son of Eupeithes, said, "The gods seem to have given you lessons in bluster and tall talking; may Jove never grant you to be chief in Ithaca as your father was before you."

Telemachus answered, "Antinous, do not chide with me, but, god willing, I will be chief
10 too if I can. Is this the worst fate you can think of for me? It is no bad thing to be a chief, for it brings both riches and honour. Still, now that Ulysses is dead there are many great men in Ithaca both old and young, and some other may take the lead among them; nevertheless I will be chief in my own house, and will rule those whom Ulysses has won for me."

Does Telemachus seem a surrogate to Ulysses?

15 Then Eurymachus, son of Polybus, answered, "It rests with heaven to decide who shall be chief among us, but you shall be master in your own house and over your own possessions; no one while there is a man in Ithaca shall do you violence nor rob you. And now, my good fellow, I want to know about this stranger. What country does he come from? Of what family is he, and where is his estate? Has he brought you news
20 about the return of your father, or was he on business of his own? He seemed a well to do man, but he hurried off so suddenly that he was gone in a moment before we could get to know him."

"My father is dead and gone," answered Telemachus, "and even if some rumour reaches me I put no more faith in it now. My mother does indeed sometimes send for a
25 soothsayer and question him, but I give his prophecyings no heed. As for the stranger, he was Mentes, son of Anchialus, chief of the Taphians, an old friend of my father's." But in his heart he knew that it had been the goddess.

The suitors then returned to their singing and dancing until the evening; but when night fell upon their pleasuring they went home to bed each in his own abode. Telemachus's
30 room was high up in a tower that looked on to the outer court; hither, then, he hied, brooding and full of thought. A good old woman, Euryclea, daughter of Ops, the son of Pisenor, went before him with a couple of blazing torches. Laertes had bought her with his own money when she was quite young; he gave the worth of twenty oxen for her, and shewed as much respect to her in his household as he did to his own wedded
35 wife, but he did not take her to his bed for he feared his wife's resentment. She it was who now lighted Telemachus to his room, and she loved him better than any of the other women in the house did, for she had nursed him when he was a baby. He opened the door of his bed room and sat down upon the bed; as he took off his shirt he gave it to the good old woman, who folded it tidily up, and hung it for him over a peg by his
40 bed side, after which she went out, pulled the door to by a silver catch, and drew the bolt home by means of the strap. But Telemachus as he lay covered with a woolen fleece kept thinking all night through of his intended voyage and of the counsel that Minerva had given him.

What goals does Minerva set for Telemachus?

BOOK II – TELEMACHUS EMBARKS TO FIND HIS FATHER

ASSEMBLY OF THE PEOPLE OF ITHACA – PEECHES OF TELEMACHUS AND OF THE SUITORS – TELEMACHUS EMBARKS UPON HIS JOURNEY TO FIND HIS FATHER, WITH MINERVA GUIDING HIS WAY AND DISGUISED AS HIS MENTOR.

Now when the child of morning, rosy-fingered Dawn, appeared Telemachus rose and dressed himself. He bound his sandals on to his comely feet, girded his sword about his shoulder, and left his room looking like an immortal god. He at once sent the criers round to call the people in assembly, so they called them and the people gathered
5 thereon; then, when they were got together, he went to the place of assembly spear in hand--not alone, for his two hounds went with him. Minerva endowed him with a presence of such divine comeliness that all marvelled at him as he went by, and when he took his place in his father's seat even the oldest councillors made way for him.

Aegyptius, a man bent double with age, and of infinite experience, was the first to speak.
10 His son Antiphus had gone with Ulysses to Ilius, land of noble steeds, but the savage Cyclops had killed him when they were all shut up in the cave. He had three sons left, of whom two still worked on their father's land, while the third, Eurynomus, was one of the suitors; nevertheless their father could not get over the loss of Antiphus, and was still weeping for him when he began his speech.

15 "Men of Ithaca," he said, "hear my words. From the day Ulysses left us there has been no meeting of our councillors until now; who then can it be, whether old or young, that finds it so necessary to convene us? Has he got wind of some host approaching, and does he wish to warn us, or would he speak upon some other matter of public moment? I am sure he is an excellent person, and I hope Jove will grant him his heart's desire."

How does Telemachus seem to resemble his father?

20 Telemachus took this speech as of good omen and rose at once, for he was bursting with what he had to say. He stood in the middle of the assembly and the good herald Pisenor brought him his staff. Then, turning to Aegyptius, "Sir," said he, "it is I, as you will shortly learn, who have convened you, for it is I who am the most aggrieved. I have not got wind of any host approaching about which I would warn you, nor is there any
25 matter of public moment on which I would speak. My grievance is purely personal, and turns on two great misfortunes which have fallen upon my house. The first of these is the loss of my excellent father, who was chief among all you here present, and was like a father to every one of you; the second is much more serious, and ere long will be the utter ruin of my estate.

30 The sons of all the chief men among you are pestering my mother to marry them against her will. They are afraid to go to her father Icarius, asking him to choose the one he likes best, and to provide marriage gifts for his daughter, but day by day they keep hanging about my father's house, sacrificing our oxen, sheep, and fat goats for their banquets, and never giving so much as a thought to the quantity of wine they drink. No
35 estate can stand such recklessness; we have now no Ulysses to ward off harm from our doors, and I cannot hold my own against them. I shall never all my days be as good a man as he was, still I would indeed defend myself if I had power to do so, for I cannot stand such treatment any longer; my house is being disgraced and ruined. Have respect, therefore, to your own consciences and to public opinion. Fear, too, the wrath of
40 heaven, lest the gods should be displeased and turn upon you. I pray you by Jove and Themis, who is the beginning and the end of councils, do not hold back, my friends, and leave me singlehanded --unless it be that my brave father Ulysses did some wrong

to the Achaeans which you would now avenge on me, by aiding and abetting these suitors. Moreover, if I am to be eaten out of house and home at all, I had rather you did the eating yourselves, for I could then take action against you to some purpose, and serve you with notices from house to house till I got paid in full, whereas now I have
5 no remedy."

With this Telemachus dashed his staff to the ground and burst into tears. Every one was very sorry for him, but they all sat still and no one ventured to make him an angry answer, save only Antinous, who spoke thus:

"Telemachus, insolent braggart that you are, how dare you try to throw the blame upon
10 us suitors? It is your mother's fault not ours, for she is a very artful woman. This three years past, and close on four, she had been driving us out of our minds, by encouraging each one of us, and sending him messages without meaning one word of what she says. And then there was that other trick she played us. She set up a great tambour frame in her room, and began to work on an enormous piece of fine needlework. 'Sweet hearts,'
15 said she, 'Ulysses is indeed dead, still do not press me to marry again immediately, wait--for I would not have skill in needlework perish unrecorded--till I have completed a pall for the hero Laertes, to be in readiness against the time when death shall take him. He is very rich, and the women of the place will talk if he is laid out without a pall.'

"This was what she said, and we assented; whereon we could see her working on her
20 great web all day long, but at night she would unpick the stitches again by torchlight. She fooled us in this way for three years and we never found her out, but as time wore on and she was now in her fourth year, one of her maids who knew what she was doing told us, and we caught her in the act of undoing her work, so she had to finish it whether she would or no. The suitors, therefore, make you this answer, that both you and the
25 Achaeans may understand-'Send your mother away, and bid her marry the man of her own and of her father's choice'; for I do not know what will happen if she goes on plaguing us much longer with the airs she gives herself on the score of the accomplishments Minerva has taught her, and because she is so clever. We never yet heard of such a woman; we know all about Tyro, Alcmena, Mycene, and the famous
30 women of old, but they were nothing to your mother any one of them. It was not fair of her to treat us in that way, and as long as she continues in the mind with which heaven has now endowed her, so long shall we go on eating up your estate; and I do not see why she should change, for she gets all the honour and glory, and it is you who pay for it, not she. Understand, then, that we will not go back to our lands, neither here
35 nor elsewhere, till she has made her choice and married some one or other of us."

Telemachus answered, "Antinous, how can I drive the mother who bore me from my father's house? My father is abroad and we do not know whether he is alive or dead. It will be hard on me if I have to pay Icarius the large sum which I must give him if I insist on sending his daughter back to him. Not only will he deal rigorously with me, but
40 heaven will also punish me; for my mother when she leaves the house will call on the Erinyes to avenge her; besides, it would not be a creditable thing to do, and I will have nothing to say to it. If you choose to take offence at this, leave the house and feast elsewhere at one another's houses at your own cost turn and turn about. If, on the other hand, you elect to persist in spunging upon one man, heaven help me, but Jove shall
45 reckon with you in full, and when you fall in my father's house there shall be no man to avenge you."

As he spoke Jove sent two eagles from the top of the mountain, and they flew on and on with the wind, sailing side by side in their own lordly flight. When they were right

In what sense is Penelope the perfect mate for Ulysses?

What loyalties does Telemachus express?

over the middle of the assembly they wheeled and circled about, beating the air with their wings and glaring death into the eyes of them that were below; then, fighting fiercely and tearing at one another, they flew off towards the right over the town. The people wondered as they saw them, and asked each other what all this might be; whereon Halitherses, who was the best prophet and reader of omens among them, spoke to them plainly and in all honesty, saying:

"Hear me, men of Ithaca, and I speak more particularly to the suitors, for I see mischief brewing for them. Ulysses is not going to be away much longer; indeed he is close at hand to deal out death and destruction, not on them alone, but on many another of us who live in Ithaca. Let us then be wise in time, and put a stop to this wickedness before he comes. Let the suitors do so of their own accord; it will be better for them, for I am not prophesying without due knowledge; everything has happened to Ulysses as I foretold when the Argives set out for Troy, and he with them. I said that after going through much hardship and losing all his men he should come home again in the twentieth year and that no one would know him; and now all this is coming true."

Eurymachus son of Polybus then said, "Go home, old man, and prophesy to your own children, or it may be worse for them. I can read these omens myself much better than you can; birds are always flying about in the sunshine somewhere or other, but they seldom mean anything. Ulysses has died in a far country, and it is a pity you are not dead along with him, instead of prating here about omens and adding fuel to the anger of Telemachus which is fierce enough as it is. I suppose you think he will give you something for your family, but I tell you--and it shall surely be--when an old man like you, who should know better, talks a young one over till he becomes troublesome, in the first place his young friend will only fare so much the worse--he will take nothing by it, for the suitors will prevent this--and in the next, we will lay a heavier fine, sir, upon yourself than you will at all like paying, for it will bear hardly upon you. As for Telemachus, I warn him in the presence of you all to send his mother back to her father, who will find her a husband and provide her with all the marriage gifts so dear a daughter may expect. Till then we shall go on harassing him with our suit; for we fear no man, and care neither for him, with all his fine speeches, nor for any fortune-telling of yours. You may preach as much as you please, but we shall only hate you the more. We shall go back and continue to eat up Telemachus's estate without paying him, till such time as his mother leaves off tormenting us by keeping us day after day on the tiptoe of expectation, each vying with the other in his suit for a prize of such rare perfection. Besides we cannot go after the other women whom we should marry in due course, but for the way in which she treats us."

The father-search is a central mythological motif. What propels Telemachus to search for his father?

Then Telemachus said, "Eurymachus, and you other suitors, I shall say no more, and entreat you no further, for the gods and the people of Ithaca now know my story. Give me, then, a ship and a crew of twenty men to take me hither and thither, and I will go to Sparta and to Pylos in quest of my father who has so long been missing. Some one may tell me something, or (and people often hear things in this way) some heaven-sent message may direct me. If I can hear of him as alive and on his way home I will put up with the waste you suitors will make for yet another twelve months. If on the other hand I hear of his death, I will return at once, celebrate his funeral rites with all due pomp, build a barrow to his memory, and make my mother marry again."

With these words he sat down, and Mentor who had been a friend of Ulysses, and had been left in charge of everything with full authority over the servants, rose to speak. He, then, plainly and in all honesty addressed them thus:

"Hear me, men of Ithaca, I hope that you may never have a kind and well-disposed ruler any more, nor one who will govern you equitably; I hope that all your chiefs henceforward may be cruel and unjust, for there is not one of you but has forgotten Ulysses, who ruled you as though he were your father. I am not half so angry with the suitors, for if they choose to do violence in the naughtiness of their hearts, and wager their heads that Ulysses will not return, they can take the high hand and eat up his estate, but as for you others I am shocked at the way in which you all sit still without even trying to stop such scandalous goings on--which you could do if you chose, for you are many and they are few."

Leiocritus, son of Evenor, answered him saying, "Mentor, what folly is all this, that you should set the people to stay us? It is a hard thing for one man to fight with many about his victuals. Even though Ulysses himself were to set upon us while we are feasting in his house, and do his best to oust us, his wife, who wants him back so very badly, would have small cause for rejoicing, and his blood would be upon his own head if he fought against such great odds. There is no sense in what you have been saying. Now, therefore, do you people go about your business, and let his father's old friends, Mentor and Halitherses, speed this boy on his journey, if he goes at all--which I do not think he will, for he is more likely to stay where he is till some one comes and tells him something."

On this he broke up the assembly, and every man went back to his own abode, while the suitors returned to the house of Ulysses.

Then Telemachus went all alone by the sea side, washed his hands in the grey waves, and prayed to Minerva.

"Hear me," he cried, "you god who visited me yesterday, and bade me sail the seas in search of my father who has so long been missing. I would obey you, but the Achaeans, and more particularly the wicked suitors, are hindering me that I cannot do so."

As he thus prayed, Minerva came close up to him in the likeness and with the voice of Mentor. "Telemachus," said she, "if you are made of the same stuff as your father you will be neither fool nor coward henceforward, for Ulysses never broke his word nor left his work half done. If, then, you take after him, your voyage will not be fruitless, but unless you have the blood of Ulysses and of Penelope in your veins I see no likelihood of your succeeding. Sons are seldom as good men as their fathers; they are generally worse, not better; still, as you are not going to be either fool or coward henceforward, and are not entirely without some share of your father's wise discernment, I look with hope upon your undertaking. But mind you never make common cause with any of those foolish suitors, for they have neither sense nor virtue, and give no thought to death and to the doom that will shortly fall on one and all of them, so that they shall perish on the same day. As for your voyage, it shall not be long delayed; your father was such an old friend of mine that I will find you a ship, and will come with you myself. Now, however, return home, and go about among the suitors; begin getting provisions ready for your voyage; see everything well stowed, the wine in jars, and the barley meal, which is the staff of life, in leathern bags, while I go round the town and beat up volunteers at once. There are many ships in Ithaca both old and new; I will run my eye over them for you and will choose the best; we will get her ready and will put out to sea without delay."

Thus spoke Minerva daughter of Jove, and Telemachus lost no time in doing as the goddess told him. He went moodily home, and found the suitors flaying goats and

How does Minerva mobilize Telemachus?

singeing pigs in the outer court. Antinous came up to him at once and laughed as he took his hand in his own, saying, "Telemachus, my fine fire-eater, bear no more ill blood neither in word nor deed, but eat and drink with us as you used to do. The Achaeans will find you in everything--a ship and a picked crew to boot--so that you can set sail for Pylos at once and get news of your noble father."

"Antinous," answered Telemachus, "I cannot eat in peace, nor take pleasure of any kind with such men as you are. Was it not enough that you should waste so much good property of mine while I was yet a boy? Now that I am older and know more about it, I am also stronger, and whether here among this people, or by going to Pylos, I will do you all the harm I can. I shall go, and my going will not be in vain--though, thanks to you suitors, I have neither ship nor crew of my own, and must be passenger not captain."

As he spoke he snatched his hand from that of Antinous. Meanwhile the others went on getting dinner ready about the buildings, jeering at him tauntingly as they did so.

"Telemachus," said one youngster, "means to be the death of us; I suppose he thinks he can bring friends to help him from Pylos, or again from Sparta, where he seems bent on going. Or will he go to Ephyra as well, for poison to put in our wine and kill us?"

Another said, "Perhaps if Telemachus goes on board ship, he will be like his father and perish far from his friends. In this case we should have plenty to do, for we could then divide up his property amongst us: as for the house we can let his mother and the man who marries her have that."

This was how they talked. But Telemachus went down into the lofty and spacious store-room where his father's treasure of gold and bronze lay heaped up upon the floor, and where the linen and spare clothes were kept in open chests. Here, too, there was a store of fragrant olive oil, while casks of old, well-ripened wine, unblended and fit for a god to drink, were ranged against the wall in case Ulysses should come home again after all. The room was closed with well-made doors opening in the middle; moreover the faithful old house-keeper Euryclea, daughter of Ops the son of Pisenor, was in charge of everything both night and day. Telemachus called her to the store-room and said:

"Nurse, draw me off some of the best wine you have, after what you are keeping for my father's own drinking, in case, poor man, he should escape death, and find his way home again after all. Let me have twelve jars, and see that they all have lids; also fill me some well-sewn leathern bags with barley meal--about twenty measures in all. Get these things put together at once, and say nothing about it. I will take everything away this evening as soon as my mother has gone upstairs for the night. I am going to Sparta and to Pylos to see if I can hear anything about the return of my dear father."

How does Antinous contrast to Ulysses?

BOOK IX – ULYSSES TELLS STORY OF HIS STRUGGLES

AFTER BEING WASHED ASHORE ON THE PHAIKIANS' COAST, ULYSSES IDENTIFIES HIMSELF AND BEGINS TO TELL HIS STORY OF HIS STRUGGLES TO RETURN HOME TO ITHACA.

Thus Ulysses announced, "King Alcinous, it is a good thing to hear a bard with such a divine voice as this man has. There is nothing better or more delightful than when a whole people make merry together, with the guests sitting orderly to listen, while the table is loaded with bread and meats, and the cup-bearer draws wine and fills his cup

5 for every man. This is indeed as fair a sight as a man can see. Now, however, since you are inclined to ask the story of my sorrows, and rekindle my own sad memories in respect of them, I do not know how to begin, nor yet how to continue and conclude my tale, for the hand of heaven has been laid heavily upon me.

"Firstly, then, I will tell you my name that you too may know it, and one day, if I outlive
10 this time of sorrow, may become my guests though I live so far away from all of you. I am Ulysses son of Laertes, renowned among mankind for all manner of subtlety, so that my fame ascends to heaven. I live in Ithaca, where there is a high mountain called Neritum, covered with forests; and not far from it there is a group of islands very near to one another--Dulichium, Same, and the wooded island of Zacynthus. It lies squat on
15 the horizon, all highest up in the sea towards the sunset, while the others lie away from it towards dawn.

Historical Narrative begins: Ulysses tells his story to the Phaikians. Note the ancient Greek concept, *nostos*, celebrated here.

It is a rugged island, but it breeds brave men, and my eyes know none that they better love to look upon. The goddess Calypso kept me with her in her cave, and wanted me to marry her, as did also the cunning Aeaean goddess Circe; but they could neither of
20 them persuade me, for there is nothing dearer to a man than his own country and his parents, and however splendid a home he may have in a foreign country, if it be far from father or mother, he does not care about it.

Note the identity between self and place, culture and country.

Now, however, I will tell you of the many hazardous adventures which by Jove's will I met with on my return from Troy. "When I had set sail thence the wind took me first
25 to Ismarus, which is the city of the Cicons. There I sacked the town and put the people to the sword. We took their wives and also much booty, which we divided equitably amongst us, so that none might have reason to complain. I then said that we had better make off at once, but my men very foolishly would not obey me, so they stayed there drinking much wine and killing great numbers of sheep and oxen on the sea shore.

What ancient Greek values can be extracted from Ulysses's tale?

30 Meanwhile the Cicons cried out for help to other Cicons who lived inland. These were more in number, and stronger, and they were more skilled in the art of war, for they could fight, either from chariots or on foot as the occasion served; in the morning, therefore, they came as thick as leaves and bloom in summer, and the hand of heaven was against us, so that we were hard pressed. They set the battle in array near the ships,
35 and the hosts aimed their bronze-shod spears at one another. So long as the day waxed and it was still morning, we held our own against them, though they were more in number than we; but as the sun went down, towards the time when men loose their oxen, the Cicons got the better of us, and we lost half a dozen men from every ship we had; so we got away with those that were left.

40 "Thence we sailed onward with sorrow in our hearts, but glad to have escaped death though we had lost our comrades, nor did we leave till we had thrice invoked each one

of the poor fellows who had perished by the hands of the Cicons. Then Jove raised the North wind against us till it blew a hurricane, so that land and sky were hidden in thick clouds, and night sprang forth out of the heavens. We let the ships run before the gale, but the force of the wind tore our sails to tatters, so we took them down for fear of
5 shipwreck, and rowed our hardest towards the land. There we lay two days and two nights suffering much alike from toil and distress of mind, but on the morning of the third day we again raised our masts, set sail, and took our places, letting the wind and steersmen direct our ship. I should have got home at that time unharmed had not the North wind and the currents been against me as I was doubling Cape Malea, and set me
10 off my course hard by the island of Cythera.

Land of Lotus Eaters.

"I was driven thence by foul winds for a space of nine days upon the sea, but on the tenth day we reached the land of the Lotus-eaters, who live on a food that comes from a kind of flower. Here we landed to take in fresh water, and our crews got their mid-day meal on the shore near the ships. When they had eaten and drunk I sent two of my
15 company to see what manner of men the people of the place might be, and they had a third man under them.

Note the impact of the lotus on the troops. Cite parallels in modern warfare.

They started at once, and went about among the Lotus-eaters, who did them no hurt, but gave them to eat of the lotus, which was so delicious that those who ate of it left off caring about home, and did not even want to go back and say what had happened
20 to them. I forced them back to the ships and made them fast under the benches. Then I told the rest to go on board at once, lest any of them should taste of the lotus and leave off wanting to get home, so they took their places and smote the grey sea with their oars.

Land of the Cyclopes.

"We sailed hence, always in much distress, till we came to the land of the lawless and
25 inhuman Cyclopes. Now the Cyclopes neither plant nor plough, but trust in providence, and live on such wheat, barley, and grapes as grow wild without any kind of tillage, and their wild grapes yield them wine as the sun and the rain may grow them. They have no laws nor assemblies of the people, but live in caves on the tops of high mountains; each is lord and master in his family, and they take no account of their neighbours.

Troops hunt wild goats and sack city of Cicons.

30 "Now off their harbour there lies a wooded and fertile island not quite close to the land of the Cyclopes, but still not far. It is over-run with wild goats, that breed there in great numbers and are never disturbed by foot of man; for sportsmen--who as a rule will suffer so much hardship in forest or among mountain precipices--do not go there, nor yet again is it ever ploughed or fed down, but it lies a wilderness untilled and unsown
35 from year to year, and has no living thing upon it but only goats. For the Cyclopes have no ships, nor yet shipwrights who could make ships for them; they cannot therefore go from city to city, or sail over the sea to one another's country as people who have ships can do; if they had had these they would have colonised the island, for it is a very good one, and would yield everything in due season. There are meadows that in some places
40 come right down to the sea shore, well watered and full of luscious grass; grapes would do there excellently; there is level land for ploughing, and it would always yield heavily at harvest time, for the soil is deep. There is a good harbour where no cables are wanted, nor yet anchors, nor need a ship be moored, but all one has to do is to beach one's vessel and stay there till the wind becomes fair for putting out to sea again. At the head
45 of the harbour there is a spring of clear water coming out of a cave, and there are poplars growing all round it.

"Here we entered, but so dark was the night that some god must have brought us in, for there was nothing whatever to be seen. A thick mist hung all round our ships; the moon was hidden behind a mass of clouds so that no one could have seen the island if he had looked for it, nor were there any breakers to tell us we were close in shore before we found ourselves upon the land itself; when, however, we had beached the ships, we took down the sails, went ashore and camped upon the beach till daybreak.

5   "When the child of morning, rosy-fingered Dawn appeared, we admired the island and wandered all over it, while the nymphs Jove's daughters roused the wild goats that we might get some meat for our dinner. On this we fetched our spears and bows and arrows from the ships, and dividing ourselves into three bands began to shoot the goats. Heaven sent us excellent sport; I had twelve ships with me, and each ship got nine goats,
10   while my own ship had ten; thus through the livelong day to the going down of the sun we ate and drank our fill, and we had plenty of wine left, for each one of us had taken many jars full when we sacked the city of the Cicons, and this had not yet run out. While we were feasting we kept turning our eyes towards the land of the Cyclopes, which was hard by, and saw the smoke of their stubble fires. We could almost fancy we heard their
15   voices and the bleating of their sheep and goats, but when the sun went down and it came on dark, we camped down upon the beach, and next morning I called a council.

"'Stay here, my brave fellows,' said I, 'all the rest of you, while I go with my ship and exploit these people myself: I want to see if they are uncivilised savages, or a hospitable and humane race.'

20   "I went on board, bidding my men to do so also and loose the hawsers; so they took their places and smote the grey sea with their oars. When we got to the land, which was not far, there, on the face of a cliff near the sea, we saw a great cave overhung with laurels. It was a station for a great many sheep and goats, and outside there was a large yard, with a high wall round it made of stones built into the ground and of trees both
25   pine and oak. This was the abode of a huge monster who was then away from home shepherding his flocks. He would have nothing to do with other people, but led the life of an outlaw. He was a horrid creature, not like a human being at all, but resembling rather some crag that stands out boldly against the sky on the top of a high mountain.

Cave of Cyclops.

"I told my men to draw the ship ashore, and stay where they were, all but the twelve
30   best among them, who were to go along with myself. I also took a goatskin of sweet black wine which had been given me by Maron, son of Euanthes, who was priest of Apollo the patron god of Ismarus, and lived within the wooded precincts of the temple. When we were sacking the city we respected him, and spared his life, as also his wife and child; so he made me some presents of great value--seven talents of fine gold, and
35   a bowl of silver, with twelve jars of sweet wine, unblended, and of the most exquisite flavour. Not a man nor maid in the house knew about it, but only himself, his wife, and one housekeeper: when he drank it he mixed twenty parts of water to one of wine, and yet the fragrance from the mixing-bowl was so exquisite that it was impossible to refrain from drinking. I filled a large skin with this wine, and took a wallet full of provisions
40   with me, for my mind misgave me that I might have to deal with some savage who would be of great strength, and would respect neither right nor law.

"We soon reached his cave, but he was out shepherding, so we went inside and took stock of all that we could see. His cheese-racks were loaded with cheeses, and he had more lambs and kids than his pens could hold. They were kept in separate flocks; first
45   there were the hoggets, then the oldest of the younger lambs and lastly the very young ones all kept apart from one another; as for his dairy, all the vessels, bowls, and milk pails into which he milked, were swimming with whey. When they saw all this, my men begged me to let them first steal some cheeses, and make off with them to the ship;

Troops enter cave of Cyclops.

they would then return, drive down the lambs and kids, put them on board and sail away with them. It would have been indeed better if we had done so but I would not listen to them, for I wanted to see the owner himself, in the hope that he might give me a present. When, however, we saw him my poor men found him ill to deal with.

Cyclops enters cave; detects troops.

5 "We lit a fire, offered some of the cheeses in sacrifice, ate others of them, and then sat waiting till the Cyclops should come in with his sheep. When he came, he brought in with him a huge load of dry firewood to light the fire for his supper, and this he flung with such a noise on to the floor of his cave that we hid ourselves for fear at the far end of the cavern. Meanwhile he drove all the ewes inside, as well as the she-goats that he

10 was going to milk, leaving the males, both rams and he-goats, outside in the yards. Then he rolled a huge stone to the mouth of the cave--so huge that two and twenty strong four-wheeled waggons would not be enough to draw it from its place against the doorway. When he had so done he sat down and milked his ewes and goats, all in due course, and then let each of them have her own young. He curdled half the milk and set

15 it aside in wicker strainers, but the other half he poured into bowls that he might drink it for his supper. When he had got through with all his work, he lit the fire, and then caught sight of us, whereon he said:

"'Strangers, who are you? Where do sail from? Are you traders, or do you sail the sea as rovers, with your hands against every man, and every man's hand against you?'

Ulysses seeks *nostos* from Cyclops.

20 "We were frightened out of our senses by his loud voice and monstrous form, but I managed to say, 'We are Achaeans on our way home from Troy, but by the will of Jove, and stress of weather, we have been driven far out of our course. We are the people of Agamemnon, son of Atreus, who has won infinite renown throughout the whole world, by sacking so great a city and killing so many people. We therefore humbly pray you to

25 show us some hospitality, and otherwise make us such presents as visitors may reasonably expect. May your excellency fear the wrath of heaven, for we are your suppliants, and Jove takes all respectable travellers under his protection, for he is the avenger of all suppliants and foreigners in distress.'

"To this he gave me but a pitiless answer, 'Stranger,' said he, 'you are a fool, or else you

30 know nothing of this country. Talk to me, indeed, about fearing the gods or shunning their anger? We Cyclopes do not care about Jove or any of your blessed gods, for we are ever so much stronger than they. I shall not spare either yourself or your companions out of any regard for Jove, unless I am in the humour for doing so. And now tell me where you made your ship fast when you came on shore. Was it round the

35 point, or is she lying straight off the land?'

Ulysses lies to Cyclops.

"He said this to draw me out, but I was too cunning to be caught in that way, so I answered with a lie; 'Neptune,' said I, 'sent my ship on to the rocks at the far end of your country, and wrecked it. We were driven on to them from the open sea, but I and those who are with me escaped the jaws of death.'

Cyclops kills two troops, then sleeps.

40 "The cruel wretch vouchsafed me not one word of answer, but with a sudden clutch he gripped up two of my men at once and dashed them down upon the ground as though they had been puppies. Their brains were shed upon the ground, and the earth was wet with their blood. Then he tore them limb from limb and supped upon them. He gobbled them up like a lion in the wilderness, flesh, bones, marrow, and entrails, without leaving

45 anything uneaten. As for us, we wept and lifted up our hands to heaven on seeing such a horrid sight, for we did not know what else to do; but when the Cyclops had filled his

huge paunch, and had washed down his meal of human flesh with a drink of neat milk, he stretched himself full length upon the ground among his sheep, and went to sleep. I was at first inclined to seize my sword, draw it, and drive it into his vitals, but I reflected that if I did we should all certainly be lost, for we should never be able to shift the stone
5 which the monster had put in front of the door. So we stayed sobbing and sighing where we were till morning came.

"When the child of morning, rosy-fingered dawn, appeared, he again lit his fire, milked his goats and ewes, all quite rightly, and then let each have her own young one; as soon as he had got through with all his work, he clutched up two more of my men, and began
10 eating them for his morning's meal. Presently, with the utmost ease, he rolled the stone away from the door and drove out his sheep, but he at once put it back again--as easily as though he were merely clapping the lid on to a quiver full of arrows. As soon as he had done so he shouted, and cried 'Shoo, shoo,' after his sheep to drive them on to the mountain; so I was left to scheme some way of taking my revenge and covering myself
15 with glory.

Cyclops wakes in morning; eats more troops. Ulysses seeks glory.

"In the end I deemed it would be the best plan to do as follows: The Cyclops had a great club which was lying near one of the sheep pens; it was of green olive wood, and he had cut it intending to use it for a staff as soon as it should be dry. It was so huge that we could only compare it to the mast of a twenty-oared merchant vessel of large
20 burden, and able to venture out into open sea. I went up to this club and cut off about six feet of it; I then gave this piece to the men and told them to fine it evenly off at one end, which they proceeded to do, and lastly I brought it to a point myself, charring the end in the fire to make it harder. When I had done this I hid it under dung, which was lying about all over the cave, and told the men to cast lots which of them should venture
25 along with myself to lift it and bore it into the monster's eye while he was asleep. The lot fell upon the very four whom I should have chosen, and I myself made five. In the evening the wretch came back from shepherding, and drove his flocks into the cave-- this time driving them all inside, and not leaving any in the yards; I suppose some fancy must have taken him, or a god must have prompted him to do so. As soon as he had
30 put the stone back to its place against the door, he sat down, milked his ewes and his goats all quite rightly, and then let each have her own young one; when he had got through with all this work, he gripped up two more of my men, and made his supper off them. So I went up to him with an ivy-wood bowl of black wine in my hands:

Ulysses plans revenge & escape.

"'Look here, Cyclops,' said I, you have been eating a great deal of man's flesh, so take
35 this and drink some wine, that you may see what kind of liquor we had on board my ship. I was bringing it to you as a drink-offering, in the hope that you would take compassion upon me and further me on my way home, whereas all you do is to go on ramping and raving most intolerably. You ought to be ashamed of yourself; how can you expect people to come see you any more if you treat them in this way?'

Ulysses schemes against Cyclops.

40 "He then took the cup and drank. He was so delighted with the taste of the wine that he begged me for another bowl full. 'Be so kind,' he said, 'as to give me some more, and tell me your name at once. I want to make you a present that you will be glad to have. We have wine even in this country, for our soil grows grapes and the sun ripens them, but this drinks like Nectar and Ambrosia all in one.'

Ulysses is "Noman".

"I then gave him some more; three times did I fill the bowl for him, and three times did he drain it without thought or heed; then, when I saw that the wine had got into his head, I said to him as plausibly as I could: 'Cyclops, you ask my name and I will tell it you; give me, therefore, the present you promised me; my name is Noman; this is what
5 my father and mother and my friends have always called me.'

"But the cruel wretch said, 'Then I will eat all Noman's comrades before Noman himself, and will keep Noman for the last. This is the present that I will make him.'

Troops blind the Cyclops.

"As he spoke he reeled, and fell sprawling face upwards on the ground. His great neck hung heavily backwards and a deep sleep took hold upon him. Presently he turned sick,
10 and threw up both wine and the gobbets of human flesh on which he had been gorging, for he was very drunk. Then I thrust the beam of wood far into the embers to heat it, and encouraged my men lest any of them should turn faint-hearted. When the wood, green though it was, was about to blaze, I drew it out of the fire glowing with heat, and my men gathered round me, for heaven had filled their hearts with courage. We drove
15 the sharp end of the beam into the monster's eye, and bearing upon it with all my weight I kept turning it round and round as though I were boring a hole in a ship's plank with an auger, which two men with a wheel and strap can keep on turning as long as they choose. Even thus did we bore the red hot beam into his eye, till the boiling blood bubbled all over it as we worked it round and round, so that the steam from the burning
20 eyeball scalded his eyelids and eyebrows, and the roots of the eye sputtered in the fire. As a blacksmith plunges an axe or hatchet into cold water to temper it--for it is this that gives strength to the iron--and it makes a great hiss as he does so, even thus did the Cyclops' eye hiss round the beam of olive wood, and his hideous yells made the cave ring again. We ran away in a fright, but he plucked the beam all besmirched with gore
25 from his eye, and hurled it from him in a frenzy of rage and pain, shouting as he did so to the other Cyclopes who lived on the bleak headlands near him; so they gathered from all quarters round his cave when they heard him crying, and asked what was the matter with him.

Other Cyclopes approach. Word game saves troops.

"'What ails you, Polyphemus,' said they, 'that you make such a noise, breaking the
30 stillness of the night, and preventing us from being able to sleep? Surely no man is carrying off your sheep? Surely no man is trying to kill you either by fraud or by force?'

"But Polyphemus shouted to them from inside the cave, 'Noman is killing me by fraud; no man is killing me by force.'

"'Then,' said they, 'if no man is attacking you, you must be ill; when Jove makes people
35 ill, there is no help for it, and you had better pray to your father Neptune.'

Ulysses: brains beats brawn.

"Then they went away, and I laughed inwardly at the success of my clever stratagem, but the Cyclops, groaning and in an agony of pain, felt about with his hands till he found the stone and took it from the door; then he sat in the doorway and stretched his hands in front of it to catch anyone going out with the sheep, for he thought I might be foolish
40 enough to attempt this.

"As for myself I kept on puzzling to think how I could best save my own life and those of my companions; I schemed and schemed, as one who knows that his life depends upon it, for the danger was very great. In the end I deemed that this plan would be the best; the male sheep were well grown, and carried a heavy black fleece, so I bound them
45 noiselessly in threes together, with some of the withies on which the wicked monster

used to sleep. There was to be a man under the middle sheep, and the two on either side were to cover him, so that there were three sheep to each man. As for myself there was a ram finer than any of the others, so I caught hold of him by the back, esconced myself in the thick wool under his belly, and hung on patiently to his fleece, face upwards, keeping a firm hold on it all the time.

"Thus, then, did we wait in great fear of mind till morning came, but when the child of morning, rosy-fingered Dawn, appeared, the male sheep hurried out to feed, while the ewes remained bleating about the pens waiting to be milked, for their udders were full to bursting; but their master in spite of all his pain felt the backs of all the sheep as they stood upright, without being sharp enough to find out that the men were underneath their bellies. As the ram was going out, last of all, heavy with its fleece and with the weight of my crafty self, Polyphemus laid hold of it and said:

Polyphemus tenderly addresses ram.

"'My good ram, what is it that makes you the last to leave my cave this morning? You are not wont to let the ewes go before you, but lead the mob with a run whether to flowery mead or bubbling fountain, and are the first to come home again at night; but now you lag last of all. Is it because you know your master has lost his eye, and are sorry because that wicked Noman and his horrid crew has got him down in his drink and blinded him? But I will have his life yet. If you could understand and talk, you would tell me where the wretch is hiding, and I would dash his brains upon the ground till they flew all over the cave. I should thus have some satisfaction for the harm this no-good Noman has done me.'

"As he spoke he drove the ram outside, but when we were a little way out from the cave and yards, I first got from under the ram's belly, and then freed my comrades; as for the sheep, which were very fat, by constantly heading them in the right direction we managed to drive them down to the ship. The crew rejoiced greatly at seeing those of us who had escaped death, but wept for the others whom the Cyclops had killed. However, I made signs to them by nodding and frowning that they were to hush their crying, and told them to get all the sheep on board at once and put out to sea; so they went aboard, took their places, and smote the grey sea with their oars. Then, when I had got as far out as my voice would reach, I began to jeer at the Cyclops.

Troops escape.

"'Cyclops,' said I, 'you should have taken better measure of your man before eating up his comrades in your cave. You wretch, eat up your visitors in your own house? You might have known that your sin would find you out, and now Jove and the other gods have punished you.'

Ulysses cannot hold his tongue.

"He got more and more furious as he heard me, so he tore the top from off a high mountain, and flung it just in front of my ship so that it was within a little of hitting the end of the rudder. The sea quaked as the rock fell into it, and the wash of the wave it raised carried us back towards the mainland, and forced us towards the shore. But I snatched up a long pole and kept the ship off, making signs to my men by nodding my head, that they must row for their lives, whereon they laid out with a will. When we had got twice as far as we were before, I was for jeering at the Cyclops again, but the men begged and prayed of me to hold my tongue.

"'Do not,' they exclaimed, 'be mad enough to provoke this savage creature further; he has thrown one rock at us already which drove us back again to the mainland, and we made sure it had been the death of us; if he had then heard any further sound of voices he would have pounded our heads and our ship's timbers into a jelly with the rugged rocks he would have heaved at us, for he can throw them a long way.'

Kleos? Or misguided hubris?

"But I would not listen to them, and shouted out to him in my rage, 'Cyclops, if any one asks you who it was that put your eye out and spoiled your beauty, say it was the
5 valiant warrior Ulysses, son of Laertes, who lives in Ithaca.'

"On this he groaned, and cried out, 'Alas, alas, then the old prophecy about me is coming true. There was a prophet here, at one time, a man both brave and of great stature, Telemus son of Eurymus, who was an excellent seer, and did all the prophesying for the Cyclopes till he grew old; he told me that all this would happen to me some day,
10 and said I should lose my sight by the hand of Ulysses. I have been all along expecting some one of imposing presence and superhuman strength, whereas he turns out to be a little insignificant weakling, who has managed to blind my eye by taking advantage of me in my drink; come here, then, Ulysses, that I may make you presents to show my hospitality, and urge Neptune to help you forward on your journey--for Neptune and I
15 are father and son. He, if he so will, shall heal me, which no one else neither god nor man can do.'

"Then I said, 'I wish I could be as sure of killing you outright and sending you down to the house of Hades, as I am that it will take more than Neptune to cure that eye of yours.'

Cyclops delivers curse upon troops.
20 "On this he lifted up his hands to the firmament of heaven and prayed, saying, 'Hear me, great Neptune; if I am indeed your own true begotten son, grant that Ulysses may never reach his home alive; or if he must get back to his friends at last, let him do so late and in sore plight after losing all his men let him reach his home in another man's ship and find trouble in his house.'

25 "Thus did he pray, and Neptune heard his prayer. Then he picked up a rock much larger than the first, swung it aloft and hurled it with prodigious force. It fell just short of the ship, but was within a little of hitting the end of the rudder. The sea quaked as the rock fell into it, and the wash of the wave it raised drove us onwards on our way towards the shore of the island.

30 "When at last we got to the island where we had left the rest of our ships, we found our comrades lamenting us, and anxiously awaiting our return. We ran our vessel upon the sands and got out of her on to the sea shore; we also landed the Cyclops' sheep, and divided them equitably amongst us so that none might have reason to complain. As for the ram, my companions agreed that I should have it as an extra share; so I sacrificed it
35 on the sea shore, and burned its thigh bones to Jove, who is the lord of all. But he heeded not my sacrifice, and only thought how he might destroy both my ships and my comrades.

"Thus through the livelong day to the going down of the sun we feasted our fill on meat and drink, but when the sun went down and it came on dark, we camped upon the
40 beach. When the child of morning rosy-fingered Dawn appeared, I bade my men on board and loose the hawsers. Then they took their places and smote the grey sea with their oars; so we sailed on with sorrow in our hearts, but glad to have escaped death though we had lost our comrades.

BOOK X – AEOLUS, THE LAESTRYGONES, CIRCE

AEOLUS, THE LAESTRYGONES, CIRCE.

Thence we went on to the Aeolian island where lives Aeolus son of Hippotas, dear to the immortal gods. It is an island that floats (as it were) upon the sea, iron bound with a wall that girds it. Now, Aeolus has six daughters and six lusty sons, so he made the sons marry the daughters, and they all live with their dear father and mother, feasting
5 and enjoying every conceivable kind of luxury. All day long the atmosphere of the house is loaded with the savour of roasting meats till it groans again, yard and all; but by night they sleep on their well made bedsteads, each with his own wife between the blankets. These were the people among whom we had now come.

"Aeolus entertained me for a whole month asking me questions all the time about Troy,
10 the Argive fleet, and the return of the Achaeans. I told him exactly how everything had happened, and when I said I must go, and asked him to further me on my way, he made no sort of difficulty, but set about doing so at once. Moreover, he flayed me a prime ox-hide to hold the ways of the roaring winds, which he shut up in the hide as in a sack- -for Jove had made him captain over the winds, and he could stir or still each one of
15 them according to his own pleasure. He put the sack in the ship and bound the mouth so tightly with a silver thread that not even a breath of a side-wind could blow from any quarter. The West wind which was fair for us did he alone let blow as it chose; but it all came to nothing, for we were lost through our own folly.

"Nine days and nine nights did we sail, and on the tenth day our native land showed on
20 the horizon. We got so close in that we could see the stubble fires burning, and I, being then dead beat, fell into a light sleep, for I had never let the rudder out of my own hands, that we might get home the faster. On this the men fell to talking among themselves, and said I was bringing back gold and silver in the sack that Aeolus had given me. 'Bless my heart,' would one turn to his neighbour, saying, 'how this man gets
25 honoured and makes friends to whatever city or country he may go. See what fine prizes he is taking home from Troy, while we, who have travelled just as far as he has, come back with hands as empty as we set out with--and now Aeolus has given him ever so much more. Quick--let us see what it all is, and how much gold and silver there is in the sack he gave him.'

Troops display disloyalty; pay price.

30 "Thus they talked and evil counsels prevailed. They loosed the sack, whereupon the wind flew howling forth and raised a storm that carried us weeping out to sea and away from our own country. Then I awoke, and knew not whether to throw myself into the sea or to live on and make the best of it; but I bore it, covered myself up, and lay down in the ship, while the men lamented bitterly as the fierce winds bore our fleet back to
35 the Aeolian island.

"When we reached it we went ashore to take in water, and dined hard by the ships. Immediately after dinner I took a herald and one of my men and went straight to the house of Aeolus, where I found him feasting with his wife and family; so we sat down as suppliants on the threshold. They were astounded when they saw us and said,
40 'Ulysses, what brings you here? What god has been ill-treating you? We took great pains to further you on your way home to Ithaca, or wherever it was that you wanted to go to.'

Assess the relationship between Ulysses and his troops.

"Thus did they speak, but I answered sorrowfully, 'My men have undone me; they, and cruel sleep, have ruined me. My friends, mend me this mischief, for you can if you will.'

"I spoke as movingly as I could, but they said nothing, till their father answered, 'Vilest of mankind, get you gone at once out of the island; him whom heaven hates will I in no
5 wise help. Be off, for you come here as one abhorred of heaven.' And with these words he sent me sorrowing from his door.

"Thence we sailed sadly on till the men were worn out with long and fruitless rowing, for there was no longer any wind to help them. Six days, night and day did we toil, and on the seventh day we reached the rocky stronghold of Lamus--Telepylus, the city of
10 the Laestrygonians, where the shepherd who is driving in his sheep and goats to be milked salutes him who is driving out his flock to feed and this last answers the salute. In that country a man who could do without sleep might earn double wages, one as a herdsman of cattle, and another as a shepherd, for they work much the same by night as they do by day.

The troops reach Laestrygonians harbor.

15 "When we reached the harbour we found it land-locked under steep cliffs, with a narrow entrance between two headlands. My captains took all their ships inside, and made them fast close to one another, for there was never so much as a breath of wind inside, but it was always dead calm. I kept my own ship outside, and moored it to a rock at the very end of the point; then I climbed a high rock to reconnoitre, but could see no sign neither
20 of man nor cattle, only some smoke rising from the ground. So I sent two of my company with an attendant to find out what sort of people the inhabitants were.

"The men when they got on shore followed a level road by which the people draw their firewood from the mountains into the town, till presently they met a young woman who had come outside to fetch water, and who was daughter to a Laestrygonian named
25 Antiphates. She was going to the fountain Artacia from which the people bring in their water, and when my men had come close up to her, they asked her who the king of that country might be, and over what kind of people he ruled; so she directed them to her father's house, but when they got there they found his wife to be a giantess as huge as a mountain, and they were horrified at the sight of her.

30 "She at once called her husband Antiphates from the place of assembly, and forthwith he set about killing my men. He snatched up one of them, and began to make his dinner off him then and there, whereon the other two ran back to the ships as fast as ever they could. But Antiphates raised a hue-and-cry after them, and thousands of sturdy Laestrygonians sprang up from every quarter--ogres, not men. They threw vast rocks at
35 us from the cliffs as though they had been mere stones, and I heard the horrid sound of the ships crunching up against one another, and the death cries of my men, as the Laestrygonians speared them like fishes and took them home to eat them. While they were thus killing my men within the harbour I drew my sword, cut the cable of my own ship, and told my men to row with all their might if they too would not fare like the
40 rest; so they laid out for their lives, and we were thankful enough when we got into open water out of reach of the rocks they hurled at us. As for the others there was not one of them left.

"Thence we sailed sadly on, glad to have escaped death, though we had lost our comrades, and came to the Aeaean island, where Circe lives--a great and cunning goddess who is own sister to the magician Aeetes--for they are both children of the sun by Perse, who is daughter to Oceanus. We brought our ship into a safe harbour without 5 a word, for some god guided us thither, and having landed we lay there for two days and two nights, worn out in body and mind. When the morning of the third day came I took my spear and my sword, and went away from the ship to reconnoitre, and see if I could discover signs of human handiwork, or hear the sound of voices. Climbing to the top of a high look-out I espied the smoke of Circe's house rising upwards amid a 10 dense forest of trees, and when I saw this I doubted whether, having seen the smoke, I would not go on at once and find out more, but in the end I deemed it best to go back to the ship, give the men their dinners, and send some of them instead of going myself.

Troops travel on to Circe's island.

"When I had nearly got back to the ship some god took pity upon my solitude, and sent a fine antlered stag right into the middle of my path. I struck him in the middle of the 15 back; the bronze point of the spear went clean through him, and he lay groaning in the dust until the life went out of him. I bound the four feet of the noble creature together; having so done I hung him round my neck and walked back to the ship leaning upon my spear, for the stag was much too big for me to be able to carry him on my shoulder. As I threw him down in front of the ship, I called the men and spoke cheeringly man 20 by man to each of them. 'Look here my friends,' said I, 'we are not going to die so much before our time after all.' On this they uncovered their heads upon the sea shore and admired the stag, for he was indeed a splendid fellow. Then, when they had feasted their eyes upon him sufficiently, they washed their hands and began to cook him for dinner.

Ulysses hunts a stag.

"Thus through the livelong day to the going down of the sun we stayed there eating and 25 drinking our fill, but when the sun went down and it came on dark, we camped upon the sea shore. When the child of morning, rosy-fingered Dawn, appeared, I called a council and said, 'My friends, we are in very great difficulties; listen therefore to me. We have no idea where the sun either sets or rises, so that we do not even know East from West. I see no way out of it; nevertheless, we must try and find one. We are certainly 30 on an island, for I went as high as I could this morning, and saw the sea reaching all round it to the horizon; it lies low, but towards the middle I saw smoke rising from out of a thick forest of trees.'

Ulysses counsels his troops.

"Their hearts sank as they heard me, for they remembered how they had been treated by the Laestrygonian Antiphates, and by the savage ogre Polyphemus. They wept 35 bitterly in their dismay, but there was nothing to be got by crying, so I divided them into two companies and set a captain over each; I gave one company to Eurylochus, while I took command of the other myself. Then we cast lots in a helmet, and the lot fell upon Eurylochus; so he set out with his twenty-two men, and they wept, as also did we who were left behind.

40 "When they reached Circe's house they found it built of cut stones, on a site that could be seen from far, in the middle of the forest. There were wild mountain wolves and lions prowling all round it--poor bewitched creatures whom she had tamed by her enchantments and drugged into subjection. They did not attack my men, but wagged their great tails and rubbed their noses lovingly against them. As hounds crowd round 45 their master when they see him coming from dinner--for they know he will bring them something--even so did these wolves and lions with their great claws fawn upon my men, but the men were terribly frightened at seeing such strange creatures. Presently they reached the gates of the goddess's house, and as they stood there they could hear Circe within, singing most beautifully as she worked at her loom, making a web so fine,

Assess Circe's powers over nature, beasts and the troops.

so soft, and of such dazzling colours as no one but a goddess could weave. On this Polites, whom I valued and trusted more than any other of my men, said, 'There is some one inside working at a loom and singing most beautifully; the whole place resounds with it, let us call her and see whether she is woman or goddess.'

Circe turns troops into pigs. Why?

5 "They called her and she came down, unfastened the door, and bade them enter. They, thinking no evil, followed her, all except Eurylochus, who suspected mischief and staid outside. When she had got them into her house, she set them upon benches and seats and mixed them a mess with cheese, honey, meal, and Pramnian wine, but she drugged it with wicked poisons to make them forget their homes, and when they had drunk she
10 turned them into pigs by a stroke of her wand, and shut them up in her pig-styes. They were like pigs--head, hair, and all, and they grunted just as pigs do; but their senses were the same as before, and they remembered everything.

"Thus then were they shut up squealing, and Circe threw them some acorns and beech masts such as pigs eat, but Eurylochus hurried back to tell me about the sad fate of our
15 comrades. He was so overcome with dismay that though he tried to speak he could find no words to do so; his eyes filled with tears and he could only sob and sigh, till at last we forced his story out of him, and he told us what had happened to the others.

One of troops reports event to Ulysses.

"'We went,' said he, 'as you told us, through the forest, and in the middle of it there was a fine house built with cut stones in a place that could be seen from far. There we found
20 a woman, or else she was a goddess, working at her loom and singing sweetly; so the men shouted to her and called her, whereon she at once came down, opened the door, and invited us in. The others did not suspect any mischief so they followed her into the house, but I staid where I was, for I thought there might be some treachery. From that moment I saw them no more, for not one of them ever came out, though I sat a long
25 time watching for them.'

"Then I took my sword of bronze and slung it over my shoulders; I also took my bow, and told Eurylochus to come back with me and shew me the way. But he laid hold of me with both his hands and spoke piteously, saying, 'Sir, do not force me to go with you, but let me stay here, for I know you will not bring one of them back with you, nor
30 even return alive yourself; let us rather see if we cannot escape at any rate with the few that are left us, for we may still save our lives.'

"'Stay where you are, then,' answered I, 'eating and drinking at the ship, but I must go, for I am most urgently bound to do so.'

Mercury warns Ulysses about Circe.

"With this I left the ship and went up inland. When I got through the charmed grove,
35 and was near the great house of the enchantress Circe, I met Mercury with his golden wand, disguised as a young man in the hey-day of his youth and beauty with the down just coming upon his face. He came up to me and took my hand within his own, saying, 'My poor unhappy man, whither are you going over this mountain top, alone and without knowing the way? Your men are shut up in Circe's pig styes, like so many wild
40 boars in their lairs. You surely do not fancy that you can set them free? I can tell you that you will never get back and will have to stay there with the rest of them. But never mind, I will protect you and get you out of your difficulty. Take this herb, which is one of great virtue, and keep it about you when you go to Circe's house, it will be a talisman to you against every kind of mischief.

"'And I will tell you of all the wicked witchcraft that Circe will try to practice upon you. She will mix a mess for you to drink, and she will drug the meal with which she makes it, but she will not be able to charm you, for the virtue of the herb that I shall give you will prevent her spells from working. I will tell you all about it. When Circe strikes you

5 with her wand, draw your sword and spring upon her as though you were going to kill her. She will then be frightened, and will desire you to go to bed with her; on this you must not point blank refuse her, for you want her to set your companions free, and to take good care also of yourself, but you must make her swear solemnly by all the blessed gods that she will plot no further mischief against you, or else when she has got you

10 naked she will unman you and make you fit for nothing.'

"As he spoke he pulled the herb out of the ground and shewed me what it was like. The root was black, while the flower was as white as milk; the gods call it Moly, and mortal men cannot uproot it, but the gods can do whatever they like.

"Then Mercury went back to high Olympus passing over the wooded island; but I fared

15 onward to the house of Circe, and my heart was clouded with care as I walked along. When I got to the gates I stood there and called the goddess, and as soon as she heard me she came down, opened the door, and asked me to come in; so I followed her-- much troubled in my mind. She set me on a richly decorated seat inlaid with silver, there was a footstool also under my feet, and she mixed a mess in a golden goblet for me to

20 drink; but she drugged it, for she meant me mischief. When she had given it me, and I had drunk it without its charming me, she struck me with her wand. 'There now,' she cried, 'be off to the pigstye, and make your lair with the rest of them.'

"But I rushed at her with my sword drawn as though I would kill her, whereon she fell   Ulysses seduced by Circe.
with a loud scream, clasped my knees, and spoke piteously, saying, 'Who and whence

25 are you? from what place and people have you come? How can it be that my drugs have no power to charm you? Never yet was any man able to stand so much as a taste of the herb I gave you; you must be spell-proof; surely you can be none other than the bold hero Ulysses, who Mercury always said would come here some day with his ship while on his way home from Troy; so be it then; sheathe your sword and let us go to bed, that

30 we may make friends and learn to trust each other.'

"And I answered, 'Circe, how can you expect me to be friendly with you when you have just been turning all my men into pigs? And now that you have got me here myself, you mean me mischief when you ask me to go to bed with you, and will unman me and make me fit for nothing. I shall certainly not consent to go to bed with you unless you

35 will first take your solemn oath to plot no further harm against me.'

"So she swore at once as I had told her, and when she had completed her oath then I went to bed with her.

"Meanwhile her four servants, who are her housemaids, set about their work. They are   Servants bathe Ulysses.
the children of the groves and fountains, and of the holy waters that run down into the

40 sea. One of them spread a fair purple cloth over a seat, and laid a carpet underneath it. Another brought tables of silver up to the seats, and set them with baskets of gold. A third mixed some sweet wine with water in a silver bowl and put golden cups upon the tables, while the fourth brought in water and set it to boil in a large cauldron over a good fire which she had lighted. When the water in the cauldron was boiling, she poured

45 cold into it till it was just as I liked it, and then she set me in a bath and began washing me from the cauldron about the head and shoulders, to take the tire and stiffness out

of my limbs. As soon as she had done washing me and anointing me with oil, she arrayed me in a good cloak and shirt and led me to a richly decorated seat inlaid with silver; there was a footstool also under my feet. A maid servant then brought me bread and offered me many things of what there was in the house, and then Circe bade me eat, but I would not, and sat without heeding what was before me, still moody and suspicious.

"When Circe saw me sitting there without eating, and in great grief, she came to me and said, 'Ulysses, why do you sit like that as though you were dumb, gnawing at your own heart, and refusing both meat and drink? Is it that you are still suspicious? You ought not to be, for I have already sworn solemnly that I will not hurt you.'

"And I said, 'Circe, no man with any sense of what is right can think of either eating or drinking in your house until you have set his friends free and let him see them. If you want me to eat and drink, you must free my men and bring them to me that I may see them with my own eyes.'

Circe frees troops.

"When I had said this she went straight through the court with her wand in her hand and opened the pigstye doors. My men came out like so many prime hogs and stood looking at her, but she went about among them and anointed each with a second drug, whereon the bristles that the bad drug had given them fell off, and they became men again, younger than they were before, and much taller and better looking. They knew me at once, seized me each of them by the hand, and wept for joy, and Circe herself was so sorry for them that she came up to me and said, 'Ulysses, noble son of Laertes, go back at once to the sea where you have left your ship, and first draw it on to the land. Then, hide all your ship's gear and property in some cave, and come back here with your men.'

"I agreed to this, so I went back to the sea shore, and found the men at the ship weeping and wailing most piteously. When they saw me the silly blubbering fellows began frisking round me as calves break out and gambol round their mothers, when they see them coming home to be milked after they have been feeding all day, and the homestead resounds with their lowing. They seemed as glad to see me as though they had got back to their own rugged Ithaca, where they had been born and bred. 'Sir,' said the affectionate creatures, 'we are as glad to see you back as though we had got safe home to Ithaca; but tell us all about the fate of our comrades.'

"I spoke comfortingly to them and said, 'We must draw our ship on to the land, and hide the ship's gear with all our property in some cave; then come with me all of you as fast as you can to Circe's house, where you will find your comrades eating and drinking in the midst of great abundance.'

Note the tension between Ulysses & troops.

"On this the men would have come with me at once, but Eurylochus tried to hold them back and said, 'Alas, poor wretches that we are, what will become of us? Rush not on your ruin by going to the house of Circe, who will turn us all into pigs or wolves or lions, and we shall have to keep guard over her house. Remember how the Cyclops treated us when our comrades went inside his cave, and Ulysses with them. It was all through his sheer folly that those men lost their lives.'

"When I heard him I was in two minds whether or no to draw the keen blade that hung by my sturdy thigh and cut his head off in spite of his being a near relation of my own;

but the men interceded for him and said, 'Sir, if it may so be, let this fellow stay here and mind the ship, but take the rest of us with you to Circe's house.'

"On this we all went inland, and Eurylochus was not left behind after all, but came on too, for he was frightened by the severe reprimand that I had given him.

5   "Meanwhile Circe had been seeing that the men who had been left behind were washed and anointed with olive oil; she had also given them woollen cloaks and shirts, and when we came we found them all comfortably at dinner in her house. As soon as the men saw each other face to face and knew one another, they wept for joy and cried aloud till the whole palace rang again. Thereon Circe came up to me and said, 'Ulysses, noble son
10   of Laertes, tell your men to leave off crying; I know how much you have all of you suffered at sea, and how ill you have fared among cruel savages on the mainland, but that is over now, so stay here, and eat and drink till you are once more as strong and hearty as you were when you left Ithaca; for at present you are weakened both in body and mind; you keep all the time thinking of the hardships you have suffered during your
15   travels, so that you have no more cheerfulness left in you.'

"Thus did she speak and we assented. We stayed with Circe for a whole twelvemonth feasting upon an untold quantity both of meat and wine. But when the year had passed in the waning of moons and the long days had come round, my men called me apart and said, 'Sir, it is time you began to think about going home, if so be you are to be
20   spared to see your house and native country at all.'

Troops delayed by Circe. Why?

"Thus did they speak and I assented. Thereon through the livelong day to the going down of the sun we feasted our fill on meat and wine, but when the sun went down and it came on dark the men laid themselves down to sleep in the covered cloisters. I, however, after I had got into bed with Circe, besought her by her knees, and the goddess
25   listened to what I had got to say. 'Circe,' said I, 'please to keep the promise you made me about furthering me on my homeward voyage. I want to get back and so do my men, they are always pestering me with their complaints as soon as ever your back is turned.'

Ulysses must descend to the underworld.

"And the goddess answered, 'Ulysses, noble son of Laertes, you shall none of you stay
30   here any longer if you do not want to, but there is another journey which you have got to take before you can sail homewards. You must go to the house of Hades and of dread Proserpine to consult the ghost of the blind Theban prophet Teiresias, whose reason is still unshaken. To him alone has Proserpine left his understanding even in death, but the other ghosts flit about aimlessly.'

35   "I was dismayed when I heard this. I sat up in bed and wept, and would gladly have lived no longer to see the light of the sun, but presently when I was tired of weeping and tossing myself about, I said, 'And who shall guide me upon this voyage--for the house of Hades is a port that no ship can reach.'

"'You will want no guide,' she answered; 'raise your mast, set your white sails, sit quite
40   still, and the North Wind will blow you there of itself. When your ship has traversed the waters of Oceanus, you will reach the fertile shore of Proserpine's country with its groves of tall poplars and willows that shed their fruit untimely; here beach your ship upon the shore of Oceanus, and go straight on to the dark abode of Hades. You will find it near the place where the rivers Pyriphlegethon and Cocytus (which is a branch

of the river Styx) flow into Acheron, and you will see a rock near it, just where the two roaring rivers run into one another.

"'When you have reached this spot, as I now tell you, dig a trench a cubit or so in length, breadth, and depth, and pour into it as a drink-offering to all the dead, first, honey
5   mixed with milk, then wine, and in the third place water--sprinkling white barley meal over the whole. Moreover you must offer many prayers to the poor feeble ghosts, and promise them that when you get back to Ithaca you will sacrifice a barren heifer to them, the best you have, and will load the pyre with good things. More particularly you must promise that Teiresias shall have a black sheep all to himself, the finest in all your
10 flocks.

"'When you shall have thus besought the ghosts with your prayers, offer them a ram and a black ewe, bending their heads towards Erebus; but yourself turn away from them as though you would make towards the river. On this, many dead men's ghosts will come to you, and you must tell your men to skin the two sheep that you have just killed,
15 and offer them as a burnt sacrifice with prayers to Hades and to Proserpine. Then draw your sword and sit there, so as to prevent any other poor ghost from coming near the spilt blood before Teiresias shall have answered your questions. The seer will presently come to you, and will tell you about your voyage--what stages you are to make, and how you are to sail the sea so as to reach your home.'

20 "It was day-break by the time she had done speaking, so she dressed me in my shirt and cloak. As for herself she threw a beautiful light gossamer fabric over her shoulders, fastening it with a golden girdle round her waist, and she covered her head with a mantle. Then I went about among the men everywhere all over the house, and spoke kindly to each of them man by man: 'You must not lie sleeping here any longer,' said I
25 to them, 'we must be going, for Circe has told me all about it.' And on this they did as I bade them.

"Even so, however, I did not get them away without misadventure. We had with us a certain youth named Elpenor, not very remarkable for sense or courage, who had got drunk and was lying on the house-top away from the rest of the men, to sleep off his
30 liquor in the cool. When he heard the noise of the men bustling about, he jumped up on a sudden and forgot all about coming down by the main staircase, so he tumbled right off the roof and broke his neck, and his soul went down to the house of Hades.

Ulysses informs troops of next journey.

"When I had got the men together I said to them, 'You think you are about to start home again, but Circe has explained to me that instead of this, we have got to go to the
35 house of Hades and Proserpine to consult the ghost of the Theban prophet Teiresias.'

"The men were broken-hearted as they heard me, and threw themselves on the ground groaning and tearing their hair, but they did not mend matters by crying. When we reached the sea shore, weeping and lamenting our fate, Circe brought the ram and the ewe, and we made them fast hard by the ship. She passed through the midst of us
40 without our knowing it, for who can see the comings and goings of a god, if the god does not wish to be seen?

BOOK XI – THE VISIT TO THE DEAD

THE VISIT TO THE DEAD.

Then, when we had got down to the sea shore we drew our ship into the water and got her mast and sails into her; we also put the sheep on board and took our places, weeping and in great distress of mind. Circe, that great and cunning goddess, sent us a fair wind that blew dead aft and staid steadily with us keeping our sails all the time well filled; so

5   we did whatever wanted doing to the ship's gear and let her go as the wind and helmsman headed her. All day long her sails were full as she held her course over the sea, but when the sun went down and darkness was over all the earth, we got into the deep waters of the river Oceanus, where lie the land and city of the Cimmerians who live enshrouded in mist and darkness which the rays of the sun never pierce neither at

10 his rising nor as he goes down again out of the heavens, but the poor wretches live in one long melancholy night. When we got there we beached the ship, took the sheep out of her, and went along by the waters of Oceanus till we came to the place of which Circe had told us.

"Here Perimedes and Eurylochus held the victims, while I drew my sword and dug the

15 trench a cubit each way. I made a drink-offering to all the dead, first with honey and milk, then with wine, and thirdly with water, and I sprinkled white barley meal over the whole, praying earnestly to the poor feckless ghosts, and promising them that when I got back to Ithaca I would sacrifice a barren heifer for them, the best I had, and would load the pyre with good things. I also particularly promised that Teiresias should have

20 a black sheep to himself, the best in all my flocks. When I had prayed sufficiently to the dead, I cut the throats of the two sheep and let the blood run into the trench, whereon the ghosts came trooping up from Erebus--brides, young bachelors, old men worn out with toil, maids who had been crossed in love, and brave men who had been killed in battle, with their armour still smirched with blood; they came from every quarter and

25 flitted round the trench with a strange kind of screaming sound that made me turn pale with fear. When I saw them coming I told the men to be quick and flay the carcasses of the two dead sheep and make burnt offerings of them, and at the same time to repeat prayers to Hades and to Proserpine; but I sat where I was with my sword drawn and would not let the poor feckless ghosts come near the blood till Teiresias should have

30 answered my questions.

"The first ghost that came was that of my comrade Elpenor, for he had not yet been laid beneath the earth. We had left his body unwaked and unburied in Circe's house, for we had had too much else to do. I was very sorry for him, and cried when I saw him: 'Elpenor,' said I, 'how did you come down here into this gloom and darkness? You have

35 got here on foot quicker than I have with my ship.'

Ulysses meets a forgotten troop.

"'Sir,' he answered with a groan, 'it was all bad luck, and my own unspeakable drunkenness. I was lying asleep on the top of Circe's house, and never thought of coming down again by the great staircase but fell right off the roof and broke my neck, so my soul came down to the house of Hades. And now I beseech you by all those

40 whom you have left behind you, though they are not here, by your wife, by the father who brought you up when you were a child, and by Telemachus who is the one hope of your house, do what I shall now ask you. I know that when you leave this limbo you will again hold your ship for the Aeaean island. Do not go thence leaving me unwaked and unburied behind you, or I may bring heaven's anger upon you; but burn me with

45 whatever armour I have, build a barrow for me on the sea shore, that may tell people

in days to come what a poor unlucky fellow I was, and plant over my grave the oar I used to row with when I was yet alive and with my messmates.' And I said, 'My poor fellow, I will do all that you have asked of me.'

"Thus, then, did we sit and hold sad talk with one another, I on the one side of the
5   trench with my sword held over the blood, and the ghost of my comrade saying all this to me from the other side. Then came the ghost of my dead mother Anticlea, daughter to Autolycus. I had left her alive when I set out for Troy and was moved to tears when I saw her, but even so, for all my sorrow I would not let her come near the blood till I had asked my questions of Teiresias.

Ulysses interviews prophet,   10   "Then came also the ghost of Theban Teiresias, with his golden sceptre in his hand. He
Teiresias.   knew me and said, 'Ulysses, noble son of Laertes, why, poor man, have you left the light of day and come down to visit the dead in this sad place? Stand back from the trench and withdraw your sword that I may drink of the blood and answer your questions truly.'

15   "So I drew back, and sheathed my sword, whereon when he had drank of the blood he began with his prophecy.

"'You want to know,' said he, 'about your return home, but heaven will make this hard for you. I do not think that you will escape the eye of Neptune, who still nurses his bitter grudge against you for having blinded his son. Still, after much suffering you may
20   get home if you can restrain yourself and your companions when your ship reaches the Thrinacian island, where you will find the sheep and cattle belonging to the sun, who sees and gives ear to everything. If you leave these flocks unharmed and think of nothing but of getting home, you may yet after much hardship reach Ithaca; but if you harm them, then I forewarn you of the destruction both of your ship and of your men.
25   Even though you may yourself escape, you will return in bad plight after losing all your men, in another man's ship, and you will find trouble in your house, which will be overrun by high-handed people, who are devouring your substance under the pretext of paying court and making presents to your wife.

Note cultural values: Teiresias   "'When you get home you will take your revenge on these suitors; and after you have
recommends revenge upon   30   killed them by force or fraud in your own house, you must take a well made oar and
suitors.   carry it on and on, till you come to a country where the people have never heard of the sea and do not even mix salt with their food, nor do they know anything about ships, and oars that are as the wings of a ship. I will give you this certain token which cannot escape your notice. A wayfarer will meet you and will say it must be a winnowing shovel
35   that you have got upon your shoulder; on this you must fix the oar in the ground and sacrifice a ram, a bull, and a boar to Neptune. Then go home and offer hecatombs to all the gods in heaven one after the other. As for yourself, death shall come to you from the sea, and your life shall ebb away very gently when you are full of years and peace of mind, and your people shall bless you. All that I have said will come true.'

40   "'This,' I answered, 'must be as it may please heaven, but tell me and tell me and tell me true, I see my poor mother's ghost close by us; she is sitting by the blood without saying a word, and though I am her own son she does not remember me and speak to me; tell me, Sir, how I can make her know me.'

"'That,' said he, 'I can soon do. Any ghost that you let taste of the blood will talk with you like a reasonable being, but if you do not let them have any blood they will go away again.'

"On this the ghost of Teiresias went back to the house of Hades, for his prophecyings had now been spoken, but I sat still where I was until my mother came up and tasted the blood. Then she knew me at once and spoke fondly to me, saying, 'My son, how did you come down to this abode of darkness while you are still alive? It is a hard thing for the living to see these places, for between us and them there are great and terrible waters, and there is Oceanus, which no man can cross on foot, but he must have a good ship to take him. Are you all this time trying to find your way home from Troy, and have you never yet got back to Ithaca nor seen your wife in your own house?'

Osysseus speaks with his dead mother.

"'Mother,' said I, 'I was forced to come here to consult the ghost of the Theban prophet Teiresias. I have never yet been near the Achaean land nor set foot on my native country, and I have had nothing but one long series of misfortunes from the very first day that I set out with Agamemnon for Ilius, the land of noble steeds, to fight the Trojans. But tell me, and tell me true, in what way did you die? Did you have a long illness, or did heaven vouchsafe you a gentle easy passage to eternity? Tell me also about my father, and the son whom I left behind me, is my property still in their hands, or has some one else got hold of it, who thinks that I shall not return to claim it? Tell me again what my wife intends doing, and in what mind she is; does she live with my son and guard my estate securely, or has she made the best match she could and married again?'

"My mother answered, 'Your wife still remains in your house, but she is in great distress of mind and spends her whole time in tears both night and day. No one as yet has got possession of your fine property, and Telemachus still holds your lands undisturbed. He has to entertain largely, as of course he must, considering his position as a magistrate, and how every one invites him; your father remains at his old place in the country and never goes near the town. He has no comfortable bed nor bedding; in the winter he sleeps on the floor in front of the fire with the men and goes about all in rags, but in summer, when the warm weather comes on again, he lies out in the vineyard on a bed of vine leaves thrown any how upon the ground. He grieves continually about your never having come home, and suffers more and more as he grows older. As for my own end it was in this wise: heaven did not take me swiftly and painlessly in my own house, nor was I attacked by any illness such as those that generally wear people out and kill them, but my longing to know what you were doing and the force of my affection for you--this it was that was the death of me.'

Mother advises Ulysses about Penelope.

"Then I tried to find some way of embracing my poor mother's ghost. Thrice I sprang towards her and tried to clasp her in my arms, but each time she flitted from my embrace as it were a dream or phantom, and being touched to the quick I said to her, 'Mother, why do you not stay still when I would embrace you? If we could throw our arms around one another we might find sad comfort in the sharing of our sorrows even in the house of Hades; does Proserpine want to lay a still further load of grief upon me by mocking me with a phantom only?'

Note the dead/living & mother/son relationship.

"'My son,' she answered, 'most ill-fated of all mankind, it is not Proserpine that is beguiling you, but all people are like this when they are dead. The sinews no longer hold the flesh and bones together; these perish in the fierceness of consuming fire as soon as life has left the body, and the soul flits away as though it were a dream. Now, however, go back to the light of day as soon as you can, and note all these things that you may tell them to your wife hereafter.'

"Thus did we converse, and anon Proserpine sent up the ghosts of the wives and daughters of all the most famous men. They gathered in crowds about the blood, and I considered how I might question them severally. In the end I deemed that it would be best to draw the keen blade that hung by my sturdy thigh, and keep them from all
5 drinking the blood at once. So they came up one after the other, and each one as I questioned her told me her race and lineage.

Ulysses speaks with Achilles and dead troops.

"As we two sat weeping and talking thus sadly with one another the ghost of Achilles came up to us with Patroclus, Antilochus, and Ajax who was the finest and goodliest man of all the Danaans after the son of Peleus. The fleet descendant of Aeacus knew
10 me and spoke piteously, saying, 'Ulysses, noble son of Laertes, what deed of daring will you undertake next, that you venture down to the house of Hades among us silly dead, who are but the ghosts of them that can labour no more?'

"And I said, 'Achilles, son of Peleus, foremost champion of the Achaeans, I came to consult Teiresias, and see if he could advise me about my return home to Ithaca, for I
15 have never yet been able to get near the Achaean land, nor to set foot in my own country, but have been in trouble all the time. As for you, Achilles, no one was ever yet so fortunate as you have been, nor ever will be, for you were adored by all us Argives as long as you were alive, and now that you are here you are a great prince among the dead. Do not, therefore, take it so much to heart even if you are dead.'

Observe the higher value Achilles places on life. Why?

20 "'Say not a word,' he answered, 'in death's favour; I would rather be a paid servant in a poor man's house and be above ground than king of kings among the dead. But give me news about my son; is he gone to the wars and will he be a great soldier, or is this not so? Tell me also if you have heard anything about my father Peleus--does he still rule among the Myrmidons, or do they show him no respect throughout Hellas and
25 Phthia now that he is old and his limbs fail him? Could I but stand by his side, in the light of day, with the same strength that I had when I killed the bravest of our foes upon the plain of Troy--could I but be as I then was and go even for a short time to my father's house, any one who tried to do him violence or supersede him would soon rue it.'

How does Ulysses characterize Achilles' son?

30 "'I have heard nothing,' I answered, 'of Peleus, but I can tell you all about your son Neoptolemus, for I took him in my own ship from Scyros with the Achaeans. In our councils of war before Troy he was always first to speak, and his judgement was unerring. Nestor and I were the only two who could surpass him; and when it came to fighting on the plain of Troy, he would never remain with the body of his men, but
35 would dash on far in front, foremost of them all in valour. Many a man did he kill in battle--I cannot name every single one of those whom he slew while fighting on the side of the Argives, but will only say how he killed that valiant hero Eurypylus son of Telephus, who was the handsomest man I ever saw except Memnon; many others also of the Ceteians fell around him by reason of a woman's bribes. Moreover, when all the
40 bravest of the Argives went inside the horse that Epeus had made, and it was left to me to settle when we should either open the door of our ambuscade, or close it, though all the other leaders and chief men among the Danaans were drying their eyes and quaking in every limb, I never once saw him turn pale nor wipe a tear from his cheek; he was all the time urging me to break out from the horse--grasping the handle of his sword and
45 his bronze-shod spear, and breathing fury against the foe. Yet when we had sacked the city of Priam he got his handsome share of the prize money and went on board (such is the fortune of war) without a wound upon him, neither from a thrown spear nor in close combat, for the rage of Mars is a matter of great chance.'

"When I had told him this, the ghost of Achilles strode off across a meadow full of asphodel, exulting over what I had said concerning the prowess of his son.

"After him I saw mighty Hercules, but it was his phantom only, for he is feasting ever with the immortal gods, and has lovely Hebe to wife, who is daughter of Jove and Juno.
5 The ghosts were screaming round him like scared birds flying all whithers. He looked black as night with his bare bow in his hands and his arrow on the string, glaring around as though ever on the point of taking aim. About his breast there was a wondrous golden belt adorned in the most marvellous fashion with bears, wild boars, and lions with gleaming eyes; there was also war, battle, and death. The man who made that belt,
10 do what he might, would never be able to make another like it. Hercules knew me at once when he saw me, and spoke piteously, saying, 'My poor Ulysses, noble son of Laertes, are you too leading the same sorry kind of life that I did when I was above ground? I was son of Jove, but I went through an infinity of suffering, for I became bondsman to one who was far beneath me--a low fellow who set me all manner of
15 labours. He once sent me here to fetch the hell-hound--for he did not think he could find anything harder for me than this, but I got the hound out of Hades and brought him to him, for Mercury and Minerva helped me.'

Ulysses sees the shade of Hercules.

BOOK XII – THE SIRENS, SCYLLA AND CHARYBDIS

THE SIRENS, SCYLLA AND CHARYBDIS, THE CATTLE OF THE SUN.

After we were clear of the river Oceanus, and had got out into the open sea, we went on till we reached the Aeaean island where there is dawn and sun-rise as in other places. We then drew our ship on to the sands and got out of her on to the shore, where we went to sleep and waited till day should break.

5 "Then, when the child of morning, rosy-fingered Dawn, appeared, I sent some men to Circe's house to fetch the body of Elpenor. We cut firewood from a wood where the headland jutted out into the sea, and after we had wept over him and lamented him we performed his funeral rites. When his body and armour had been burned to ashes, we raised a cairn, set a stone over it, and at the top of the cairn we fixed the oar that he had
10 been used to row with.

Ithacans return to Aiaia; prepare burial for fellow-warrior, Elpenor.

"While we were doing all this, Circe, who knew that we had got back from the house of Hades, dressed herself and came to us as fast as she could; and her maid servants came with her bringing us bread, meat, and wine. Then she stood in the midst of us and said, 'You have done a bold thing in going down alive to the house of Hades, and you will
15 have died twice, to other people's once; now, then, stay here for the rest of the day, feast your fill, and go on with your voyage at daybreak tomorrow morning. In the meantime I will tell Ulysses about your course, and will explain everything to him so as to prevent your suffering from misadventure either by land or sea.'

"We agreed to do as she had said, and feasted through the livelong day to the going
20 down of the sun, but when the sun had set and it came on dark, the men laid themselves down to sleep by the stern cables of the ship. Then Circe took me by the hand and bade me be seated away from the others, while she reclined by my side and asked me all about our adventures.

Circe advises Ulysses about SIRENS.

"'So far so good,' said she, when I had ended my story, 'and now pay attention to what
25 I am about to tell you--heaven itself, indeed, will recall it to your recollection. First you will come to the Sirens who enchant all who come near them. If any one unwarily draws in too close and hears the singing of the Sirens, his wife and children will never welcome him home again, for they sit in a green field and warble him to death with the sweetness of their song. There is a great heap of dead men's bones lying all around, with the flesh
30 still rotting off them. Therefore pass these Sirens by, and stop your men's ears with wax that none of them may hear; but if you like you can listen yourself, for you may get the men to bind you as you stand upright on a cross piece half way up the mast, and they must lash the rope's ends to the mast itself, that you may have the pleasure of listening. If you beg and pray the men to unloose you, then they must bind you faster.

35 "'When your crew have taken you past these Sirens, I cannot give you coherent directions as to which of two courses you are to take; I will lay the two alternatives before you, and you must consider them for yourself. On the one hand there are some overhanging rocks against which the deep blue waves of Amphitrite beat with terrific fury; the blessed gods call these rocks the Wanderers. Here not even a bird may pass,
40 no, not even the timid doves that bring ambrosia to Father Jove, but the sheer rock always carries off one of them, and Father Jove has to send another to make up their number; no ship that ever yet came to these rocks has got away again, but the waves

and whirlwinds of fire are freighted with wreckage and with the bodies of dead men. The only vessel that ever sailed and got through, was the famous Argo on her way from the house of Aetes, and she too would have gone against these great rocks, only that Juno piloted her past them for the love she bore to Jason.

5   "'Of these two rocks the one reaches heaven and its peak is lost in a dark cloud. This never leaves it, so that the top is never clear not even in summer and early autumn. No man though he had twenty hands and twenty feet could get a foothold on it and climb it, for it runs sheer up, as smooth as though it had been polished. In the middle of it there is a large cavern, looking West and turned towards Erebus; you must take your 10   ship this way, but the cave is so high up that not even the stoutest archer could send an arrow into it. Inside it Scylla sits and yelps with a voice that you might take to be that of a young hound, but in truth she is a dreadful monster and no one--not even a god-- could face her without being terror-struck. She has twelve mis-shapen feet, and six necks of the most prodigious length; and at the end of each neck she has a frightful 15   head with three rows of teeth in each, all set very close together, so that they would crunch any one to death in a moment, and she sits deep within her shady cell thrusting out her heads and peering all round the rock, fishing for dolphins or dogfish or any larger monster that she can catch, of the thousands with which Amphitrite teems. No ship ever yet got past her without losing some men, for she shoots out all her heads at 20   once, and carries off a man in each mouth.

Circe advises troops about female monster, Scylla.

"'You will find the other rock lie lower, but they are so close together that there is not more than a bow-shot between them. A large fig tree in full leaf grows upon it, and under it lies the sucking whirlpool of Charybdis. Three times in the day does she vomit forth her waters, and three times she sucks them down again; see that you be not there 25   when she is sucking, for if you are, Neptune himself could not save you; you must hug the Scylla side and drive ship by as fast as you can, for you had better lose six men than your whole crew.'

Circe advises troops about Charybdis.

"'Is there no way,' said I, 'of escaping Charybdis, and at the same time keeping Scylla off when she is trying to harm my men?'

30   "'You dare devil,' replied the goddess, 'you are always wanting to fight somebody or something; you will not let yourself be beaten even by the immortals. For Scylla is not mortal; moreover she is savage, extreme, rude, cruel and invincible. There is no help for it; your best chance will be to get by her as fast as ever you can, for if you dawdle about her rock while you are putting on your armour, she may catch you with a second cast 35   of her six heads, and snap up another half dozen of your men; so drive your ship past her at full speed, and roar out lustily to Crataiis who is Scylla's dam, bad luck to her; she will then stop her from making a second raid upon you.'

"'You will now come to the Thrinacian island, and here you will see many herds of cattle and flocks of sheep belonging to the sun-god--seven herds of cattle and seven flocks of 40   sheep, with fifty head in each flock. They do not breed, nor do they become fewer in number, and they are tended by the goddesses Phaethusa and Lampetie, who are children of the sun-god Hyperion by Neaera. Their mother when she had borne them and had done suckling them sent them to the Thrinacian island, which was a long way off, to live there and look after their father's flocks and herds. If you leave these flocks 45   unharmed, and think of nothing but getting home, you may yet after much hardship reach Ithaca; but if you harm them, then I forewarn you of the destruction both of your ship and of your comrades; and even though you may yourself escape, you will return late, in bad plight, after losing all your men.'

Circe advises troops not to eat cattle.

Troops set sail with Circe's help.

"Here she ended, and dawn enthroned in gold began to show in heaven, whereon she returned inland. I then went on board and told my men to loose the ship from her moorings; so they at once got into her, took their places, and began to smite the grey sea with their oars. Presently the great and cunning goddess Circe befriended us with a
5 fair wind that blew dead aft, and staid steadily with us, keeping our sails well filled, so we did whatever wanted doing to the ship's gear, and let her go as wind and helmsman headed her.

Ulysses repeats Circe's warnings to troops; they approach the SIRENS.

"Then, being much troubled in mind, I said to my men, 'My friends, it is not right that one or two of us alone should know the prophecies that Circe has made me, I will
10 therefore tell you about them, so that whether we live or die we may do so with our eyes open. First she said we were to keep clear of the Sirens, who sit and sing most beautifully in a field of flowers; but she said I might hear them myself so long as no one else did. Therefore, take me and bind me to the crosspiece half way up the mast; bind me as I stand upright, with a bond so fast that I cannot possibly break away, and lash
15 the rope's ends to the mast itself. If I beg and pray you to set me free, then bind me more tightly still.'

"I had hardly finished telling everything to the men before we reached the island of the two Sirens, for the wind had been very favourable. Then all of a sudden it fell dead calm; there was not a breath of wind nor a ripple upon the water, so the men furled the
20 sails and stowed them; then taking to their oars they whitened the water with the foam they raised in rowing. Meanwhile I took a large wheel of wax and cut it up small with my sword. Then I kneaded the wax in my strong hands till it became soft, which it soon did between the kneading and the rays of the sun-god son of Hyperion. Then I stopped the ears of all my men, and they bound me hands and feet to the mast as I stood upright
25 on the cross piece; but they went on rowing themselves. When we had got within earshot of the land, and the ship was going at a good rate, the Sirens saw that we were getting in shore and began with their singing.

SIRENS try to seduce Ulysses.

"'Come here,' they sang, 'renowned Ulysses, honour to the Achaean name, and listen to our two voices. No one ever sailed past us without staying to hear the enchanting
30 sweetness of our song--and he who listens will go on his way not only charmed, but wiser, for we know all the ills that the gods laid upon the Argives and Trojans before Troy, and can tell you everything that is going to happen over the whole world.'

"They sang these words most musically, and as I longed to hear them further I made signs by frowning to my men that they should set me free; but they quickened their
35 stroke, and Eurylochus and Perimedes bound me with still stronger bonds till we had got out of hearing of the Sirens' voices. Then my men took the wax from their ears and unbound me.

"Immediately after we had got past the island I saw a great wave from which spray was rising, and I heard a loud roaring sound. The men were so frightened that they loosed
40 hold of their oars, for the whole sea resounded with the rushing of the waters, but the ship stayed where it was, for the men had left off rowing. I went round, therefore, and exhorted them man by man not to lose heart.

"'My friends,' said I, 'this is not the first time that we have been in danger, and we are in nothing like so bad a case as when the Cyclops shut us up in his cave; nevertheless,
45 my courage and wise counsel saved us then, and we shall live to look back on all this as well. Now, therefore, let us all do as I say, trust in Jove and row on with might and

main. As for you, coxswain, these are your orders; attend to them, for the ship is in your hands; turn her head away from these steaming rapids and hug the rock, or she will give you the slip and be over yonder before you know where you are, and you will be the death of us.'

5 "So they did as I told them; but I said nothing about the awful monster Scylla, for I knew the men would not go on rowing if I did, but would huddle together in the hold. In one thing only did I disobey Circe's strict instructions--I put on my armour. Then seizing two strong spears I took my stand on the ship's bows, for it was there that I expected first to see the monster of the rock, who was to do my men so much harm;
10 but I could not make her out anywhere, though I strained my eyes with looking the gloomy rock all over and over.

Note how Ulysses disobeys Circe.

"Then we entered the Straits in great fear of mind, for on the one hand was Scylla, and on the other dread Charybdis kept sucking up the salt water. As she vomited it up, it was like the water in a cauldron when it is boiling over upon a great fire, and the spray
15 reached the top of the rocks on either side. When she began to suck again, we could see the water all inside whirling round and round, and it made a deafening sound as it broke against the rocks. We could see the bottom of the whirlpool all black with sand and mud, and the men were at their wits ends for fear. While we were taken up with this, and were expecting each moment to be our last, Scylla pounced down suddenly upon
20 us and snatched up my six best men. I was looking at once after both ship and men, and in a moment I saw their hands and feet ever so high above me, struggling in the air as Scylla was carrying them off, and I heard them call out my name in one last despairing cry. As a fisherman, seated, spear in hand, upon some jutting rock throws bait into the water to deceive the poor little fishes, and spears them with the ox's horn with which
25 his spear is shod, throwing them gasping on to the land as he catches them one by one--even so did Scylla land these panting creatures on her rock and munch them up at the mouth of her den, while they screamed and stretched out their hands to me in their mortal agony. This was the most sickening sight that I saw throughout all my voyages.

"When we had passed the Wandering rocks, with Scylla and terrible Charybdis, we
30 reached the noble island of the sun-god, where were the goodly cattle and sheep belonging to the sun Hyperion. While still at sea in my ship I could hear the cattle lowing as they came home to the yards, and the sheep bleating. Then I remembered what the blind Theban prophet Teiresias had told me, and how carefully Aeaean Circe had warned me to shun the island of the blessed sun-god. So being much troubled I said to
35 the men, 'My men, I know you are hard pressed, but listen while I tell you the prophecy that Teiresias made me, and how carefully Aeaean Circe warned me to shun the island of the blessed sun-god, for it was here, she said, that our worst danger would lie. Head the ship, therefore, away from the island.'

"The men were in despair at this, and Eurylochus at once gave me an insolent answer.
40 'Ulysses,' said he, 'you are cruel; you are very strong yourself and never get worn out; you seem to be made of iron, and now, though your men are exhausted with toil and want of sleep, you will not let them land and cook themselves a good supper upon this island, but bid them put out to sea and go faring fruitlessly on through the watches of the flying night. It is by night that the winds blow hardest and do so much damage; how
45 can we escape should one of those sudden squalls spring up from South West or West, which so often wreck a vessel when our lords the gods are unpropitious? Now, therefore, let us obey the behests of night and prepare our supper here hard by the ship; to-morrow morning we will go on board again and put out to sea.'

Dissent from the troops; note the commander's response.

"Thus spoke Eurylochus, and the men approved his words. I saw that heaven meant us a mischief and said, 'You force me to yield, for you are many against one, but at any rate each one of you must take his solemn oath that if he meet with a herd of cattle or a large flock of sheep, he will not be so mad as to kill a single head of either, but will be
5 satisfied with the food that Circe has given us.'

"They all swore as I bade them, and when they had completed their oath we made the ship fast in a harbour that was near a stream of fresh water, and the men went ashore and cooked their suppers. As soon as they had had enough to eat and drink, they began talking about their poor comrades whom Scylla had snatched up and eaten; this set them
10 weeping and they went on crying till they fell off into a sound sleep.

"In the third watch of the night when the stars had shifted their places, Jove raised a great gale of wind that flew a hurricane so that land and sea were covered with thick clouds, and night sprang forth out of the heavens. When the child of morning, rosy-fingered Dawn, appeared, we brought the ship to land and drew her into a cave wherein
15 the sea-nymphs hold their courts and dances, and I called the men together in council.

"'My friends,' said I, 'we have meat and drink in the ship, let us mind, therefore, and not touch the cattle, or we shall suffer for it; for these cattle and sheep belong to the mighty sun, who sees and gives ear to everything.' And again they promised that they would obey.

20 "For a whole month the wind blew steadily from the South, and there was no other wind, but only South and East. As long as corn and wine held out the men did not touch the cattle when they were hungry; when, however, they had eaten all there was in the ship, they were forced to go further afield, with hook and line, catching birds, and taking whatever they could lay their hands on; for they were starving. One day,
25 therefore, I went up inland that I might pray heaven to show me some means of getting away. When I had gone far enough to be clear of all my men, and had found a place that was well sheltered from the wind, I washed my hands and prayed to all the gods in Olympus till by and by they sent me off into a sweet sleep.

"Meanwhile Eurylochus had been giving evil counsel to the men, 'Listen to me,' said he,
30 'my poor comrades. All deaths are bad enough but there is none so bad as famine. Why should not we drive in the best of these cows and offer them in sacrifice to the immortal gods? If we ever get back to Ithaca, we can build a fine temple to the sun-god and enrich it with every kind of ornament; if, however, he is determined to sink our ship out of revenge for these horned cattle, and the other gods are of the same mind, I for one
35 would rather drink salt water once for all and have done with it, than be starved to death by inches in such a desert island as this is.'

Troops disobey Circe and eat the cattle.

"Thus spoke Eurylochus, and the men approved his words. Now the cattle, so fair and goodly, were feeding not far from the ship; the men, therefore, drove in the best of them, and they all stood round them saying their prayers, and using young oak-shoots
40 instead of barley-meal, for there was no barley left. When they had done praying they killed the cows and dressed their carcasses; they cut out the thigh bones, wrapped them round in two layers of fat, and set some pieces of raw meat on top of them. They had no wine with which to make drink-offerings over the sacrifice while it was cooking, so they kept pouring on a little water from time to time while the inward meats were being
45 grilled; then, when the thigh bones were burned and they had tasted the inward meats, they cut the rest up small and put the pieces upon the spits.

"By this time my deep sleep had left me, and I turned back to the ship and to the sea shore. As I drew near I began to smell hot roast meat, so I groaned out a prayer to the immortal gods. 'Father Jove,' I exclaimed, 'and all you other gods who live in everlasting bliss, you have done me a cruel mischief by the sleep into which you have sent me; see
5   what fine work these men of mine have been making in my absence.'

"Meanwhile Lampetie went straight off to the sun and told him we had been killing his cows, whereon he flew into a great rage, and said to the immortals, 'Father Jove, and all you other gods who live in everlasting bliss, I must have vengeance on the crew of Ulysses' ship: they have had the insolence to kill my cows, which were the one thing I
10   loved to look upon, whether I was going up heaven or down again. If they do not square accounts with me about my cows, I will go down to Hades and shine there among the dead.'

Troops punished for eating cattle.

"'Sun,' said Jove, 'go on shining upon us gods and upon mankind over the fruitful earth. I will shiver their ship into little pieces with a bolt of white lightning as soon as they get
15   out to sea.'

"I was told all this by Calypso, who said she had heard it from the mouth of Mercury.

"As soon as I got down to my ship and to the sea shore I rebuked each one of the men separately, but we could see no way out of it, for the cows were dead already. And indeed the gods began at once to show signs and wonders among us, for the hides of
20   the cattle crawled about, and the joints upon the spits began to low like cows, and the meat, whether cooked or raw, kept on making a noise just as cows do.

Ulysses rebukes troops too late; Gods deliver deadly storm.

"For six days my men kept driving in the best cows and feasting upon them, but when Jove the son of Saturn had added a seventh day, the fury of the gale abated; we therefore went on board, raised our masts, spread sail, and put out to sea. As soon as we were
25   well away from the island, and could see nothing but sky and sea, the son of Saturn raised a black cloud over our ship, and the sea grew dark beneath it. We did not get on much further, for in another moment we were caught by a terrific squall from the West that snapped the forestays of the mast so that it fell aft, while all the ship's gear tumbled about at the bottom of the vessel. The mast fell upon the head of the helmsman in the
30   ship's stern, so that the bones of his head were crushed to pieces, and he fell overboard as though he were diving, with no more life left in him.

"Then Jove let fly with his thunderbolts, and the ship went round and round, and was filled with fire and brimstone as the lightning struck it. The men all fell into the sea; they were carried about in the water round the ship, looking like so many sea-gulls, but the
35   god presently deprived them of all chance of getting home again.

"I stuck to the ship till the sea knocked her sides from her keel (which drifted about by itself) and struck the mast out of her in the direction of the keel; but there was a backstay of stout ox-thong still hanging about it, and with this I lashed the mast and keel together, and getting astride of them was carried wherever the winds chose to take me.

Ulysses battles with nature & the immortals.

40   "The gale from the West had now spent its force, and the wind got into the South again, which frightened me lest I should be taken back to the terrible whirlpool of Charybdis. This indeed was what actually happened, for I was borne along by the waves all night, and by sunrise had reached the rock of Scylla, and the whirlpool. She was then sucking down the salt sea water, but I was carried aloft toward the fig tree, which I caught hold

of and clung on to like a bat. I could not plant my feet anywhere so as to stand securely, for the roots were a long way off and the boughs that overshadowed the whole pool were too high, too vast, and too far apart for me to reach them; so I hung patiently on, waiting till the pool should discharge my mast and raft again--and a very long while it
5 seemed. A jury-man is not more glad to get home to supper, after having been long detained in court by troublesome cases, than I was to see my raft beginning to work its way out of the whirlpool again. At last I let go with my hands and feet, and fell heavily into the sea, hard by my raft on to which I then got, and began to row with my hands. As for Scylla, the father of gods and men would not let her get further sight of me--
10 otherwise I should have certainly been lost.

Ulysses saved/taken prisoner by Calypso for 7 years.

"Hence I was carried along for nine days till on the tenth night the gods stranded me on the Ogygian island, where dwells the great and powerful goddess Calypso. She took me in and was kind to me, but I need say no more about this, for I told you and your noble wife all about it yesterday, and I hate saying the same thing over and over again."

BOOK XIII – ULYSSES RETURNS TO ITHACA

ULYSSES LEAVES SCHERIA AND RETURNS TO ITHACA

Thus did he speak, and they all held their peace throughout the covered cloister, enthralled by the charm of his story, till presently Alcinous began to speak.

"Ulysses," said he, "now that you have reached my house I doubt not you will get home without further misadventure no matter how much you have suffered in the past. To
5 you others, however, who come here night after night to drink my choicest wine and listen to my bard, I would insist as follows. Our guest has already packed up the clothes, wrought gold, and other valuables which you have brought for his acceptance; let us now, therefore, present him further, each one of us, with a large tripod and a cauldron. We will recoup ourselves by the levy of a general rate; for private individuals cannot be
10 expected to bear the burden of such a handsome present."

Narrative ends; returns to real time.

Every one approved of this, and then they went home to bed each in his own abode. When the child of morning, rosy-fingered Dawn, appeared they hurried down to the ship and brought their cauldrons with them. Alcinous went on board and saw everything so securely stowed under the ship's benches that nothing could break adrift
15 and injure the rowers. Then they went to the house of Alcinous to get dinner, and he sacrificed a bull for them in honour of Jove who is the lord of all.

Phaikians prepare to send Ulysses home.

"Sir, and all of you, farewell. Make your drink-offerings and send me on my way rejoicing, for you have fulfilled my heart's desire by giving me an escort, and making me presents, which heaven grant that I may turn to good account; may I find my admirable
20 wife living in peace among friends, and may you whom I leave behind me give satisfaction to your wives and children; may heaven vouchsafe you every good grace, and may no evil thing come among your people."

As he spoke he crossed the threshold, and Alcinous sent a man to conduct him to his ship and to the sea shore. Arete also sent some maidservants with him. When they got
25 to the water side the crew took these things and put them on board, with all the meat and drink; but for Ulysses they spread a rug and a linen sheet on deck that he might sleep soundly in the stern of the ship. Then he too went on board and lay down without a word, but the crew took every man his place and loosed the hawser from the pierced stone to which it had been bound. Thereon, when they began rowing out to sea, Ulysses
30 fell into a deep, sweet, and almost deathlike slumber.

Troops set sail; Ulysses sleeps.

The ship bounded forward on her way as a four in hand chariot flies over the course when the horses feel the whip. Her prow curvetted as it were the neck of a stallion, and a great wave of dark blue water seethed in her wake. She held steadily on her course, and even a falcon, swiftest of all birds, could not have kept pace with her. Thus, then,
35 she cut her way through the water, carrying one who was as cunning as the gods, but who was now sleeping peacefully, forgetful of all that he had suffered both on the field of battle and by the waves of the weary sea.

When the bright star that heralds the approach of dawn began to show, the ship drew near to land. Into this harbour, then, they took their ship, for they knew the place. She
40 had so much way upon her that she ran half her own length on to the shore; when, however, they had landed, the first thing they did was to lift Ulysses with his rug and

linen sheet out of the ship, and lay him down upon the sand still fast asleep. Then they took out the presents which Minerva had persuaded the Phaeacians to give him when he was setting out on his voyage homewards. They put these all together by the root of the olive tree, away from the road, for fear some passer by might come and steal them
5   before Ulysses awoke; and then they made the best of their way home again.

Ulysses does not recognize his homeland. Why not? Goddess escorts him.

Then Minerva came up to him disguised as a young shepherd of delicate and princely mien, with a good cloak folded double about her shoulders; she had sandals on her comely feet and held a javelin in her hand. Ulysses was glad when he saw her,and went straight up to her.

10   "My friend," said he, "you are the first person whom I have met with in this country; I salute you, therefore, and beg you to be well disposed towards me. Protect these my goods, and myself too, for I embrace your knees and pray to you as though you were a god. Tell me, then, and tell me truly, what land and country is this? Who are its inhabitants? Am I on an island, or is this the sea board of some continent?"

15   Minerva answered, "Stranger, you must be very simple, or must have come from somewhere a long way off, not to know what country this is. It is a very celebrated place, and everybody knows it East and West. It is rugged and not a good driving country, but it is by no means a bad island for what there is of it. It grows any quantity of corn and also wine, for it is watered both by rain and dew; it breeds cattle also and
20   goats; all kinds of timber grow here, and there are watering places where the water never runs dry; so, sir, the name of Ithaca is known even as far as Troy, which I understand to be a long way off from this Achaean country."

Ulysses lies & disguises himself.

Ulysses was glad at finding himself, as Minerva told him, in his own country, and he began to answer, but he did not speak the truth, and made up a lying story in the
25   instinctive wiliness of his heart.

"I heard of Ithaca," said he, "when I was in Crete beyond the seas, and now it seems I have reached it with all these treasures. I have left as much more behind me for my children, but am flying because I killed Orsilochus son of Idomeneus, the fleetest runner in Crete. I killed him because he wanted to rob me of the spoils I had got from Troy
30   with so much trouble and danger both on the field of battle and by the waves of the weary sea; he said I had not served his father loyally at Troy as vassal, but had set myself up as an independent ruler, so I lay in wait for him with one of my followers by the road side, and speared him as he was coming into town from the country. It was a very dark night and nobody saw us; it was not known, therefore, that I had killed him, but
35   as soon as I had done so I went to a ship and besought the owners, who were Phoenicians, to take me on board and set me in Pylos or in Elis where the Epeans rule, giving them as much spoil as satisfied them. They meant no guile, but the wind drove them off their course, and we sailed on till we came hither by night. It was all we could do to get inside the harbour, and none of us said a word about supper though we wanted
40   it badly, but we all went on shore and lay down just as we were. I was very tired and fell asleep directly, so they took my goods out of the ship, and placed them beside me where I was lying upon the sand. Then they sailed away to Sidonia, and I was left here in great distress of mind."

Minerva asks why Ulysses cannot be honest in his own country. Why not?

Such was his story, but Minerva smiled and caressed him with her hand. Then she took
45   the form of a woman, fair, stately, and wise, "He must be indeed a shifty lying fellow," said she, "who could surpass you in all manner of craft even though you had a god for

your antagonist. Dare devil that you are, full of guile, unwearying in deceit, can you not drop your tricks and your instinctive falsehood, even now that you are in your own country again? Did you not know Jove's daughter Minerva--me, who have been ever with you, who kept watch over you in all your troubles, and who made the Phaeacians
5 take so great a liking to you? And now, again, I am come here to talk things over with you, and help you to hide the treasure I made the Phaeacians give you; I want to tell you about the troubles that await you in your own house; you have got to face them, but tell no one, neither man nor woman, that you have come home again. Bear everything, and put up with every man's insolence, without a word."

10 And Ulysses answered, "A man, goddess, may know a great deal, but you are so constantly changing your appearance that when he meets you it is a hard matter for him to know whether it is you or not. This much, however, I know exceedingly well; you were very kind to me as long as we Achaeans were fighting before Troy, but from the day on which we went on board ship after having sacked the city of Priam, and heaven
15 dispersed us--from that day, Minerva, I saw no more of you, and cannot ever remember your coming to my ship to help me in a difficulty; I had to wander on sick and sorry till the gods delivered me from evil and I reached the city of the Phaeacians, where you encouraged me and took me into the town. And now, I beseech you in your father's name, tell me the truth, for I do not believe I am really back in Ithaca. I am in some
20 other country and you are mocking me and deceiving me in all you have been saying. Tell me then truly, have I really got back to my own country?"

Note the god/mortal relationship portrayed here.

"You are always taking something of that sort in your head," replied Minerva, "and that is why I cannot desert you in your afflictions; you are so plausible, shrewd and shifty. Any one but yourself on returning from so long a voyage would at once have gone
25 home to see his wife and children, but you do not seem to care about asking after them or hearing any news about them till you have exploited your wife, who remains at home vainly grieving for you, and having no peace night or day for the tears she sheds on your behalf. As for my not coming near you, I was never uneasy about you, for I was certain you would get back safely though you would lose all your men, and I did not wish to
30 quarrel with my uncle Neptune, who never forgave you for having blinded his son. I will now, however, point out to you the lie of the land, and you will then perhaps believe me. This is the haven of the old merman Phorcys, and here is the olive tree that grows at the head of it; here too is the overarching cavern in which you have offered many an acceptable hecatomb to the nymphs, and this is the wooded mountain Neritum."

A god's loyalty to an epic hero. What spiritual/social values are portrayed?

35 As she spoke the goddess dispersed the mist and the land appeared. Then Ulysses rejoiced at finding himself again in his own land, and kissed the bounteous soil; he lifted up his hands and prayed to the nymphs, saying, "Naiad nymphs, daughters of Jove, I made sure that I was never again to see you, now therefore I greet you with all loving salutations, and I will bring you offerings as in the old days, if Jove's redoubtable
40 daughter will grant me life, and bring my son to manhood."

"Take heart, and do not trouble yourself about that," rejoined Minerva, "let us rather set about stowing your things at once in the cave, where they will be quite safe. Let us see how we can best manage it all."

Therewith she went down into the cave to look for the safest hiding places, while
45 Ulysses brought up all the treasure of gold, bronze, and good clothing which the Phaeacians had given him. They stowed everything carefully away, and Minerva set a stone against the door of the cave. Then the two sat down by the root of the great olive, and consulted how to compass the destruction of the wicked suitors.

"Ulysses," said Minerva, "noble son of Laertes, think how you can lay hands on these disreputable people who have been lording it in your house these three years, courting your wife and making wedding presents to her, while she does nothing but lament your absence, giving hope and sending encouraging messages to every one of them, but meaning the very opposite of all she says."

⁵

And Ulysses answered, "In good truth, goddess, it seems I should have come to much the same bad end in my own house as Agamemnon did, if you had not given me such timely information. Advise me how I shall best avenge myself. Stand by my side and put your courage into my heart as on the day when we loosed Troy's fair diadem from her brow. Help me now as you did then, and I will fight three hundred men, if you, goddess, will be with me."

¹⁰

"Trust me for that," said she, "I will not lose sight of you when once we set about it, and I imagine that some of those who are devouring your substance will then bespatter the pavement with their blood and brains. I will begin by disguising you so that no human being shall know you; I will cover your body with wrinkles; you shall lose all your yellow hair; I will blear your fine eyes for you, and make you an unseemly object in the sight of the suitors, of your wife, and of the son whom you left behind you. Then go at once to the swineherd who is in charge of your pigs; he has been always well affected towards you, and is devoted to Penelope and your son; you will find him feeding his pigs near the rock that is called Raven by the fountain Arethusa. Stay with him and find out how things are going, while I proceed to Sparta and see your son, who is with Menelaus at Lacedaemon, where he has gone to try and find out whether you are still alive."

¹⁵

²⁰

"But why," said Ulysses, "did you not tell him, for you knew all about it? Did you want him too to go sailing about amid all kinds of hardship while others are eating up his estate?"

²⁵

Minerva answered, "Never mind about him, I sent him that he might be well spoken of for having gone. He is in no sort of difficulty, but is staying quite comfortably with Menelaus, and is surrounded with abundance of every kind. The suitors have put out to sea and are lying in wait for him, for they mean to kill him before he can get home. I do not much think they will succeed, but rather that some of those who are now eating up your estate will first find a grave themselves."

³⁰

As she spoke Minerva touched him with her wand and covered him with wrinkles, took away all his yellow hair, and withered the flesh over his whole body; she bleared his eyes, which were naturally very fine ones; she changed his clothes and threw an old rag of a wrap about him, and a tunic, tattered, filthy, and begrimed with smoke; she also gave him an undressed deer skin as an outer garment, and furnished him with a staff and a wallet all in holes, with a twisted thong for him to sling it over his shoulder.

³⁵

When the pair had thus laid their plans they parted, and the goddess went straight to Lacedaemon to fetch Telemachus.

⁴⁰

Ulysses asks for god's guidance in returning to his home.

Note the nature of Ulysses's questions for the goddess.

BOOK XVI – FATHER-SON REUNION

FATHER-SON REUNION: ULYSSES REVEALS HIMSELF TO TELEMACHUS.

Meanwhile Ulysses and the swineherd had lit a fire in the hut and were were getting breakfast ready at daybreak, for they had sent the men out with the pigs. When Telemachus came up, the dogs did not bark but fawned upon him, so Ulysses, hearing the sound of feet and noticing that the dogs did not bark, said to Eumaeus:

5 "Eumaeus, I hear footsteps; I suppose one of your men or someone of your acquaintance is coming here, for the dogs are fawning upon him and not barking."

The words were hardly out of his mouth before his son stood at the door. Eumaeus sprang to his feet, and the bowls in which he was mixing wine fell from his hands, as he made towards his master. He kissed his head and both his beautiful eyes, and wept
10 for joy. A father could not be more delighted at the return of an only son, the child of his old age, after ten years' absence in a foreign country and after having gone through much hardship. He embraced him, kissed him all over as though he had come back from the dead, and spoke fondly to him saying:

"Stranger"-Son Reunion.

"So you are come, Telemachus, light of my eyes that you are. When I heard you had
15 gone to Pylos I made sure I was never going to see you any more. Come in, my dear child, and sit down, that I may have a good look at you now you are home again; it is not very often you come into the country to see us herdsmen; you stick pretty close to the town generally. I suppose you think it better to keep an eye on what the suitors are doing."

20 "So be it, old friend," answered Telemachus, "but I am come now because I want to see you, and to learn whether my mother is still at her old home or whether some one else has married her, so that the bed of Ulysses is without bedding and covered with cobwebs."

"She is still at the house," replied Eumaeus, "grieving and breaking her heart, and doing
25 nothing but weep, both night and day continually."

As he spoke he took Telemachus' spear, whereon he crossed the stone threshold and came inside. Ulysses rose from his seat to give him place as he entered, but Telemachus checked him; "Sit down, stranger," said he, "I can easily find another seat, and there is one here who will lay it for me."

30 Ulysses went back to his own place, and Eumaeus strewed some green brushwood on the floor and threw a sheepskin on top of it for Telemachus to sit upon. Then the swineherd brought them platters of cold meat, the remains from what they had eaten the day before, and he filled the bread baskets with bread as fast as he could. He mixed wine also in bowls of ivy-wood, and took his seat facing Ulysses. Then they laid their
35 hands on the good things that were before them, and as soon as they had had enough to eat and drink Telemachus said to Eumaeus, "Old friend, where does this stranger come from? How did his crew bring him to Ithaca, and who were they?--for assuredly he did not come here by land."

To this you answered, O swineherd Eumaeus, "My son, I will tell you the real truth. He says he is a Cretan, and that he has been a great traveller. At this moment he is running away from a Thesprotian ship, and has taken refuge at my station, so I will put him into your hands. Do whatever you like with him, only remember that he is your suppliant."

5 "I am very much distressed," said Telemachus, "by what you have just told me. How can I take this stranger into my house? I am as yet young, and am not strong enough to hold my own if any man attacks me. My mother cannot make up her mind whether to stay where she is and look after the house out of respect for public opinion and the memory of her husband, or whether the time is now come for her to take the best man 10 of those who are wooing her, and the one who will make her the most advantageous offer; still, as the stranger has come to your station I will find him a cloak and shirt of good wear, with a sword and sandals, and will send him wherever he wants to go. Or if you like you can keep him here at the station, and I will send him clothes and food that he may be no burden on you and on your men; but I will not have him go near the 15 suitors, for they are very insolent, and are sure to ill treat him in a way that would greatly grieve me; no matter how valiant a man may be he can do nothing against numbers, for they will be too strong for him."

Note the nature of Ulysses's inquiry here.

Then Ulysses said, "Sir, it is right that I should say something myself. I am much shocked about what you have said about the insolent way in which the suitors are 20 behaving in despite of such a man as you are. Tell me, do you submit to such treatment tamely, or has some god set your people against you? May you not complain of your brothers--for it is to these that a man may look for support, however great his quarrel may be? I wish I were as young as you are and in my present mind; if I were son to Ulysses, or, indeed, Ulysses himself, I would rather some one came and cut my head 25 off, but I would go to the house and be the bane of every one of these men. If they were too many for me--I being single-handed--I would rather die fighting in my own house than see such disgraceful sights day after day, strangers grossly maltreated, and men dragging the women servants about the house in an unseemly way, wine drawn recklessly, and bread wasted all to no purpose for an end that shall never be 30 accomplished."

And Telemachus answered, "I will tell you truly everything. There is no enmity between me and my people, nor can I complain of brothers, to whom a man may look for support however great his quarrel may be. Jove has made us a race of only sons. Laertes was the only son of Arceisius, and Ulysses only son of Laertes. I am myself the only son 35 of Ulysses who left me behind him when he went away, so that I have never been of any use to him. Hence it comes that my house is in the hands of numberless marauders; for the chiefs from all the neighbouring islands...

"I understand and heed you," replied Eumaeus; "you need instruct me no further, only as I am going that way say whether I had not better let poor Laertes know that you are 40 returned.

"More's the pity," answered Telemachus, "I am sorry for him, but we must leave him to himself just now. If people could have everything their own way, the first thing I should choose would be the return of my father; but go, and give your message; then make haste back again, and do not turn out of your way to tell Laertes. Tell my mother 45 to send one of her women secretly with the news at once, and let him hear it from her."

Thus did he urge the swineherd; Eumaeus, therefore, took his sandals, bound them to his feet, and started for the town. Minerva watched him well off the station, and then came up to it in the form of a woman--fair, stately, and wise. She stood against the side of the entry, and revealed herself to Ulysses, but Telemachus could not see her, and

5 knew not that she was there, for the gods do not let themselves be seen by everybody. Ulysses saw her, and so did the dogs, for they did not bark, but went scared and whining off to the other side of the yards. She nodded her head and motioned to Ulysses with her eyebrows; whereon he left the hut and stood before her outside the main wall of the yards. Then she said to him:

10 "Ulysses, noble son of Laertes, it is now time for you to tell your son: do not keep him in the dark any longer, but lay your plans for the destruction of the suitors, and then make for the town. I will not be long in joining you, for I too am eager for the fray."

> Goddess instructs Ulysses to identify himself to his son.

As she spoke she touched him with her golden wand. First she threw a fair clean shirt and cloak about his shoulders; then she made him younger and of more imposing

15 presence; she gave him back his colour, filled out his cheeks, and let his beard become dark again. Then she went away and Ulysses came back inside the hut. His son was astounded when he saw him, and turned his eyes away for fear he might be looking upon a god.

"Stranger," said he, "how suddenly you have changed from what you were a moment

20 or two ago. You are dressed differently and your color is not the same. Are you someone or other of the gods that live in heaven? If so, be propitious to me till I can make you due sacrifice and offerings of wrought gold. Have mercy upon me."

And Ulysses said, "I am no god, why should you take me for one? I am your father, on whose account you grieve and suffer so much at the hands of lawless men."

25 As he spoke he kissed his son, and a tear fell from his cheek on to the ground, for he had restrained all tears till now. But Telemachus could not yet believe that it was his father, and said:

> Telemachus mistrusts; does not recognize father.

"You are not my father, but some god is flattering me with vain hopes that I may grieve the more hereafter; no mortal man could of himself contrive to do as you have been

30 doing, and make yourself old and young at a moment's notice, unless a god were with him. A second ago you were old and all in rags, and now you are like some god come down from heaven."

Ulysses answered, "Telemachus, you ought not to be so immeasurably astonished at my being really here. There is no other Ulysses who will come hereafter. Such as I am, it is

35 I, who after long wandering and much hardship have got home in the twentieth year to my own country. What you wonder at is the work of the redoubtable goddess Minerva, who does with me whatever she will, for she can do what she pleases. At one moment she makes me like a beggar, and the next I am a young man with good clothes on my back; it is an easy matter for the gods who live in heaven to make any man look either

40 rich or poor."

As he spoke he sat down, and Telemachus threw his arms about his father and wept. They were both so much moved that they cried aloud like eagles or vultures with crooked talons that have been robbed of their half fledged young by peasants. Thus piteously did they weep, and the sun would have gone down upon their mourning if

> Father-Son Reunion and Catharsis.

Telemachus had not suddenly said, "In what ship, my dear father, did your crew bring you to Ithaca? Of what nation did they declare themselves to be--for you cannot have come by land?"

Ulysses shares brief history with his son. Why?

"I will tell you the truth, my son," replied Ulysses. "It was the Phaeacians who brought
5   me here. They are great sailors, and are in the habit of giving escorts to any one who reaches their coasts. They took me over the sea while I was fast asleep, and landed me in Ithaca, after giving me many presents in bronze, gold, and raiment. These things by heaven's mercy are lying concealed in a cave, and I am now come here on the suggestion of Minerva that we may consult about killing our enemies. First, therefore, give me a
10 list of the suitors, with their number, that I may learn who, and how many, they are. I can then turn the matter over in my mind, and see whether we two can fight the whole body of them ourselves, or whether we must find others to help us."

To this Telemachus answered, "Father, I have always heard of your renown both in the field and in council, but the task you talk of is a very great one: I am awed at the mere
15 thought of it; two men cannot stand against many and brave ones. There are not ten suitors only, nor twice ten, but ten many times over; you shall learn their number at once. There are fifty-two chosen youths from Dulichium, and they have six servants; from Same there are twenty-four; twenty young Achaeans from Zacynthus, and twelve from Ithaca itself, all of them well born. They have with them a servant Medon, a bard,
20 and two men who can carve at table. If we face such numbers as this, you may have bitter cause to rue your coming, and your revenge. See whether you cannot think of some one who would be willing to come and help us."

Father-son plan retaliation on suitors.

"Listen to me," replied Ulysses, "and think whether Minerva and her father Jove may seem sufficient, or whether I am to try and find some one else as well."

25 "Those whom you have named," answered Telemachus, "are a couple of good allies, for though they dwell high up among the clouds they have power over both gods and men."

"These two," continued Ulysses, "will not keep long out of the fray, when the suitors and we join fight in my house. Now, therefore, return home early to-morrow morning,
30 and go about among the suitors as before. Later on the swineherd will bring me to the city disguised as a miserable old beggar. If you see them ill treating me, steel your heart against my sufferings; even though they drag me feet foremost out of the house, or throw things at me, look on and do nothing beyond gently trying to make them behave more reasonably; but they will not listen to you, for the day of their reckoning is at hand.
35 Furthermore I say, and lay my saying to your heart; when Minerva shall put it in my mind, I will nod my head to you, and on seeing me do this you must collect all the armour that is in the house and hide it in the strong store room. Make some excuse when the suitors ask you why you are removing it; say that you have taken it to be out of the way of the smoke, inasmuch as it is no longer what it was when Ulysses went
40 away, but has become soiled and begrimed with soot. Add to this more particularly that you are afraid Jove may set them on to quarrel over their wine, and that they may do each other some harm which may disgrace both banquet and wooing, for the sight of arms sometimes tempts people to use them. But leave a sword and a spear apiece for yourself and me, and a couple of oxhide shields so that we can snatch them up at any
45 moment; Jove and Minerva will then soon quiet these people. There is also another matter; if you are indeed my son and my blood runs in your veins, let no one know that Ulysses is within the house--neither Laertes, nor yet the swineherd, nor any of the servants, nor even Penelope herself. Let you and me exploit the women alone, and let

us also make trial of some other of the men servants, to see who is on our side and whose hand is against us."

"Father," replied Telemachus, "you will come to know me by and by, and when you do you will find that I can keep your counsel. I do not think, however, the plan you propose
5 will turn out well for either of us. Think it over. It will take us a long time to go the round of the farms and exploit the men, and all the time the suitors will be wasting your estate with impunity and without compunction. Prove the women by all means, to see who are disloyal and who guiltless, but I am not in favour of going round and trying the men. We can attend to that later on, if you really have some sign from Jove that he will
10 support you."

Then, when they had finished their work and the meal was ready, they ate it, and every man had his full share so that all were satisfied. As soon as they had had enough to eat and drink, they laid down to rest and enjoyed the boon of sleep.

Son advises father.

BOOK XVII – TELEMACHUS AND HIS MOTHER MEET

TELEMACHUS AND HIS MOTHER MEET--ULYSSES AND EUMAEUS COME DOWN TO THE TOWN, AND ULYSSES IS INSULTED BY MELANTHIUS--HE IS RECOGNISED BY THE DOG ARGOS--HE IS INSULTED AND PRESENTLY STRUCK BY ANTINOUS WITH A STOOL--PENELOPE DESIRES THAT HE SHALL BE SENT TO HER.

When Telemachus reached home he stood his spear against a bearing-post of the cloister, crossed the stone floor of the cloister itself, and went inside. Penelope came out of her room looking like Diana or Venus, and wept as she flung her arms about her son. She kissed his forehead and both his beautiful eyes, "Light of my eyes," she cried
5 as she spoke fondly to him, "so you are come home again; I made sure I was never going to see you any more. To think of your having gone off to Pylos without saying anything about it or obtaining my consent. But come, tell me what you saw."

"Do not scold me, mother," answered Telemachus, "nor vex me, seeing what a narrow escape I have had, but wash your face, change your dress, go upstairs with your maids,
10 and promise full and sufficient hecatombs to all the gods if Jove will only grant us our revenge upon the suitors. I must now go to the place of assembly to invite a stranger who has come back with me from Pylos. I sent him on with my crew, and told Piraeus to take him home and look after him till I could come for him myself."

Son orders mother to retreat.

She heeded her son's words, washed her face, changed her dress, and vowed full and
15 sufficient hecatombs to all the gods if they would only vouchsafe her revenge upon the suitors.

"Telemachus, I shall go upstairs and lie down on that sad couch, which I have not ceased to water with my tears, from the day Ulysses set out for Troy with the sons of Atreus. You failed, however, to make it clear to me before the suitors came back to the
20 house, whether or no you had been able to hear anything about the return of your father."

Telemachus lies to mother. Why?

"I will tell you then truth," replied her son. "We went to Pylos and saw Nestor, who took me to his house and treated me as hospitably as though I were a son of his own who had just returned after a long absence; so also did his sons; but he said he had not
25 heard a word from any human being about Ulysses, whether he was alive or dead. He sent me, therefore, with a chariot and horses to Menelaus. There I saw Helen, for whose sake so many, both Argives and Trojans, were in heaven's wisdom doomed to suffer. Menelaus asked me what it was that had brought me to Lacedaemon, and I told him the whole truth, whereon he said, 'So, then, these cowards would usurp a brave man's
30 bed? A hind might as well lay her new-born young in the lair of a lion, and then go off to feed in the forest or in some grassy dell. The lion, when he comes back to his lair, will make short work with the pair of them, and so will Ulysses with these suitors. By father Jove, Minerva, and Apollo, if Ulysses is still the man that he was when he wrestled with Philomeleides in Lesbos, and threw him so heavily that all the Greeks cheered him-
35 -if he is still such, and were to come near these suitors, they would have a short shrift and a sorry wedding. As regards your question, however, I will not prevaricate nor deceive you, but what the old man of the sea told me, so much will I tell you in full. He said he could see Ulysses on an island sorrowing bitterly in the house of the nymph Calypso, who was keeping him prisoner, and he could not reach his home, for he had
40 no ships nor sailors to take him over the sea.' This was what Menelaus told me, and

when I had heard his story I came away; the gods then gave me a fair wind and soon brought me safe home again." With these words he moved the heart of Penelope.

Immediately afterwards Ulysses came inside, looking like a poor miserable old beggar, leaning on his staff and with his clothes all in rags. He sat down upon the threshold of 5 ash-wood just inside the doors leading from the outer to the inner court, and against a bearing-post of cypress-wood which the carpenter had skilfully planed, and had made to join truly with rule and line. Telemachus took a whole loaf from the bread-basket, with as much meat as he could hold in his two hands, and said to Eumaeus, "Take this to the stranger, and tell him to go the round of the suitors, and beg from them; a beggar 10 must not be shamefaced."

So Eumaeus went up to him and said, "Stranger, Telemachus sends you this, and says you are to go the round of the suitors begging, for beggars must not be shamefaced."

Ulysses answered, "May King Jove grant all happiness to Telemachus, and fulfil the desire of his heart."

15 Then with both hands he took what Telemachus had sent him, and laid it on the dirty old wallet at his feet. He went on eating it while the bard was singing, and had just finished his dinner as he left off. The suitors applauded the bard, whereon Minerva went up to Ulysses and prompted him to beg pieces of bread from each one of the suitors, that he might see what kind of people they were, and tell the good from the 20 bad; but come what might she was not going to save a single one of them. Ulysses, therefore, went on his round, going from left to right, and stretched out his hands to beg as though he were a real beggar. Some of them pitied him, and were curious about him, asking one another who he was and where he came from; whereon the goatherd Melanthius said, "Suitors of my noble mistress, I can tell you something about him, for 25 I have seen him before. The swineherd brought him here, but I know nothing about the man himself, nor where he comes from."

On this Antinous began to abuse the swineherd. "You precious idiot," he cried, "what have you brought this man to town for? Have we not tramps and beggars enough already to pester us as we sit at meat? Do you think it a small thing that such people 30 gather here to waste your master's property--and must you needs bring this man as well?"

And Eumaeus answered, "Antinous, your birth is good but your words evil. It was no doing of mine that he came here. Who is likely to invite a stranger from a foreign country, unless it be one of those who can do public service as a seer, a healer of hurts, 35 a carpenter, or a bard who can charm us with his singing? Such men are welcome all the world over, but no one is likely to ask a beggar who will only worry him. You are always harder on Ulysses' servants than any of the other suitors are, and above all on me, but I do not care so long as Telemachus and Penelope are alive and here."

But Telemachus said, "Hush, do not answer him; Antinous has the bitterest tongue of 40 all the suitors, and he makes the others worse."

Then turning to Antinous he said, "Antinous, you take as much care of my interests as though I were your son. Why should you want to see this stranger turned out of the house? Heaven forbid; take something and give it him yourself; I do not grudge it; I bid you take it. Never mind my mother, nor any of the other servants in the house; but I

Ulysses, disguised as beggar, enters home in Ithaca.

Ulysses evaluates the suitors as he begs.

know you will not do what I say, for you are more fond of eating things yourself than of giving them to other people."

"What do you mean, Telemachus," replied Antinous, "by this swaggering talk? If all the suitors were to give him as much as I will, he would not come here again for another
5   three months."

As he spoke he drew the stool on which he rested his dainty feet from under the table, and made as though he would throw it at Ulysses, but the other suitors all gave him something, and filled his wallet with bread and meat

On this Ulysses began to move off, and said, "Your looks, my fine sir, are better than
10   your breeding; if you were in your own house you would not spare a poor man so much as a pinch of salt, for though you are in another man's, and surrounded with abundance, you cannot find it in you to give him even a piece of bread."

This made Antinous very angry, and he scowled at him saying, "You shall pay for this before you get clear of the court." With these words he threw a footstool at him, and
15   hit him on the right shoulder blade near the top of his back. Ulysses stood firm as a rock and the blow did not even stagger him, but he shook his head in silence as he brooded on his revenge. Then he went back to the threshold and sat down there, laying his well filled wallet at his feet.

What cultural code does Ulysses offer here?

"Listen to me," he cried, "you suitors of Queen Penelope, that I may speak even as I
20   am minded. A man knows neither ache nor pain if he gets hit while fighting for his money, or for his sheep or his cattle; and even so Antinous has hit me while in the service of my miserable belly, which is always getting people into trouble. Still, if the poor have gods and avenging deities at all, I pray them that Antinous may come to a bad end before his marriage."

25   "Sit where you are, and eat your victuals in silence, or be off elsewhere," shouted Antinous. "If you say more I will have you dragged hand and foot through the courts, and the servants shall flay you alive."

The other suitors were much displeased at this, and one of the young men said, "Antinous, you did ill in striking that poor wretch of a tramp: it will be worse for you if
30   he should turn out to be some god--and we know the gods go about disguised in all sorts of ways as people from foreign countries, and travel about the world to see who do amiss and who righteously."

Note Telemachus's restraint.

Thus said the suitors, but Antinous paid them no heed. Meanwhile Telemachus was furious about the blow that had been given to his father, and though no tear fell from
35   him, he shook his head in silence and brooded on his revenge.

Penelope pities begger and summons him.

"Call him here, then," said Penelope, "that I too may hear his story. As for the suitors, let them take their pleasure indoors or out as they will, for they have nothing to fret about. Their corn and wine remain unwasted in their houses with none but servants to consume them, while they keep hanging about our house day after day sacrificing our
40   oxen, sheep, and fat goats for their banquets, and never giving so much as a thought to the quantity of wine they drink. No estate can stand such recklessness, for we have now no Ulysses to protect us. If he were to come again, he and his son would soon have their revenge."

BOOK XIX – ULYSSES INTERVIEWS PENELOPE

TELEMACHUS AND ULYSSES REMOVE THE ARMOUR--ULYSSES INTERVIEWS PENELOPE--
EURYCLEA WASHES HIS FEET AND RECOGNISES THE SCAR ON HIS LEG--PENELOPE TELLS
HER DREAM TO ULYSSES.

Ulysses was left in the cloister, pondering on the means whereby with Minerva's help he might be able to kill the suitors. Presently he said to Telemachus, "Telemachus, we must get the armour together and take it down inside. Make some excuse when the suitors ask you why you have removed it. Say that you have taken it to be out of the
5 way of the smoke, inasmuch as it is no longer what it was when Ulysses went away, but has become soiled and begrimed with soot. Add to this more particularly that you are afraid Jove may set them on to quarrel over their wine, and that they may do each other some harm which may disgrace both banquet and wooing, for the sight of arms sometimes tempts people to use them."

10 Telemachus approved of what his father had said, so he called nurse Euryclea and said, "Nurse, shut the women up in their room, while I take the armour that my father left behind him down into the store room. No one looks after it now my father is gone, and it has got all smirched with soot during my own boyhood. I want to take it down where the smoke cannot reach it."

15 Euryclea did as she was told, and bolted the women inside their room. Then Ulysses and his son made all haste to take the helmets, shields, and spears inside; and Minerva went before them with a gold lamp in her hand that shed a soft and brilliant radiance, whereon Telemachus said, "Father, my eyes behold a great marvel: the walls, with the rafters, crossbeams, and the supports on which they rest are all aglow as with a flaming
20 fire. Surely there is some god here who has come down from heaven."

"Hush," answered Ulysses, "hold your peace and ask no questions, for this is the manner of the gods. Get you to your bed, and leave me here to talk with your mother and the maids. Your mother in her grief will ask me all sorts of questions."

Ulysses instructs son about the gods.

On this Telemachus went by torch-light to the other side of the inner court, to the room
25 in which he always slept. There he lay in his bed till morning, while Ulysses was left in the cloister pondering on the means whereby with Minerva's help he might be able to kill the suitors.

Then Penelope came down from her room looking like Venus or Diana, and they set her a seat inlaid with scrolls of silver and ivory near the fire in her accustomed place. It
30 had been made by Icmalius and had a footstool all in one piece with the seat itself; and it was covered with a thick fleece: on this she now sat, and the maids came from the women's room to join her. They set about removing the tables at which the wicked suitors had been dining, and took away the bread that was left, with the cups from which they had drunk. They emptied the embers out of the braziers, and heaped much wood
35 upon them to give both light and heat; but Melantho began to rail at Ulysses a second time and said, "Stranger, do you mean to plague us by hanging about the house all night and spying upon the women? Be off, you wretch, outside, and eat your supper there, or you shall be driven out with a firebrand."

Penelope does not recognize her husband.

Ulysses scowled at her and answered, "My good woman, why should you be so angry with me? Is it because I am not clean, and my clothes are all in rags, and because I am obliged to go begging about after the manner of tramps and beggars generally? I too was a rich man once, and had a fine house of my own; in those days I gave to many a
5 tramp such as I now am, no matter who he might be nor what he wanted. I had any number of servants, and all the other things which people have who live well and are accounted wealthy, but it pleased Jove to take all away from me; therefore, woman, beware lest you too come to lose that pride and place in which you now wanton above your fellows; have a care lest you get out of favour with your mistress, and lest Ulysses
10 should come home, for there is still a chance that he may do so. Moreover, though he be dead as you think he is, yet by Apollo's will he has left a son behind him, Telemachus, who will note anything done amiss by the maids in the house, for he is now no longer in his boyhood."

Penelope heard what he was saying and scolded the maid, "Impudent baggage," said
15 she, "I see how abominably you are behaving, and you shall smart for it. You knew perfectly well, for I told you myself, that I was going to see the stranger and ask him about my husband, for whose sake I am in such continual sorrow."

Penelope asks "stranger" his identity.

Eurynome brought the seat at once and set a fleece upon it, and as soon as Ulysses had sat down Penelope began by saying, "Stranger, I shall first ask you who and whence are
20 you? Tell me of your town and parents."

"Madam," answered Ulysses, "who on the face of the whole earth can dare to chide with you? Your fame reaches the firmament of heaven itself; you are like some blameless king, who upholds righteousness, as the monarch over a great and valiant nation: the earth yields its wheat and barley, the trees are loaded with fruit, the ewes bring forth
25 lambs, and the sea abounds with fish by reason of his virtues, and his people do good deeds under him. Nevertheless, as I sit here in your house, ask me some other question and do not seek to know my race and family, or you will recall memories that will yet more increase my sorrow. I am full of heaviness, but I ought not to sit weeping and wailing in another person's house, nor is it well to be thus grieving continually. I shall
30 have one of the servants or even yourself complaining of me, and saying that my eyes swim with tears because I am heavy with wine."

Penelope offers truthful story.

Then Penelope answered, "Stranger, heaven robbed me of all beauty, whether of face or figure, when the Argives set sail for Troy and my dear husband with them. If he were to return and look after my affairs I should be both more respected and should show a
35 better presence to the world. As it is, I am oppressed with care, and with the afflictions which heaven has seen fit to heap upon me. The chiefs from all our islands--Dulichium, Same, and Zacynthus, as also from Ithaca itself, are wooing me against my will and are wasting my estate. I can therefore show no attention to strangers, nor suppliants, nor to people who say that they are skilled artisans, but am all the time broken-hearted about
40 Ulysses. They want me to marry again at once, and I have to invent stratagems in order to deceive them. In the first place heaven put it in my mind to set up a great tambour-frame in my room, and to begin working upon an enormous piece of fine needlework. Then I said to them, 'Sweethearts, Ulysses is indeed dead, still, do not press me to marry again immediately; wait--for I would not have my skill in needlework perish unrecorded-
45 -till I have finished making a pall for the hero Laertes, to be ready against the time when death shall take him. He is very rich, and the women of the place will talk if he is laid out without a pall.' This was what I said, and they assented; whereon I used to keep working at my great web all day long, but at night I would unpick the stitches again by torch light. I fooled them in this way for three years without their finding it out, but as

time wore on and I was now in my fourth year, in the waning of moons, and many days had been accomplished, those good for nothing hussies my maids betrayed me to the suitors, who broke in upon me and caught me; they were very angry with me, so I was forced to finish my work whether I would or no. And now I do not see how I can find
5 any further shift for getting out of this marriage. My parents are putting great pressure upon me, and my son chafes at the ravages the suitors are making upon his estate, for he is now old enough to understand all about it and is perfectly able to look after his own affairs, for heaven has blessed him with an excellent disposition. Still, notwithstanding all this, tell me who you are and where you come from--for you must
10 have had father and mother of some sort; you cannot be the son of an oak or of a rock."

Then Ulysses answered, "Madam, wife of Ulysses, since you persist in asking me about my family, I will answer, no matter what it costs me: people must expect to be pained when they have been exiles as long as I have, and suffered as much among as many peoples. Nevertheless, as regards your question I will tell you all you ask. There is a fair
15 and fruitful island in mid-ocean called Crete; it is thickly peopled and there are ninety cities in it: the people speak many different languages which overlap one another, for there are Achaeans, brave Eteocretans, Dorians of three-fold race, and noble Pelasgi. There is a great town there, Cnossus, where Minos reigned who every nine years had a conference with Jove himself. Minos was father to Deucalion, whose son I am, for
20 Deucalion had two sons Idomeneus and myself. Idomeneus sailed for Troy, and I, who am the younger, am called Aethon; my brother, however, was at once the older and the more valiant of the two; hence it was in Crete that I saw Ulysses and showed him hospitality, for the winds took him there as he was on his way to Troy, carrying him out of his course from cape Malea and leaving him in Amnisus off the cave of Ilithuia,
25 where the harbours are difficult to enter and he could hardly find shelter from the winds that were then raging. As soon as he got there he went into the town and asked for Idomeneus, claiming to be his old and valued friend, but Idomeneus had already set sail for Troy some ten or twelve days earlier, so I took him to my own house and showed him every kind of hospitality, for I had abundance of everything. Moreover, I fed the
30 men who were with him with barley meal from the public store, and got subscriptions of wine and oxen for them to sacrifice to their heart's content. They stayed with me twelve days, for there was a gale blowing from the North so strong that one could hardly keep one's feet on land. I suppose some unfriendly god had raised it for them, but on the thirteenth day the wind dropped, and they got away."

35 Many a plausible tale did Ulysses further tell her, and Penelope wept as she listened, for her heart was melted. As the snow wastes upon the mountain tops when the winds from South East and West have breathed upon it and thawed it till the rivers run bank full with water, even so did her cheeks overflow with tears for the husband who was all the time sitting by her side. Ulysses felt for her and was sorry for her, but he kept his eyes
40 as hard as horn or iron without letting them so much as quiver, so cunningly did he restrain his tears. Then, when she had relieved herself by weeping, she turned to him again and said: "Now, stranger, I shall put you to the test and see whether or no you really did entertain my husband and his men, as you say you did. Tell me, then, how he was dressed, what kind of a man he was to look at, and so also with his companions."

45 "Madam," answered Ulysses, "it is such a long time ago that I can hardly say. Twenty years are come and gone since he left my home, and went elsewhither; but I will tell you as well as I can recollect. Ulysses wore a mantle of purple wool, double lined, and it was fastened by a gold brooch with two catches for the pin. On the face of this there was a device that shewed a dog holding a spotted fawn between his fore paws, and watching
50 it as it lay panting upon the ground. Every one marvelled at the way in which these

Assess the psychological value of this tale-telling for the husband-wife reunion.

things had been done in gold, the dog looking at the fawn, and strangling it, while the fawn was struggling convulsively to escape. As for the shirt that he wore next his skin, it was so soft that it fitted him like the skin of an onion, and glistened in the sunlight to the admiration of all the women who beheld it. Furthermore I say, and lay my saying to
5 your heart, that I do not know whether Ulysses wore these clothes when he left home, or whether one of his companions had given them to him while he was on his voyage; or possibly some one at whose house he was staying made him a present of them, for he was a man of many friends and had few equals among the Achaeans. I myself gave him a sword of bronze and a beautiful purple mantle, double lined, with a shirt that
10 went down to his feet, and I sent him on board his ship with every mark of honour. He had a servant with him, a little older than himself, and I can tell you what he was like; his shoulders were hunched, he was dark, and he had thick curly hair. His name was Eurybates, and Ulysses treated him with greater familiarity than he did any of the others, as being the most like-minded with himself."

15 Penelope was moved still more deeply as she heard the indisputable proofs that Ulysses laid before her; and when she had again found relief in tears she said to him, "Stranger, I was already disposed to pity you, but henceforth you shall be honoured and made welcome in my house. It was I who gave Ulysses the clothes you speak of. I took them out of the store room and folded them up myself, and I gave him also the gold brooch
20 to wear as an ornament. Alas! I shall never welcome him home again. It was by an ill fate that he ever set out for that detested city whose very name I cannot bring myself even to mention."

Then Ulysses answered, "Madam, wife of Ulysses, do not disfigure yourself further by grieving thus bitterly for your loss, though I can hardly blame you for doing so. A
25 woman who has loved her husband and borne him children, would naturally be grieved at losing him, even though he were a worse man than Ulysses, who they say was like a god. Still, cease your tears and listen to what I can tell you. I will hide nothing from you, and can say with perfect truth that I have lately heard of Ulysses as being alive and on his way home; he is among the Thesprotians, and is bringing back much valuable
30 treasure that he has begged from one and another of them; but his ship and all his crew were lost as they were leaving the Thrinacian island, for Jove and the sun-god were angry with him because his men had slaughtered the sun-god's cattle, and they were all drowned to a man. But Ulysses stuck to the keel of the ship and was drifted on to the land of the Phaeacians, who are near of kin to the immortals, and who treated him as
35 though he had been a god, giving him many presents, and wishing to escort him home safe and sound. In fact Ulysses would have been here long ago, had he not thought better to go from land to land gathering wealth; for there is no man living who is so wily as he is; there is no one can compare with him. Pheidon king of the Thesprotians told me all this, and he swore to me--making drink-offerings in his house as he did so-
40 -that the ship was by the water side and the crew found who would take Ulysses to his own country. He sent me off first, for there happened to be a Thesprotian ship sailing for the wheat-growing island of Dulichium, but he showed me all the treasure Ulysses had got together, and he had enough lying in the house of king Pheidon to keep his family for ten generations; but the king said Ulysses had gone to Dodona that he might
45 learn Jove's mind from the high oak tree, and know whether after so long an absence he should return to Ithaca openly or in secret. So you may know he is safe and will be here shortly; he is close at hand and cannot remain away from home much longer; nevertheless I will confirm my words with an oath, and call Jove who is the first and mightiest of all gods to witness, as also that hearth of Ulysses to which I have now
50 come, that all I have spoken shall surely come to pass. Ulysses will return in this self same year; with the end of this moon and the beginning of the next he will be here."

"May it be even so," answered Penelope; "if your words come true you shall have such gifts and such good will from me that all who see you shall congratulate you; but I know very well how it will be. Ulysses will not return, neither will you get your escort hence, for so surely as that Ulysses ever was, there are now no longer any such masters in the
5 house as he was, to receive honourable strangers or to further them on their way home. And now, you maids, wash his feet for him, and make him a bed on a couch with rugs and blankets, that he may be warm and quiet till morning. Then, at day break wash him and anoint him again, that he may sit in the cloister and take his meals with Telemachus. It shall be the worse for any one of these hateful people who is uncivil to him; like it or
10 not, he shall have no more to do in this house. For how, sir, shall you be able to learn whether or no I am superior to others of my sex both in goodness of heart and understanding, if I let you dine in my cloisters squalid and ill clad? Men live but for a little season; if they are hard, and deal hardly, people wish them ill so long as they are alive, and speak contemptuously of them when they are dead, but he that is righteous
15 and deals righteously, the people tell of his praise among all lands, and many shall call him blessed."

Ulysses answered, "Madam, I have foresworn rugs and blankets from the day that I left the snowy ranges of Crete to go on shipboard. I will lie as I have lain on many a sleepless night hitherto. Night after night have I passed in any rough sleeping place, and waited
20 for morning. Nor, again, do I like having my feet washed; I shall not let any of the young hussies about your house touch my feet; but, if you have any old and respectable woman who has gone through as much trouble as I have, I will allow her to wash them."

Then Ulysses answered, "Madam, wife of Ulysses, you need not defer your tournament, for Ulysses will return ere ever they can string the bow, handle it how they will, and
25 send their arrows through the iron."

To this Penelope said, "As long, sir, as you will sit here and talk to me, I can have no desire to go to bed. Still, people cannot do permanently without sleep, and heaven has appointed us dwellers on earth a time for all things. I will therefore go upstairs and recline upon that couch which I have never ceased to flood with my tears from the day
30 Ulysses set out for the city with a hateful name."

She then went upstairs to her own room, not alone, but attended by her maidens, and when there, she lamented her dear husband till Minerva shed sweet sleep over her eyelids.

BOOK XX – ULYSSES CANNOT SLEEP, SIGNS FROM HEAVEN

ULYSSES CANNOT SLEEP--PENELOPE'S PRAYER TO DIANA--THE TWO SIGNS FROM HEAVEN--EUMAEUS AND PHILOETIUS ARRIVE--THE SUITORS DINE--CTESIPPUS THROWS AN OX'S FOOT AT ULYSSES--THEOCLYMENUS FORETELLS DISASTER AND LEAVES THE HOUSE.

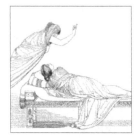

Ulysses slept in the cloister upon an undressed bullock's hide, on the top of which he threw several skins of the sheep the suitors had eaten, and Eurynome threw a cloak over him after he had laid himself down. There, then, Ulysses lay wakefully brooding upon the way in which he should kill the suitors; and by and by, the women who had
5 been in the habit of misconducting themselves with them, left the house giggling and laughing with one another. This made Ulysses very angry, and he doubted whether to get up and kill every single one of them then and there, or to let them sleep one more and last time with the suitors.

Thus he chided with his heart, and checked it into endurance, but he tossed about as
10 one who turns a paunch full of blood and fat in front of a hot fire, doing it first on one side and then on the other, that he may get it cooked as soon as possible, even so did he turn himself about from side to side, thinking all the time how, single handed as he was, he should contrive to kill so large a body of men as the wicked suitors. But by and by Minerva came down from heaven in the likeness of a woman, and hovered over his
15 head saying, "My poor unhappy man, why do you lie awake in this way? This is your house: your wife is safe inside it, and so is your son who is just such a young man as any father may be proud of."

Ulysses strategizes; struggles with his emotions.

"Goddess," answered Ulysses, "all that you have said is true, but I am in some doubt as to how I shall be able to kill these wicked suitors single handed, seeing what a number
20 of them there always are. And there is this further difficulty, which is still more considerable. Supposing that with Jove's and your assistance I succeed in killing them, I must ask you to consider where I am to escape to from their avengers when it is all over."

Gods assure us.

"For shame," replied Minerva, "why, anyone else would trust a worse ally than myself,
25 even though that ally were only a mortal and less wise than I am. Am I not a goddess, and have I not protected you throughout in all your troubles? I tell you plainly that even though there were fifty bands of men surrounding us and eager to kill us, you should take all their sheep and cattle, and drive them away with you. But go to sleep; it is a very bad thing to lie awake all night, and you shall be out of your troubles before long."

30 As she spoke she shed sleep over his eyes, and then went back to Olympus.

Note the new battle Ulysses fights at home.

As this the day broke, Ulysses heard the sound of Penelope weeping, and it puzzled him, for it seemed as though she already knew him and was by his side. Then he gathered up the cloak and the fleeces on which he had lain, and set them on a seat in the cloister, but he took the bullock's hide out into the open. He lifted up his hands to
35 heaven, and prayed, saying "Father Jove, since you have seen fit to bring me over land and sea to my own home after all the afflictions you have laid upon me, give me a sign out of the mouth of someone or other of those who are now waking within the house, and let me have another sign of some kind from outside."

Thus did he pray. Jove heard his prayer and forthwith thundered high up among the clouds from the splendour of Olympus, and Ulysses was glad when he heard it.

Meanwhile the suitors were hatching a plot to murder Telemachus: but a bird flew near them on their left hand—an eagle with a dove in its talons. On this Amphinomus said, "My friends,this plot of ours to murder Telemachus will not succeed; let us go to dinner instead."

Suitors plot to kill Telemachus.

But Minerva would not let the suitors for one moment drop their insolence, for she wanted Ulysses to become still more bitter against them. Now there happened to be among them a ribald fellow, whose name was Ctesippus, and who came from Same. This man, confident in his great wealth, was paying court to the wife of Ulysses, and said to the suitors, "Hear what I have to say. The stranger has already had as large a portion as any one else; this is well, for it is not right nor reasonable to ill-treat any guest of Telemachus who comes here. I will, however, make him a present on my own account, that he may have something to give to the bath-woman, or to some other of Ulysses' servants."

Note the "justice" that the gods want.

BOOK XXI – TRIAL OF AXES, ULYSSES REVEALS HIMSELF

THE TRIAL OF THE AXES, DURING WHICH ULYSSES REVEALS HIMSELF TO EUMAEUS AND PHILOETIUS

Minerva now put it in Penelope's mind to make the suitors try their skill with the bow and with the iron axes, in contest among themselves, as a means of bringing about their destruction. She went upstairs and got the store-room key, which was made of bronze and had a handle of ivory; she then went with her maidens into the store-room at the
5 end of the house, where her husband's treasures of gold, bronze, and wrought iron were kept, and where was also his bow, and the quiver full of deadly arrows that had been given him by a friend whom he had met in Lacedaemon--Iphitus the son of Eurytus. This bow, then, given him by Iphitus, had not been taken with him by Ulysses when he sailed for Troy; he had used it so long as he had been at home, but had left it behind as
10 having been a keepsake from a valued friend.

She sat down with it on her knees, weeping bitterly as she took the bow out of its case, and when her tears had relieved her, she went to the cloister where the suitors were, carrying the bow and the quiver, with the many deadly arrows that were inside it. Along with her came her maidens, bearing a chest that contained much iron and bronze which
15 her husband had won as prizes. When she reached the suitors, she stood by one of the bearing-posts supporting the roof of the cloister, holding a veil before her face, and with a maid on either side of her. Then she said:

Penelope sets the bow & oxen contest.

"Listen to me you suitors, who persist in abusing the hospitality of this house because its owner has been long absent, and without other pretext than that you want to marry
20 me; this, then, being the prize that you are contending for, I will bring out the mighty bow of Ulysses, and whomsoever of you shall string it most easily and send his arrow through each one of twelve axes, him will I follow and quit this house of my lawful husband, so goodly, and so abounding in wealth. But even so I doubt not that I shall remember it in my dreams."

None of the suitors can string the bow.

25 The rest agreed, and Leiodes son of Oenops was the first to rise. He was sacrificial priest to the suitors, and sat in the corner near the mixing-bowl. He was the only man who hated their evil deeds and was indignant with the others. He was now the first to take the bow and arrow, so he went on to the pavement to make his trial, but he could not string the bow, for his hands were weak and unused to hard work, they therefore
30 soon grew tired, and he said to the suitors, "My friends, I cannot string it; let another have it, this bow shall take the life and soul out of many a chief among us, for it is better to die than to live after having missed the prize that we have so long striven for, and which has brought us so long together. Some one of us is even now hoping and praying that he may marry Penelope, but when he has seen this bow and tried it, let him woo
35 and make bridal offerings to some other woman, and let Penelope marry whoever makes her the best offer and whose lot it is to win her."

Ulysses asserts his bravado.

The rest approved his words, and thereon men servants poured water over the hands of the guests, while pages filled the mixing-bowls with wine and water and handed it round after giving every man his drink-offering. Then, when they had made their
40 offerings and had drunk each as much as he desired, Ulysses craftily said:--

"Suitors of the illustrious queen, listen that I may speak even as I am minded. I appeal more especially to Eurymachus, and to Antinous who has just spoken with so much reason. Cease shooting for the present and leave the matter to the gods, but in the morning let heaven give victory to whom it will. For the moment, however, give me the bow that I may prove the power of my hands among you all, and see whether I still have as much strength as I used to have, or whether travel and neglect have made an end of it."

This made them all very angry, for they feared he might string the bow, Antinous therefore rebuked him fiercely saying, "Wretched creature, you have not so much as a grain of sense in your whole body; you ought to think yourself lucky in being allowed to dine unharmed among your betters, without having any smaller portion served you than we others have had, and in being allowed to hear our conversation. No other beggar or stranger has been allowed to hear what we say among ourselves; the wine must have been doing you a mischief, as it does with all those who drink immoderately.

Penelope then spoke to him. "Antinous," said she, "it is not right that you should ill-treat any guest of Telemachus who comes to this house. If the stranger should prove strong enough to string the mighty bow of Ulysses, can you suppose that he would take me home with him and make me his wife? Even the man himself can have no such idea in his mind: none of you need let that disturb his feasting; it would be out of all reason."

"Queen Penelope," answered Eurymachus, "we do not suppose that this man will take you away with him; it is impossible; but we are afraid lest some of the baser sort, men or women among the Achaeans, should go gossiping about and say, 'These suitors are a feeble folk; they are paying court to the wife of a brave man whose bow not one of them was able to string, and yet a beggarly tramp who came to the house strung it at once and sent an arrow through the iron.' This is what will be said, and it will be a scandal against us."

"Eurymachus," Penelope answered, "people who persist in eating up the estate of a great chieftain and dishonouring his house must not expect others to think well of them. Why then should you mind if men talk as you think they will? This stranger is strong and well-built, he says moreover that he is of noble birth. Give him the bow, and let us see whether he can string it or no. I say--and it shall surely be--that if Apollo vouchsafes him the glory of stringing it, I will give him a cloak and shirt of good wear, with a javelin to keep off dogs and robbers, and a sharp sword. I will also give him sandals, and will see him sent safely wherever he wants to go."

Note Penelope's wit.

Another said, "I hope he may be no more successful in other things than he is likely to be in stringing this bow."

But Ulysses, when he had taken it up and examined it all over, strung it as easily as a skilled bard strings a new peg of his lyre and makes the twisted gut fast at both ends. Then he took it in his right hand to prove the string, and it sang sweetly under his touch like the twittering of a swallow. The suitors were dismayed, and turned color as they heard it; at that moment, moreover, Jove thundered loudly as a sign, and the heart of Ulysses rejoiced as he heard the omen that the son of scheming Saturn had sent him.

Ulysses proves his god-like skill.

He took an arrow that was lying upon the table--for those which the Achaeans were so shortly about to taste were all inside the quiver--he laid it on the centre-piece of the bow, and drew the notch of the arrow and the string toward him, still seated on his seat.

When he had taken aim he let fly, and his arrow pierced every one of the handle-holes of the axes from the first onwards till it had gone right through them, and into the outer courtyard. Then he said to Telemachus:

"Your guest has not disgraced you, Telemachus. I did not miss what I aimed at, and I
5 was not long in stringing my bow. I am still strong, and not as the suitors twit me with being. Now, however, it is time for the Achaeans to prepare supper while there is still daylight, and then otherwise to disport themselves with song and dance which are the crowning ornaments of a banquet."

As he spoke he made a sign with his eyebrows, and Telemachus girded on his sword,
10 grasped his spear, and stood armed beside his father's seat.

BOOK XXII – THE KILLING OF THE SUITORS

THE KILLING OF THE SUITORS--THE MAIDS WHO HAVE MISCONDUCTED THEMSELVES ARE MADE TO CLEANSE THE CLOISTERS AND ARE THEN HANGED.

Then Ulysses tore off his rags, and sprang on to the broad pavement with his bow and his quiver full of arrows. He shed the arrows on to the ground at his feet and said, "The mighty contest is at an end. I will now see whether Apollo will vouchsafe it to me to hit another mark which no man has yet hit."

5 On this he aimed a deadly arrow at Antinous, who was about to take up a two-handled gold cup to drink his wine and already had it in his hands. He had no thought of death--who amongst all the revellers would think that one man, however brave, would stand alone among so many and kill him? The arrow struck Antinous in the throat, and the point went clean through his neck, so that he fell over and the cup dropped from his
10 hand, while a thick stream of blood gushed from his nostrils. He kicked the table from him and upset the things on it, so that the bread and roasted meats were all soiled as they fell over on to the ground. The suitors were in an uproar when they saw that a man had been hit; they sprang in dismay one and all of them from their seats and looked everywhere towards the walls, but there was neither shield nor spear, and they rebuked
15 Ulysses very angrily. "Stranger," said they, "you shall pay for shooting people in this way: you shall see no other contest; you are a doomed man; he whom you have slain was the foremost youth in Ithaca, and the vultures shall devour you for having killed him."

Thus they spoke, for they thought that he had killed Antinous by mistake, and did not
20 perceive that death was hanging over the head of every one of them. But Ulysses glared at them and said:

"Dogs, did you think that I should not come back from Troy? You have wasted my substance, have forced my women servants to lie with you, and have wooed my wife while I was still living. You have feared neither God nor man, and now you shall die."

Ulysses lists cultural crimes of suitors.

25 They turned pale with fear as he spoke, and every man looked round about to see whither he might fly for safety, but Eurymachus alone spoke.

Suitors ask for mercy.

"If you are Ulysses," said he, "then what you have said is just. We have done much wrong on your lands and in your house. But Antinous who was the head and front of the offending lies low already. It was all his doing. It was not that he wanted to marry
30 Penelope; he did not so much care about that; what he wanted was something quite different, and Jove has not vouchsafed it to him; he wanted to kill your son and to be chief man in Ithaca. Now, therefore, that he has met the death which was his due, spare the lives of your people. We will make everything good among ourselves, and pay you in full for all that we have eaten and drunk. Each one of us shall pay you a fine worth
35 twenty oxen, and we will keep on giving you gold and bronze till your heart is softened. Until we have done this no one can complain of your being enraged against us."

Ulysses again glared at him and said, "Though you should give me all that you have in the world both now and all that you ever shall have, I will not stay my hand till I have paid all of you in full. You must fight, or fly for your lives; and fly, not a man of you
40 shall."

Suitors accept the fight

Their hearts sank as they heard him, but Eurymachus again spoke saying:

"My friends, this man will give us no quarter. He will stand where he is and shoot us down till he has killed every man among us. Let us then show fight; draw your swords, and hold up the tables to shield you from his arrows. Let us have at him with a rush, to
5 drive him from the pavement and doorway: we can then get through into the town, and raise such an alarm as shall soon stay his shooting."

As he spoke he drew his keen blade of bronze, sharpened on both sides, and with a loud cry sprang towards Ulysses, but Ulysses instantly shot an arrow into his breast that caught him by the nipple and fixed itself in his liver. He dropped his sword and fell
10 doubled up over his table. The cup and all the meats went over on to the ground as he smote the earth with his forehead in the agonies of death, and he kicked the stool with his feet until his eyes were closed in darkness.

Telemachus assists Ulysses.

Then Amphinomus drew his sword and made straight at Ulysses to try and get him away from the door; but Telemachus was too quick for him, and struck him from
15 behind; the spear caught him between the shoulders and went right through his chest, so that he fell heavily to the ground and struck the earth with his forehead. Then Telemachus sprang away from him, leaving his spear still in the body, for he feared that if he stayed to draw it out, some one of the Achaeans might come up and hack at him with his sword, or knock him down, so he set off at a run, and immediately was at his
20 father's side. Then he said:

"Father, let me bring you a shield, two spears, and a brass helmet for your temples. I will arm myself as well, and will bring other armour for the swineherd and the stockman, for we had better be armed."

"Run and fetch them," answered Ulysses, "while my arrows hold out, or when I am
25 alone they may get me away from the door."

Telemachus did as his father said, and went off to the store room where the armour was kept.

Suitors beg goddess not to help Ulysses.

But all the time he felt sure it was Minerva, and the suitors from the other side raised an uproar when they saw her. Agelaus was the first to reproach her. "Mentor," he cried,
30 "do not let Ulysses beguile you into siding with him and fighting the suitors. This is what we will do: when we have killed these people, father and son, we will kill you too. You shall pay for it with your head, and when we have killed you, we will take all you have, in doors or out, and bring it into hotch-pot with Ulysses' property; we will not let your sons live in your house, nor your daughters, nor shall your widow continue to live
35 in the city of Ithaca."

Goddess makes Ulysses prove himself before helping. Why?

But she would not give him full victory as yet, for she wished still further to prove his own prowess and that of his brave son, so she flew up to one of the rafters in the roof of the cloister and sat upon it in the form of a swallow.

Meanwhile Agelaus son of Damastor, Eurynomus, Amphimedon, Demoptolemus,
40 Pisander, and Polybus son of Polyctor bore the brunt of the fight upon the suitors' side; of all those who were still fighting for their lives they were by far the most valiant, for the others had already fallen under the arrows of Ulysses.

They threw their spears as he bade them, but Minerva made them all of no effect. One hit the door post; another went against the door; the pointed shaft of another struck the wall; and as soon as they had avoided all the spears of the suitors Ulysses said to his own men, "My friends, I should say we too had better let drive into the middle of them, or they will crown all the harm they have done us by killing us outright."

They therefore aimed straight in front of them and threw their spears. Ulysses killed Demoptolemus, Telemachus Euryades, Eumaeus Elatus, while the stockman killed Pisander. These all bit the dust, and as the others drew back into a corner Ulysses and his men rushed forward and regained their spears by drawing them from the bodies of the dead.

The suitors now aimed a second time, but again Minerva made their weapons for the most part without effect. They made a horrible groaning as their brains were being battered in, and the ground seethed with their blood.

Leiodes then caught the knees of Ulysses and said, "Ulysses I beseech you have mercy upon me and spare me. I never wronged any of the women in your house either in word or deed, and I tried to stop the others. I saw them, but they would not listen, and now they are paying for their folly. I was their sacrificing priest; if you kill me, I shall die without having done anything to deserve it, and shall have got no thanks for all the good that I did."

Ulysses delivers "justice" upon priest.

Ulysses looked sternly at him and answered, "If you were their sacrificing priest, you must have prayed many a time that it might be long before I got home again, and that you might marry my wife and have children by her. Therefore you shall die."

With these words he picked up the sword that Agelaus had dropped when he was being killed, and which was lying upon the ground. Then he struck Leiodes on the back of his neck, so that his head fell rolling in the dust while he was yet speaking.

The minstrel Phemius son of Terpes--he who had been forced by the suitors to sing to them--now tried to save his life. He was standing near towards the trap door, and held his lyre in his hand. He did not know whether to fly out of the cloister and sit down by the altar of Jove that was in the outer court, and on which both Laertes and Ulysses had offered up the thigh bones of many an ox, or whether to go straight up to Ulysses and embrace his knees, but in the end he deemed it best to embrace Ulysses' knees. So he laid his lyre on the ground between the mixing bowl and the silver-studded seat; then going up to Ulysses he caught hold of his knees and said, "Ulysses, I beseech you have mercy on me and spare me. You will be sorry for it afterwards if you kill a bard who can sing both for gods and men as I can. I make all my lays myself, and heaven visits me with every kind of inspiration. I would sing to you as though you were a god, do not therefore be in such a hurry to cut my head off. Your own son Telemachus will tell you that I did not want to frequent your house and sing to the suitors after their meals, but they were too many and too strong for me, so they made me."

Ulysses and Telemachus distinguish innocent from guilty.

Telemachus heard him, and at once went up to his father. "Hold!" he cried, "the man is guiltless, do him no hurt; and we will spare Medon too, who was always good to me when I was a boy, unless Philoetius or Eumaeus has already killed him, or he has fallen in your way when you were raging about the court."

Medon caught these words of Telemachus, for he was crouching under a seat beneath which he had hidden by covering himself up with a freshly flayed heifer's hide, so he threw off the hide, went up to Telemachus, and laid hold of his knees.

"Here I am, my dear sir," said he, "stay your hand therefore, and tell your father, or he
5 will kill me in his rage against the suitors for having wasted his substance and been so foolishly disrespectful to yourself."

Ulysses smiled at him and answered, "Fear not; Telemachus has saved your life, that you may know in future, and tell other people, how greatly better good deeds prosper than evil ones. Go, therefore, outside the cloisters into the outer court, and be out of
10 the way of the slaughter--you and the bard--while I finish my work here inside."

The pair went into the outer court as fast as they could, and sat down by Jove's great altar, looking fearfully round, and still expecting that they would be killed. Then Ulysses searched the whole court carefully over, to see if anyone had managed to hide himself and was still living, but he found them all lying in the dust and weltering in their blood.
15 They were like fishes which fishermen have netted out of the sea, and thrown upon the beach to lie gasping for water till the heat of the sun makes an end of them. Even so were the suitors lying all huddled up one against the other.

Ulysses, in the meantime, he called Telemachus, the stockman, and the swineherd.
"Begin," said he, "to remove the dead, and make the women help you. Then, get
20 sponges and clean water to swill down the tables and seats. When you have thoroughly cleansed the whole cloisters, take the women into the space between the domed room and the wall of the outer court, and run them through with your swords till they are quite dead, and have forgotten all about love and the way in which they used to lie in secret with the suitors."

25 On this the women came down in a body, weeping and wailing bitterly. First they carried the dead bodies out, and propped them up against one another in the gatehouse. Ulysses ordered them about and made them do their work quickly, so they had to carry the bodies out. When they had done this, they cleaned all the tables and seats with sponges and water, while Telemachus and the two others shovelled up the blood and dirt from
30 the ground, and the women carried it all away and put it out of doors.

Then when they had made the whole place quite clean and orderly, they took the women out and hemmed them in the narrow space between the wall of the domed room and that of the yard, so that they could not get away: and Telemachus said to the other two, "I shall not let these women die a clean death, for they were insolent to me and my
35 mother, and used to sleep with the suitors."

So saying he made a ship's cable fast to one of the bearing-posts that supported the roof of the domed room, and secured it all around the building, at a good height, lest any of the women's feet should touch the ground; and as thrushes or doves beat against a net that has been set for them in a thicket just as they were getting to their nest, and a
40 terrible fate awaits them, even so did the women have to put their heads in nooses one after the other and die most miserably. Their feet moved convulsively for a while, but not for very long.

When they had done this they washed their hands and feet and went back into the house, for all was now over; and Ulysses said to the dear old nurse Euryclea, "Bring me

Ulysses orders "criminal" women killed; other women to clean palace.

Telemachus delivers his own brand of justice upon criminal women.

sulphur, which cleanses all pollution, and fetch fire also that I may burn it, and purify the cloisters. Go, moreover, and tell Penelope to come here with her attendants, and also all the maidservants that are in the house."

"All that you have said is true," answered Euryclea, "but let me bring you some clean
5 clothes--a shirt and cloak. Do not keep these rags on your back any longer. It is not right."

"First light me a fire," replied Ulysses.

She brought the fire and sulphur, as he had bidden her, and Ulysses thoroughly purified the cloisters and both the inner and outer courts. Then she went inside to call the
10 women and tell them what had happened; whereon they came from their apartment with torches in their hands, and pressed round Ulysses to embrace him, kissing his head and shoulders and taking hold of his hands. It made him feel as if he should like to weep, for he remembered every one of them.

BOOK XXIII – PENELOPE RECOGNISES HER HUSBAND

PENELOPE EVENTUALLY RECOGNISES HER HUSBAND--EARLY IN THE MORNING ULYSSES, TELEMACHUS, EUMAEUS, AND PHILOETIUS LEAVE THE TOWN.

Maidens joyfully inform Penelope that Ulysses has returned.

Why does Penelope distrust the news?

Euryclea now went upstairs laughing to tell her mistress that her dear husband had come home. Her aged knees became young again and her feet were nimble for joy as she went up to her mistress and bent over her head to speak to her. "Wake up Penelope, my dear child," she exclaimed, "and see with your own eyes something that you have 5 been wanting this long time past. Ulysses has at last indeed come home again, and has killed the suitors who were giving so much trouble in his house, eating up his estate and ill treating his son."

"My good nurse," answered Penelope, "you must be mad. The gods sometimes send some very sensible people out of their minds, and make foolish people become sensible. 10 This is what they must have been doing to you; for you always used to be a reasonable person. Why should you thus mock me when I have trouble enough already--talking such nonsense, and waking me up out of a sweet sleep that had taken possession of my eyes and closed them? I have never slept so soundly from the day my poor husband went to that city with the ill-omened name. Go back again into the women's room; if it 15 had been any one else who had woke me up to bring me such absurd news I should have sent her away with a severe scolding. As it is your age shall protect you."

"My dear child," answered Euryclea, "I am not mocking you. It is quite true as I tell you that Ulysses is come home again. He was the stranger whom they all kept on treating so badly in the cloister. Telemachus knew all the time that he was come back, but kept 20 his father's secret that he might have his revenge on all these wicked people."

Then Penelope sprang up from her couch, threw her arms round Euryclea, and wept for joy. "But my dear nurse," said she, "explain this to me; if he has really come home as you say, how did he manage to overcome the wicked suitors single handed, seeing what a number of them there always were?"

25 "I was not there," answered Euryclea, "and do not know; I only heard them groaning while they were being killed. We sat crouching and huddled up in a corner of the women's room with the doors closed, till your son came to fetch me because his father sent him. Then I found Ulysses standing over the corpses that were lying on the ground all round him, one on top of the other. You would have enjoyed it if you could have 30 seen him standing there all bespattered with blood and filth, and looking just like a lion. But the corpses are now all piled up in the gatehouse that is in the outer court, and Ulysses has lit a great fire to purify the house with sulphur. He has sent me to call you, so come with me that you may both be happy together after all; for now at last the desire of your heart has been fulfilled; your husband is come home to find both wife 35 and son alive and well, and to take his revenge in his own house on the suitors who behaved so badly to him."

Note Penelope's reticence.

"My dear nurse," said Penelope, "do not exult too confidently over all this. You know how delighted everyone would be to see Ulysses come home--more particularly myself, and the son who has been born to both of us; but what you tell me cannot be really 40 true. It is some god who is angry with the suitors for their great wickedness, and has made an end of them; for they respected no man in the whole world, neither rich nor poor, who came near them, and they have come to a bad end in consequence of their iniquity; Ulysses is dead far away from the Achaean land; he will never return home again."

Then nurse Euryclea said, "My child, what are you talking about? but you were all hard
5 of belief and have made up your mind that your husband is never coming, although he is in the house and by his own fire side at this very moment. Besides I can give you another proof; when I was washing him I perceived the scar which the wild boar gave him, and I wanted to tell you about it, but in his wisdom he would not let me, and clapped his hands over my mouth; so come with me and I will make this bargain with
10 you--if I am deceiving you, you may have me killed by the most cruel death you can think of."

"My dear nurse," said Penelope, "however wise you may be you can hardly fathom the counsels of the gods. Nevertheless, we will go in search of my son, that I may see the corpses of the suitors, and the man who has killed them."

15 On this she came down from her upper room, and while doing so she considered whether she should keep at a distance from her husband and question him, or whether she should at once go up to him and embrace him. When, however, she had crossed the stone floor of the cloister, she sat down opposite Ulysses by the fire, against the wall at right angles to that by which she had entered, while Ulysses sat near one of the
20 bearing-posts, looking upon the ground, and waiting to see what his brave wife would say to him when she saw him. For a long time she sat silent and as one lost in amazement. At one moment she looked him full in the face, but then again directly, she was misled by his shabby clothes and failed to recognize him, till Telemachus began to reproach her and said:

Why does Penelope not recognize her husband?

25 "Mother--but you are so hard that I cannot call you by such a name--why do you keep away from my father in this way? Why do you not sit by his side and begin talking to him and asking him questions? No other woman could bear to keep away from her husband when he had come back to her after twenty years of absence, and after having gone through so much; but your heart always was as hard as a stone."

How do we explain Penelope's "hardness"?

30 Penelope answered, "My son, I am so lost in astonishment that I can find no words in which either to ask questions or to answer them. I cannot even look him straight in the face. Still, if he really is Ulysses come back to his own home again, we shall get to understand one another better by and by, for there are tokens with which we two are alone acquainted, and which are hidden from all others."

35 Ulysses smiled at this, and said to Telemachus, "Let your mother put me to any proof she likes; she will make up her mind about it presently. She rejects me for the moment and believes me to be somebody else, because I am covered with dirt and have such bad clothes on; let us, however, consider what we had better do next. When one man has killed another--even though he was not one who would leave many friends to take
40 up his quarrel--the man who has killed him must still say good bye to his friends and fly the country; whereas we have been killing the stay of a whole town, and all the picked youth of Ithaca. I would have you consider this matter."

"Look to it yourself, father," answered Telemachus, "for they say you are the wisest counsellor in the world, and that there is no other mortal man who can compare with you. We will follow you with right good will, nor shall you find us fail you in so far as our strength holds out."

Ulysses washes self and asks for music to conceal the killings.

"I will say what I think will be best," answered Ulysses. "First wash and put your shirts on; tell the maids also to go to their own room and dress; Phemius shall then strike up
5 a dance tune on his lyre, so that if people outside hear, or any of the neighbours, or some one going along the street happens to notice it, they may think there is a wedding in the house, and no rumours about the death of the suitors will get about in the town, before we can escape to the woods upon my own land. Once there, we will settle which of the courses heaven vouchsafes us shall seem wisest."

10 Thus did he speak, and they did even as he had said. First they washed and put their shirts on, while the women got ready. Then Phemius took his lyre and set them all longing for sweet song and stately dance. The house re-echoed with the sound of men and women dancing, and the people outside said, "I suppose the queen has been getting married at last. She ought to be ashamed of herself for not continuing to protect her
15 husband's property until he comes home."

Note Ulysses's inability to woo Penelope. Why?

This was what they said, but they did not know what it was that had been happening. The upper servant Eurynome washed and anointed Ulysses in his own house and gave him a shirt and cloak, while Minerva made him look taller and stronger than before; she also made the hair grow thick on the top of his head, and flow down in curls like
20 hyacinth blossoms; she glorified him about the head and shoulders just as a skilful workman who has studied art of all kinds under Vulcan or Minerva--and his work is full of beauty--enriches a piece of silver plate by gilding it. He came from the bath looking like one of the immortals, and sat down opposite his wife on the seat he had left. "My dear," said he, "heaven has endowed you with a heart more unyielding than woman ever
25 yet had. No other woman could bear to keep away from her husband when he had come back to her after twenty years of absence, and after having gone through so much. But come, nurse, get a bed ready for me; I will sleep alone, for this woman has a heart as hard as iron."

Penelope tests Ulysses regarding their bed.

"My dear," answered Penelope, "I have no wish to set myself up, nor to depreciate you;
30 but I am not struck by your appearance, for I very well remember what kind of a man you were when you set sail from Ithaca. Nevertheless, Euryclea, take his bed outside the bed chamber that he himself built. Bring the bed outside this room, and put bedding upon it with fleeces, good coverlets, and blankets."

She said this to try him, but Ulysses was very angry and said, "Wife, I am much
35 displeased at what you have just been saying. Who has been taking my bed from the place in which I left it? He must have found it a hard task, no matter how skilled a workman he was, unless some god came and helped him to shift it. There is no man living, however strong and in his prime, who could move it from its place, for it is a marvellous curiosity which I made with my very own hands. There was a young olive
40 growing within the precincts of the house, in full vigour, and about as thick as a bearing-post. I built my room round this with strong walls of stone and a roof to cover them, and I made the doors strong and well-fitting. Then I cut off the top boughs of the olive tree and left the stump standing. This I dressed roughly from the root upwards and then worked with carpenter's tools well and skilfully, straightening my work by drawing a line
45 on the wood, and making it into a bed-prop. I then bored a hole down the middle, and made it the centre-post of my bed, at which I worked till I had finished it, inlaying it with gold and silver; after this I stretched a hide of crimson leather from one side of it

to the other. So you see I know all about it, and I desire to learn whether it is still there, or whether any one has been removing it by cutting down the olive tree at its roots."

When she heard the sure proofs Ulysses now gave her, she fairly broke down. She flew weeping to his side, flung her arms about his neck, and kissed him. "Do not be angry
5 with me Ulysses," she cried, "you, who are the wisest of mankind. We have suffered, both of us. Heaven has denied us the happiness of spending our youth, and of growing old, together; do not then be aggrieved or take it amiss that I did not embrace you thus as soon as I saw you. I have been shuddering all the time through fear that someone might come here and deceive me with a lying story; for there are many very wicked
10 people going about. Jove's daughter Helen would never have yielded herself to a man from a foreign country, if she had known that the sons of Achaeans would come after her and bring her back. Heaven put it in her heart to do wrong, and she gave no thought to that sin, which has been the source of all our sorrows. Now, however, that you have convinced me by showing that you know all about our bed (which no human being has
15 ever seen but you and I and a single maidservant, the daughter of Actor, who was given me by my father on my marriage, and who keeps the doors of our room) hard of belief though I have been I can mistrust no longer."

Catharsis for Penelope.

Then Ulysses in his turn melted, and wept as he clasped his dear and faithful wife to his bosom. As the sight of land is welcome to men who are swimming towards the shore,
20 when Neptune has wrecked their ship with the fury of his winds and waves; a few alone reach the land, and these, covered with brine, are thankful when they find themselves on firm ground and out of danger--even so was her husband welcome to her as she looked upon him, and she could not tear her two fair arms from about his neck. Indeed they would have gone on indulging their sorrow till rosy-fingered morn appeared, had
25 not Minerva determined otherwise, and held night back in the far west, while she would not suffer Dawn to leave Oceanus, nor to yoke the two steeds Lampus and Phaethon that bear her onward to break the day upon mankind.

Reunion of husband and wife.

At last, however, Ulysses said, "Wife, we have not yet reached the end of our troubles. I have an unknown amount of toil still to undergo. It is long and difficult, but I must
30 go through with it, for thus the shade of Teiresias prophesied concerning me, on the day when I went down into Hades to ask about my return and that of my companions. But now let us go to bed, that we may lie down and enjoy the blessed boon of sleep."

Note Ulysses's comment: I have other wars ahead of me.

"You shall go to bed as soon as you please," replied Penelope, "now that the gods have sent you home to your own good house and to your country. But as heaven has put it
35 in your mind to speak of it, tell me about the task that lies before you. I shall have to hear about it later, so it is better that I should be told at once."

"My dear," answered Ulysses, "why should you press me to tell you? Still, I will not conceal it from you, though you will not like it. I do not like it myself, for Teiresias bade me travel far and wide, carrying an oar, till I came to a country where the people have
40 never heard of the sea, and do not even mix salt with their food. They know nothing about ships, nor oars that are as the wings of a ship. He gave me this certain token which I will not hide from you. He said that a wayfarer should meet me and ask me whether it was a winnowing shovel that I had on my shoulder. On this, I was to fix my oar in the ground and sacrifice a ram, a bull, and a boar to Neptune; after which I was
45 to go home and offer hecatombs to all the gods in heaven, one after the other. As for myself, he said that death should come to me from the sea, and that my life should ebb away very gently when I was full of years and peace of mind, and my people should bless me. All this, he said, should surely come to pass."

And Penelope said, "If the gods are going to vouchsafe you a happier time in your old age, you may hope then to have some respite from misfortune."

Penelope and Ulysses recap their histories together.

When Ulysses and Penelope had had their fill of love they fell talking with one another. She told him how much she had had to bear in seeing the house filled with a crowd of wicked suitors who had killed so many sheep and oxen on her account, and had drunk so many casks of wine. Ulysses in his turn told her what he had suffered, and how much trouble he had himself given to other people. He told her everything, and she was so delighted to listen that she never went to sleep till he had ended his whole story.

Ulysses instructs Penelope to hide until trouble subsides.

Then Minerva bethought her of another matter. When she deemed that Ulysses had had both of his wife and of repose, she bade gold-enthroned Dawn rise out of Oceanus that she might shed light upon mankind. On this, Ulysses rose from his comfortable bed and said to Penelope, "Wife, we have both of us had our full share of troubles, you, here, in lamenting my absence, and I in being prevented from getting home though I was longing all the time to do so. Now, however, that we have at last come together, take care of the property that is in the house. As for the sheep and goats which the wicked suitors have eaten, I will take many myself by force from other people, and will compel the Achaeans to make good the rest till they shall have filled all my yards. I am now going to the wooded lands out in the country to see my father who has so long been grieved on my account, and to yourself I will give these instructions, though you have little need of them. At sunrise it will at once get abroad that I have been killing the suitors; go upstairs, therefore, and stay there with your women. See nobody and ask no questions."

As he spoke he girded on his armour. Then he roused Telemachus, Philoetius, and Eumaeus, and told them all to put on their armour also. This they did, and armed themselves. When they had done so, they opened the gates and sallied forth, Ulysses leading the way. It was now daylight, but Minerva nevertheless concealed them in darkness and led them quickly out of the town.

BOOK XXIV – MINERVA CALLS FOR PEACE

ULYSSES AND HIS MEN GO TO THE HOUSE OF LAERTES, ULYSSES'S FATHER --THE PEOPLE
OF ITHACA COME OUT TO ATTACK ULYSSES, BUT MINERVA CONCLUDES A PEACE.

As he went down into the great orchard, he did not see Dolius, nor any of his sons nor
of the other bondsmen, for they were all gathering thorns to make a fence for the
vineyard, at the place where the old man had told them; he therefore found his father
alone, hoeing a vine. He had on a dirty old shirt, patched and very shabby;his legs were
5 bound round with thongs of oxhide to save him from the brambles, and he also wore
sleeves of leather; he had a goat skin cap on his head, and was looking very woe-begone.
When Ulysses saw him so worn, so old and full of sorrow, he stood still under a tall
pear tree and began to weep. He doubted whether to embrace him, kiss him, and tell
him all about his having come home, or whether he should first question him and see
10 what he would say. In the end he deemed it best to be crafty with him, so in this mind
he went up to his father, who was bending down and digging about a plant.

"I see, sir," said Ulysses, "that you are an excellent gardener--what pains you take with
it, to be sure. There is not a single plant, not a fig tree, vine, olive, pear, nor flower bed,
but bears the trace of your attention. I trust, however, that you will not be offended if
15 I say that you take better care of your garden than of yourself. You are old, unsavory,
and very meanly clad. It cannot be because you are idle that your master takes such poor
care of you, indeed your face and figure have nothing of the slave about them, and
proclaim you of noble birth. I should have said that you were one of those who should
wash well, eat well, and lie soft at night as old men have a right to do; but tell me, and
20 tell me true, whose bondman are you, and in whose garden are you working? Tell me
also about another matter. Is this place that I have come to really Ithaca? I met a man
just now who said so, but he was a dull fellow, and had not the patience to hear my
story out when I was asking him about an old friend of mine, whether he was still living,
or was already dead and in the house of Hades. Believe me when I tell you that this man
25 came to my house once when I was in my own country and never yet did any stranger
come to me whom I liked better. He said that his family came from Ithaca and that his
father was Laertes, son of Arceisius. I received him hospitably, making him welcome to
all the abundance of my house, and when he went away I gave him all customary
presents. I gave him seven talents of fine gold, and a cup of solid silver with flowers
30 chased upon it. I gave him twelve light cloaks, and as many pieces of tapestry; I also
gave him twelve cloaks of single fold, twelve rugs, twelve fair mantles, and an equal
number of shirts. To all this I added four good looking women skilled in all useful arts,
and I let him take his choice."

His father shed tears and answered, "Sir, you have indeed come to the country that you
35 have named, but it is fallen into the hands of wicked people. All this wealth of presents
has been given to no purpose. If you could have found your friend here alive in Ithaca,
he would have entertained you hospitably and would have requited your presents amply
when you left him--as would have been only right considering what you had already
given him. But tell me, and tell me true, how many years is it since you entertained this
40 guest--my unhappy son, as ever was? Alas! He has perished far from his own country;
the fishes of the sea have eaten him, or he has fallen a prey to the birds and wild beasts
of some continent. Neither his mother, nor I his father, who were his parents, could
throw our arms about him and wrap him in his shroud, nor could his excellent and
richly dowered wife Penelope bewail her husband as was natural upon his death bed,
45 and close his eyes according to the offices due to the departed. But now, tell me truly

What philosophical message
does Ulysses present here?

for I want to know. Who and whence are you--tell me of your town and parents? Where is the ship lying that has brought you and your men to Ithaca? Or were you a passenger on some other man's ship, and those who brought you here have gone on their way and left you?"

Ulysses lies to his father.

5 "I will tell you everything," answered Ulysses, "quite truly. I come from Alybas, where I have a fine house. I am son of king Apheidas, who is the son of Polypemon. My own name is Eperitus; heaven drove me off my course as I was leaving Sicania, and I have been carried here against my will. As for my ship it is lying over yonder, off the open country outside the town, and this is the fifth year since Ulysses left my country. Poor 10 fellow, yet the omens were good for him when he left me. The birds all flew on our right hands, and both he and I rejoiced to see them as we parted, for we had every hope that we should have another friendly meeting and exchange presents."

Ulysses reveals himself to his father; father requires proof.

A dark cloud of sorrow fell upon Laertes as he listened. He filled both hands with the dust from off the ground and poured it over his grey head, groaning heavily as he did 15 so. The heart of Ulysses was touched, and his nostrils quivered as he looked upon his father; then he sprang towards him, flung his arms about him and kissed him, saying, "I am he, father, about whom you are asking--I have returned after having been away for twenty years. But cease your sighing and lamentation--we have no time to lose, for I should tell you that I have been killing the suitors in my house, to punish them for their 20 insolence and crimes."

"If you really are my son Ulysses," replied Laertes, "and have come back again, you must give me such manifest proof of your identity as shall convince me."

"First observe this scar," answered Ulysses, "which I got from a boar's tusk when I was hunting on Mt. Parnassus. You and my mother had sent me to Autolycus, my mother's 25 father, to receive the presents which when he was over here he had promised to give me. Furthermore I will point out to you the trees in the vineyard which you gave me, and I asked you all about them as I followed you round the garden. We went over them all, and you told me their names and what they all were. You gave me thirteen pear trees, ten apple trees, and forty fig trees; you also said you would give me fifty rows of vines; 30 there was corn planted between each row, and they yield grapes of every kind when the heat of heaven has been laid heavy upon them."

Laertes' strength failed him when he heard the convincing proofs which his son had given him. He threw his arms about him, and Ulysses had to support him, or he would have gone off into a swoon; but as soon as he came to, and was beginning to recover 35 his senses, he said, "O father Jove, then you gods are still in Olympus after all, if the suitors have really been punished for their insolence and folly. Nevertheless, I am much afraid that I shall have all the townspeople of Ithaca up here directly, and they will be sending messengers everywhere throughout the cities of the Cephallenians."

Ulysses answered, "Take heart and do not trouble yourself about that, but let us go into 40 the house hard by your garden. I have already told Telemachus, Philoetius, and Eumaeus to go on there and get dinner ready as soon as possible."

Thus conversing the two made their way towards the house. When they got there they found Telemachus with the stockman and the swineherd cutting up meat and mixing wine with water.

While they were thus busy getting their dinner ready, Rumor went round the town, and noised abroad the terrible fate that had befallen the suitors; as soon, therefore, as the people heard of it they gathered from every quarter, groaning and hooting before the house of Ulysses. They took the dead away, buried every man his own, and put the
5   bodies of those who came from elsewhere on board the fishing vessels, for the fishermen to take each of them to his own place. They then met angrily in the place of assembly, and when they were got together Eupeithes rose to speak. He was overwhelmed with grief for the death of his son Antinous, who had been the first man killed by Ulysses, so he said, weeping bitterly, "My friends, this man has done the
10 Achaeans great wrong. He took many of our best men away with him in his fleet, and he has lost both ships and men; now, moreover, on his return he has been killing all the foremost men among the Cephallenians. Let us be up and doing before he can get away to Pylos or to Elis where the Epeans rule, or we shall be ashamed of ourselves for ever afterwards. It will be an everlasting disgrace to us if we do not avenge the murder of
15 our sons and brothers. For my own part I should have no more pleasure in life, but had rather die at once. Let us be up, then, and after them, before they can cross over to the main land."

He wept as he spoke and every one pitied him. But Medon and the bard Phemius had now woke up, and came to them from the house of Ulysses. Every one was astonished
20 at seeing them, but they stood in the middle of the assembly, and Medon said, "Hear me, men of Ithaca. Ulysses did not do these things against the will of heaven. I myself saw an immortal god take the form of Mentor and stand beside him. This god appeared, now in front of him encouraging him, and now going furiously about the court and attacking the suitors whereon they fell thick on one another."

25 "Men of Ithaca, it is all your own fault that things have turned out as they have; you would not listen to me, nor yet to Mentor, when we bade you check the folly of your sons who were doing much wrong in the wantonness of their hearts--wasting the substance and dishonouring the wife of a chieftain who they thought would not return. Now, however, let it be as I say, and do as I tell you. Do not go out against Ulysses, or
30 you may find that you have been drawing down evil on your own heads."

Then Minerva said to Jove, "Father, son of Saturn, king of kings, answer me this question--What do you propose to do? Will you set them fighting still further, or will you make peace between them?"

And Jove answered, "My child, why should you ask me? Was it not by your own
35 arrangement that Ulysses came home and took his revenge upon the suitors? Do whatever you like, but I will tell you what I think will be most reasonable arrangement. Now that Ulysses is revenged, let them swear to a solemn covenant, in virtue of which he shall continue to rule, while we cause the others to forgive and forget the massacre of their sons and brothers. Let them then all become friends as heretofore, and let peace
40 and plenty reign."

This was what Minerva was already eager to bring about, so down she darted from off the topmost summits of Olympus.

Then Jove's daughter Minerva came up to the Ithacans, having assumed the form and voice of Mentor. Ulysses was glad when he saw her, and said to his son Telemachus,
45 "Telemachus, now that you are about to fight in an engagement, which will show every

Rumor spreads regarding massacre of suitors.

Citizens side with the justice of the gods.

Gods convene regarding how to deliver justice.

man's mettle, be sure not to disgrace your ancestors, who were eminent for their strength and courage all the world over."

"You say truly, my dear father," answered Telemachus, "and you shall see, if you will, that I am in no mind to disgrace your family."

5 Laertes was delighted when he heard this. "Good heavens," he exclaimed, "what a day I am enjoying: I do indeed rejoice at it. My son and grandson are vying with one another in the matter of valour."

Goddess proclaims that justice has been delivered; restores peace.

Meantime Ulysses and his son fell upon the front line of the foe and smote them with their swords and spears; indeed, they would have killed every one of them, and 10 prevented them from ever getting home again, only Minerva raised her voice aloud, and made every one pause. "Men of Ithaca," she cried, "cease this dreadful war, and settle the matter at once without further bloodshed."

On this pale fear seized every one; they were so frightened that their arms dropped from their hands and fell upon the ground at the sound of the goddess' voice, and they fled 15 back to the city for their lives. But Ulysses gave a great cry, and gathering himself together swooped down like a soaring eagle. Then the son of Saturn sent a thunderbolt of fire that fell just in front of Minerva, so she said to Ulysses, "Ulysses, noble son of Laertes, stop this warful strife, or Jove will be angry with you."

Thus spoke Minerva, and Ulysses obeyed her gladly. Then Minerva assumed the form 20 and voice of Mentor, and presently made a covenant of peace between the two contending parties.

THE END

SAPPHO'S LYRICS

BY SAPPHO

TRANSLATED FROM THE GREEK BY BLISS CARMAN

Introduction by M. B. McLatchey

Perhaps the greatest lyric poet of ancient Greece, Sappho (630 – 570 B.C.) addresses themes of the heart in her poems. In contrast to the great epic poems that celebrate national heroes, her poems celebrate the complex emotions of ordinary lives. With simple language and sharp images, her poems offer snapshots of myriad emotions: love and heart ache; jealousy and passion; and longing and loss. Her lyrics, named such because they were sung to the accompaniment of the lyre, remind us of the ancient Greek's deep interest in human psychology and emotions.

Fig. 3: Sappho

LYRIC XXX

    Love shakes my soul, like a mountain wind
      Falling upon the trees,
    When they are swayed and whitened and bowed
5   As the great gusts will.

      I know why Daphne sped through the grove
      When the bright god came by,
    And shut herself in the laurel's heart
10   For her silent doom.

      Love fills my heart, like my lover's breath
      Filling the hollow flute,
    Till the magic wood awakes and cries
15   With remembrance and joy.

      Ah, timid Syrinx, do I not know
      Thy tremor of sweet fear?
    For a beautiful and imperious player
20   Is the lord of life.

LYRIC XXXVI

When I pass thy door at night
I a benediction breathe:
"Ye who have the sleeping world
5   In your care,

"Guard the linen sweet and cool,
Where a lovely golden head
With its dreams of mortal bliss
10   Slumbers now!"

LYRIC XLII

O heart of insatiable longing,
15 What spell, what enchantment allures thee
Over the rim of the world
With the sails of the sea-going ships?

And when the rose-petals are scattered
20 At dead of still noon on the grass-plot,
What means this passionate grief,—
This infinite ache of regret?

25 ## LYRIC LV

Soul of sorrow, why this weeping?
What immortal grief hath touched thee
With the poignancy of sadness,—
  Testament of tears?
30

Have the high gods deigned to show thee
Destiny, and disillusion
Fills thy heart at all things human,
  Fleeting and desired?
35

Nay, the gods themselves are fettered
By one law which links together
Truth and nobleness and beauty,

Man and stars and sea.

     And they only shall find freedom
Who with courage rise and follow
5 Where love leads beyond all peril,
    Wise beyond all words.

LYRIC LX

10   When I have departed,
Say but this behind me,
"Love was all her wisdom,
    All her care.

15   "Well she kept love's secret
Dared and never faltered,—
Laughed and never doubted
    Love would win.

20   "Let the world's rough triumph
Trample by above her,
She is safe forever
    From all harm.

25   "In a land that knows not
Bitterness nor sorrow,
She has found out all Of truth at last."

PLATO'S READINGS

INTRODUCTION BY EDWARD BROOKS, JR.

Of all writers of speculative philosophy, both ancient and modern, there is probably no one who has attained so eminent a position as Plato. What Homer was to Epic poetry, what Cicero and Demosthenes were to oratory, and what Shakespeare was to the drama of England, Plato was to ancient philosophy, not unapproachable nor unapproached, but possessing an inexplicable but unquestioned supremacy.

Fig. 4: Plato

The authentic records of his life are meagre, and much that has been written concerning him is of a speculative nature. He was born at Athens in the year 427 B.C. His father's name was Ariston, and his mother's family, which claimed its descent from Solon, included among its members many Athenian notables, among whom was Oritias, one of the thirty tyrants.

In his early youth Plato applied himself to poetry and painting, both of which pursuits he relinquished to become the disciple and follower of Socrates. It is said that his name was originally Aristocles, but that it was changed to Plato on account of the breadth of his shoulders and forehead. He is also said to have been an expert wrestler and to have taken part in several important battles.

He was the devoted friend and pupil of Socrates, and during the imprisonment of his master he attended him constantly, and committed to writing his last discourses on the immortality of the soul.

After the death of Socrates it is supposed that Plato took refuge with Euclides in Megara, and subsequently extended his travels into Magna Graecia and Egypt.

Upon his return to Athens he taught those who came to him for instruction in the grove named Academus, near the Cephisus, and thus founded the first great philosophical school, over which he continued to preside until the day of his death. Above the entrance to this grove was inscribed the legend: "Let no one ignorant of geometry enter here." Here he was attended by persons of every description, among the more illustrious of whom were Aristotle, Lycurgus, Demosthenes and Isocrates.

There is a story to the effect that Plato three times visited Sicily, once upon the invitation of the elder Dionysius, and twice at the earnest solicitations of the younger. The former he is said to have so seriously offended as to cause the tyrant to have him seized on his return home and sold as a slave, from which state of bondage he was, however, released by Anicerius of Cyrene.

The people of his time thought more of him than they did of all their other philosophers, and called him the Divine Plato. So great was the regard and veneration for him that it was considered better to err with Plato than be right with any one else.

The writings of Plato are numerous, and most of them are in the form of dialogues. The following pages contain translations of three of his works, viz.: "The Apologia", "The Crito"and "The Phædo", all of which have reference to the trial, imprisonment and death of Socrates.

"The Apologia" represents Socrates on trial for his life, undertaking his own defence, though unaccustomed to the language of the courts, the occasion being, as he says, the first time he has ever been before a court of justice, though seventy years of age. Plato was present at the trial, and no doubt gives us the very arguments used by the accused. Two charges were brought against Socrates—one that he did not believe in the gods recognized by the State, the other that he had corrupted the Athenian youth by his teachings.

Socrates does not have recourse to the ordinary methods adopted by orators on similar occasions. He prefers to stand upon his own integrity and innocence, uninfluenced by the fear of that imaginary evil, death. He, therefore, does not firmly grapple with either of the charges preferred against him. He neither denies nor confesses the first accusation, but shows that in several instances he conformed to the religious customs of his country, and that he believes in God more than he fears man. The second charge he meets by a cross-examination of his accuser, Melitus, whom he reduces to the dilemma of charging him with corrupting the youth designedly, which would be absurd, or with doing so undesignedly, for which he could not be liable to punishment.

His defence, however, avails him nothing, and he is condemned by the judges to die by drinking the poisonous hemlock. In the closing part of "The Apologia" Socrates is represented as commenting upon the sentence which has been passed upon him, and as expressing his belief that in going to his death he is only passing to a better and a happier life.

In "The Crito" Socrates is represented in conversation with a friend of his named Crito, who had been present at his trial, and who had offered to assist Socrates in paying a fine, had a fine been the sentence imposed. Crito visits Socrates in his confinement to bring to him the intelligence that the ship, the arrival of which was to be the signal for his death upon the following day, would arrive forthwith, and to urge him to adopt the means of escape which had already been prepared. Socrates promises to follow the advice of Crito if, upon a full discussion of the matter, it seems right to do so. In the conversation which ensues Socrates argues that it is wrong to return evil for evil and that the obligations which a citizen owes to his State are more binding than those which a child owes his parents or a slave his master, and, therefore, it is his duty to submit to the laws of Athens at whatever cost to himself. Crito has no answer to make to this argument, and Socrates thereupon decides to submit to his fate.

Plato is said to have had two objects in writing this dialogue: First, to acquit Socrates of the charge of corrupting the Athenian youth; and, second, to establish the fact that it is necessary under all circumstances to submit to the established laws of his country.

"The Phædo" relates the manner in which Socrates spent the last day of his life and the circumstances attending his death. He is visited by a number of his friends, among whom are Phædo, Simmias and Crito. He remarks upon the unaccountable connection between pleasure and pain, and from this the conversation gradually turns to a consideration of the question of the immortality of the soul. He convinces his listeners of the pre-existence of the soul; but they are still skeptical as to its immortality, urging that its pre-existence and the fact that it is more durable than the body does not preclude the possibility of its being mortal. Socrates, however, argues that contraries cannot exist in the same thing at the same time. Life and death are contraries and can never coexist; but wherever there is life there is soul, so that the soul contains that which is contrary to death and can never admit death; consequently the soul is immortal.

Having convinced his listeners, Socrates bathes and takes leave of his children and the women of his family. Thereupon the officer appears and tells him it is time for him to drink the poison. At this his friends commence to weep and are rebuked by Socrates for their weakness. He drinks the poison calmly and without hesitation, and then begins to walk about, still conversing with his friends. His limbs soon grow stiff and heavy and he lays himself down upon his back. His last words are: "Crito, we owe a cock to Æsculapius; pay it, therefore, and do not neglect it."

APOLOGY

BY PLATO

TRANSLATED FROM THE GREEK BY HENRY CARY, M.A., WORCESTER COLLEGE, OXFORD.

I know not, O Athenians! how far you have been influenced by my accusers for my part, in listening to them I almost forgot myself, so plausible were their arguments however, so to speak, they have said nothing true. But of the many falsehoods which they uttered I wondered at one of them especially, that in which they said that you ought
5 to be on your guard lest you should be deceived by me, as being eloquent in speech. For that they are not ashamed of being forthwith convicted by me in fact, when I shall show that I am not by any means eloquent, this seemed to me the most shameless thing in them, unless indeed they call him eloquent who speaks the truth. For, if they mean this, then I would allow that I am an orator, but not after their fashion for they, as I
10 affirm, have said nothing true, but from me you shall hear the whole truth.

Not indeed, Athenians, arguments highly wrought, as theirs were, with choice phrases and expressions, nor adorned, but you shall hear a speech uttered without premeditation in such words as first present themselves. For I am confident that what I say will be just, and let none of you expect otherwise, for surely it would not become my time of
15 life to come before you like a youth with a got up speech. Above all things, therefore, I beg and implore this of you, O Athenians! if you hear me defending myself in the same language as that in which I am accustomed to speak both in the forum at the counters, where many of you have heard me, and elsewhere, not to be surprised or disturbed on this account. For the case is this: I now for the first time come before a court of justice,
20 though more than seventy years old; I am therefore utterly a stranger to the language here. As, then, if I were really a stranger, you would have pardoned me if I spoke in the language and the manner in which I had been educated, so now I ask this of you as an act of justice, as it appears to me, to disregard the manner of my speech, for perhaps it may be somewhat worse, and perhaps better, and to consider this only, and to give your
25 attention to this, whether I speak what is just or not; for this is the virtue of a judge, but of an orator to speak the truth.

First, then, O Athenians! I am right in defending myself against the first false accusations alleged against me, and my first accusers, and then against the latest accusations, and the latest accusers.

30 For many have been accusers of me to you, and for many years, who have asserted nothing true, of whom I am more afraid than of Anytus and his party, although they too are formidable; but those are still more formidable, Athenians, who, laying hold of many of you from childhood, have persuaded you, and accused me of what is not true: "that there is one Socrates, a wise man, who occupies himself about celestial matters,
35 and has explored every thing under the earth, and makes the worse appear the better reason." Those, O Athenians! who have spread abroad this report are my formidable accusers; for they who hear them think that such as search into these things do not believe that there are gods. In the next place, these accusers are numerous, and have accused me now for a long time; moreover, they said these things to you at that time of
40 life in which you were most credulous, when you were boys and some of you youths, and they accused me altogether in my absence, when there was no one to defend me.

Socrates warns against the fancy and false rhetoric of his accusers as opposed to the plain truth that he presents. He admits he is not accustomed to the language of the courts, but he is confident that the truth will prevail.

Socrates claims that his accusers question his belief in gods of the state because he questions accepted wisdom. The pre-Socratic philosophers faced similar charges when they explored scientific, rather than religious, explanations for universal phenomenon. As we shall see, however, Socrates is NOT interested in scientific questions. The fact that his accusers link him to this other branch of philosophers indicates to him that they have not actually examined his ideas. Thus, it is the man they want to put on trial and not his ideas.

But the most unreasonable thing of all is, that it is not possible to learn and mention their names, except that one of them happens to be a comic poet. [1] Such, however, as, influenced by envy and calumny, have persuaded you, and those who, being themselves persuaded, have persuaded others, all these are most difficult to deal with; for it is not
5 possible to bring any of them forward here, nor to confute any; but it is altogether necessary to fight, as it were with a shadow, in making my defense, and to convict when there is no one to answer. Consider, therefore, as I have said, that my accusers are twofold, some who have lately accused me, and others long since, whom I have made mention of; and believe that I ought to defend myself against these first; for you heard
10 them accusing me first, and much more than these last.

Well. I must make my defense, then, O Athenians! and endeavor in this so short a space of time to remove from your minds the calumny which you have long entertained. I wish, indeed, it might be so, if it were at all better both for you and me, and that in making my defense I could effect something more advantageous still: I think, however,
15 that it will be difficult, and I am not entirely ignorant what the difficulty is. Nevertheless, let this turn out as may be pleasing to God, I must obey the law and make my defense.

Let us, then, repeat from the beginning what the accusation is from which the calumny against me has arisen, and relying on which Melitus has preferred this indictment against me. Well. What, then, do they who charge me say in their charge?

20 For it is necessary to read their deposition as of public accusers. "Socrates acts wickedly, and is criminally curious in searching into things under the earth, and in the heavens, and in making the worse appear the better cause, and in teaching these same things to others." Such is the accusation: for such things you have yourselves seen in the comedy of Aristophanes, one Socrates there carried about, saying that he walks in the air, and
25 acting many other buffooneries, of which I understand nothing whatever. Nor do I say this as disparaging such a science, if there be any one skilled in such things, only let me not be prosecuted by Melitus on a charge of this kind; but I say it, O Athenians! because I have nothing to do with such matters. And I call upon most of you as witnesses of this, and require you to inform and tell each other, as many of you as have ever heard
30 me conversing; and there are many such among you. Therefore tell each other, if any one of you has ever heard me conversing little or much on such subjects. And from this you will know that other things also, which the multitude assert of me, are of a similar nature.

However not one of these things is true; nor, if you have heard from any one that I
35 attempt to teach men, and require payment, is this true.

Though this, indeed, appears to me to be an honorable thing, if one should be able to instruct men, like Gorgias the Leontine, Prodicus the Cean, and Hippias the Elean. For each of these, O Athenians! is able, by going through the several cities, to persuade the young men, who can attach themselves gratuitously to such of their own fellow-citizens
40 as they please, to abandon their fellow-citizens and associate with them, giving them money and thanks besides. There is also another wise man here, a Parian, who, I hear, is staying in the city. For I happened to visit a person who spends more money on the sophists than all others together: I mean Callias, son of Hipponicus. I therefore asked him, for he has two sons, "Callias," I said, "if your two sons were colts or calves, we
45 should have had to choose a master for them, and hire a person who would make them excel in such qualities as belong to their nature; and he would have been a groom or an agricultural laborer. But now, since your sons are men, what master do you intend to choose for them? Who is there skilled in the qualities that become a man and a citizen?

Socrates observes that his accusers have remained nameless, thus he cannot fairly defend himself in an intellectual debate with them.

Socrates refutes his accusers' charges that he investigates scientific phenomenon. He claims that his interest is in human nature, not nature.

Socrates refutes his accusers' charges that he teaches for financial gain. In fact, he associates modest living and his own poverty with a life of virtue.

For I suppose you must have considered this, since you have sons. Is there any one," I said, "or not?" "Certainly," he answered. "Who is he?" said I, "and whence does he come? and on what terms does he teach?" He replied, "Evenus the Parian, Socrates, for five minæ." And I deemed Evenus happy, if he really possesses this art, and teaches

5 admirably. And I too should think highly of myself, and be very proud, if I possessed this knowledge, but I possess it not, O Athenians.

Perhaps, one of you may now object: "But, Socrates, what have you done, then? Whence have these calumnies against you arisen? For surely if you had not busied yourself more than others, such a report and story would never have got abroad, unless you had done

10 something different from what most men do. Tell us, therefore, what it is, that we may not pass a hasty judgment on you." He who speaks thus appears to me to speak justly, and I will endeavor to show you what it is that has occasioned me this character and imputation. Listen, then: to some of you perhaps I shall appear to jest, yet be assured that I shall tell you the whole truth. For I, O Athenians! have acquired this character

15 through nothing else than a certain wisdom.

Socrates claims that his accusers mistake his wisdom for arrogance.

Of what kind, then, is this wisdom? Perhaps it is merely human wisdom. For in this, in truth, I appear to be wise. They probably, whom I have just now mentioned, possessed a wisdom more than human, otherwise I know not what to say about it; for I am not acquainted with it, and whosoever says I am, speaks falsely, and for the purpose of

20 calumniating me. But, O Athenians! do not cry out against me, even though I should seem to you to speak somewhat arrogantly. For the account which I am going to give you is not my own; but I shall refer to an authority whom you will deem worthy of credit. For I shall adduce to you the god at Delphi as a witness of my wisdom, if I have any, and of what it is. You doubtless know Chærepho: he was my associate from youth,

25 and the associate of most of you; he accompanied you in your late exile, and returned with you. You know, then, what kind of a man Chærepho was, how earnest in whatever he undertook. Having once gone to Delphi, he ventured to make the following inquiry of the oracle (and, as I said, O Athenians! do not cry out), for he asked if there was any one wiser than I. The Pythian thereupon answered that there was not one wiser; and of

30 this, his brother here will give you proofs, since he himself is dead.

Consider, then, why I mention these things: it is because I am going to show you whence the calumny against me arose. For when I heard this, I reasoned thus with myself, What does the god mean? What enigma is this? For I am not conscious to myself that I am wise, either much or little. What, then, does he mean by saying that I am the wisest? For

35 assuredly he does not speak falsely: that he could not do. And for a long time I was in doubt what he meant; afterward, with considerable difficulty, I had recourse to the following method of searching out his meaning.

In the following passage, Socrates arrives at his key claim: The wise man is the one who knows what he does not know. Furthermore, men who are revealed as unwise or as misguided will choose to kill the messenger of truth.

I went to one of those who have the character of being wise, thinking that there, if anywhere, I should confute the oracle, and show in answer to the response that This

40 man is wiser than I, though you affirmed that I was the wisest. Having, then, examined this man (for there is no occasion to mention his name; he was, however, one of our great politicians, in examining whom I felt as I proceed to describe, O Athenians!), having fallen into conversation with him, this man appeared to be wise in the opinion of most other men, and especially in his own opinion, though in fact he was not so. I

45 thereupon endeavored to show him that he fancied himself to be wise, but really was not. Hence I became odious, both to him and to many others who were present. When I left him, I reasoned thus with myself: I am wiser than this man, for neither of us appears to know anything great and good; but he fancies he knows something, although he knows nothing; whereas I, as I do not know anything, so I do not fancy I do. In this

trifling particular, then, I appear to be wiser than he, because I do not fancy I know what I do not know. After that I went to another who was thought to be wiser than the former, and formed the very same opinion. Hence I became odious to him and to many others.

5   After this I went to others in turn, perceiving indeed, and grieving and alarmed, that I was making myself odious; however, it appeared necessary to regard the oracle of the god as of the greatest moment, and that, in order to discover its meaning, I must go to all who had the reputation of possessing any knowledge.

And by the dog, O Athenians! for I must tell you the truth, I came to some such
10   conclusion as this: those who bore the highest reputation appeared to me to be most deficient, in my researches in obedience to the god, and others who were considered inferior more nearly approaching to the possession of understanding. But I must relate to you my wandering, and the labors which I underwent, in order that the oracle might prove incontrovertible. For after the politicians I went to the poets, as well the tragic as
15   the dithyrambic and others, expecting that here I should in very fact find myself more ignorant than they. Taking up, therefore, some of their poems, which appeared to me most elaborately finished, I questioned them as to their meaning, that at the same time I might learn something from them. I am ashamed, O Athenians! to tell you the truth; however, it must be told. For, in a word, almost all who were present could have given
20   a better account of them than those by whom they had been composed. I soon discovered this, therefore, with regard to the poets, that they do not effect their object by wisdom, but by a certain natural inspiration, and under the influence of enthusiasm, like prophets and seers; for these also say many fine things, but they understand nothing that they say. The poets appeared to me to be affected in a similar manner; and at the
25   same time I perceived that they considered themselves, on account of their poetry, to be the wisest of men in other things, in which they were not. I left them, therefore, under the persuasion that I was superior to them, in the same way that I was to the politicians.

At last, therefore, I went to the artisans.

30   For I was conscious to myself that I knew scarcely anything, but I was sure that I should find them possessed of much beautiful knowledge. And in this I was not deceived; for they knew things which I did not, and in this respect they were wiser than I. But, O Athenians! even the best workmen appeared to me to have fallen into the same error as the poets; for each, because he excelled in the practice of his art, thought that he was
35   very wise in other most important matters, and this mistake of theirs obscured the wisdom that they really possessed. I therefore asked myself, in behalf of the oracle, whether I should prefer to continue as I am, possessing none, either of their wisdom or their ignorance, or to have both as they have. I answered, therefore, to myself and to the oracle, that it was better for me to continue as I am.

40   From this investigation, then, O Athenians! many enmities have arisen against me, and those the most grievous and severe, so that many calumnies have sprung from them, and among them this appellation of being wise; for those who are from time to time present think that I am wise in those things, with respect to which I expose the ignorance of others.

Socrates on politicians: They are the most reputed, yet the most intellectually and spiritually deficient. On poets: They say fine things, but understand nothing.

Socrates on craftsmen: Because they are wise in their practice of art, they think they are wise in all other matters.

Socrates chooses the truth over popularity.

The god, however, O Athenians! appears to be really wise, and to mean this by his oracle: that human wisdom is worth little or nothing; and it is clear that he did not say this to Socrates, but made use of my name, putting me forward as an example, as if he had said, that man is the wisest among you, who, like Socrates, knows that he is in reality
5   worth nothing with respect to wisdom. Still, therefore, I go about and search and inquire into these things, in obedience to the god, both among citizens and strangers, if I think any one of them is wise; and when he appears to me not to be so, I take the part of the god, and show that he is not wise. And, in consequence of this occupation, I have no leisure to attend in any considerable degree to the affairs of the state or my own; but I
10 am in the greatest poverty through my devotion to the service of the god.

In addition to this, young men, who have much leisure and belong to the wealthiest families, following me of their own accord, take great delight in hearing men put to the test, and often imitate me, and themselves attempt to put others to the test; and then, I think, they find a great abundance of men who fancy they know something, although
15 they know little or nothing.

Socrates refutes charges that he has corrupted the minds of the youth. Secondly, he maintains that his accusers do not know what he teaches.

Hence those who are put to the test by them are angry with me, and not with them, and say that "there is one Socrates, a most pestilent fellow, who corrupts the youth." And when any one asks them by doing or teaching what, they have nothing to say, for they do not know; but, that they may not seem to be at a loss, they say such things as are
20 ready at hand against all philosophers; "that he searches into things in heaven and things under the earth, that he does not believe there are gods, and that he makes the worse appear the better reason." For they would not, I think, be willing to tell the truth that they have been detected in pretending to possess knowledge, whereas they know nothing. Therefore, I think, being ambitions and vehement and numerous, and speaking
25 systematically and persuasively about me, they have filled your ears, for a long time and diligently calumniating me. From among these, Melitus, Anytus and Lycon have attacked me; Melitus being angry on account of the poets, Anytus on account of the artisans and politicians, and Lycon on account of the rhetoricians. So that, as I said in the beginning, I should wonder if I were able in so short a time to remove from your
30 minds a calumny that has prevailed so long. This, O Athenians! is the truth; and I speak it without concealing or disguising anything from you, much or little; though I very well know that by so doing I shall expose myself to odium. This, however, is a proof that I speak the truth, and that this is the nature of the calumny against me, and that these are its causes. And if you will investigate the matter, either now or hereafter, you will find
35 it to be so.

With respect, then, to the charges which my first accusers have alleged against me, let this be a sufficient apology to you. To Melitus, that good and patriotic man, as he says, and to my later accusers, I will next endeavor to give an answer; and here, again, as there are different accusers, let us take up their deposition. It is pretty much as follows:
40 "Socrates," it says, "acts unjustly in corrupting the youth, and in not believing in those gods in whom the city believes, but in other strange divinities."

Socrates accuses his accusers: They are the ones, not him – that corrupt the youth because they model hypocrisy and love of power.

Such is the accusation; let us examine each particular of it. It says that I act unjustly in corrupting the youth. But I, O Athenians! say that Melitus acts unjustly, because he jests on serious subjects, rashly putting men upon trial, under pretense of being zealous and
45 solicitous about things in which he never at any time took any concern. But that this is the case I will endeavor to prove to you.

Come, then, Melitus, tell me, do you not consider it of the greatest importance that the youth should be made as virtuous as possible?

Mel. I do.

Socr. Well, now, tell the judges who it is that makes them better, for it is evident
5 that you know, since it concerns you so much; for, having detected me in corrupting them, as you say, you have cited me here, and accused me: come, then, say, and inform the judges who it is that makes them better. Do you see, Melitus, that you are silent, and have nothing to say? But does it not appear to you to be disgraceful, and a sufficient proof of what I say, that you never took any concern about the matter? But tell me,
10 friend, who makes them better?

Mel. The laws.

Socr. I do not ask this, most excellent sir, but what man, who surely must first know this very thing, the laws?

Mel. These, Socrates, the judges.

15 *Socr.* How say you, Melitus? Are these able to instruct the youth, and make them better?

Mel. Certainly.

Socr. Whether all, or some of them, and others not?

Mel. All.

20 *Socr.* You say well, by Juno! and have found a great abundance of those that confer benefit. But what further? Can these hearers make them better, or not?

Mel. They, too, can.

Socr. And what of the senators?

Mel. The senators, also.

25 *Socr.* But, Melitus, do those who attend the public assemblies corrupt the younger men? or do they all make them better?

Mel. They too.

Socr. All the Athenians, therefore, as it seems, make them honorable and good, except me; but I alone corrupt them. Do you say so?

30 *Mel.* I do assert this very thing.

Socrates embarks upon his method of inquiry to discover the truth with the help of his accuser. This is the so-called Socratic method of questions and answers sustained by logic.

By comparing himself to a trainer of horses, Socrates shines light on the difference between himself and the multitude – in this case, his accusers. Like the horse-trainer, the teacher aims to groom excellent performance – not corrupt performance. Furthermore, Socrates says, only a very few are qualified to train horses or to tutor children in the arts and sciences. Socrates concludes by claiming that his accusers care nothing about the virtue of youth, and solely about persecuting him.

Socr. You charge me with great ill-fortune. But answer me: does it appear to you to be the same, with respect to horses? Do all men make them better, and is there only some one that spoils them? or does quite the contrary of this take place? Is there some one person who can make them better, or very few; that is, the trainers? But if the
5 generality of men should meddle with and make use of horses, do they spoil them? Is not this the case, Melitus, both with respect to horses and all other animals? It certainly is so, whether you and Anytus deny it or not. For it would be a great good-fortune for the youth if only one person corrupted, and the rest benefited them.

However, Melitus, you have sufficiently shown that you never bestowed any care upon
10 youth; and you clearly evince your own negligence, in that you have never paid any attention to the things with respect to which you accuse me.

Tell us further, Melitus, in the name of Jupiter, whether is it better to dwell with good or bad citizens? Answer, my friend; for I ask you nothing difficult. Do not the bad work some evil to those that are continually near them, but the good some good?

15 **Mel.** Certainly.

Socrates proves that his accusers have not examined the logic of their own charges: Why would a man corrupt young people and then have to live among them?

Socr. Is there any one that wishes to be injured rather than benefited by his associates? Answer, good man; for the law requires you to answer. Is there any one who wishes to be injured?

Mel. No, surely.

20 **Socr.** Come, then, whether do you accuse me here, as one that corrupts the youth, and makes them more depraved, designedly or undesignedly?

Mel. Designedly, I say.

Socr. What, then, Melitus, are you at your time of life so much wiser than I at my time of life, as to know that the evil are always working some evil to those that are most
25 near to them, and the good some good; but I have arrived at such a pitch of ignorance as not to know that if I make any one of my associates depraved, I shall be in danger of receiving some evil from him; and yet I designedly bring about this so great evil, as you say? In this I can not believe you, Melitus, nor do I think would any other man in the world. But either I do not corrupt the youth, or, if I do corrupt them, I do it
30 undesignedly: so that in both cases you speak falsely. But if I corrupt them undesignedly, for such involuntary offenses it is not usual to accuse one here, but to take one apart, and teach and admonish one. For it is evident that if I am taught, I shall cease doing what I do undesignedly. But you shunned me, and were not willing to associate with and instruct me; but you accuse me here, where it is usual to accuse those who need
35 punishment, and not instruction.

Thus, then, O Athenians! this now is clear that I have said; that Melitus never paid any attention to these matters, much or little. However, tell us, Melitus, how you say I corrupt the youth? Is it not evidently, according to the indictment which you have preferred, by teaching them not to believe in the gods in whom the city believes, but in
40 other strange deities? Do you not say that, by teaching these things, I corrupt the youth?

Mel. Certainly I do say so.

Socr. By those very gods, therefore, Melitus, of whom the discussion now is, speak still more clearly both to me and to these men. For I can not understand whether you say that I teach them to believe that there are certain gods (and in that case I do believe that there are gods, and am not altogether an atheist, nor in this respect to blame), not,
5   however, those which the city believes in, but others; and this it is that you accuse me of, that I introduce others. Or do you say outright that I do not myself believe that there are gods, and that I teach others the same?

Mel. I say this: that you do not believe in any gods at all.

Socr. O wonderful Melitus, how come you to say this? Do I not, then, like the
10   rest of mankind, believe that the sun and moon are gods?

Mel. No, by Jupiter, O judges! for he says that the sun is a stone, and the moon an earth.

Socr. You fancy that you are accusing Anaxagoras, my dear Melitus, and thus you put a slight on these men, and suppose them to be so illiterate as not to know that the
15   books of Anaxagoras of Clazomene are full of such assertions.

And the young, moreover, learn these things from me, which they might purchase for a drachma, at most, in the orchestra, and so ridicule Socrates, if he pretended they were his own, especially since they are so absurd? I ask then, by Jupiter, do I appear to you to believe that there is no god?

To his accusers, Socrates in effect says, "You have the wrong man. I am not teaching scientific ideas that would cause children to question the existence of god!"

20   ***Mel.*** No, by Jupiter, none whatever.

Socr. You say what is incredible, Melitus, and that, as appears to me, even to yourself. For this man, O Athenians! appears to me to be very insolent and intemperate and to have preferred this indictment through downright insolence, intemperance, and wantonness. For he seems, as it were, to have composed an enigma for the purpose of
25   making an experiment. Whether will Socrates the wise know that I am jesting, and contradict myself, or shall I deceive him and all who hear me? For, in my opinion, he clearly contradicts himself in the indictment, as if he should say, Socrates is guilty of wrong in not believing that there are gods, and in believing that there are gods. And this, surely, is the act of one who is trifling.

30   Consider with me now, Athenians, in what respect he appears to me to say so. And do you, Melitus, answer me; and do ye, as I besought you at the outset, remember not to make an uproar if I speak after my usual manner.

Is there any man, Melitus, who believes that there are human affairs, but does not believe that there are men? Let him answer, judges, and not make so much noise. Is
35   there any one who does not believe that there are horses, but that there are things pertaining to horses? or who does not believe that there are pipers, but that there are things pertaining to pipes? There is not, O best of men! for since you are not willing to answer, I say it to you and to all here present. But answer to this at least: is there any one who believes that there are things relating to demons, but does not believe that
40   there are demons?

Socrates proves that his accusers have not examined the logical nature of their own charges: How can a man believe in demons, as Socrates and his accusers do, but not believe in gods?

Mel. There is not.

Socr. How obliging you are in having hardly answered; though compelled by these judges! You assert, then, that I do believe and teach things relating to demons, whether they be new or old; therefore, according to your admission, I do believe in things relating to demons, and this you have sworn in the bill of indictment. If, then, I believe in things

5   relating to demons, there is surely an absolute necessity that I should believe that there are demons. Is it not so? It is. For I suppose you to assent, since you do not answer. But with respect to demons, do we not allow that they are gods, or the children of gods? Do you admit this or not?

Mel. Certainly.

10   *Socr.* Since, then, I allow that there are demons, as you admit, if demons are a kind of gods, this is the point in which I say you speak enigmatically and divert yourself in saying that I do not allow there are gods, and again that I do allow there are, since I allow that there are demons? But if demons are the children of gods, spurious ones, either from nymphs or any others, of whom they are reported to be, what man can

15   think that there are sons of gods, and yet that there are not gods? For it would be just as absurd as if any one should think that there are mules, the offspring of horses and asses, but should not think there are horses and asses. However, Melitus, it can not be otherwise than that you have preferred this indictment for the purpose of trying me, or because you were at a loss what real crime to allege against me; for that you should

20   persuade any man who has the smallest degree of sense that the same person can think that there are things relating to demons and to gods, and yet that there are neither demons, nor gods, not heroes, is utterly impossible.

That I am not guilty, then, O Athenians! according to the indictment of Melitus, appears to me not to require a lengthened defense; but what I have said is sufficient.

Socrates asks Athenian citizens to beware of setting a precedent of condemning to death men whom we do not like.

25   And as to what I said at the beginning, that there is a great enmity toward me among the multitude, be assured it is true. And this it is which will condemn me, if I am condemned, not Melitus, nor Anytus, but the calumny and envy of the multitude, which have already condemned many others, and those good men, and will, I think, condemn others also; for there is no danger that it will stop with me.

In the argument that follows, Socrates draws his example from Homer's *Iliad* of a man who chose to die for a noble cause, rather than live as a coward. Martin Luther King, Jr. said the same thing, "A man who has nothing to die for has nothing to live for."

30   Perhaps, however, some one may say, "Are you not ashamed, Socrates, to have pursued a study from which you are now in danger of dying?" To such a person I should answer with good reason, You do not say well, friend, if you think that a man, who is even of the least value, ought to take into the account the risk of life or death, and ought not to consider that alone when be performs any action, whether he is acting justly or unjustly,

35   and the part of a good man or bad man. For, according to your reasoning, all those demi-gods that died at Troy would be vile characters, as well all the rest as the son of Thetis, who so far despised danger in comparison of submitting to disgrace, that when his mother, who was a goddess, spoke to him, in his impatience to kill Hector, something to this effect, as I think,[2] "My son, if you revenge the death of your friend

40   Patroclus, and slay Hector, you will yourself die, for," she said, "death awaits you immediately after Hector;" but he, on hearing this, despised death and danger, and dreading much more to live as a coward, and not avenge his friend, said, "May I die immediately when I have inflicted punishment on the guilty, that I may not stay here an object of ridicule, by the curved ships, a burden to the ground?"—do you think that he

45   cared for death and danger? For thus it is, O Athenians! in truth: wherever any one has posted himself, either thinking it to be better, or has been posted by his chief, there, as it appears to me, he ought to remain and meet danger, taking no account either of death or anything else in comparison with disgrace.

I then should be acting strangely, O Athenians! if, when the generals whom you chose to command me assigned me my post at Potidæa, at Amphipolis, and at Delium, I then remained where they posted me, like any other person, and encountered the danger of death; but when the deity, as I thought and believed, assigned it as my duty to pass my
5   life in the study of philosophy, and examining myself and others, I should on that occasion, through fear of death or any thing else whatsoever, desert my post, strange indeed would it be; and then, in truth, any one might justly bring me to trial, and accuse me of not believing in the gods, from disobeying the oracle, fearing death, and thinking myself to be wise when I am not.

10   For to fear death, O Athenians! is nothing else than to appear to be wise, without being so; for it is to appear to know what one does not know. For no one knows but that death is the greatest of all good to man; but men fear it, as if they well knew that it is the greatest of evils. And how is not this the most reprehensible ignorance, to think that one knows what one does not know? But I, O Athenians! in this, perhaps, differ from
15   most men; and if I should say that I am in any thing wiser than another, it would be in this, that not having a competent knowledge of the things in Hades, I also think that I have not such knowledge. But to act unjustly, and to disobey my superior, whether God or man, I know is evil and base. I shall never, therefore, fear or shun things which, for aught I know, maybe good, before evils which I know to be evils. So that, even if you
20   should now dismiss me, not yielding to the instances of Anytus, who said that either I should not ² appear here at all, or that, if I did appear, it was impossible not to put me to death, telling you that if I escaped, your sons, studying what Socrates teaches, would all be utterly corrupted; if you should address me thus, "Socrates, we shall not now yield to Anytus, but dismiss you, on this condition, however, that you no longer persevere in
25   your researches nor study philosophy; and if hereafter you are detected in so doing, you shall die"—if, as I said, you should dismiss, me on these terms, I should say to you, "O Athenians! I honor and love you; but I shall obey God rather than you!"

"And so long as I breathe and am able, I shall not cease studying philosophy, and exhorting you and warning any one of you I may happen to meet, saying, as I have been
30   accustomed to do: 'O best of men! seeing you are an Athenian, of a city the most powerful and most renowned for wisdom and strength, are you not ashamed of being careful for riches, how you may acquire them in greatest abundance, and for glory, and honor, but care not nor take any thought for wisdom and truth, and for your soul, how it maybe made most perfect?'"

35   And if any one of you should question my assertion, and affirm that he does care for these things, I shall not at once let him go, nor depart, but I shall question him, sift and prove him. And if he should appear to me not to possess virtue, but to pretend that he does, I shall reproach him for that he sets the least value on things of the greatest worth, but the highest on things that are worthless. Thus I shall act to all whom I meet, both
40   young and old, stranger and citizen, but rather to you, my fellow-citizens, because ye are more nearly allied to me. For be well assured, this the deity commands. And I think that no greater good has ever befallen you in the city than my zeal for the service of the god. For I go about doing nothing else than persuading you, both young and old, to take no care either for the body, or for riches, prior to or so much as for the soul, how
45   it may be made most perfect, telling you that virtue does not spring from riches, but riches and all other human blessings, both private and public, from virtue. If, then, by saying these things, I corrupt the youth, these things must be mischievous; but if any one says that I speak other things than these, he misleads you. ⁴ Therefore I must say, O Athenians! either yield to Anytus, or do not, either dismiss me or not, since I shall
50   not act otherwise, even though I must die many deaths.

Socrates maintains that it would be strange for him to ignore his calling to teach simply to preserve his own life. This would be strange because it would effectively contradict the core value that he teaches – namely, the importance of living a life of principle, or being ready to die for the preservation of certain principles.

Socrates states that the laws he ultimately obeys issue from an eternal judge, God – not from men.

Socrates puts his accusers on trial. He accuses them of choosing wealth over wisdom; power over virtue; material things over spiritual.

Murmur not, O Athenians! but continue to attend to my request, not to murmur at what I say, but to listen, for, as I think, you will derive benefit from listening.

For I am going to say other things to you, at which, perhaps, you will raise a clamor; but on no account do so. Be well assured, then, if you put me to death, being such a
5 man as I say I am, you will not injure me more than yourselves. For neither will Melitus nor Anytus harm me; nor have they the power; for I do not think that it is possible for a better man to be injured by a worse. He may perhaps have me condemned to death, or banished, or deprived of civil rights; and he or others may perhaps consider these as mighty evils; I, how ever, do not consider them so, but that it is much more so to do
10 what he is now doing, to endeavor to put a man to death unjustly. Now, therefore, O Athenians! I am far from making a defense on my behalf, as any one might think, but I do so on your own behalf, lest by condemning me you should offend at all with respect to the gift of the deity to you. For, if you should put me to death, you will not easily find such another, though it may be ridiculous to say so, altogether attached by the deity
15 to this city as to a powerful and generous horse, somewhat sluggish from his size, and requiring to be roused by a gad-fly; so the deity appears to have united me, being such a person as I am, to the city, that I may rouse you, and persuade and reprove every one of you, nor ever cease besetting you throughout the whole day. Such another man, O Athenians! will not easily be found; therefore, if you will take my advice, you will spare
20 me. But you, perhaps, being irritated like drowsy persons who are roused from sleep, will strike me, and, yielding to Anytus, will unthinkingly condemn me to death; and then you will pass the rest of your life in sleep, unless the deity, caring for you, should send some one else to you. But that I am a person who has been given by the deity to this city, you may discern from hence; for it is not like the ordinary conduct of men, that I
25 should have neglected all my own affairs, and suffered my private interest to be neglected for so many years, and that I should constantly attend to your concerns, addressing myself to each of you separately, like a father, or elder brother, persuading you to the pursuit of virtue. And if I had derived any profit from this course, and had received pay for my exhortations, there would have been some reason for my conduct;
30 but now you see yourselves that my accusers, who have so shamelessly calumniated me in everything else, have not had the impudence to charge me with this, and to bring witnesses to prove that I ever either exacted or demanded any reward.

And I think I produce a sufficient proof that I speak the truth, namely, my poverty.

Perhaps, however, it may appear absurd that I, going about, thus advise you in private
35 and make myself busy, but never venture to present myself in public before your assemblies and give advice to the city.

The cause of this is that which you have often and in many places heard me mention; because I am moved by a certain divine and spiritual influence, which also Melitus, through mockery, has set out in the indictment. This began with me from childhood,
40 being a kind of voice which, when present, always diverts me from what I am about to do, but never urges me on. This it is which opposed my meddling in public politics; and it appears to me to have opposed me very properly. For be well assured, O Athenians! if I had long since attempted to intermeddle with politics, I should have perished long ago, and should not have at all benefited you or myself. And be not angry with me for
45 speaking the truth. For it is not possible that any man should be safe who sincerely opposes either you, or any other multitude, and who prevents many unjust and illegal actions from being committed in a city; but it is necessary that he who in earnest contends for justice, if he will be safe for but a short time, should live privately, and take no part in public affairs.

I will give you strong proofs of this, not words, but what you value, facts. Hear, then, what has happened to me, that you may know that I would not yield to any one contrary to what is just, through fear of death, at the same time by not yielding I must perish. I shall tell you what will be displeasing and wearisome, ⁵ yet true. For I, O Athenians!

5 never bore any other magisterial office in the city, but have been a senator: and our Antiochean tribe happened to supply the Prytanes when you chose to condemn in a body the ten generals who had not taken off those that perished in the sea-fight, in violation of the law, as you afterward all thought. At that time I alone of the Prytanes opposed your doing anything contrary to the laws, and I voted against you; and when

10 the orators were ready to denounce me, and to carry me before a magistrate, and you urged and cheered them on, I thought I ought rather to meet the danger with law and justice on my side, than through fear of imprisonment or death, to take part with you in your unjust designs. And this happened while the city was governed by a democracy. But when it became an oligarchy, the Thirty, having sent for me with four others to the

15 Tholus, ordered us to bring Leon the Salaminian from Salamis, that he might be put to death; and they gave many similar orders to many others, wishing to involve as many as they could in guilt.

Then, however, I showed, not in word but in deed, that I did not care for death, if the expression be not too rude, in the smallest degree; but that all my care was to do nothing

20 unjust or unholy. For that government, strong as it was, did not so overawe me as to make me commit an unjust action; but when we came out from the Tholus, the four went to Salamis, and brought back Leon; but I went away home. And perhaps for this I should have been put to death, if that government had not been speedily broken up. And of this you can have many witnesses.

25 Do you think, then, that I should have survived so many years if I had engaged in public affairs, and, acting as becomes a good man, had aided the cause of justice, and, as I ought, had deemed this of the highest importance? Far from it, O Athenians! nor would any other man have done so. But I, through the whole of my life, if I have done anything in public, shall be found to be a man, and the very same in private, who has

30 never made a concession to any one contrary to justice, neither to any other, nor to any one of these whom my calumniators say are my disciples. I, however, was never the preceptor of any one; but if any one desired to hear me speaking, and to see me busied about my own mission, whether he were young or old, I never refused him. Nor do I discourse when I receive money, and not when I do not receive any, but I allow both

35 rich and poor alike to question me, and, if any one wishes it, to answer me and hear what I have to say. And for these, whether any one proves to be a good man or not, I cannot justly be responsible, because I never either promised them any instruction or taught them at all. But if any one says that he has ever learned or heard anything from me in private which all others have not, be well assured that he does not speak the truth.

40 But why do some delight to spend so long a time with me? Ye have heard, O Athenians! I have told you the whole truth, that they delight to hear those closely questioned who think that they are wise but are not; for this is by no means disagreeable. But this duty, as I say, has been enjoined me by the deity, by oracles, by dreams, and by every mode by which any other divine decree has ever enjoined anything to man to do. These things,

45 O Athenians! are both true, and easily confuted if not true.

Socrates condemns hypocrisy: "May the outward and inward man be the same."

Socrates challenges the "corrupted" youth to rise up against him to demonstrate their displeasure with what he has taught them. Let this be the evidence that is brought against him.

For if I am now corrupting some of the youths, and have already corrupted others, it were fitting, surely, that if any of them, having become advanced in life, had discovered that I gave them bad advice when they were young, they should now rise up against me, accuse me, and have me punished; or if they were themselves unwilling to do this, some
5 of their kindred, their fathers, or brothers, or other relatives, if their kinsman have ever sustained any damage from me, should now call it to mind. Many of them, however, are here present, whom I see: first, Crito, my contemporary and fellow-burgher, father of this Critobulus; then Lysanias of Sphettus, father of this Æschines; again, Antiphon of Cephisus, father of Epigenes. There are those others, too, whose brothers maintained
10 the same intimacy with me, namely, Nicostratus, son of Theodotus, brother of Theodotus—Theodotus indeed is dead, so that he could not deprecate his brother's proceedings—and Paralus here, son of Demodocus, whose brother was Theages; and Adimantus, son of Ariston, whose brother is this Plato; and Æantodorus, whose brother is this Apollodorus. I could also mention many others to you, some one of whom
15 certainly Melitus ought to have adduced in his speech as a witness. If, however, he then forgot to do so, let him now adduce them; I give him leave to do so, and let him say it, if he has anything of the kind to allege. But, quite contrary to this, you will find, O Athenians! all ready to assist me, who have corrupted and injured their relatives, as Melitus and Anytus say. For those who have been themselves corrupted might perhaps
20 have some reason for assisting me; but those who have not been corrupted, men now advanced in life, their relatives, what other reason can they have for assisting me, except that right and just one, that they know that Melitus speaks falsely, and that I speak the truth.

Well, then, Athenians, these are pretty much the things I have to say in my defense, and
25 others perhaps of the same kind.

Socrates points out that he has not asked for a pity release: he has not marched his family before the judges. Why? He respects the law, but not these men.

Perhaps, however, some among you will be indignant on recollecting his own case, if he, when engaged in a cause far less than this, implored and besought the judges with many tears, bringing forward his children in order that he might excite their utmost compassion, and many others of his relatives and friends, whereas I do none of these
30 things, although I may appear to be incurring the extremity of danger. Perhaps, therefore, some one, taking notice of this, may become more determined against me, and, being enraged at this very conduct of mine, may give his vote under the influence of anger. If, then, any one of you is thus affected—I do not, however, suppose that there is—but if there should be, I think I may reasonably say to him: "I, too, O best of
35 men, have relatives; for, to make use of that saying of Homer, I am not sprung from an oak, nor from a rock, but from men, so that I, too, O Athenians! have relatives, and three sons, one now grown up, and two boys: I shall not, however, bring any one of them forward and implore you to acquit me." Why, then, shall I not do this? Not from contumacy, O Athenians! nor disrespect toward you. Whether or not I am undaunted
40 at the prospect of death is another question; but, out of regard to my own character, and yours, and that of the whole city, it does not appear to me to be honorable that I should do any thing of this kind at my age, and with the reputation I have, whether true or false. For it is commonly agreed that Socrates in some respects excels the generality of men. If, then, those among you who appear to excel either in wisdom, or fortitude,
45 or any other virtue whatsoever, should act in such a manner as I have often seen some when they have been brought to trial, it would be shameful, who appearing indeed to be something, have conducted themselves in a surprising manner, as thinking they should suffer something dreadful by dying, and as if they would be immortal if you did not put them to death. Such men appear to me to bring disgrace on the city, so that any
50 stranger might suppose that such of the Athenians as excel in virtue, and whom they themselves choose in preference to themselves for magistracies and other honors, are

in no respect superior to women. For these things, O Athenians! neither ought we to do who have attained to any height of reputation, nor, should we do them, ought you to suffer us; but you should make this manifest, that you will much rather condemn him who introduces these piteous dramas, and makes the city ridiculous, than him who
5 quietly awaits your decision.

But, reputation apart, O Athenians! it does not appear to me to be right to entreat a judge, or to escape by entreaty; but one ought to inform and persuade him.

For a judge does not sit for the purpose of administering justice out of favor, but that he may judge rightly, and he is sworn not to show favor to whom he pleases, but that
10 he will decide according to the laws. It is, therefore, right that neither should we accustom you, nor should you accustom yourselves, to violate your oaths; for in so doing neither of us would act righteously. Think not then, O Athenians! that I ought to adopt such a course toward you as I neither consider honorable, nor just, nor holy, as well, by Jupiter! on any other occasion, and now especially when I am accused of impiety
15 by this Melitus. For clearly, if I should persuade you, and by my entreaties should put a constraint on you who are bound by an oath, I should teach you to think that there are no gods, and in reality, while making my defense, should accuse myself of not believing in the gods. This, however, is far from being the case; for I believe, O Athenians! as none of my accusers do, and I leave it to you and to the deity to judge concerning me
20 in such way as will be best both for me and for you.

[Socrates here concludes his defense, and, the votes being taken, he is declared guilty by a majority of voices. He thereupon resumes his address.]

That I should not be grieved, O Athenians! at what has happened—namely, that you have condemned me—as well many other circumstances concur in bringing to pass;
25 and, moreover this, that what has happened has not happened contrary to my expectation; but I much rather wonder at the number of votes on either side. For I did not expect that I should be condemned by so small a number, but by a large majority; but now, as it seems, if only three more votes had changed sides, I should have been acquitted. So far as Melitus is concerned, as it appears to me, I have been already
30 acquitted; and not only have I been acquitted, but it is clear to every one that had not Anytus and Lycon come forward to accuse me, he would have been fined a thousand drachmas, for not having obtained a fifth part of the votes.

The man, then, awards me the penalty of death. Well. But what shall I, on my part, O Athenians! award myself? Is it not clear that it will be such as I deserve? What, then, is
35 that? Do I deserve to suffer, or to pay a fine? for that I have purposely during my life not remained quiet, but neglecting what most men seek after, money-making, domestic concerns, military command, popular oratory, and, moreover, all the magistracies, conspiracies, and cabals that are met with in the city, thinking that I was in reality too upright a man to be safe if I took part in such things, I therefore did not apply myself
40 to those pursuits, by attending to which I should have been of no service either to you or to myself; but in order to confer the greatest benefit on each of you privately, as I affirm, I thereupon applied myself to that object, endeavoring to persuade every one of you not to take any care of his own affairs before he had taken care of himself in what way he may become the best and wisest, nor of the affairs of the city before he took
45 care of the city itself; and that he should attend to other things in the same manner. What treatment, then, do I deserve, seeing I am such a man? Some reward, O Athenians! if, at least, I am to be estimated according to my real deserts; and, moreover, such a reward as would be suitable to me. What, then, is suitable to a poor man, a benefactor,

Socrates advises Athenians to never beg for mercy when accused falsely. Instead, they should educate their accusers and persuade with reason.

and who has need of leisure in order to give you good advice? There is nothing so suitable, O Athenians! as that such a man should be maintained in the Prytaneum, and this much more than if one of you had been victorious at the Olympic games in a horserace, or in the two or four horsed chariot race: for such a one makes you appear
5 to be happy, but I, to be so; and he does not need support, but I do. If, therefore, I must award a sentence according to my just deserts, I award this, maintenance in the Prytaneum.

Perhaps, however, in speaking to you thus, I appear to you to speak in the same presumptuous manner as I did respecting commiseration and entreaties; but such is not
10 the case, O Athenians! it is rather this: I am persuaded that I never designedly injured any man, though I can not persuade you of this, for we have conversed with each other but for a short time. For if there were the same law with you as with other men, that in capital cases the trial should list not only one day, but many, I think you would be persuaded; but it is not easy in a short time to do away with, great calumnies. Being
15 persuaded, then, that I have injured no one, I am far from intending to injure myself, and of pronouncing against myself that I am deserving of punishment, and from awarding myself any thing of the kind. Through fear of what? lest I should suffer that which Melitus awards me, of which I say I know not whether it be good or evil? Instead of this, shall I choose what I well know to be evil, and award that? Shall I choose
20 imprisonment? And why should I live in prison, a slave to the established magistracy, the Eleven? Shall I choose a fine, and to be imprisoned until I have paid it? But this is the same as that which I just now mentioned, for I have not money to pay it. Shall I, then, award myself exile? For perhaps you would consent to this award. I should indeed be very fond of life, O Athenians! if I were so devoid of reason as not to be able to
25 reflect that you, who are my fellow-citizens, have been unable to endure my manner of life and discourses, but they have become so burdensome and odious to you that you now seek to be rid of them: others, however, will easily bear them. Far from it, O Athenians! A fine life it would be for me at my age to go out wandering, and driven from city to city, and so to live. For I well know that, wherever I may go, the youth will
30 listen to me when I speak, as they do here. And if I repulse them, they will themselves drive me out, persuading the elders; and if I do not repulse them, their fathers and kindred will banish me on their account.

Perhaps, however, some one will say, Can you not, Socrates, when you have gone from us, live a silent and quiet life? This is the most difficult thing of all to persuade some of
35 you. For if I say that that would be to disobey the deity, and that, therefore, it is impossible for me to live quietly, you would not believe me, thinking I spoke ironically.

If, on the other hand, I say that this is the greatest good to man, to discourse daily on virtue, and other things which you have heard me discussing, examining both myself and others, but that a life without investigation is not worth living for, still less would
40 you believe me if I said this. Such, however, is the case, as I affirm, O Athenians! though it is not easy to persuade you. And at the same time I am not accustomed to think myself deserving of any ill. If, indeed, I were rich, I would amerce myself in such a sum as I should be able to pay; for then I should have suffered no harm, but now—for I can not, unless you are willing to amerce me in such a sum as I am able to pay. But perhaps
45 I could pay you a mina of silver: in that sum, then, I amerce myself. But Plato here, O Athenians! and Crito Critobulus, and Apollodorus bid me amerce myself in thirty minæ, and they offer to be sureties. I amerce myself, then, to you in that sum; and they will be sufficient sureties for the money.

[The judges now proceeded to pass the sentence, and condemned Socrates to death; whereupon he continued:]

For the sake of no long space of time, O Athenians! you will incur the character and reproach at the hands of those who wish to defame the city, of having put that wise
5 man, Socrates, to death. For those who wish to defame you will assert that I am wise, though I am not. If, then, you had waited for a short time, this would have happened of its own accord; for observe my age, that it is far advanced in life, and near death.

But I say this not to you all, but to those only who have condemned me to die. And I say this, too, to the same persons. Perhaps you think, O Athenians! that I have been
10 convicted through the want of arguments, by which I might have persuaded you, had I thought it right to do and say any thing, so that I might escape punishment. Far otherwise: I have been convicted through want indeed, yet not of arguments, but of audacity and impudence, and of the inclination to say such things to you as would have been most agreeable for you to hear, had I lamented and bewailed and done and said
15 many other things unworthy of me, as I affirm, but such as you are accustomed to hear from others. But neither did I then think that I ought, for the sake of avoiding danger, to do any thing unworthy of a freeman, nor do I now repent of having so defended myself; but I should much rather choose to die, having so defended myself, than to live in that way. For neither in a trial nor in battle is it right that I or any one else should
20 employ every possible means whereby he may avoid death; for in battle it is frequently evident that a man might escape death by laying down his arms, and throwing himself on the mercy of his pursuers. And there are many other devices in every danger, by which to avoid death, if a man dares to do and say every thing. But this is not difficult, O Athenians! to escape death; but it is much more difficult to avoid depravity, for it
25 runs swifter than death. And now I, being slow and aged, am overtaken by the slower of the two; but my accusers, being strong and active, have been overtaken by the swifter, wickedness. And now I depart, condemned by you to death; but they condemned by truth, as guilty of iniquity and injustice: and I abide my sentence, and so do they. These things, perhaps, ought so to be, and I think that they are for the best.

30 In the next place, I desire to predict to you who have condemned me, what will be your fate; for I am now in that condition in which men most frequently prophesy—namely, when they are about to die.

I say, then, to you, O Athenians! who have condemned me to death, that immediately after my death a punishment will overtake you, far more severe, by Jupiter! than that
35 which you have inflicted on me. For you have done this, thinking you should be freed from the necessity of giving an account of your lives. The very contrary, however, as I affirm, will happen to you. Your accusers will be more numerous, whom I have now restrained, though you did not perceive it; and they will be more severe, inasmuch as they are younger, and you will be more indignant. For if you think that by putting men
40 to death you will restrain any one from upbraiding you because you do not live well, you are much mistaken; for this method of escape is neither possible nor honorable; but that other is most honorable and most easy, not to put a check upon others, but for a man to take heed to himself how he may be most perfect. Having predicted thus much to those of you who have condemned me, I take my leave of you.

45 But with you who have voted for my acquittal I would gladly hold converse on what has now taken place, while the magistrates are busy, and I am not yet carried to the place where I must die.

Socrates claims that a man who does not live according to his principles is a walking dead man.

Socrates' famous statement, "The unexamined life is not worth living" emerges here. What does he mean by this statement?

Socrates predicts that his accusers will face accusers of their own after they kill him.

Socrates goes to his death
peacefully and with a clear
conscience.

Stay with me, then, so long, O Athenians! for nothing hinders our conversing with each other, while we are permitted to do so; for I wish to make known to you, as being my friends, the meaning of that which has just now befallen me. To me, then, O my judges! and in calling you judges I call you rightly—a strange thing has happened. For the
5 wonted prophetic voice of my guardian deity on every former occasion, even in the most trifling affairs, opposed me if I was about to do any thing wrong; but now that has befallen me which ye yourselves behold, and which any one would think, and which is supposed to be the extremity of evil; yet neither when I departed from home in the morning did the warning of the god oppose me, nor when I came up here to the place
10 of trial, nor in my address when I was about to say any thing; yet on other occasions it has frequently restrained me in the midst of speaking. But now it has never, throughout this proceeding, opposed me, either in what I did or said. What, then, do I suppose to be the cause of this? I will tell you: what has befallen me appears to be a blessing; and it is impossible that we think rightly who suppose that death is an evil. A great proof of
15 this to me is the fact that it is impossible but that the accustomed signal should have opposed me, unless I had been about to meet with some good.

Moreover, we may hence conclude that there is great hope that death is a blessing. For to die is one of two things: for either the dead may be annihilated, and have no sensation of any thing whatever; or, as it is said, there are a certain change and passage of the soul
20 from one place to another. And if it is a privation of all sensation, as it were a sleep in which the sleeper has no dream, death would be a wonderful gain. For I think that if any one, having selected a night in which he slept so soundly as not to have had a dream, and having compared this night with all the other nights and days of his life, should be required, on consideration, to say how many days and nights he had passed better and
25 more pleasantly than this night throughout his life, I think that not only a private person, but even the great king himself, would find them easy to number, in comparison with other days and nights. If, therefore, death is a thing of this kind, I say it is a gain; for thus all futurity appears to be nothing more than one night. But if, on the other hand, death is a removal from hence to another place, and what is said be true, that all the
30 dead are there, what greater blessing can there be than this, my judges? For if, on arriving at Hades, released from these who pretend to be judges, one shall find those who are true judges, and who are said to judge there, Minos and Rhadamanthus, Æacus and Triptolemus, and such others of the demi-gods as were just during their own life, would this be a sad removal? At what price would you not estimate a conference with Orpheus
35 and Musæus, Hesiod and Homer? I indeed should be willing to die often, if this be true. For to me the sojourn there would be admirable, when I should meet with Palamedes, and Ajax, son of Telamon, and any other of the ancients who has died by an unjust sentence. The comparing my sufferings with theirs would, I think, be no unpleasing occupation. But the greatest pleasure would be to spend my time in questioning and
40 examining the people there as I have done those here, and discovering who among them is wise, and who fancies himself to be so, but is not. At what price, my judges, would not any one estimate the opportunity of questioning him who led that mighty army against Troy, or Ulysses, or isyphus, or ten thousand others whom one might mention both men and women—with whom to converse and associate, and to question
45 them, would be an inconceivable happiness? Surely for that the judges there do not condemn to death; for in other respects those who live there are more happy than those who are here, and are henceforth immortal, if, at least, what is said be true.

You, therefore, O my judges! ought to entertain good hopes with respect to death, and to meditate on this one truth, that to a good man nothing is evil, neither while living
50 nor when dead, nor are his concerns neglected by the gods.

And what has befallen me is not the effect of chance; but this is clear to me, that now to die, and be freed from my cares is better for me On this account the warning in no way turned me aside; and I bear no resentment toward those who condemned me, or against my accusers, although they did not condemn and accuse me with this intention,
5 but thinking to injure me: in this they deserve to be blamed.

Thus much, however, I beg of them. Punish my sons when they grow up, O judges! paining them as I have pained you, if they appear to you to care for riches or anything else before virtue; and if they think themselves to be something when they are nothing, reproach them as I have done you, for not attending to what they ought, and for
10 conceiving themselves to be something when they are worth nothing. If ye do this, both I and my sons shall have met with just treatment at your hands.

But it is now time to depart—for me to die, for you to live. But which of us is going to a better state is unknown to every one but God.

Socrates proclaims that no harm can come to a good man. He makes his final request: to kill his sons if they grow up to resemble his accusers – loving wealth more than good character; cherishing the material world more than the spiritual.

CRITO

BY PLATO

TRANSLATED FROM THE GREEK BY HENRY CARY, M.A., WORCESTER COLLEGE, OXFORD.

INTRODUCTION BY EDWARD BROOKS, JR

It has been remarked by Stallbaum that Plato had a twofold design in this dialogue—one, and that the primary one, to free Socrates from the imputation of having attempted to corrupt the Athenian youth; the other, to establish the principle that under all circumstances it is the duty of a good citizen to obey the laws of his country. These two points, however, are so closely interwoven with each other, that the general principle appears only to be illustrated by the example of Socrates.

Crito was one of those friends of Socrates who had been present at his trial, and had offered to assist in paying a fine, had a fine been imposed instead of the sentence of death. He appears to have frequently visited his friend in prison after his condemnation; and now, having obtained access to his cell very early in the morning, finds him composed in a quiet sleep. He brings intelligence that the ship, the arrival of which would be the signal for his death on the following day, is expected to arrive forthwith, and takes occasion to entreat Socrates to make his escape, the means of which were already prepared. Socrates thereupon, having promised to follow the advice of Crito if, after the matter had been fully discussed, it should appear to be right to do so, proposes to consider the duty of a citizen toward his country; and having established the divine principle that it is wrong to return evil for evil, goes on to show that the obligations of a citizen to his country are even more binding than those of a child to its parent, or a slave to his master, and that therefore it is his duty to obey the established laws, at whatever cost to himself.

At length Crito admits that he has no answer to make, and Socrates resolves to submit himself to the will of Providence.

CRITO VISITS SOCRATES IN PRISON

Socr. Why have you come at this hour, Crito? Is it not very early?

Cri. It is.

Socr. About what time?

5   *Cri.* Scarce day-break.

Socr. I wonder how the keeper of the prison came to admit you.

Cri. He is familiar with me, Socrates, from my having frequently come hither; and he is under some obligations to me.

Socr. Have you just now come, or some time since?

10   *Cri.* A considerable time since.

Socr. Why, then, did you not wake me at once, instead of sitting down by me in silence?

Cri. By Jupiter! Socrates, I should not myself like to be so long awake, and in such affliction. But I have been for some time wondering at you, perceiving how sweetly you
5 slept; and I purposely did not awake you, that you might pass your time as pleasantly as possible.

And, indeed, I have often before throughout your whole life considered you happy in your disposition, but far more so in the present calamity, seeing how easily and meekly you bear it.

10 *Socr.* However, Crito, it would be disconsonant for a man at my time of life to repine because he must needs die.

Cri. But others, Socrates, at your age have been involved in similar calamities, yet their age has not hindered their repining at their present fortune.

Socr. So it is. But why did you come so early?

15 *Cri.* Bringing sad tidings, Socrates, not sad to you, as it appears, but to me, and all your friends, sad and heavy, and which I, I think, shall bear worst of all.

Socr. What tidings? Has the ship ⁶ arrived from Delos, on the arrival of which I must die?

Cri. It has not yet arrived, but it appears to me that it will come to-day, from what
20 certain persons report who have come from Sunium, ⁷ and left it there. It is clear, therefore, from these messengers, that it will come to day, and consequently it will be necessary, Socrates, for you to die to-morrow.

Socr. But with good fortune, Crito, and if so it please the gods, so be it. I do not think, however, that it will come to day.

25 *Cri.* Whence do you form this conjecture?

Socr. I will tell you. I must die on the day after that on which the ship arrives.

Cri. So they say who have the control of these things.

Socr. I do not think, then, that it will come to-day, but to-morrow. I conjecture this from a dream which I had this very night, not long ago, and you seem very
30 opportunely to have refrained from waking me.

Cri. But what was this dream?

Socr. A beautiful and majestic woman, clad in white garments seemed to approach me, and to call to me and say, "Socrates, three days hence you will reach fertile Pythia".

Cri. What a strange dream, Socrates!

Crito asks Socrates why he does not seem afraid to die.

Socr. Very clear, however, as it appears to me, Crito.

Cri. Very much so, as it seems. But, my dear Socrates, even now be persuaded by me, and save yourself.

Crito begs Socrates to save himself by bribing the judges with money, but Socrates refuses.

For if you die, not only a single calamity will befall me, but, besides being deprived of
5 such a friend as I shall never meet with again, I shall also appear to many who do not know you and me well, when I might have saved you had I been willing to spend my money, to have neglected to do so. And what character can be more disgraceful than this—to appear to value one's riches more than one's friends? For the generality of men will not be persuaded that you were unwilling to depart hence, when we urged you to
10 it.

Socr. But why, my dear Crito, should we care so much for the opinion of the many? For the most worthy men, whom we ought rather to regard, will think that matters have transpired as they really have.

Crito asks Socrates to notice the damage that men can do to one another. Socrates claims no man's opinion can change the true character of another man – unless he allows it.

Cri. Yet you see, Socrates, that it is necessary to attend to the opinion of the many.
15 For the very circumstances of the present case show that the multitude are able to effect not only the smallest evils, but even the greatest, if any one is calumniated to them.

Socr. Would, O Crito that the multitude could effect the greatest evils, that they might also effect the greatest good, for then it would be well. But now they can do neither; for they can make a man neither wise nor foolish; but they do whatever chances.

20 *Cri.* So let it be, then. But answer me this, Socrates: are you not anxious for me and other friends, lest, if you should escape from hence, informers should give us trouble, as having secretly carried you off, and so we should be compelled either to lose all our property, or a very large sum, or to suffer something else besides this?

For, if you fear any thing of the kind, dismiss your fears; for we are justified in running
25 the risk to save you—and, if need be, even a greater risk than this. But be persuaded by me, and do not refuse.

Socr. I am anxious about this, Crito, and about many other things.

Cri. Do not fear this, however; for the sum is not large on receipt of which certain persons are willing to save you, and take you hence. In the next place, do you not see
30 how cheap these informers are, so that there would be no need of a large sum for them? My fortune is at your service, sufficient, I think, for the purpose; then if, out of regard to me, you do not think right to spend my money, these strangers here are ready to spend theirs. One of them, Simmias the Theban, has brought with him a sufficient sum for the very purpose. Cebes, too, is ready, and very many others. So that, as I said, do
35 not, through fears of this kind, hesitate to save yourself, nor let what you said in court give you any trouble, that if you went from hence you would not know what to do with yourself. For in many places, and wherever you go, men will love you; and if you are disposed to go to Thessaly, I have friends there who will esteem you very highly, and will insure your safety, so that no one in Thessaly will molest you.

Moreover, Socrates, you do not appear to me to pursue a just course in giving yourself up when you might be saved; and you press on the very results with respect to yourself which your enemies would press, and have pressed, in their anxiety to destroy you.

Besides this, too, you appear to me to betray your own sons, whom, when it is in your
5 power to rear and educate them, you will abandon, and, so far as you are concerned, they will meet with such a fate as chance brings them, and, as is probable, they will meet with such things as orphans are wont to experience in a state of orphanage. Surely one ought not to have children, or one should go through the toil of rearing and instructing them. But you appear to me to have chosen the most indolent course; though you ought
10 to have chosen such a course as a good and brave man would have done, since you profess to have made virtue your study through the whole of your life; so that I am ashamed both for you and for us who are your friends, lest this whole affair of yours should seem to be the effect of cowardice on our part—your appearing to stand your trial in the court, since you appeared when it was in your power not to have done so,
15 the very manner in which the trial was conducted, and this last circumstance, as it were, a ridiculous consummation of the whole business; your appearing to have escaped from us through our indolence and cowardice, who did not save you; nor did you save yourself, when it was practicable and possible, had we but exerted ourselves a little. Think of these things, therefore, Socrates, and beware, lest, besides the evil *that will result*,
20 they be disgraceful both to you and to us; advise, then, with yourself; though, indeed, there is no longer time for advising—your resolve should be already made. And there is but one plan; for in the following night the whole must be accomplished. If we delay, it will be impossible and no longer practicable. By all means, therefore, Socrates, be persuaded by me, and on no account refuse.

25 **Socr.** My dear Crito, your zeal would be very commendable were it united with right principle; otherwise, by how much the more earnest it is, by so much is it the more sad. We must consider, therefore, whether this plan should be adopted or not. For I not now only, but always, am a person who will obey nothing within me but reason, according as it appears to me on mature deliberation to be best. And the reasons which
30 I formerly professed I can not now reject, because this misfortune has befallen me; but they appear to me in much the same light, and I respect and honor them as before; so that if we are unable to adduce any better at the present time, be assured that I shall not give in to you, even though the power of the multitude should endeavor to terrify us like children, by threatening more than it does now, bonds and death, and confiscation
35 of property. How, therefore, may we consider the matter most conveniently? First of all, if we recur to the argument which you used about opinions, whether on former occasions it was rightly resolved or not, that we ought to pay attention to some opinions, and to others not; or whether, before it was necessary that I should die, it was rightly resolved; but now it has become clear that it was said idly for argument's sake, though
40 in reality it was merely jest and trifling. I desire then, Crito, to consider, in common with you, whether it will appear to me in a different light, now that I am in this condition, or the same, and whether we shall give it up or yield to it. It was said, I think, on former occasions, by those who were thought to speak seriously, as I just now observed, that of the opinions which men entertain some should be very highly esteemed and others
45 not. By the gods! Crito, does not this appear to you to be well said? For you, in all human probability, are out of all danger of dying tomorrow, and the present calamity will not lead your judgment astray. Consider, then; does it not appear to you to have been rightly settled that we ought not to respect all the opinions of men, but some we should, and others not? Nor yet the opinions of all men, but of some we should, and
50 of others not? What say you? Is not this rightly resolved?

Crito tries to persuade Socrates to save himself for the following reasons: (1) his children's welfare, (2) his students' welfare, and (3) his legacy.

Cri. It is.

Socr. Therefore we should respect the good, but not the bad?

Cri. Yes.

Socr. And are not the good those of the wise, and the bad those of the foolish?

5 *Cri.* How can it be otherwise?

Socr. Come, then: how, again, were the following points settled? Does a man who practices gymnastic exercises and applies himself to them, pay attention to the praise and censure and opinion of every one, or of that one man only who happens to be a physician, or teacher of the exercises?

10 *Cri.* Of that one only.

Socr. He ought, therefore, to fear the censures and covet the praises of that one, but not those of the multitude.

Cri. Clearly.

Socr. He ought, therefore, so to practice and exercise himself, and to eat and 15 drink, as seems fitting to the one who presides and knows, rather than to all others together.

Cri. It is so.

Socr. Well, then, if he disobeys the one, and disregards his opinion and praise, but respects that of the multitude and of those who know nothing, will he not suffer some 20 evil?

Cri. How should he not?

Socr. But what is this evil? Whither does it tend, and on what part of him that disobeys will it fall?

Cri. Clearly on his body, for this it ruins.

Socrates reasons that men should NOT follow the opinion of the multitude in areas that they do not understand. In the areas of justice and honor, Crito should follow Socrates' opinions, not those of the multitude.

25 *Socr.* You say well. The case is the same, too, Crito, with all other things, not to go through them all. With respect then, to things just and unjust, base and honorable, good and evil, about which we are now consulting, ought we to follow the opinion of the multitude, and to respect it, or that of one, if there is any one who understands, whom we ought to reverence and respect rather than all others together? And if we do 30 not obey him, shall we not corrupt and injure that part of ourselves which becomes better by justice, but is ruined by injustice? Or is this nothing?

Cri. I agree with you, Socrates.

Socr. Come, then, if we destroy that which becomes better by what is wholesome, but is impaired by what is unwholesome, through being persuaded by those who do not understand, can we enjoy life when that is impaired? And this is the body we are speaking of, is it not?

5   *Cri.* Yes.

Socr. Can we, then, enjoy life with a diseased and impaired body?

Cri. By no means.

Socr. But can we enjoy life when that is impaired which injustice ruins but justice benefits? Or do we think that to be of less value than the body, whatever part of us it
10   may be, about which injustice and justice are concerned'

Cri. By no means.

Socr. But of more value?

Cri. Much more.

Socr. We must not then, my excellent friend, so much regard what the multitude
15   will say of us, but what he will say who understands the just and the unjust, the one, even truth itself. So that at first you did not set out with a right principle, when you laid it down that we ought to regard the opinion of the multitude with respect to things just and honorable and good, and their contraries. How ever, some one may say, are not the multitude able to put us to death?

20   *Cri.* This, too, is clear, Socrates, any one might say so.

Socr. You say truly. But, my admirable friend, this principle which we have just discussed appears to me to be the same as it was before.

And consider this, moreover, whether it still holds good with us or not, that we are not to be anxious about living but about living well.

25   *Cri.* It does hold good.

Socr. And does this hold good or not, that to live well and Honorable and justly are the same thing?

Cri. It does.

Socr. From what has been admitted, then, this consideration arises, whether it is
30   just or not that I should endeavor to leave this place without the permission of the Athenians. And should it appear to be just, we will make the attempt, but if not, we will give it up. But as to the considerations which you mention, of an outlay of money, reputation, and the education of children, beware, Crito, lest such considerations as these in reality belong to these multitudes, who rashly put one to death, and would
35   restore one to life, if they could do so, without any reason at all. But we, since reason

Socrates advises Crito: Do not be anxious about living, but about living well. Should we modify our core principles if it means saving our lives?

so requires, must consider nothing else than what we just now mentioned, whether we shall act justly in paying money and contracting obligations to those who will lead me hence, as well they who lead me as we who are led hence, or whether, in truth, we shall not act unjustly in doing all these things. And if we should appear in so doing to be
5 acting unjustly, observe that we must not consider whether from remaining here and continuing quiet we must needs die, or suffer any thing else, rather than whether we shall be acting unjustly.

Cri. You appear to me to speak wisely, Socrates, but see what we are to do.

Socr. Let us consider the matter together, my friend, and if you have any thing to
10 object to what I say, make good your objection, and I will yield to you, but if not, cease, my excellent friend, to urge upon me the same thing so often, that I ought to depart hence against the will of the Athenians. For I highly esteem your endeavors to persuade me thus to act, so long as it is not against my will Consider, then, the beginning of our inquiry, whether it is stated to your entire satisfaction, and endeavor to answer the
15 question put to you exactly as you think right.

Cri. I will endeavor to do so.

Socr. Say we, then, that we should on no account deliberately commit injustice, or may we commit injustice under certain circumstances, under others not?

Or is it on no account either good or honorable to commit injustice, as we have often
20 agreed on former occasions, and as we just now said? Or have all those our former admissions been dissipated in these few days, and have we, Crito, old men as we are, been for a long time seriously conversing with each other without knowing that we in no respect differ from children? Or does the case, beyond all question, stand as we then determined? Whether the multitude allow it or not, and whether we must suffer a more
25 severe or a milder punishment than this, still is injustice on every account both evil and disgraceful to him who commits it? Do we admit this, or not?

Cri. We do admit it.

Socr. On no account, therefore, ought we to act unjustly.

Cri. Surely not.

30 *Socr.* Neither ought one who is injured to return the injury, as the multitude think, since it is on no account right to act unjustly.

Cri. It appears not.

Socr. What, then? Is it right to do evil, Crito, or not?

Cri. Surely it is not right, Socrates.

35 *Socr.* But what? To do evil in return when one has been evil-entreated, is that right, or not?

Socrates challenges Crito to consider the value of having principles. May we commit injustices under certain conditions? Or, are injustices always injustices?

Cri. By no means.

Socr. For to do evil to men differs in no respect from committing injustice.

Cri. You say truly.

Socr. It is not right, therefore, to return an injury, or to do evil to any man,
5 however one may have suffered from him.

But take care, Crito, that in allowing these things you do not allow them contrary to
your opinion, for I know that to some few only these things both do appear, and will
appear, to be true. They, then, to whom these things appear true, and they to whom
they do not, have no sentiment in common, and must needs despise each other, while
10 they look to each other's opinions. Consider well, then, whether you coincide and think
with me, and whether we can begin our deliberations from this point—that it is never
right either to do an injury or to return an injury, or when one has been evil-entreated,
to revenge one's self by doing evil in return, or do you dissent from, and not coincide
in this principle? For so it appears to me, both long since and now, but if you in any
15 respect think otherwise, say so and inform me. But if you persist in your former
opinions, hear what follows.

Cri. I do persist in them, and think with you. Speak on, then.

Socr. I say next, then, or rather I ask; whether when a man has promised to do
things that are just he ought to do them, or evade his promise?

20 *Cri.* He ought to do them.

Socr. Observe, then, what follows. By departing hence without the leave of the
city, are we not doing evil to some, and that to those to whom we ought least of all to
do it, or not? And do we abide by what we agreed on as being just, or do we not?

Cri. I am unable to answer your question, Socrates; for I do not understand it.

25 *Socr.* Then, consider it thus. If, while we were preparing to run away, or by
whatever name we should call it, the laws and commonwealth should come, and,
presenting themselves before us, should say, "Tell me, Socrates, what do you purpose
doing? Do you design any thing else by this proceeding in which you are engaged than
to destroy us, the laws, and the whole city, so far as you are able? Or do you think it
30 possible for that city any longer to subsist, and not be subverted, in which judgments
that are passed have no force, but are set aside and destroyed by private persons?"—
what should we say, Crito, to these and similar remonstrances? For any one, especially
an orator, would have much to say on the violation of the law, which enjoins that
judgments passed shall be enforced. Shall we say to them that the city has done us an
35 injustice, and not passed a right sentence? Shall we say this, or what else?

Cri. This, by Jupiter! Socrates.

Socr. What, then, if the laws should say, "Socrates, was it not agreed between us
that you should abide by the judgments which the city should pronounce?" And if we
should wonder at their speaking thus, perhaps they would say, "Wonder not, Socrates,

Socrates points to the immutable
nature of principles like "just" and
"unjust". Can an unjust act be made
just if the majority decides it is
just?

at what we say, but answer, since you are accustomed to make use of questions and answers. For, come, what charge have you against us and the city, that you attempt to destroy us? Did we not first give you being? and did not your father, through us, take your mother to wife and beget you? Say, then, do you find fault with those laws among
5 us that relate to marriage as being bad?" I should say, "I do not find fault with them." "Do you with those that relate to your nurture when born, and the education with which you were instructed? Or did not the laws, ordained on this point, enjoin rightly, in requiring your father to instruct you in music and gymnastic exercises?" I should say, rightly. Well, then, since you were born, nurtured, and educated through our means, can
10 you say, first of all, that you are not both our offspring and our slave, as well you as your ancestors? And if this be so, do you think that there are equal rights between us? and whatever we attempt to do to you, do you think you may justly do to us in turn?

Or had you not equal rights with your father, or master, if you happened to have one, so as to return what you suffered, neither to retort when found fault with, nor, when
15 stricken, to strike again, nor many other things of the kind; but that with your country and the laws you may do so; so that if we attempt to destroy you, thinking it to be just, you also should endeavor, so far as you are able, in return, to destroy us, the laws, and your country; and in doing this will you say that you act justly—you who, in reality, make virtue your chief object? Or are you so wise as not to know that one's country is
20 more honorable, venerable, and sacred, and more highly prized both by gods, and men possessed of understanding, than mother and father, and all other progenitors; and that one ought to reverence, submit to, and appease one's country, when angry, rather than one's father; and either persuade it or do what it orders, and to suffer quietly if it bids one suffer, whether to be beaten, or put in bonds; or if it sends one out to battle there
25 to be wounded or slain, this must be done; for justice so requires, and one must not give way, or retreat, or leave one's post; but that both in war and in a court of justice, and everywhere one must do what one's city and country enjoin, or persuade it in such manner as justice allows; but that to offer violence either to one's mother or father is not holy, much less to one's country? What shall we say to these things, Crito? That the
30 laws speak the truth, or not?

   Cri. It seems so to me.

   Socr. "Consider, then, Socrates," the laws perhaps might say, "whether we say truly that in what you are now attempting you are attempting to do what is not just toward us. For we, having given you birth, nurtured, instructed you, and having
35 imparted to you and all other citizens all the good in our power, still proclaim, by giving the power to every Athenian who pleases, when he has arrived at years of discretion, and become acquainted with the business of the state, and us, the laws, that any one who is not satisfied with us may take his property, and go wherever he pleases. And if any one of you wishes to go to a colony, if he is not satisfied with us and the city, or to
40 migrate and settle in another country, none of us, the laws, hinder or forbid him going whithersoever he pleases, taking with him all his property. But whoever continues with us after he has seen the manner in which we administer justice, and in other respects govern the city, we now say that he has in fact entered into a compact with us to do what we order; and we affirm that he who does not obey is in three respects guilty of
45 injustice—because he does not obey us who gave him being, and because he does not obey us who nurtured him, and because, having made a compact that he would obey us, he neither does so, nor does he persuade us if we do any thing wrongly; though we propose for his consideration, and do not rigidly command him to do what we order, but leave him the choice of one of two things, either to persuade us, or to do what we
50 require, and yet he does neither of these."

Given the chance to escape from prison, Socrates rejects it. He maintains that it is more important to obey the law – even when the charges against him are false. What would you do if you were him?

"And we say that you, O Socrates! will be subject to these charges if you accomplish your design, and that not least of the Athenians, but most so of all." And if I should ask, "For what reason?" they would probably justly retort on me by saying that, among all the Athenians, I especially made this compact with them.

5 For they would say, "Socrates, we have strong proof of this, that you were satisfied both with us and the city; for, of all the Athenians, you especially would never have dwelt in it if it had not been especially agreeable to you; for you never went out of the city to any of the public spectacles, except once to the Isthmian games, nor anywhere else, except on military service, nor have you ever gone abroad as other men do, nor had you ever 10 had any desire to become acquainted with any other city or other laws, but we and our city were sufficient for you; so strongly were you attached to us, and so far did you consent to submit to our government, both in other respects and in begetting children in this city, in consequence of your being satisfied with it. Moreover, in your very trial, it was in your power to have imposed on yourself a sentence of exile, if you pleased, 15 and might then have done, with the consent of the city, what you now attempt against its consent. Then, indeed, you boasted yourself as not being grieved if you must needs die; but you preferred, as you said, death to exile. Now, however, you are neither ashamed of those professions, nor do you revere us, the laws, since you endeavor to destroy us, and you act as the vilest slave would act, by endeavoring to make your escape 20 contrary to the conventions and the compacts by which you engaged to submit to our government. First, then, therefore, answer us this, whether we speak the truth or not in affirming that you agreed to be governed by us in deed, though not in word?" What shall we say to this, Crito? Can we do otherwise than assent?

Cri. We must needs do so, Socrates.

25 *Socr.* "What else, then," they will say, "are you doing but violating the conventions and compacts which you made with us, though you did not enter into them from compulsion or through deception, or from being compelled to determine in a short time but during the space of seventy years, in which you might have departed if you had been dissatisfied with us, and the compacts had not appeared to you to be just? You, 30 however, preferred neither Lacedæmon nor Crete, which you several times said are governed by good laws, nor any other of the Grecian or barbarian cities; but you have been less out of Athens than the lame and the blind, and other maimed persons. So much, it is evident, were you satisfied with the city and us, the laws, beyond the rest of the Athenians; for who can be satisfied with a city without laws? But now will you not 35 abide by your compacts? You will, if you are persuaded by us, Socrates, and will not make yourself ridiculous by leaving the city."

"For consider, by violating these compacts and offending against any of them, what good you will do to yourself or your friends. For that your friends will run the risk of being themselves banished, and deprived of the rights of citizenship, or of forfeiting 40 their property, is pretty clear. And as for yourself, if you should go to one of the neighboring cities, either Thebes or Megara, for both are governed by good laws, you will go there, Socrates, as an enemy to their polity; and such as have any regard for their country will look upon you with suspicion, regarding you as a corrupter of the laws; and you will confirm the opinion of the judges, so that they will appear to have condemned 45 you rightly, for whose is a corrupter of the laws will appear in all likelihood to be a corrupter of youths and weak-minded men. Will you, then, avoid these well-governed cities, and the best-ordered men? And should you do so, will it be worth your while to live? Or will you approach them, and have the effrontery to converse with them, Socrates, on subjects the same as you did here—that virtue and justice, legal institutions

Socrates claims that, although he has been wrongly sentenced to death, he cannot escape from prison because that would be breaking the law. How does breaking the law, in Socrates' mind, also mean breaking a promise or contract he made to his family, friends, and country? Do you agree with his position?

and laws, should be most highly valued by men? And do you not think that this conduct of Socrates would be very indecorous? You must think so. But you will keep clear of these places, and go to Thessaly, to Crito's friends, for there are the greatest disorder and licentiousness; and perhaps they will gladly hear you relating how drolly you escaped
5 from prison, clad in some dress or covered with a skin, or in some other disguise such as fugitives are wont to dress themselves in, having so changed your usual appearance. And will no one say that you, though an old man, with but a short time to live, in all probability, have dared to have such a base desire of life as to violate the most sacred laws? Perhaps not, should you not offend any one. But if you should, you will hear,
10 Socrates, many things utterly unworthy of you. You will live, too, in a state of abject dependence on all men, and as their slave. But what will you do in Thessaly besides feasting, as if you had gone to Thessaly to a banquet? And what will become of those discourses about justice and all other virtues? But do you wish to live for the sake of your children, that you may rear and educate them? What then? Will you take them to
15 Thessaly, and there rear and educate them, making them aliens to their country, that they may owe you this obligation too? Or, if not so, being reared here, will they be better reared and educated while you are living, though not with them, for your friends will take care of them? Whether, if you go to Thessaly, will they take care of them, but if you go to Hades will they not take care of them? If, however, any advantage is to be
20 derived from those that say they are your friends, we must think they will."

Socrates advises us to never value our own lives more than justice. Do you agree?

"Then, O Socrates! be persuaded by us who have nurtured you, and do not set a higher value on your children, or on life, or on any thing else than justice, that, when you arrive in Hades, you may have all this to say in your defense before those who have dominion there.

25 For neither here in this life, if you do what is proposed, does it appear to be better, or more just, or more holy to yourself, or any of your friends; nor will it be better for you when you arrive there.

Socrates says he has been unjustly treated not by laws, but by men. What does he mean by this?

But now you depart, if you do depart, unjustly treated, not by us, the laws, but by men; but should you escape, having thus disgracefully returned injury for injury, and evil for
30 evil, having violated your own compacts and conventions which you made with us, and having done evil to those to whom you least of all should have done it—namely, yourself, your friends, your country, and us—both we shall be indignant with you as long as you live, and there our brothers, the laws in Hades, will not receive you favorably knowing that you attempted, so far as you were able, to destroy us. Let not Crito, then,
35 persuade you to do what he advises, rather than we."

These things, my dear friend Crito, be assured, I seem to hear as the votaries of Cybele seem to hear the flutes. And the sound of these words booms in my ear, and makes me incapable of hearing any thing else. Be sure, then, so long as I retain my present opinions, if you should say any thing contrary to these, you will speak in vain. If,
40 however, you think that you can prevail at all, say on.

Cri. But, Socrates, I have nothing to say.

Socr. Desist, then, Crito, and let us pursue this course, since this way the deity leads us.

PHÆDO

Or, The Immortality Of The Soul

BY PLATO

TRANSLATED FROM THE GREEK BY HENRY CARY, M.A., WORCESTER COLLEGE, OXFORD.

Fig. 5: The Death of Socrates

IN ATTENDANCE: ECHECRATES, PHÆDO, SOCRATES, APOLLODORUS, CEBES, SIMMIAS, AND CRITO.

Ech. Were you personally present, Phædo, with Socrates on that day when he drank the poison in prison, or did you hear an account of it from someone else?

Phæd. I was there myself, Echecrates.

Ech. And what, Phædo, were the circumstances of his death? What was said and done? and who of his friends were with him? or would not the magistrates allow them to be present, but did he die destitute of friends?

Phæd. I was, indeed, wonderfully affected by being present, for I was not impressed with a feeling of pity, like one present at the death of a friend; for the man appeared to me to be happy, Echecrates, both from his manner and discourse, so fearlessly and nobly did he meet his death: so much so, that it occurred to me that in going to Hades he was not going without a divine destiny, but that when he arrived there he would be happy, if any one ever was.

Ech. But who were present, Phædo?

Phæd. Of his fellow-countrymen, this Apollodorus was present, and Critobulus, and his father, Crito; moreover, Hermogenes, Epigenes, Æschines and Antisthenes; Ctesippus the Pæanian, Menexenus, and some others of his countrymen, were also there: Plato, I think, was sick.

5   *Ech.* Were any strangers present?

Phæd. Yes; Simmias, the Theban, Cebes and Phædondes; and from Megara, Euclides and Terpsion.

Ech. Well, now, what do you say was the subject of conversation?

Phæd. When we entered, we found Socrates just freed from his bonds, and Xantippe,
10   you know her, holding his little boy, and sitting by him. As soon as Xantippe saw us she wept aloud, and said such things as women usually do on such occasions—as, "Socrates, your friends will now converse with you for the last time, and you with them." But Socrates, looking towards Crito, said: "Crito, let someone take her home." Upon which some of Crito's attendants led her away, wailing and beating herself. But Socrates, sitting
15   up in bed, drew up his leg, and rubbed it with his hand, and as he rubbed it, said: "What an unaccountable thing, my friends, that seems to be, which men call pleasure! and how wonderfully is it related toward that which appears to be its contrary, pain, in that they will not both be present to a man at the same time! Yet if any one pursues and attains the one, he is almost always compelled to receive the other, as if they were both united
20   together from one head."

"But I depart, as it seems, to-day; for so the Athenians order."

Student asks Socrates about the lawfulness of suicide.

Cebes then asked Socrates, "What do you mean, Socrates, by saying that it is not lawful to commit violence on one's self, but that a philosopher should be willing to follow one who is dying?"   "Why, Socrates, do they say that it is not allowable to kill one's self?

25   "Then, you should consider it attentively," said Socrates, "for perhaps you may hear. Probably, however, it will appear wonderful to you, if this alone, of all other things, is a universal truth, and it never happens to a man, as is the case in all other things, that at some times and to some persons only it is better to die than to live; yet that these men for whom it is better to die—this probably will appear wonderful to you—may not
30   without impiety do this good to themselves, but must await another benefactor."

Socrates compares the body to the soul's prison.

"And, indeed," said Socrates, "it would appear to be unreasonable; yet still, perhaps, it has some reason on its side. The maxim, indeed, given on this subject in the mystical doctrines, that we men are in a kind of prison, and that we ought not to free ourselves from it and escape, appears to me difficult to be understood, and not easy to penetrate.
35   This, however, appears to me, Cebes, to be well said: that the gods take care of us, and that we men are one of their possessions. Does it not seem so to you?"

"It does," replied Cebes.

"Therefore," said Socrates, "if one of your slaves were to kill himself, without your having intimated that you wished him to die, should you not be angry with him, and
40   should you not punish him if you could?"

"Certainly," he replied.

"Perhaps, then, in this point of view, it is not unreasonable to assert that a man ought not to kill himself before the deity lays him under a necessity of doing so, such as that now laid on me."

Socrates justifies suicide if god requires it. How can we translate his meaning?

5 "Come, then," said he, "I will endeavor to defend myself more successfully before you than before the judges. For," he proceeded, "Simmias and Cebes, if I did not think that I should go, first of all, among other deities who are both wise and good, and, next, among men who have departed this life, better than any here, I should be wrong in not grieving at death; but now, be assured, I hope to go among good men, though I would
10 not positively assert it. That, however, I shall go among gods who are perfectly good masters, be assured I can positively assert this, if I can anything of the kind. So that, on this account, I am not so much troubled, but I entertain a good hope that something awaits those who die, and that, as was said long since, it will be far better for the good than the evil."

15 "But now I wish to render an account to you, my judges, of the reason why a man who has really devoted his life to philosophy, when he is about to die, appears to me, on good grounds, to have confidence, and to entertain a firm hope that the greatest good will befall him in the other world when he has departed this life. How, then, this comes to pass, Simmias and Cebes, I will endeavor to explain."

20 But," Socrates said, "let us speak to one another. Do we think that death is anything?"

"Certainly," replied Simmias.

"Is it anything else than the separation of the soul from the body? And is not this to die, for the body to be apart by itself separated from the soul, and for the soul to subsist apart by itself separated from the body? Is death anything else than this?"

25 "No, but this," he replied.

"Consider, then, my good friend, whether you are of the same opinion as I; for thus, I think, we shall understand better the subject we are considering. Does it appear to you to be becoming in a philosopher to be anxious about pleasures, as they are called, such as meats and drinks?"

Socrates reminds his students to value the soul more than the body.

30 "By no means, Socrates," said Simmias.

"But what? about the pleasures of love?"

"Not at all."

"What, then? Does such a man appear to you to think other bodily indulgences of value? For instance, does he seem to you to value or despise the possession of magnificent
35 garments and sandals, and other ornaments of the body except so far as necessity compels him to use them?"

"The true philosopher," he answered, "appears to me to despise them."

"Does not, then," he continued, "the whole employment of such a man appear to you to be, not about the body, but to separate himself from it as much as possible, and be occupied about his soul?"

"It does."

5 "First of all, then, in such matters, does not the philosopher, above all other men, evidently free his soul as much as he can from communion with the body?"

"It appears so."

"And it appears, Simmias, to the generality of men, that he who takes no pleasure in such things, and who does not use them, does not deserve to live; but that he nearly
10 approaches to death who cares nothing for the pleasures that subsist through the body."

"You speak very truly."

Socrates maintains that care for the body distracts from care for the soul.

"But what with respect to the acquisition of wisdom? Is the body an impediment, or not, if any one takes it with him as a partner in the search? What I mean is this: Do sight and hearing convey any truth to men, or are they such as the poets constantly sing, who
15 say that we neither hear nor see anything with accuracy? If, however, these bodily senses are neither accurate nor clear, much less can the others be so; for they are all far inferior to these. Do they not seem so to you?"

"Certainly," he replied.

"When, then," said he, "does the soul light on the truth? for when it attempts to consider
20 any thing in conjunction with the body, it is plain that it is then led astray by it."

"You say truly."

"Must it not, then, be by reasoning, if at all, that any of the things that really are become known to it?"

"Yes."

25 "And surely the soul then reasons best when none of these things disturb it—neither hearing, nor sight, nor pain, nor pleasure of any kind; but it retires as much as possible within itself, taking leave of the body; and, so far as it can, not communicating or being in contact with it, it aims at the discovery of that which is."

"Such is the case."

30 "Does not, then, the soul of the philosopher, in these cases, despise the body, and flee from it, and seek to retire within itself?"

"It appears so."

Socrates views death as an extension of life.

"Do you, then," Socrates said, "describe to me in the same manner with respect to life and death? Do you not say that life is contrary to death?"

"I do," said CEBES. "And that they are produced from each other?" "Yes." "What, then, is produced from life?" "Death," he replied. "What, then," said he "is produced from death?" "I must need confess," he replied, "that life is." "From the dead, then, O Cebes! living things and living men are produced." "It appears so," he said. "Our souls, 5 therefore," said Socrates, "exist in Hades."

"But it is right, my friends," Socrates said, "that we should consider this – that if the soul is immortal, it requires our care not only for the present time, which we call life, but for all time; and the danger would now appear to be dreadful if one should neglect it. For if death were a deliverance from everything, it would be a great gain for the 10 wicked, when they die, to be delivered at the same time from the body, and from their vices together with the soul; but now, since it appears to be immortal, it can have no other refuge from evils, nor safety, except by becoming as good and wise as possible. "But, for the sake of these things which we have described, we should use every endeavor, Simmias, so as to acquire virtue and wisdom in this life, for the reward is 15 noble, and the hope great."

Socrates recommends caring for the soul during life. How so?

When he had said thus, he rose, and went into a chamber to bathe, and Crito followed him, but he directed us to wait for him. We waited, therefore, conversing among ourselves about what had been said, and considering it again, and sometimes speaking about our calamity, how severe it would be to us, sincerely thinking that, like those who 20 are deprived of a father, we should pass the rest of our life as orphans. When he had bathed, and his children were brought to him (for he had two little sons and one grown up), and the women belonging to his family were come, having conversed with them in the presence of Crito, and given them such injunctions as he wished, he directed the women and children to go away, and then returned to us. And it was now near sunset; 25 for he spent a considerable time within.

Socrates bathes and prepares to die.

But when he came from bathing he sat down, and did not speak much afterward; then the officer came in, and, standing near him, said, "Socrates, I shall not have to find that fault with you that I do with others, that they are angry with me, and curse me, when, by order of the archons, I bid them drink the poison. But you, on all other occasions 30 during the time you have been here, I have found to be the most noble, meek, and excellent man of all that ever came into this place; and, therefore, I am now well convinced that you will not be angry with me (for you know who are to blame), but with them. Now, then (for you know what I came to announce to you), farewell, and endeavor to bear what is inevitable as easily as possible." And at the same time, bursting 35 into tears, he turned away and withdrew.

And Socrates, looking after him, said, "And thou, too, farewell. We will do as you direct." At the same time turning to us, he said, "How courteous the man is! During the whole time I have been here he has visited me, and conversed with me sometimes, and proved the worthiest of men; and now how generously he weeps for me! But come, 40 Crito, let us obey him, and let someone bring the poison, if it is ready pounded; but if not, let the man pound it."

Then Crito said, "But I think, Socrates, that the sun is still on the mountains, and has not yet set. Besides, I know that others have drunk the poison very late, after it had been announced to them, and have supped and drunk freely, and some even have 45 enjoyed the objects of their love. Do not hasten, then, for there is yet time."

Upon this Socrates replied, "These men whom you mention, Crito, do these things with good reason, for they think they shall gain by so doing; and I, too, with good reason, shall not do so; for I think I shall gain nothing by drinking a little later, except to become ridiculous to myself, in being so fond of life, and sparing of it, when none any longer
5 remains. Go then," he said, "obey, and do not resist."

Crito, having heard this, nodded to the boy that stood near. And the boy, having gone out and staid for some time, came, bringing with him the man that was to administer the poison, who brought it ready pounded in a cup. And Socrates, on seeing the man, said, "Well, my good friend, as you are skilled in these matters, what must I do?"

10 "Nothing else," he replied, "than, when you have drunk it, walk about until there is a heaviness in your legs; then lie down: thus it will do its purpose." And at the same time he held out the cup to Socrates. And he having received it very cheerfully, Echecrates neither trembling, nor changing at all in color or countenance, but, as he was wont, looking steadfastly at the man, said, "What say you of this potion, with respect to making
15 a libation to any one, is it lawful or not?"

"We only pound so much, Socrates," he said, "as we think sufficient to drink."

"I understand you," he said; "but it is certainly both lawful and right to pray to the gods, that my departure hence thither may be happy; which, therefore, I pray, and so may it be." And as he said this, he drank it off readily and calmly. Thus far, most of us were
20 with difficulty able to restrain ourselves from weeping; but when we saw him drinking, and having finished the draught, we could do so no longer; but, in spite of myself, the tears came in full torrent, so that, covering my face, I wept for myself. Apollodorus, pierced the heart of every one present, except Socrates himself. But he said, "What are you doing, my admirable friends? I have heard that it is right to die with good omens.
25 Be quiet, therefore, and bear up."

When we heard this, we were ashamed, and restrained our tears. But he, having walked about, when he said that his legs were growing heavy, lay down on his back; for the man had so directed him. And, at the same time, he who gave the poison taking hold of him, after a short interval, examined his feet and legs; and then, having pressed his foot hard,
30 he asked if he felt it: he said that he did not. And after this he pressed his thighs; and, thus going higher, he showed us that he was growing cold and stiff. Then Socrates touched himself, and said that when the poison reached his heart he should then depart. But now the parts around the lower belly were almost cold; when, uncovering himself, for he had been covered over, he said (and they were his last words), "Crito, we owe a
35 cock to Æsculapius; pay it, therefore; and do not neglect it."

"It shall be done," said Crito; "but consider whether you have anything else to say."

To this question he gave no reply; but, shortly after, he gave a convulsive movement, and the man covered him, and his eyes were fixed; and Crito, perceiving it, closed his mouth and eyes.

40 This, Echecrates, was the end of our friend,—a man, as we may say, the best of all of his time that we have known, and, moreover, the most wise and just.

THE REPUBLIC

BY PLATO

TRANSLATED FROM THE GREEK BY BENJAMIN JOWETT

Introduction by M. B. McLatchey

By definition, an allegory presents a story that teaches us a lesson regarding how to live our lives. It could be said that Plato's "Allegory of the Cave" recalls the central life lessons that Plato learned from his teacher and friend, Socrates. The questions that this allegory examines also defined the lives of these two men: What is the nature of the truth? How do we regard the one who delivers the truth? Do we welcome him or do we kill the messenger? What is an enlightened life, and what hard choices will we have to make to achieve it? Like Socrates, Plato was more interested in human nature than nature itself. And, like his teacher, he felt the scorn of those who questioned his ambitions and motives. Nevertheless, Plato's writings leave us a record of his teacher's lessons that continue to inform our cultural values and ideals today.

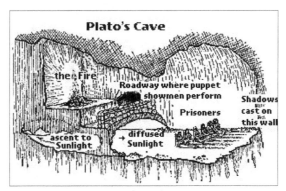

Fig. 6: Plato's Cave

BOOK VII – THE ALLEGORY OF THE CAVE

And now, I said, let me show in a figure how far our nature is enlightened or unenlightened: Behold! Human beings living in a underground den, which has a mouth open towards the light and reaching all along the den; here they have been from their childhood, and have their legs and necks chained so that they cannot move, and can
5   only see before them, being prevented by the chains from turning round their heads. Above and behind them a fire is blazing at a distance, and between the fire and the prisoners there is a raised way; and you will see, if you look, a low wall built along the

way, like the screen which marionette players have in front of them, over which they show the puppets.

I see.

5 And do you see, I said, men passing along the wall carrying all sorts of vessels, and statues and figures of animals made of wood and stone and various materials, which appear over the wall? Some of them are talking, others silent

You have shown me a strange image, and they are strange prisoners.

Like ourselves, I replied; and they see only their own shadows, or the shadows of one another, which the fire throws on the opposite wall of the cave?

10 True, he said; how could they see anything but the shadows if they were never allowed to move their heads?

And of the objects which are being carried in like manner they would only see the shadows?

Yes, he said.

15 And if they were able to converse with one another, would they not suppose that they were naming what was actually before them?

Very true.

And suppose further that the prison had an echo which came from the other side, would they not be sure to fancy when one of the passers-by spoke that the voice which they 20 heard came from the passing shadow?

No question, he replied.

To them, I said, the truth would be literally nothing but the shadows of the images.

That is certain.

And now look again, and see what will naturally follow if the prisoners are released and 25 disabused of their error. At first, when any of them is liberated and compelled suddenly to stand up and turn his neck round and walk and look towards the light, he will suffer sharp pains; the glare will distress him, and he will be unable to see the realities of which in his former state he had seen the shadows; and then conceive some one saying to him, that what he saw before was an illusion, but that now, when he is approaching nearer 30 to being and his eye is turned towards more real existence, he has a clearer vision,— what will be his reply? And you may further imagine that his instructor is pointing to the objects as they pass and requiring him to name them,—will he not be perplexed? Will he not fancy that the shadows which he formerly saw are truer than the objects which are now shown to him?

35 Far truer.

In terms of Plato's thinking here, in what sense might an individual in today's world be regarded as a "prisoner" or a "cave dweller"? Conversely, in what sense might an individual be regarded as one who has been "liberated"?

And if he is compelled to look straight at the light, will he not have a pain in his eyes which will make him turn away to take refuge in the objects of vision which he can see, and which he will conceive to be in reality clearer than the things which are now being shown to him?

How is it that the cave dweller is blinded by the light? In what sense will the truth hurt if we are not accustomed to it?

5   True, he said.

And suppose once more, that he is reluctantly dragged up a steep and rugged ascent, and held fast until he is forced into the presence of the sun himself, is he not likely to be pained and irritated? When he approaches the light his eyes will be dazzled, and he will not be able to see anything at all of what are now called realities.

10 Not all in a moment, he said.

He will require to grow accustomed to the sight of the upper world. And first he will see the shadows best, next the reflections of men and other objects in the water, and then the objects themselves; then he will gaze upon the light of the moon and the stars and the spangled heaven; and he will see the sky and the stars by night better than the
15 sun or the light of the sun by day?

Certainly.

Last of all he will be able to see the sun, and not mere reflections of him in the water, but he will see him in his own proper place, and not in another; and he will contemplate him as he is.

20 Certainly.

He will then proceed to argue that this is he who gives the season and the years, and is the guardian of all that is in the visible world, and in a certain way the cause of all things which he and his fellows have been accustomed to behold?

Clearly, he said, he would first see the sun and then reason about him.

25 And when he remembered his old habitation, and the wisdom of the den and his fellow-prisoners, do you not suppose that he would felicitate himself on the change, and pity them?

What motivates the liberated cave-dweller to return to his compatriots and tell them what he has discovered?

Certainly, he would.

And if they were in the habit of conferring honours among themselves on those who
30 were quickest to observe the passing shadows and to remark which of them went before, and which followed after, and which were together; and who were therefore best able to draw conclusions as to the future, do you think that he would care for such honours and glories, or envy the possessors of them? Would he not say with Homer,

'Better to be the poor servant of a poor master,'

35 And to endure anything, rather than think as they do and live after their manner?

Yes, he said, I think that he would rather suffer anything than entertain these false notions and live in this miserable manner.

Imagine once more, I said, such an one coming suddenly out of the sun to be replaced in his old situation; would he not be certain to have his eyes full of darkness?

5 To be sure, he said.

Why would the cave dwellers kill the "enlightened" messenger? Can you think of a modern-day analogy?

And if there were a contest, and he had to compete in measuring the shadows with the prisoners who had never moved out of the den, while his sight was still weak, and before his eyes had become steady (and the time which would be needed to acquire this new habit of sight might be very considerable), would he not be ridiculous? Men would say
10 of him that up he went and down he came without his eyes; and that it was better not even to think of ascending; and if any one tried to loose another and lead him up to the light, let them only catch the offender, and they would put him to death.

No question, he said.

What price does the enlightened one pay for choosing to live an enlightened life? How does this allegory recall the life of Socrates?

This entire allegory, I said, you may now append, dear Glaucon, to the previous
15 argument; the prison-house is the world of sight, the light of the fire is the sun, and you will not misapprehend me if you interpret the journey upwards to be the ascent of the soul into the intellectual world according to my poor belief, which, at your desire, I have expressed—whether rightly or wrongly God knows.

What recommendation regarding how we should live our lives does Socrates offer in these last lines?

But, whether true or false, my opinion is that in the world of knowledge the idea of
20 good appears last of all, and is seen only with an effort; and, when seen, is also inferred to be the universal author of all things beautiful and right, parent of light and of the lord of light in this visible world, and the immediate source of reason and truth in the intellectual; and that this is the power upon which he who would act rationally either in public or private life must have his eye fixed.

NICOMACHEAN ETHICS

BY ARISTOTLE

TRANSLATED FROM THE GREEK BY W. D. ROSS

Introduction by M. B. McLatchey

Aristotle's "Ethics of Happiness" examines questions that remain the root questions of our lives today. What makes a person happy? What constitutes a happy life? When can we say that a person has lived a good and happy life?

In Greek, the word *ethos* – from which we derive the term *ethics* – means *character*. In his "Ethics of Happiness", Aristotle examines not just the character of happiness, but also the character of human beings. If, as Aristotle notes, different things make different individuals happy, then none of these things can – in themselves – be the elements that universally define a happy life. Therefore, the concept of happiness itself must be scrutinized for its meaning and for its place in our lives.

Fig. 7: Aristotle

As a philosopher, logician, and even a nation-builder of a sort, Aristotle prefers to examine universal ideas – basic values and beliefs that unite us as human beings. For this reason, he is less interested in the different activities that make men cheerful and more interested in the commonly-shared drive men exhibit to go on in life when they cannot always be cheerful. From this perspective, he recognizes that the question he should be asking is not what makes a life *cheerful*, but what makes a life *fulfilled*? What constitutes a *happy* life, for Aristotle, is what constitutes a *fulfilled* life.

BOOK I – THE ETHICS OF HAPPINESS

Let us resume our inquiry and state, in view of the fact, that all knowledge and every pursuit aims at some good …. Verbally there is very general agreement; for both the general run of men and people of superior refinement say that it is happiness, and identify living well and doing well with being happy; but with regard to what happiness is they differ, and the many do not give the same account as the wise.

For the former think it is some plain and obvious thing, like pleasure, wealth, or honour; they differ, however, from one another- and often even the same man identifies it with different things, with health when he is ill, with wealth when he is poor; but, conscious of their ignorance, they admire those who proclaim some great ideal that is above their comprehension. Now some thought that apart from these many goods there is another which is self-subsistent and causes the goodness of all these as well. To examine all the opinions that have been held were perhaps somewhat fruitless; enough to examine those that are most prevalent or that seem to be arguable.

Aristotle asks, "What makes people happy?" and then establishes four basic points: (1) When asked why they engage in learning and other pursuits, people from all social classes offer the same answer -- to achieve happiness, and they identify living well and doing well with being happy; (2) While they all pursue happiness, people differ in their definitions of happiness; (3) The same man will define happiness differently at different times in his life; (4) Given these different definitions of happiness, it seems more productive to look for commonalities among men.

***

To judge from the lives that men lead, most men, and men of the most vulgar type, seem (not without some ground) to identify the good, or happiness, with pleasure; which is the reason why they love the life of enjoyment.

For there are, we may say, three prominent types of life- that just mentioned the vulgar life, the life of labor, the political, and thirdly the contemplative life. Now the mass of mankind are evidently quite slavish in their tastes, preferring a life suitable to beasts....

A consideration of the prominent types of life shows that people of superior refinement and of active disposition identify happiness with honour; for this is, roughly speaking, the end of the political life. But it seems too superficial to be what we are looking for, since it is thought to depend on those who bestow honour rather than on him who receives it, but the good we divine to be something proper to a man and not easily taken from him.

Further, men seem to pursue honour in order that they may be assured of their goodness; at least it is by men of practical wisdom that they seek to be honoured, and among those who know them, and on the ground of their virtue; clearly, then, according to them, at any rate, virtue is better.

The life of money-making is one undertaken under compulsion, and wealth is evidently not the good we are seeking; for it is merely useful and for the sake of something else. And so one might rather take the aforenamed objects to be ends; for they are loved for themselves. But it is evident that not even these are ends; yet many arguments have been thrown away in support of them. Let us leave this subject, then.

***

We had perhaps better consider the universal good and discuss thoroughly what is meant by it.... Clearly, then, goods must be spoken of in two ways, and some must be good in themselves, the others by reason of these. Let us separate, then, things good in themselves from things useful, and consider whether the former are called good by reference to a single Idea. What sort of goods would one call good in themselves?

Let us again return to the good we are seeking, and ask what it can be. It seems different in different actions and arts; it is different in medicine, in strategy, and in the other arts likewise. What then is the good of each? Surely that for whose sake everything else is done. In medicine this is health, in strategy victory, in architecture a house, in any other sphere something else, and in every action and pursuit the end; for it is for the sake of this that all men do whatever else they do. Therefore, if there is an end for all that we do, this will be the good achievable by action, and if there are more than one, these will be the goods achievable by action.

So the argument has by a different course reached the same point; but we must try to state this even more clearly. Since there are evidently more than one end, and we choose some of these (e.g. wealth, flutes, and in general instruments) for the sake of something else, clearly not all ends are final ends; but the chief good is evidently something final.

Margin notes:

Aristotle observes that most people define a good or happy life in accordance with how much pleasure they enjoy. Thus, for most people, "happy" = "cheerful".

5

Aristotle notes that while most people equate happiness with physical pleasures, other more cultured people equate happiness with honor.

10

Aristotle suggests that, since men seem to pursue honor in order that they can be characterized as good, then it is not honor but good character that should be equated with happiness.

15

As long as honor or money-making are means to an end – good character or high status in life – they can not be the things that in themselves make people happy. Rather, they are conditions that lead to some better condition in life.

20

25

Aristotle explores the question of what things in themselves make people happy. For example, does money make us happy? Or is money simply a means to happiness? Is it possible to have all the money one needs and still be unhappy in life? It appears so. So, what elements are needed in a life such that we would call it a good or happy life?

30

35

40

Now such a thing happiness, above all else, is held to be; for this we choose always for self and never for the sake of something else, but honour, pleasure, reason, and every virtue we choose indeed for themselves (for if nothing resulted from them we should still choose each of them), but we choose them also for the sake of happiness, judging that by means of them we shall be happy. Happiness, on the other hand, no one chooses for the sake of these, nor, in general, for anything other than itself.

***

But we must add 'in a complete life.' For one swallow does not make a summer, nor does one day; and so too one day, or a short time, does not make a man blessed and happy.

Aristotle observes that, just as we cannot call a summer a happy summer based upon one beautiful day and we cannot call an Olympic competitor happy until he has completed his performance, so too we cannot call a life happy until it is completed.

And as in the Olympic Games it is not the most beautiful and the strongest that are crowned but those who compete (for it is some of these that are victorious), so those who act win, and rightly win, the noble and good things in life.

Must no one at all, then, be called happy while he lives; must we, as Solon says, see the end? Certainly the future is obscure to us, while happiness, we claim, is an end and something in every way final. If so, we shall call happy those among living men in whom these conditions are, and are to be, fulfilled.

Aristotle notes that, because the future is unknown for each one of us and because pleasant and unpleasant circumstances may come our way, we cannot call our lives happy until they come to their end and we evaluate how we faced these circumstances. Therefore, he suggests, a life of obstacles may turn out to be the happier life if these obstacles elicited from us our nobler selves.

Now many events happen by chance, and events differing in importance; small pieces of good fortune or of its opposite clearly do not weigh down the scales of life one way or the other, but a multitude of great events if they turn out well will make life happier (for not only are they themselves such as to add beauty to life, but the way a man deals with them may be noble and good), while if they turn out ill they crush and maim happiness; for they both bring pain with them and hinder many activities. Yet even in these nobility shines through, when a man bears with resignation many great misfortunes, not through insensibility to pain but through nobility and greatness of soul.

If activities are, as we said, what gives life its character, no happy man can become miserable; for he will never do the acts that are hateful and mean.

According to Aristotle, the question is not WHAT happens to us in life but HOW WE DEAL with events that determines if our lives will be happy. Therefore, a life of hardships need not make a man miserable, nor his life unhappy.

For the man who is truly good and wise, we think, bears all the chances in life becomingly and always makes the best of circumstances, as a good general makes the best military use of the army at his command and a good shoemaker makes the best shoes out of the hides that are given him; and so with all other craftsmen. And if this is the case, the happy man can never become miserable;

Freedom is participation in power.

— *Marcus Tullius Cicero*

PART II: THE ROMAN REPUBLIC AND EMPIRE

TREATISE ON FRIENDSHIP

BY MARCUS TULLIUS CICERO

TRANSLATED FROM THE LATIN BY E. S. SHUCKBURGH

Introduction by M. B. McLatchey

An attorney. A scholar. A contemporary to Julius Caesar, although not always an ally. The most renown public speaker in an age when the art of oration was revered. Marcus Tullius Cicero embodied the principles of the Roman Republic in the 1st century B.C. Before his assassination – an event that signaled an assault on his ideals – Cicero was Rome's spokesman for the glory of the Roman Republic and for every citizen's duty first to his country, then his family, and lastly his friends.

In his "Treatise on Friendship", we hear Cicero's most personal and deeply-felt reflections on the value of friendships among citizens. With a typically-Roman pragmatism, Cicero advises his readers on how to choose friends and when to abandon them. He vigorously rejects the adage that "a friend in need is a friend indeed", insisting that "friendships can only exist between good men" and that the glue of all friendships is virtue. In his final analysis, he concludes that a good friend must also be a good citizen. Conversely, the man who presents himself as an enemy to the values of the state must be our enemies as well.

Fig. 8: Cicero

As a guardian of the Roman Republic, Cicero challenged Roman citizens to examine their allegiances to one another and to the core values of their society. His "Treatise on Friendship" explores the questions that all citizens inevitably consider as an aspect of living among others: Will the friendships that we cultivate make us better human beings? Will our associations with others benefit or burden the society? What contribution will we make to the growth of a civilization? It is as though Cicero is speaking to us today.

ON FRIENDSHIP

You have often urged me to write something on Friendship, and I quite acknowledged that the subject seemed one worth everybody's investigation, and specially suited to the close intimacy that has existed between you and me. Accordingly I was quite ready to benefit the public at your request.

Cicero casts his essay in the dramatic voice of Laelius, a legal scholar under whom he studied. This grants him a disinterested tone regarding a subject he felt deeply about and that wounded his own career.

5 Finally, as I sent the former essay to you as a gift from one old man to another, so I have dedicated this *On Friendship* as a most affectionate friend to his friend. In the former Cato spoke, who was the oldest and wisest man of his day; in this Laelius speaks on friendship—Laelius, who was at once a wise man (that was the title given him) and eminent for his famous friendship. Please forget me for a while; imagine Laelius to be
10 speaking.

But I must at the very beginning lay down this principle—*friendship can only exist between good men.* I do not, however, press this too closely, like the philosophers who push their definitions to a superfluous accuracy. They have truth on their side, perhaps, but it is of no practical advantage. Those, I mean, who say that no one but the "wise" is "good."
5 Granted, by all means. But the "wisdom" they mean is one to which no mortal ever yet attained. We must concern ourselves with the facts of everyday life as we find it—not imaginary and ideal perfections. Even Gaius Fannius, Manius Curius, and Tiberius Coruncanius, whom our ancestors decided to be "wise," I could never declare to be so according to their standard. Let them, then, keep this word "wisdom" to themselves.
10 Everybody is irritated by it; no one understands what it means. Let them but grant that the men I mentioned were "good." No, they won't do that either. No one but the "wise" can be allowed that title, say they. Well, then, let us dismiss them and manage as best we may with our own poor mother wit, as the phrase is.

We mean then by the "good" *those whose actions and lives leave no question as to their honour,*
15 *purity, equity, and liberality; who are free from greed, lust, and violence; and who have the courage of their convictions.* The men I have just named may serve as examples. Such men as these being generally accounted "good," let us agree to call them so, on the ground that to the best of human ability they follow nature as the most perfect guide to a good life.

Now this truth seems clear to me, that nature has so formed us that a certain tie unites
20 us all, but that this tie becomes stronger from proximity. So it is that fellow-citizens are preferred in our affections to foreigners, relations to strangers; for in their case Nature herself has caused a kind of friendship to exist, though it is one which lacks some of the elements of permanence. Friendship excels relationship in this, that whereas you may eliminate affection from relationship, you cannot do so from friendship. Without
25 it relationship still exists in name, friendship does not. You may best understand this friendship by considering that, whereas the merely natural ties uniting the human race are indefinite, this one is so concentrated, and confined to so narrow a sphere, that affection is ever shared by two persons only or at most by a few.

Now friendship may be thus defined: a complete accord on all subjects human and
30 divine, joined with mutual goodwill and affection. And with the exception of wisdom, I am inclined to think nothing better than this has been given to man by the immortal gods. There are people who give the palm to riches or to good health, or to power and office, many even to sensual pleasures. This last is the ideal of brute beasts; and of the others we may say that they are frail and uncertain, and depend less on our own
35 prudence than on the caprice of fortune. Then there are those who find the "chief good" in virtue. Well, that is a noble doctrine. But the very virtue they talk of is the parent and preserver of friendship, and without it friendship cannot possibly exist.

Let us, I repeat, use the word virtue in the ordinary acceptation and meaning of the term, and do not let us define it in high-flown language. Let us account as good the
40 persons usually considered so, such as Paulus, Cato, Gallus, Scipio, and Philus. Such men as these are good enough for everyday life; and we need not trouble ourselves about those ideal characters which are nowhere to be met with.

Well, between men like these the advantages of friendship are almost more than I can say. To begin with, how can life be worth living, to use the words of Ennius, which

For the sake of clarity and his practical purposes, Cicero dismisses the lofty ideas of the ancient philosophers. In fact he challenges their notion that only a wise man can be a good man. From Cicero's perspective, a good man might not be wise at all, but he must certainly embody the traits that he lists in the next paragraph.

Cicero examines how the seeds of true friendships get planted, and how they bloom. Physical proximity – our nearness to one another, as neighbors or fellow citizens – can initiate friendships. In fact, Cicero seems to advocate friendships among fellow citizens rather than with foreigners.

Cicero offers two points: (1) he believes that the most natural and appropriate friendships grow between two people who share cultural and religious values, who share what he calls "a complete accord on all subjects human and divine". Thus, Romans befriend Romans. And (2) that, because of the intensity, we can only have a few true friendships; the rest are merely relationships and acquaintances.

Cicero identifies what he believes must be the glue of all true friendships: virtue. He sees friendships between people as opportunities for mutual growth and mutual benefit. Therefore, both individuals in the relationship must embody good character traits. We may claim that we have many friends, some more admirable in character than others. But, from Cicero's perspective, our "friends" are only those who share our honorable values; all the rest are merely acquaintances with whom we sometimes waste our time.

Cicero lists the advantages of friendships: sharing our joys and hardships; our friends double our joys and bear our hardships for us.

lacks that repose which is to be found in the mutual good-will of a friend? What can be more delightful than to have some one to whom you can say everything with the same absolute confidence as to yourself? Is not prosperity robbed of half its value if you have no one to share your joy? On the other hand, misfortunes would be hard to bear if there
5　were not some one to feel them even more acutely than yourself. In a word, other objects of ambition serve for particular ends—riches for use, power for securing homage, office for reputation, pleasure for enjoyment, health for' freedom from pain and the full use of the functions of the body. But friendship embraces innumerable advantages. Turn which way you please, you will find it at hand. It is everywhere; and
10　yet never out of place, never unwelcome. Fire and water themselves, to use a common expression, are not of more universal use than friendship. I am not now speaking of the common or modified form of it, though even that is a source of pleasure and profit, but of that true and complete friendship which existed between the select few who are known to fame. Such friendship enhances prosperity, and relieves adversity of its
15　burden by halving and sharing it.

According to Cicero, friendships sustain us. They give us hope and forbid despair.

And great and numerous as are the blessings of friendship, this certainly is the sovereign one, that it gives us bright hopes for the future and forbids weakness and despair. In the face of a true friend a man sees as it were a second self. So that where his friend is he is; if his friend be rich, he is not poor; though he be weak, his friend's strength is his;
20　and in his friend's life he enjoys a second life after his own is finished. This last is perhaps the most difficult to conceive. But such is the effect of the respect, the loving remembrance, and the regret of friends which follow us to the grave. While they take the sting out of death, they add a glory to the life of the survivors. Nay, if you eliminate from nature the tie of affection, there will be an end of house and city, nor will so much
25　as the cultivation of the soil be left. If you don't see the virtue of friendship and harmony, you may learn it by observing the effects of quarrels and feuds. Was any family ever so well established, any State so firmly settled, as to be beyond the reach of utter destruction from animosities and factions? This may teach you the immense advantage of friendship.

Cicero examines what makes friends come together. Is it a mutual need? Is a friendship formed because one person is strong and the other is weak? Do friends complement one another? No, Cicero says. Friendships are based on something nobler: a mutual affection, a love. Friends see in one another the values that they admire.

30　Well, then, it has very often occurred to me when thinking about friendship, that the chief point to be considered was this: is it weakness and want of means that make friendship desired? I mean, is its object an interchange of good offices, so that each may give that in which he is strong, and receive that in which he is weak? Or is it not rather true that, although this is an advantage naturally belonging to friendship, yet its original
35　cause is quite other, prior in time, more noble in character, and springing more directly from our nature itself? The Latin word for friendship—*amicitia*—is derived from that for love— *amor*; and love is certainly the prime mover in contracting mutual affection. For as to material advantages, it often happens that those are obtained even by men who are courted by a mere show of friendship and treated with respect from interested
40　motives.

Cicero dismisses the notion that a friend in need is a friend indeed. Friends do not look for what they can gain materially or any other way from one another. They come together out of a mutual respect and love inspired by the virtue that they see in one another. Friends enoble us and appeal to our higher qualities: honesty, truth, and the courage to stand by our convictions.

But friendship by its nature admits of no feigning, no pretence: as far as it goes it is both genuine and spontaneous. Therefore I gather that friendship springs from a natural impulse rather than a wish for help: from an inclination of the heart, combined with a certain instinctive feeling of love, rather than from a deliberate calculation of the
45　material advantage it was likely to confer. The strength of this feeling you may notice in certain animals. They show such love to their offspring for a certain period, and are so beloved by them, that they clearly have a share in this natural, instinctive affection. But of course it is more evident in the case of man: first, in the natural affection between children and their parents, an affection which only shocking wickedness can sunder;
50　and next, when the passion of love has attained to a like strength—on our finding, that

is, some one person with whose character and nature we are in full sympathy, because we think that we perceive in him what I may call the beacon-light of virtue. For nothing inspires love, nothing conciliates affection, like virtue. Why, in a certain sense we may be said to feel affection even for men we have never seen, owing to their honesty and
5   virtue. Who, for instance, fails to dwell on the memory of Gaius Fabricius and Manius Curius with some affection and warmth of feeling, though he has never seen them? Or who but loathes Tarquinius Superbus, Spurius Cassius, Spurius Maelius? We have fought for empire in Italy with two great generals, Pyrrhus and Hannibal. For the former, owing to his probity, we entertain no great feelings of enmity: the latter, owing
10 to his cruelty, our country has detested and always will detest.

Far different is the view of those who, like brute beasts, refer everything to sensual pleasure. And no wonder. Men who have degraded all their powers of thought to an object so mean and contemptible can of course raise their eyes to nothing lofty, to nothing grand and divine. Such persons indeed let us leave out of the present question.
15 And let us accept the doctrine that the sensation of love and the warmth of inclination have their origin in a spontaneous feeling which arises directly the presence of probity is indicated. When once men have conceived the inclination, they of course try to attach themselves to the object of it, and move themselves nearer and nearer to him. Their aim is that they may be on the same footing and the same level in regard to affection,
20 and be more inclined to do a good service than to ask a return, and that there should be this noble rivalry between them. Thus both truths will be established. We shall get the most important material advantages from friendship; and its origin from a natural impulse rather than from a sense of need will be at once more dignified and more in accordance with fact. For if it were true that its material advantages cemented
25 friendship, it would be equally true that any change in them would dissolve it. But nature being incapable of change, it follows that genuine friendships are eternal.

We may then lay down this rule of friendship—neither ask nor consent to do what is wrong. For the plea "for friendship's sake" is a discreditable one, and not to be admitted for a moment. This rule holds good for all wrong-doing, but more especially in such as
30 involves disloyalty to the republic. For things have come to such a point with us, my dear Fannius and Scaevola, that we are bound to look somewhat far ahead to what is likely to happen to the republic. The constitution, as known to our ancestors, has already swerved somewhat from the regular course and the lines marked out for it. Tiberius Gracchus made an attempt to obtain the power of a king, or, I might rather say, enjoyed
35 that power for a few months. Had the Roman people ever heard or seen the like before? What the friends and connexions that followed him, even after his death, have succeeded in doing in the case of Publius Scipio I cannot describe without tears. As for Carbo, thanks to the punishment recently inflicted on Tiberius Gracchus, we have by hook or by crook managed to hold out against his attacks. But what to expect of the
40 tribuneship of Caius Gracchus I do not like to forecast. One thing leads to another; and once set going, the downward course proceeds with ever-increasing velocity. There is the case of the ballot: what a blow was inflicted first by the lex Gabinia, and two years afterwards by the lex Cassia! I seem already to see the people estranged from the Senate, and the most important affairs at the mercy of the multitude. For you may be sure that
45 more people will learn how to set such things in motion than how to stop them.

What is the point of these remarks? This: no one ever makes any attempt of this sort without friends to help him. We must therefore impress upon good men that, should they become inevitably involved in friendships with men of this kind, they ought not to consider themselves under any obligation to stand by friends who are disloyal to the
50 republic. Bad men must have the fear of punishment before their eyes: a punishment

Cicero dismisses as false friends those who form friendships for material gain or for political advantage or for sensual pleasures. These friendships come and go, while true friendships are eternal.

Cicero maintains, the enemy is the one who asks us to choose between friendship or our core values. He then explores the link between political unrest and disloyalty to the Roman Republic. His recommendation: Never stand by a man who is disloyal to the Republic.

Cicero points to virtuous characters in history who chose principle over popularity: Themistocles and Coriolanus.

not less severe for those who follow than for those who lead others to crime. Who was more famous and powerful in Greece than Themistocles? At the head of the army in the Persian war he had freed Greece; he owed his exile to personal envy: but he did not submit to the wrong done him by his ungrateful country as he ought to have done. He acted as Coriolanus had acted among us twenty years before. But no one was found to help them in their attacks upon their fatherland. Both of them accordingly committed suicide.

We conclude, then, not only that no such confederation of evilly disposed men must be allowed to shelter itself under the plea of friendship, but that, on the contrary, it must be visited with the severest punishment, lest the idea should prevail that fidelity to a friend justifies even making war upon one's country. And this is a case which I am inclined to think, considering how things are beginning to go, will sooner or later arise. And I care quite as much what the state of the constitution will be after my death as what it is now.

Let this, then, be laid down as the first law of friendship, that *we should ask from friends, and do for friends', only what is good*. But do not let us wait to be asked either: let there be ever an eager readiness, and an absence of hesitation. Let us have the courage to give advice with candour. In friendship, let the influence of friends who give good advice be paramount; and let this influence be used to enforce advice not only in plain-spoken terms, but sometimes, if the case demands it, with sharpness; and when so used, let it be obeyed.

I give you these rules because I believe that some wonderful opinions are entertained by certain persons who have, I am told, a reputation for wisdom in Greece. There is nothing in the world, by the way, beyond the reach of their sophistry. Well, some of them teach that we should avoid very close friendships, for fear that one man should have to endure the anxieties of several. Each man, say they, has enough and to spare on his own hands; it is too bad to be involved in the cares of other people. The wisest course is to hold the reins of friendship as loose as possible; you can then tighten or slacken them at your will. For the first condition of a happy life is freedom from care, which no one's mind can enjoy if it has to travail, so to speak, for others besides itself. Another sect, I am told, gives vent to opinions still less generous. I briefly touched on this subject just now. They affirm that friendships should be sought solely for the sake of the assistance they give, and not at all from motives of feeling and affection; and that therefore just in proportion as a man's power and means of support are lowest, he is most eager to gain friendships: thence it comes that weak women seek the support of friendship more than men, the poor more than the rich, the unfortunate rather than those esteemed prosperous. What noble philosophy! You might just as well take the sun out of the sky as friendship from life; for the immortal gods have given us nothing better or more delightful.

Sidenotes:

Cicero reminds us that the first rule of friendships is good character. Friends give honest advice to one another, even when it risks dissolving the friendship.

Cicero fears that the republic will dissolve under the weight of a mob culture, where men choose loyalty to one another rather than loyalty to the laws and values of the nation.

Cicero recommends that we "hold the reins of friendship as loose as possible" so that they never burden us. Also, he advises us to never cherish friends more than our own principles, which should mirror the values of the republic. For Cicero, the Roman Republic must come first, friendships second.

THE CARMINA OF CATULLUS

BY GAIUS VALERIUS CATULLUS

TRANSLATED FROM THE LATIN BY M. B. MCLATCHEY

Introduction by M. B. McLatchey

If Cicero celebrated the spirit of Rome, Gaius Valerius Catullus celebrated the flesh. Yet, in the 1st century B.C., the dynamism and diversity of the Roman Republic demanded forums for both of these men. While Cicero recommended that the citizens of Rome aspire to a Stoic virtue discovered through military triumphs and political contests, Catullus endorsed an Epicurean virtue found in the pleasure of leading a refined and charming life. For Cicero, the emphasis falls on duty; for Catullus, it falls on pleasure. Cicero's **virtus** (courage and character) versus Catullus's **venustas** (beauty and charm).

Fig. 9: Catullus

In the poems presented here, Catullus expresses a range of emotions – lust, longing, jealousy, and even bitter sarcasm – that chronicles his relationship with a woman named Lesbia, a pseudonym for the married woman he loved and who is traditionally identified as Claudia Metelli Celeris, the sister of a popular Roman politician. The practice of replacing the real names of lovers with names of identical meter was not uncommon among Roman poets – hence Les-bi-a for Clau-di-a. Furthermore, Catullus may have wanted the erotic and literary connection to Lesbos, the island where the Greek poet, Sappho, and her female lovers produced a similar canon of lyrical poems.

Distancing himself from the lofty language and formal meters of previous poets and epic verse, Catullus identified himself with a new school of poets – the "neoteroi" or moderns – whose language resembled that of the spoken word and whose verses mirrored the spontaneity and range of emotions that a young lover feels. His themes are not the national and heroic themes of Homer's epics. Nor do Catullus's poems share the goals of the Roman poet, Virgil, whose epic *The Aeneid* will later codify the Stoic and warrior ideals of the Roman empire. Whereas Virgil's epic performances champion the public man, Catullus champions the private man. His topics are the varieties of love and companionship that we experience in our personal histories. In an age when public oration codified the ideals of Roman citizens and was regarded as an art reserved for only an accomplished few, Catullus stands shoulder-to-shoulder with Cicero as one of the two major literary voices of the Roman Republic.

In my translations from Latin into English of the following selection of poems from Catullus's *Carmina* (love songs), I have generally followed the advice and texts of two Classics scholars: Robinson Ellis, Professor of Latin in University College, London and Francis Warre Cornish, Late Fellow of King's College, Cambridge. While my chief objective was to produce translations that were as literal and readable as possible, I also wanted to capture Catullus's wit and colloquial style, a modernism that reminds us of those *fin de siècle*, free-verse poets who aimed at loosening themselves from a tradition of high rhetoric and strict meters. My goal here was to be as true to the spirit as to the letter of Catullus's poetry.

LESBIA'S SPARROW

Passer, deliciae meae puellae,

quicum ludere, quem in sinu tenere,

cui primum digitum dare appetenti

et acris solet incitare morsus,

cum desiderio meo nitenti

carum nescio quid libet iocari,

credo ut, cum gravis acquiescet ardor,

sit solaciolum sui doloris,

tecum ludere sicut ipsa possem

et tristis animi levare curas!

Tam gratumst mihi quam ferunt puellae

Pernici aureolum fuisse malum,

Quod zonam soluit diu ligatam.

Sparrow, favorite of my own beloved,

whom to play with or to fondle in her arms

she delights; to whom she surrenders

her fingertip to your pecking

and does provoke your sharp bite.

When my lady, a lovely star to long for,

bends her splendor awhile to make

merriment; and perhaps to make

a little comfort for her own anguish,

might I, as she plays, play with thee!

That I might free myself from misery.

TO LESBIA

Vivamus, mea Lesbia, atque amemus,	Let us live, my Lesbia, and let us love!
Rumoresque senum severiorum	All the rumors and mutterings of old men
Omnes unius aestimemus assis.	let us price and prize not one cent's worth!
Soles occidere et redire possunt:	The Suns can westward sink again to rise
Nobis cum semel occidit brevis lux,	but we, extinguished once our tiny light,
Nox est perpetua una dormienda.	perhaps shall slumber through one lasting night!
Da mi basia mille, deinde centum,	Kiss me a thousand times, then hundred more,
Dein mille altera, dein secunda centum,	then thousand others, then a new five-score,
Deinde usque altera mille, deinde centum.	still other thousand other hundred store.
Dein, cum milia multa fecerimus,	Then when we have added many thousands,
Conturbabimus illa, ne sciamus,	the sum let's trouble till no more we know,
Aut nequis malus invidere possit,	nor let men cast their jealous eyes upon us,
Cum tantum sciet esse basiorum.	knowing how many kisses have been kissed between us.

HOW THE LOVER LOVES

Odi et amo. quare id faciam, fortasse requiris.	I hate and I love. Should you ask me how I do so
Nescio, sed fieri sentio et excrucior.	I do not know, but I feel it truly and I suffer.

THE AENEID

BY PUBLIUS VERGILIUS MARO (VIRGIL)

TRANSLATED FROM THE LATIN BY J. W. MACKAIL, M.A. FELLOW OF BALLIOL COLLEGE, OXFORD, LONDON. MACMILLAN AND CO. 1885. PRINTED BY R. & R. CLARK, EDINBURGH.

Introduction by M. B. McLatchey

Fig. 10: Virgil

Commissioned by the Roman Emperor Octavian Augustus to produce a national anthem that would rival the great poems of the Greeks, Virgil embarked upon his epic poem, *The Aeneid*. Although Virgil did not complete his epic poem before his death, he nevertheless succeeded in producing for the glory of Rome a national hero, Aeneas, who embodied the Stoic virtues that his Emperor Augustus celebrated during his reign: piety, patriotism, and poise governed by reason.

Virgil's *Aeneid* chronicles the post-war exodus of the Trojan hero Aeneas and his navy from Troy and their journey to Italy to "found a second Troy". It is a journey that foreshadows the Pheonix-like rising of a Roman Empire out of the ashes of the Trojan War and promises centuries of prosperity for the Roman people.

Of the twelve books of Latin verse that Virgil produced, four are presented here in prose translation. These excerpts highlight the metamorphoses of the hero candidate, Aeneas, from a self-absorbed navy general to an icon of Roman valor. The dramatic conflicts that these books explore are the conflicts that the Emperor Augustus wanted resolved for his Roman citizens – in every case choosing the former of these two choices: country vs. self; duty vs. pleasure; reason vs. emotions; piety versus passion; Rome vs. Carthage; stoicism vs. epicureanism. With *The Aeneid*, Virgil resolves these conflicts and delivers on his promise to his emperor to give Rome a national song.

The opening lines of *The Aeneid* – shown on the following page in the original Latin verse [Fig. 11] – foreshadow a central conflict that the hero Aeneas will wrestle with throughout this epic, namely the struggle between fate and free will. Notice how, in these opening scenes, two tiers are established – the tier of men on earth, and that of gods in the sky. The gods delivered Aeneas's destiny to him when they allowed the Greeks to seize his city of Troy. However, Aeneas – and not the gods – will decide how to cope with this defeat. Will Aeneas regard his life as riddled with unfair obstacles, or will he embrace it as rich with opportunities to manifest his talents? The ancient epics in the western world are fascinated by this tension.

If the modern-day question in popular psychology asks, "Why do bad things happen to good people?" then the ancient heroic epics respond, "Because they keep passing the test." What tests will the good Aeneas have to pass before he can emerge as a national hero? What values will he ultimately embrace such that his culture will call him the ideal Roman warrior?

COMPLETE LIST OF BOOKS FROM THE AENEID

BOOK FIRST*   The Coming of Aeneas to Carthage

BOOK SECOND   The Story of the Sack of Troy

BOOK THIRD   The Story of the Seven Years' Wandering

BOOK FOURTH*   The Love of Dido, and Her End

BOOK FIFTH   The Games of the Fleet

BOOK SIXTH*   The Vision of the Under World

BOOK SEVENTH   The Landing in Latium, and the Roll of the Armies of Italy

BOOK EIGHTH   The Embassage to Evander

BOOK NINTH   The Siege of the Trojan Camp

BOOK TENTH   The Battle on the Beach

BOOK ELEVENTH   The Council of the Latins, and the Life and Death of Camilla

BOOK TWELFTH*   The Slaying of Turnus

Arma virumque cano, Troiae qui primus ab oris
Italiam, fato profugus, Laviniaque venit
litora, multum ille et terris iactatus et alto
vi superum saevae memorem Iunonis ob iram;
multa quoque et bello passus, dum conderet urbem,
inferretque deos Latio, genus unde Latinum,

Fig. 11: The Aeneid in its original Latin form

---

* Books included in this edition of *Primary Sources.*

BOOK FIRST - THE COMING OF AENEAS TO CARTHAGE

I sing of arms and the man who of old from the coasts of Troy came, an exile of fate, to Italy and the shore of Lavinium; hard driven on land and on the deep by the violence of heaven, for cruel Juno's unforgetful anger, and hard bestead in war also, ere he might found a city and carry his gods into Latium; from whom is the Latin race, the lords of Alba, and the stately city Rome.

Muse, tell me why, for what attaint of her deity, or in what vexation, did the Queen of heaven drive one so excellent in goodness to circle through so many afflictions, to face so many toils? Is anger so fierce in celestial spirits?

There was a city of ancient days that Tyrian settlers dwelt in, Carthage, over against Italy and the Tiber mouths afar; rich of store, and mighty in war's fierce pursuits; wherein, they say, alone beyond all other lands had Juno her seat, and held Samos itself less dear. Here was her armour, here her chariot; even now, if fate permit, the goddess strives to nurture it for queen of the nations. Nevertheless she had heard a race was issuing of the blood of Troy, which sometime should overthrow her Tyrian citadel; from it should come a people, lord of lands and tyrannous in war, the destroyer of Libya: so rolled the destinies. Fearful of that, the daughter of Saturn, the old war in her remembrance that she fought at Troy for her beloved Argos long ago,—nor had the springs of her anger nor the bitterness of her vexation yet gone out of mind: deep stored in her soul lies the judgment of Paris, the insult of her slighted beauty, the hated race and the dignities of ravished Ganymede; fired with this also, she tossed all over ocean the Trojan remnant left of the Greek host and merciless Achilles, and held them afar from Latium; and many a year were they wandering driven of fate around all the seas. Such work was it to found the Roman people.

Hardly out of sight of the land of Sicily did they set their sails to sea, and merrily upturned the salt foam with brazen prow, when Juno, the undying wound still deep in her heart, thus broke out alone:

'Am I then to abandon my baffled purpose, powerless to keep the Teucrian king from Italy? and because fate forbids me? Could Pallas lay the Argive fleet in ashes, and sink the Argives in the sea, for one man's guilt, mad Oïlean Ajax? Her hand darted Jove's flying fire from the clouds, scattered their ships, upturned the seas in tempest; him, his pierced breast yet breathing forth the flame, she caught in a whirlwind and impaled on a spike of rock. But I, who move queen among immortals, I sister and wife of Jove, wage warfare all these years with a single people; and is there any who still adores Juno's divinity, or will kneel to lay sacrifice on her altars?'

Such thoughts inly revolving in her kindled bosom, the goddess reaches Aeolia, the home of storm-clouds, the land laden with furious southern gales. Here in a desolate cavern Aeolus keeps under royal dominion and yokes in dungeon fetters the struggling winds and loud storms. They with mighty moan rage indignant round their mountain barriers. In his lofty citadel Aeolus sits sceptred, assuages their temper and soothes their rage; else would they carry with them seas and lands, and the depth of heaven, and sweep them through space in their flying course. But, fearful of this, the lord omnipotent hath hidden them in caverned gloom, and laid a mountain mass high over them, and appointed them a ruler, who should know by certain law to strain and slacken the reins at command. To him now Juno spoke thus in suppliant accents:

'Aeolus—for to thee hath the father of gods and king of men given the wind that lulls and that lifts the waves—a people mine enemy sails the Tyrrhene sea, carrying into Italy
5 the conquered gods of their Ilian home. Rouse thy winds to fury, and overwhelm their sinking vessels, or drive them asunder and strew ocean with their bodies. Mine are twice seven nymphs of passing loveliness; her who of them all is most excellent in beauty, Deïopea, I will unite to thee in wedlock to be thine for ever; that for this thy service she may fulfil all her years at thy side, and make thee father of a beautiful race.'

10 Aeolus thus returned: 'Thine, O queen, the task to search whereto thou hast desire; for me it is right to do thy bidding. From thee have I this poor kingdom, from thee my sceptre and Jove's grace; thou dost grant me to take my seat at the feasts of the gods, and makest me sovereign over clouds and storms.'

Even with these words, turning his spear, he struck the side of the hollow hill, and the
15 winds, as in banded array, pour where passage is given them, and cover earth with eddying blasts. East wind and west wind together, and the gusty south-wester, falling prone on the sea, stir it up from its lowest chambers, and roll vast billows to the shore. Behind rises shouting of men and whistling of cordage. In a moment clouds blot sky and daylight from the Teucrians' eyes; black night broods over the deep. Pole thunders
20 to pole, and the air quivers with incessant flashes; all menaces them with instant death. Straightway Aeneas' frame grows unnerved and chill, and stretching either hand to heaven, he cries thus aloud: 'Ah, thrice and four times happy they who found their doom under high Troy town before their fathers' faces! Ah, son of Tydeus, bravest of the Grecian race, that I could not have fallen on the Ilian plains, and gasped out this my
25 life beneath thine hand! where under the spear of Aeacides lies fierce Hector, lies mighty Sarpedon; where Simoïs so often bore beneath his whirling wave shields and helmets and brave bodies of men.'

As the cry leaves his lips, a gust of the shrill north strikes full on the sail and raises the waves up to heaven. The oars are snapped; the prow swings away and gives her side to
30 the waves; down in a heap comes a broken mountain of water. These hang on the wave's ridge; to these the yawning billow shows ground amid the surge, where the sea churns with sand. Three ships the south wind catches and hurls on hidden rocks, rocks amid the waves which Italians call the Altars, a vast reef banking the sea. Three the east forces from the deep into shallows and quicksands, piteous to see, dashes on shoals and girdles
35 with a sandbank. One, wherein loyal Orontes and his Lycians rode, before their lord's eyes a vast sea descending strikes astern. The helmsman is dashed away and rolled forward headlong; her as she lies the billow sends spinning thrice round with it, and engulfs in the swift whirl. Scattered swimmers appear in the vast eddy, armour of men, timbers and Trojan treasure amid the water. Ere now the stout ship of Ilioneus, ere now
40 of brave Achates, and she wherein Abas rode, and she wherein aged Aletes, have yielded to the storm; through the shaken fastenings of their sides they all draw in the deadly water, and their opening seams give way.

Meanwhile Neptune discerned with astonishment the loud roaring of the vexed sea, the tempest let loose from prison, and the still water boiling up from its depths, and lifting
45 his head calm above the waves, looked forth across the deep. He sees all ocean strewn with Aeneas' fleet, the Trojans overwhelmed by the waves and the ruining heaven. Juno's guile and wrath lay clear to her brother's eye; east wind and west he calls before him, and thereon speaks thus:

Aeneas complains aloud that he will drown in a storm at sea, rather than die nobly. Meanwhile, his ships wreck and his troops drown.

'Stand you then so sure in your confidence of birth? Careless, O winds, of my deity, dare you confound sky and earth, and raise so huge a coil? you whom I—But better to still the aroused waves; for a second sin you shall pay me another penalty. Speed your flight, and say this to your king: not to him but to me was allotted the stern trident of
5   ocean empire. His fastness is on the monstrous rocks where thou and thine, east wind, dwell: there let Aeolus glory in his palace and reign over the barred prison of his winds.'

Thus he speaks, and ere the words are done he soothes the swollen seas, chases away the gathered clouds, and restores the sunlight. Cymothoë and Triton together push the ships strongly off the sharp reef; himself he eases them with his trident, channels the
10 vast quicksands, and assuages the sea, gliding on light wheels along the water. Even as when oft in a throng of people strife hath risen, and the base multitude rage in their minds, and now brands and stones are flying; madness lends arms; then if perchance they catch sight of one reverend for goodness and service, they are silent and stand by with attentive ear; he with speech sways their temper and soothes their breasts; even so
15 hath fallen all the thunder of ocean, when riding forward beneath a cloudless sky the lord of the sea wheels his coursers and lets his gliding chariot fly with loosened rein.

Aeneas and his navy take shelter in enemy harbor, off the coast of Libya. He delivers a motivational speech to his troops.

The outworn Aeneadae hasten to run for the nearest shore, and turn to the coast of Libya. There lies a spot deep withdrawn; an island forms a harbour with outstretched sides, whereon all the waves break from the open sea and part into the hollows of the
20 bay. On this side and that enormous cliffs rise threatening heaven, and twin crags beneath whose crest the sheltered water lies wide and calm; above hangs a background of flickering forest, and the dark shade of rustling groves. Beneath the seaward brow is a rock-hung cavern, within it fresh springs and seats in the living stone, a haunt of nymphs; where tired ships need no fetters to hold nor anchor to fasten them with
25 crooked bite. Here with seven sail gathered of all his company Aeneas enters; and disembarking on the land of their desire the Trojans gain the chosen beach, and set their feet dripping with brine upon the shore. At once Achates struck a spark from the flint and caught the fire on leaves, and laying dry fuel round kindled it into flame. Then, weary of fortune, they fetch out corn spoiled by the sea and weapons of corn-dressing,
30 and begin to parch over the fire and bruise in stones the grain they had rescued.

Meanwhile Aeneas scales the crag, and seeks the whole view wide over ocean, if he may see aught of Antheus storm-tossed with his Phrygian galleys, aught of Capys or of Caïcus' armour high astern. Ship in sight is none; three stags he espies straying on the shore; behind whole herds follow, and graze in long train across the valley. Stopping
35 short, he snatched up a bow and swift arrows, the arms trusty Achates was carrying; and first the leaders, their stately heads high with branching antlers, then the common herd fall to his hand, as he drives them with his shafts in a broken crowd through the leafy woods. Nor stays he till seven great victims are stretched on the sod, fulfilling the number of his ships. Thence he seeks the harbour and parts them among all his
40 company. The casks of wine that good Acestes had filled on the Trinacrian beach, the hero's gift at their departure, he thereafter shares, and calms with speech their sorrowing hearts:

'O comrades, for not now nor aforetime are we ignorant of ill, O tried by heavier fortunes, unto this last likewise will God appoint an end. The fury of Scylla and the
45 roaring recesses of her crags you have been anigh; the rocks of the Cyclops you have trodden. Recall your courage, put dull fear away. This too sometime we shall haply remember with delight. Through chequered fortunes, through many perilous ways, we steer for Latium, where destiny points us a quiet home. There the realm of Troy may rise again unforbidden. Keep heart, and endure till prosperous fortune come.'

Such words he utters, and sick with deep distress he feigns hope on his face, and keeps his anguish hidden deep in his breast. The others set to the spoil they are to feast upon, tear chine from ribs and lay bare the flesh; some cut it into pieces and pierce it still quivering with spits; others plant cauldrons on the beach and feed them with flame.
5 Then they repair their strength with food, and lying along the grass take their fill of old wine and fat venison. After hunger is driven from the banquet, and the board cleared, they talk with lingering regret of their lost companions, swaying between hope and fear, whether they may believe them yet alive, or now in their last agony and deaf to mortal call. Most does good Aeneas inly wail the loss now of valiant Orontes, now of Amycus,
10 the cruel doom of Lycus, of brave Gyas, and brave Cloanthus. And now they ceased; when from the height of air Jupiter looked down on the sail-winged sea and outspread lands, the shores and broad countries, and looking stood on the cope of heaven, and cast down his eyes on the realm of Libya. To him thus troubled at heart Venus, her bright eyes brimming with tears, sorrowfully speaks:

15 'O thou who dost sway mortal and immortal things with eternal command and the terror of thy thunderbolt, how can my Aeneas have transgressed so grievously against thee? how his Trojans? on whom, after so many deaths outgone, all the world is barred for Italy's sake. From them sometime in the rolling years the Romans were to arise indeed; from them were to be rulers who, renewing the blood of Teucer, should hold
20 sea and land in universal lordship. This thou didst promise: why, O father, is thy decree reversed? This was my solace for the wretched ruin of sunken Troy, doom balanced against doom. Now so many woes are spent, and the same fortune still pursues them; Lord and King, what limit dost thou set to their agony? Antenor could elude the encircling Achaeans, could thread in safety the Illyrian bays and inmost realms of the
25 Liburnians, could climb Timavus' source, whence through nine mouths pours the bursting tide amid dreary moans of the mountain, and covers the fields with hoarse waters. Yet here did he set Patavium town, a dwelling-place for his Teucrians, gave his name to a nation and hung up the armour of Troy; now settled in peace, he rests and is in quiet. We, thy children, we whom thou beckonest to the heights of heaven, our fleet
30 miserably cast away for a single enemy's anger, are betrayed and severed far from the Italian coasts. Is this the reward of goodness? Is it thus thou dost restore our throne?'

Smiling on her with that look which clears sky and storms, the parent of men and gods lightly kissed his daughter's lips; then answered thus:

'Spare thy fear, Cytherean; thy people's destiny abides unshaken. Thine eyes shall see
35 the city Lavinium, their promised home; thou shalt exalt to the starry heaven thy noble Aeneas; nor is my decree reversed. He thou lovest (for I will speak, since this care keeps torturing thee, and will unroll further the secret records of fate) shall wage a great war in Italy, and crush warrior nations; he shall appoint his people a law and a city; till the third summer see him reigning in Latium, and three winters' camps pass over the
40 conquered Rutulians. But the boy Ascanius, whose surname is now Iülus—Ilus he was while the Ilian state stood sovereign—thirty great circles of rolling months shall he fulfil in government; he shall carry the kingdom from its fastness in Lavinium, and make a strong fortress of Alba the Long. Here the full space of thrice an hundred years shall the kingdom endure under the race of Hector's kin, till the royal priestess Ilia from Mars'
45 embrace shall give birth to a twin progeny. Thence shall Romulus, gay in the tawny hide of the she-wolf that nursed him, take up their line, and name them Romans after his own name. I appoint to these neither period nor boundary of empire: I have given them dominion without end. Nay, harsh Juno, who in her fear now troubles earth and sea and sky, shall change to better counsels, and with me shall cherish the lords of the world,
50 the gowned race of Rome. Thus is it willed. A day will come in the lapse of cycles, when

Aeneas's goddess-mother, Venus, questions Jupiter about her son's destiny. Notice that, in doubting the gods, she displays the same lack of piety that her son displays.

Jupiter assures Venus that Aeneas will arrive in Italy, and that centuries of peace and prosperity – PAX ROMANA – will become the legacy of the divinely-descended Octavian Augustus.

the house of Assaracus shall lay Phthia and famed Mycenae in bondage, and reign over conquered Argos. From the fair line of Troy a Caesar shall arise, who shall limit his empire with ocean, his glory with the firmament, Julius, inheritor of great Iülus' name. Him one day, thy care done, thou shalt welcome to heaven loaded with Eastern spoils;

5 to him too shall vows be addressed. Then shall war cease, and the iron ages soften. Hoar Faith and Vesta, Quirinus and Remus brothers again, shall deliver statutes. The dreadful steel-riveted gates of war shall be shut fast; on murderous weapons the inhuman Fury, his hands bound behind him with an hundred fetters of brass, shall sit within, shrieking with terrible blood-stained lips.'

10 So speaking, he sends Maia's son down from above, that the land and towers of Carthage, the new town, may receive the Trojans with open welcome; lest Dido, ignorant of doom, might debar them her land. Flying through the depth of air on winged oarage, the fleet messenger alights on the Libyan coasts. At once he does his bidding; at once, for a god willed it, the Phoenicians allay their haughty temper; the queen above

15 all takes to herself grace and compassion towards the Teucrians.

Disguised as a forest-nymph, Aeneas's mother asks her son his identity and his mission. What positive impact does her intervention seem to provide him here?

But good Aeneas, nightlong revolving many and many a thing, issues forth, so soon as bountiful light is given, to explore the strange country; to what coasts the wind has borne him, who are their habitants, men or wild beasts, for all he sees is wilderness; this he resolves to search, and bring back the certainty to his comrades. The fleet he hides

20 close in embosoming groves beneath a caverned rock, amid shivering shadow of the woodland; himself, Achates alone following, he strides forward, clenching in his hand two broad-headed spears. And amid the forest his mother crossed his way, wearing the face and raiment of a maiden, the arms of a maiden of Sparta, or like Harpalyce of Thrace when she tires her coursers and outstrips the winged speed of Hebrus in her

25 flight. For huntress fashion had she slung the ready bow from her shoulder, and left her blown tresses free, bared her knee, and knotted together her garments' flowing folds. 'Ha! my men,' she begins, 'shew me if haply you have seen a sister of mine straying here girt with quiver and a lynx's dappled fell, or pressing with shouts on the track of a foaming boar.'

30 Thus Venus, and Venus' son answering thus began:

'Sound nor sight have I had of sister of thine, O maiden unnamed; for thy face is not mortal, nor thy voice of human tone; O goddess assuredly! sister of Phoebus perchance, or one of the nymphs' blood? Be thou gracious, whoso thou art, and lighten this toil of ours; deign to instruct us beneath what skies, on what coast of the world, we are thrown.

35 Driven hither by wind and desolate waves, we wander in a strange land among unknown men. Many a sacrifice shall fall by our hand before thine altars.'

Then Venus: 'Nay, to no such offerings do I aspire. Tyrian maidens are wont ever to wear the quiver, to tie the purple buskin high above their ankle. Punic is the realm thou seest, Tyrian the people, and the city of Agenor's kin; but their borders are Libyan, a

40 race unassailable in war. Dido sways the sceptre, who flying her brother set sail from the Tyrian town. Long is the tale of crime, long and intricate; but I will briefly follow its argument. Her husband was Sychaeus, wealthiest in lands of the Phoenicians, and loved of her with ill-fated passion; to whom with virgin rites her father had given her maidenhood in wedlock. But the kingdom of Tyre was in her brother Pygmalion's

45 hands, a monster of guilt unparalleled. Between these madness came; the unnatural brother, blind with lust of gold, and reckless of his sister's love, lays Sychaeus low before the altars with stealthy unsuspected weapon; and for long he hid the deed, and by many a crafty pretence cheated her love-sickness with hollow hope. But in slumber came the

very ghost of her unburied husband; lifting up a face pale in wonderful wise, he exposed the merciless altars and his breast stabbed through with steel, and unwove all the blind web of household guilt. Then he counsels hasty flight out of the country, and to aid her passage discloses treasures long hidden underground, an untold mass of silver and gold.
5 Stirred thereby, Dido gathered a company for flight. All assemble in whom hatred of the tyrant was relentless or fear keen; they seize on ships that chanced to lie ready, and load them with the gold. Pygmalion's hoarded wealth is borne overseas; a woman leads the work. They came at last to the land where thou wilt descry a city now great, New Carthage, and her rising citadel, and bought ground, called thence Byrsa, as much as a
10 bull's hide would encircle. But who, I pray, are you, or from what coasts come, or whither hold you your way?'

At her question he, sighing and drawing speech deep from his breast, thus replied:

'Ah goddess, should I go on retracing from the fountain head, were time free to hear the history of our woes, sooner would the evening star lay day asleep in the closed gates
15 of heaven. Us, as from ancient Troy (if the name of Troy hath haply passed through your ears) we sailed over alien seas, the tempest at his own wild will hath driven on the Libyan coast. I am Aeneas the good, who carry in my fleet the household gods I rescued from the enemy; my fame is known high in heaven. I seek Italy my country, my kin of Jove's supreme blood. With twenty sail did I climb the Phrygian sea; oracular tokens led
20 me on; my goddess mother pointed the way; scarce seven survive the shattering of wave and wind. Myself unknown, destitute, driven from Europe and Asia, I wander over the Libyan wilderness.'

But staying longer complaint, Venus thus broke in on his half-told sorrows:

'Whoso thou art, not hated I think of the immortals dost thou draw the breath of life,
25 who hast reached the Tyrian city. Only go on, and betake thee hence to the courts of the queen. For I declare to thee thy comrades are restored, thy fleet driven back into safety by the shifted northern gales, except my parents were pretenders, and unavailing the augury they taught me. Behold these twelve swans in joyous line, whom, stooping from the tract of heaven, the bird of Jove fluttered over the open sky; now in long train
30 they seem either to take the ground or already to look down on the ground they took. As they again disport with clapping wings, and utter their notes as they circle the sky in company, even so do these ships and crews of thine either lie fast in harbour or glide under full sail into the harbour mouth. Only go on, and turn thy steps where the pathway leads thee.'

35 Speaking she turned away, and her neck shone roseate, her immortal tresses breathed the fragrance of deity; her raiment fell flowing down to her feet, and the godhead was manifest in her tread. He knew her for his mother, and with this cry pursued her flight: 'Thou also merciless! Why mockest thou thy son so often in feigned likeness? Why is it forbidden to clasp hand in hand, to hear and utter true speech?' Thus reproaching her
40 he bends his steps towards the city. But Venus girt them in their going with dull mist, and shed round them a deep divine clothing of cloud, that none might see them, none touch them, or work delay, or ask wherefore they came. Herself she speeds through the sky to Paphos, and joyfully revisits her habitation, where the temple and its hundred altars steam with Sabaean incense, and are fresh with fragrance of chaplets in her
45 worship.

Aeneas seems to recognize his mother. How do you explain his upset reaction?

Aeneas approaches Queen Dido's palace, while recounting Carthage's grandeur and history of battles with Rome. He and his troops are in the midst of an awesome enemy civilization.

They meantime have hasted along where the pathway points, and now were climbing the hill which hangs enormous over the city, and looks down on its facing towers. Aeneas marvels at the mass of building, pastoral huts once of old, marvels at the gateways and clatter of the pavements. The Tyrians are hot at work to trace the walls,
5 to rear the citadel, and roll up great stones by hand, or to choose a spot for their dwelling and enclose it with a furrow. They ordain justice and magistrates, and the august senate. Here some are digging harbours, here others lay the deep foundations of their theatre, and hew out of the cliff vast columns, the lofty ornaments of the stage to be: even as bees when summer is fresh over the flowery country ply their task beneath the sun,
10 when they lead forth their nation's grown brood, or when they press the liquid honey and strain their cells with nectarous sweets, or relieve the loaded incomers, or in banded array drive the idle herd of drones far from their folds; they swarm over their work, and the odorous honey smells sweet of thyme. 'Happy they whose city already rises!' cries Aeneas, looking on the town roofs below. Girt in the cloud he passes amid them,
15 wonderful to tell, and mingling with the throng is descried of none.

In the heart of the town was a grove deep with luxuriant shade, wherein first the Phoenicians, buffeted by wave and whirlwind, dug up the token Queen Juno had appointed, the head of a war horse: thereby was their race to be through all ages illustrious in war and opulent in living. Here to Juno was Sidonian Dido founding a vast
20 temple, rich with offerings and the sanctity of her godhead: brazen steps rose on the threshold, brass clamped the pilasters, doors of brass swung on grating hinges. First in this grove did a strange chance meet his steps and allay his fears; first here did Aeneas dare to hope for safety and have fairer trust in his shattered fortunes. For while he closely scans the temple that towers above him, while, awaiting the queen, he admires
25 the fortunate city, the emulous hands and elaborate work of her craftsmen, he sees ranged in order the battles of Ilium, that war whose fame was already rumoured through all the world, the sons of Atreus and Priam, and Achilles whom both found pitiless. He stopped and cried weeping, 'What land is left, Achates, what tract on earth that is not full of our agony? Behold Priam! Here too is the meed of honour, here mortal estate
30 touches the soul to tears. Dismiss thy fears; the fame of this will somehow bring thee salvation.'

Aeneas weeps when he sees the tale of Troy's defeat told in architectural sculptures.

So speaks he, and fills his soul with the painted show, sighing often the while, and his face wet with a full river of tears. For he saw, how warring round the Trojan citadel here the Greeks fled, the men of Troy hard on their rear; here the Phrygians, plumed Achilles
35 in his chariot pressing their flight. Not far away he knows the snowy canvas of Rhesus' tents, which, betrayed in their first sleep, the blood-stained son of Tydeus laid desolate in heaped slaughter, and turns the ruddy steeds away to the camp ere ever they tasted Trojan fodder or drunk of Xanthus. Elsewhere Troïlus, his armour flung away in flight—luckless boy, no match for Achilles to meet!—is borne along by his horses, and
40 thrown back entangled with his empty chariot, still clutching the reins; his neck and hair are dragged over the ground, and his reversed spear scores the dust. Meanwhile the Ilian women went with disordered tresses to unfriendly Pallas' temple, and bore the votive garment, sadly beating breast with palm: the goddess turning away held her eyes fast on the ground. Thrice had Achilles whirled Hector round the walls of Troy, and was selling
45 the lifeless body for gold; then at last he heaves a loud and heart-deep groan, as the spoils, as the chariot, as the dear body met his gaze, and Priam outstretching unarmed hands. Himself too he knew joining battle with the foremost Achaeans, knew the Eastern ranks and swart Memnon's armour. Penthesilea leads her crescent-shielded Amazonian columns in furious heat with thousands around her; clasping a golden belt
50 under her naked breast, the warrior maiden clashes boldly with men.

While these marvels meet Dardanian Aeneas' eyes, while he dizzily hangs rapt in one long gaze, Dido the queen entered the precinct, beautiful exceedingly, a youthful train thronging round her. Even as on Eurotas' banks or along the Cynthian ridges Diana wheels the dance, while behind her a thousand mountain nymphs crowd to left and
5 right; she carries quiver on shoulder, and as she moves outshines them all in deity; Latona's heart is thrilled with silent joy; such was Dido, so she joyously advanced amid the throng, urging on the business of her rising empire. Then in the gates of the goddess, beneath the central vault of the temple roof, she took her seat girt with arms and high enthroned. And now she gave justice and laws to her people, and adjusted or allotted
10 their taskwork in due portion; when suddenly Aeneas sees advancing with a great crowd about them Antheus and Sergestus and brave Cloanthus, and other of his Trojans, whom the black squall had sundered at sea and borne far away on the coast. Dizzy with the shock of joy and fear he and Achates together were on fire with eagerness to clasp their hands; but in confused uncertainty they keep hidden, and clothed in the sheltering
15 cloud wait to espy what fortune befalls them, where they are leaving their fleet ashore, why they now come; for they advanced, chosen men from all the ships, praying for grace, and held on with loud cries towards the temple.

After they entered in, and free speech was granted, aged Ilioneus with placid mien thus began:

20 'Queen, to whom Jupiter hath given to found this new city, and lay the yoke of justice upon haughty tribes, we beseech thee, we wretched Trojans storm-driven over all the seas, stay the dreadful flames from our ships; spare a guiltless race, and bend a gracious regard on our fortunes. We are not come to deal slaughter through Libyan homes, or to drive plundered spoils to the coast. Such violence sits not in our mind, nor is a
25 conquered people so insolent. There is a place Greeks name Hesperia, an ancient land, mighty in arms and foison of the clod; Oenotrian men dwelt therein; now rumour is that a younger race from their captain's name have called it Italy. Thither lay our course . . . when Orion rising on us through the cloudrack with sudden surf bore us on blind shoals, and scattered us afar with his boisterous gales and whelming brine over waves
30 and trackless reefs. To these your coasts we a scanty remnant floated up. What race of men, what land how barbarous soever, allows such a custom for its own? We are debarred the shelter of the beach; they rise in war, and forbid us to set foot on the brink of their land. If you slight human kinship and mortal arms, yet look for gods unforgetful of innocence and guilt. Aeneas was our king, foremost of men in righteousness,
35 incomparable in goodness as in warlike arms; whom if fate still preserves, if he draws the breath of heaven and lies not yet low in dispiteous gloom, fear we have none; nor mayest thou repent of challenging the contest of service. In Sicilian territory too is tilth and town, and famed Acestes himself of Trojan blood. Grant us to draw ashore our storm-shattered fleet, to shape forest trees into beams and strip them for oars; so, if to
40 Italy we may steer with our king and comrades found, Italy and Latium shall we gladly seek; but if salvation is clean gone, if the Libyan gulf holds thee, dear lord of thy Trojans, and Iülus our hope survives no more, seek we then at least the straits of Sicily, the open homes whence we sailed hither, and Acestes for our king.' Thus Ilioneus, and all the Dardanian company murmured assent. . . . Then Dido, with downcast face, briefly
45 speaks:

Enter Queen Dido.

Queen Dido addresses Aeneas and his troops.

'Cheer your anxious hearts, O Teucrians; put by your care. Hard fortune in a strange realm forces me to this task, to keep watch and ward on my wide frontiers. Who can be ignorant of the race of Aeneas' people, who of Troy town and her men and deeds, or of the great war's consuming fire? Not so dull are the hearts of our Punic wearing, not

5 so far doth the sun yoke his steeds from our Tyrian town. Whether your choice be broad Hesperia, the fields of Saturn's dominion, or Eryx for your country and Acestes for your king, my escort shall speed you in safety, my arsenals supply your need. Or will you even find rest here with me and share my kingdom? The city I establish is yours; draw your ships ashore; Trojan and Tyrian shall be held by me in even balance. And

10 would that he your king, that Aeneas were here, storm-driven to this same haven! But I will send messengers along the coast, and bid them trace Libya to its limits, if haply he strays shipwrecked in forest or town.'

Stirred by these words brave Achates and lord Aeneas both ere now burned to break through the cloud. Achates first accosts Aeneas: 'Goddess-born, what purpose now

15 rises in thy spirit? Thou seest all is safe, our fleet and comrades are restored. One only is wanting, whom our eyes saw whelmed amid the waves; all else is answerable to thy mother's words.'

Scarce had he spoken when the encircling cloud suddenly parts and melts into clear air. Aeneas stood discovered in sheen of brilliant light, like a god in face and shoulders; for

20 his mother's self had shed on her son the grace of clustered locks, the radiant light of youth, and the lustre of joyous eyes; as when ivory takes beauty under the artist's hand, or when silver or Parian stone is inlaid in gold. Then breaking in on all with unexpected speech he thus addresses the queen:

Aeneas introduces himself to Dido as a valiant and divinely-descended Trojan warrior.

'I whom you seek am here before you, Aeneas of Troy, snatched from the Libyan waves.

25 O thou who alone hast pitied Troy's untold agonies, thou who with us the remnant of the Grecian foe, worn out ere now by every suffering land and sea can bring, with us in our utter want dost share thy city and home! to render meet recompense is not possible for us, O Dido, nor for all who scattered over the wide world are left of our Dardanian race. The gods grant thee worthy reward, if their deity turn any regard on goodness, if

30 aught avails justice and conscious purity of soul. What happy ages bore thee? what mighty parents gave thy virtue birth? While rivers run into the sea, while the mountain shadows move across their slopes, while the stars have pasturage in heaven, ever shall thine honour, thy name and praises endure in the unknown lands that summon me.' With these words he advances his right hand to dear Ilioneus, his left to Serestus; then

35 to the rest, brave Gyas and brave Cloanthus.

Dido the Sidonian stood astonished, first at the sight of him, then at his strange fortunes; and these words left her lips:

Dido is awed by Aeneas's grandeur and offers him comfort in her palace.

'What fate follows thee, goddess-born, through perilous ways? what violence lands thee on this monstrous coast? Art thou that Aeneas whom Venus the bountiful bore to

40 Dardanian Anchises by the wave of Phrygian Simoïs? And well I remember how Teucer came to Sidon, when exiled from his native land he sought Belus' aid to gain new realms; Belus my father even then ravaged rich Cyprus and held it under his conquering sway. From that time forth have I known the fall of the Trojan city, known thy name and the Pelasgian princes. Their very foe would extol the Teucrians with highest praises, and

45 boasted himself a branch of the ancient Teucrian stem. Come therefore, O men, and enter our house. Me too hath a like fortune driven through many a woe, and willed at last to find my rest in this land. Not ignorant of ill do I learn to succour the afflicted.'

With such speech she leads Aeneas into the royal house, and orders sacrifice in the gods' temples. Therewith she sends his company on the shore twenty bulls, an hundred great bristly-backed swine, an hundred fat lambs and their mothers with them, gifts of the day's gladness. . . . But the palace within is decked with splendour of royal state, and a
5 banquet made ready amid the halls. The coverings are curiously wrought in splendid purple; on the tables is massy silver and deeds of ancestral valour graven in gold, all the long course of history drawn through many a heroic name from the nation's primal antiquity.

Aeneas follows Dido to her palace and leaves his troops behind.

Aeneas—for a father's affection denied his spirit rest—sends Achates speeding to his
10 ships, to carry this news to Ascanius, and lead him to the town: in Ascanius is fixed all the parent's loving care. Presents likewise he bids him bring saved from the wreck of Ilium, a mantle stiff with gold embroidery, and a veil with woven border of yellow acanthus-flower, that once decked Helen of Argos, the marvel of her mother Leda's giving; Helen had borne them from Mycenae, when she sought Troy towers and a
15 lawless bridal; the sceptre too that Ilione, Priam's eldest daughter, once had worn, a beaded necklace, and a double circlet of jewelled gold. Achates, hasting on his message, bent his way towards the ships.

But in the Cytherean's breast new arts, new schemes revolve; if Cupid, changed in form and feature, may come in sweet Ascanius' room, and his gifts kindle the queen to
20 madness and set her inmost sense aflame. Verily she fears the uncertain house, the double-tongued race of Tyre; cruel Juno frets her, and at nightfall her care floods back. Therefore to winged Love she speaks these words:

Venus orders Cupid to change his form into that of Aeneas' son, Ascanius. When Dido hugs Ascanius, she will feel Cupid's spell and feel affection for Aeneas (her enemy, whom she should revile).

'Son, who art alone my strength and sovereignty, son, who scornest the mighty father's Typhoïan shafts, to thee I fly for succour, and sue humbly to thy deity. How Aeneas
25 thy brother is driven about all the sea-coasts by bitter Juno's malignity, this thou knowest, and hast often grieved in our grief. Now Dido the Phoenician holds him stayed with soft words, and I tremble to think how the welcome of Juno's house may issue; she will not be idle in this supreme turn of fortune. Wherefore I counsel to prevent her wiles and circle the queen with flame, that, unalterable by any deity, she may be held
30 fast to me by passionate love for Aeneas. Take now my thought how to do this. The boy prince, my chiefest care, makes ready at his dear father's summons to go to the Sidonian city, carrying gifts that survive the sea and the flames of Troy. Him will I hide deep asleep in my holy habitation, high on Cythera's hills or in Idalium, that he may not know nor cross our wiles. Do thou but for one night feign his form, and, boy as thou
35 art, put on the familiar face of a boy; so when in festal cheer, amid royal dainties and Bacchic juice, Dido shall take thee to her lap, shall fold thee in her clasp and kiss thee close and sweet, thou mayest imbreathe a hidden fire and unsuspected poison.'

Love obeys his dear mother's words, lays by his wings, and walks rejoicingly with Iülus' tread. But Venus pours gentle dew of slumber on Ascanius' limbs, and lifts him lulled
40 in her lap to the tall Idalian groves of her deity, where soft amaracus folds him round with the shadowed sweetness of its odorous blossoms. And now, obedient to her words, Cupid went merrily in Achates' guiding, with the royal gifts for the Tyrians. Already at his coming the queen hath sate her down in the midmost on her golden throne under the splendid tapestries; now lord Aeneas, now too the men of Troy gather, and all
45 recline on the strewn purple. Servants pour water on their hands, serve corn from baskets, and bring napkins with close-cut pile. Fifty handmaids are within, whose task is in their course to keep unfailing store and kindle the household fire. An hundred others, and as many pages all of like age, load the board with food and array the wine cups. Therewithal the Tyrians are gathered full in the wide feasting chamber, and take

Cupid obeys Venus's orders.

Queen Dido, a widow, falls in love with Aeneas.

their appointed places on the broidered cushions. They marvel at Aeneas' gifts, marvel at Iülus, at the god's face aflame and forged speech, at the mantle and veil wrought with yellow acanthus-flower. Above all the hapless Phoenician, victim to coming doom, cannot satiate her soul, but, stirred alike by the boy and the gifts, she gazes and takes
5 fire. He, when hanging clasped on Aeneas' neck he had satisfied all the deluded parent's love, makes his way to the queen; the queen clings to him with her eyes and all her soul, and ever and anon fondles him in her lap, ah, poor Dido! witless how mighty a deity sinks into her breast; but he, mindful of his mother the Acidalian, begins touch by touch to efface Sychaeus, and sows the surprise of a living love in the long-since-unstirred
10 spirit and disaccustomed heart. Soon as the noise of banquet ceased and the board was cleared, they set down great bowls and enwreathe the wine. The house is filled with hum of voices eddying through the spacious chambers; lit lamps hang down by golden chainwork, and flaming tapers expel the night. Now the queen called for a heavy cup of jewelled gold, and filled it with pure wine; therewith was the use of Belus and all of
15 Belus' race: then the hall was silenced. 'Jupiter,' she cries, 'for thou art reputed lawgiver of hospitality, grant that this be a joyful day to the Tyrians and the voyagers from Troy, a day to live in our children's memory. Bacchus, the giver of gladness, be with us, and Juno the bountiful; and you, O Tyrians, be favourable to our assembly.' She spoke, and poured liquid libation on the board, which done, she first herself touched it lightly with
20 her lips, then handed it to Bitias and bade him speed; he valiantly drained the foaming cup, and flooded him with the brimming gold. The other princes followed. Long-haired Iopas on his gilded lyre fills the chamber with songs ancient Atlas taught; he sings of the wandering moon and the sun's travails; whence is the human race and the brute, whence water and fire; of Arcturus, the rainy Hyades, and the twin Oxen; why wintry
25 suns make such haste to dip in ocean, or what delay makes the nights drag lingeringly. Tyrians and Trojans after them redouble applause. Therewithal Dido wore the night in changing talk, alas! and drank long draughts of love, asking many a thing of Priam, many a thing of Hector; now in what armour the son of the Morning came; now of what fashion were Diomede's horses; now of mighty Achilles. 'Nay, come,' she cries, 'tell to

Dido asks Aeneas to tell her his stories of victories and defeats in battle.

30 us, O guest, from their first beginning the treachery of the Grecians, thy people's woes, and thine own wanderings; for this is now the seventh summer that bears thee a wanderer over all the earth and sea.'

BOOK FOURTH – THE LOVE OF DIDO, AND HER END

But the Queen, long ere now pierced with sore distress, feeds the wound with her life-blood, and catches the fire unseen. Again and again his own valiance and his line's renown flood back upon her spirit; look and accent cling fast in her bosom, and the pain allows not rest or calm to her limbs. The morrow's dawn bore the torch of Phoebus
5 across the earth, and had rolled away the dewy darkness from the sky, when, scarce herself, she thus opens her confidence to her sister:

Anna, my sister, such dreams of terror thrill me through! What guest unknown is this who hath entered our dwelling? How high his mien! how brave in heart as in arms! I believe it well, with no vain assurance, his blood is divine. Fear proves the vulgar spirit.
10 Alas, by what destinies is he driven! what wars outgone he chronicled! Were my mind not planted, fixed and immoveable, to ally myself to none in wedlock since my love of old was false to me in the treachery of death; were I not sick to the heart of bridal torch and chamber, to this temptation alone I might haply yield. Anna, I will confess it; since Sychaeus mine husband met his piteous doom, and our household was shattered by a
15 brother's murder, he only hath touched mine heart and stirred the balance of my soul. I know the prints of the ancient flame. But rather, I pray, may earth first yawn deep for me, or the Lord omnipotent hurl me with his thunderbolt into gloom, the pallid gloom and profound night of Erebus, ere I soil thee, mine honour, or unloose thy laws. He took my love away who made me one with him long ago; he shall keep it with him, and
20 guard it in the tomb.' She spoke, and welling tears filled the bosom of her gown.

The love-sick, Queen Dido, confides in her sister.

Anna replies: 'O dearer than the daylight to thy sister, wilt thou waste, sad and alone, all thy length of youth, and know not the sweetness of motherhood, nor love's bounty? Deemest thou the ashes care for that, or the ghost within the tomb? Be it so: in days gone by no wooers bent thy sorrow, not in Libya, not ere then in Tyre; Iarbas was
25 slighted, and other princes nurtured by the triumphal land of Africa; wilt thou contend so with a love to thy liking? nor does it cross thy mind whose are these fields about thy dwelling? On this side are the Gaetulian towns, a race unconquerable in war; the reinless Numidian riders and the grim Syrtis hem thee in; on this lies a thirsty tract of desert, swept by the raiders of Barca. Why speak of the war gathering from Tyre, and thy
30 brother's menaces? . . . With gods' auspices to my thinking, and with Juno's favour, hath the Ilian fleet held on hither before the gale. What a city wilt thou discern here, O sister! what a realm will rise on such a union! the arms of Troy ranged with ours, what glory will exalt the Punic state! Do thou only, asking divine favour with peace-offerings, be bounteous in welcome and draw out reasons for delay, while the storm rages at sea and
35 Orion is wet, and his ships are shattered and the sky unvoyageable.' With these words she made the fire of love flame up in her spirit, put hope in her wavering soul, and let honour slip away.

Dido's sister advises the queen to marry Aeneas and have children with him.

First they visit the shrines, and desire grace from altar to altar; they sacrifice sheep fitly chosen to Ceres the Lawgiver, to Phoebus and lord Lyaeus, to Juno before all, guardian
40 of the marriage bond. Dido herself, excellent in beauty, holds the cup in her hand, and pours libation between the horns of a milk-white cow, or moves in state to the rich altars before the gods' presences, day by day renewing her gifts, and gazing athirst into the breasts of cattle laid open to take counsel from the throbbing entrails. Ah, witless souls of soothsayers! how may vows or shrines help her madness? all the while the
45 subtle flame consumes her inly, and deep in her breast the wound is silent and alive.

Dido abandons her duties as queen of Carthage. Her love-crazed demeanor underscores a contrast in philosophies that the epic will play out: Dido's Epicureanism vs. Rome's Stoicism.

Stung to misery, Dido wanders in frenzy all down the city, even as an arrow-stricken deer, whom, far and heedless amid the Cretan woodland, a shepherd archer hath pierced and left the flying steel in her unaware; she ranges in flight the Dictaean forest lawns; fast in her side clings the deadly reed. Now she leads Aeneas with her through the town,
5 and displays her Sidonian treasure and ordered city; she essays to speak, and breaks off half-way in utterance. Now, as day wanes, she seeks the repeated banquet, and again madly pleads to hear the agonies of Ilium, and again hangs on the teller's lips. Thereafter, when all are gone their ways, and the dim moon in turn quenches her light, and the setting stars counsel to sleep, alone in the empty house she mourns, and flings herself
10 on the couch he left: distant she hears and sees him in the distance; or enthralled by the look he has of his father, she holds Ascanius on her lap, if so she may steal the love she may not utter. No more do the unfinished towers rise, no more do the people exercise in arms, nor work for safety in war on harbour or bastion; the works hang broken off, vast looming walls and engines towering into the sky.

15 So soon as she perceives her thus fast in the toils, and madly careless of her name, Jove's beloved wife, daughter of Saturn, accosts Venus thus:

'Noble indeed is the fame and splendid the spoils you win, thou and that boy of thine, and mighty the renown of deity, if two gods have vanquished one woman by treachery. Nor am I so blind to thy terror of our town, thine old suspicion of the high house of
20 Carthage. But what shall be the end? or why all this contest now? Nay, rather let us work an enduring peace and a bridal compact. Thou hast what all thy soul desired; Dido is on fire with love, and hath caught the madness through and through. Then rule we this people jointly in equal lordship; allow her to be a Phrygian husband's slave, and to lay her Tyrians for dowry in thine hand.'

25 To her—for she knew the dissembled purpose of her words, to turn the Teucrian kingdom away to the coasts of Libya—Venus thus began in answer: 'Who so mad as to reject these terms, or choose rather to try the fortune of war with thee? if only when done, as thou sayest, fortune follow. But I move in uncertainty of Jove's ordinance, whether he will that Tyrians and wanderers from Troy be one city, or approve the
30 mingling of peoples and the treaty of union. Thou art his wife, and thy prayers may essay his soul. Go on; I will follow.'

Then Queen Juno thus rejoined: 'That task shall ·be mine. Now, by what means the present need may be fulfilled, attend and I will explain in brief. Aeneas and Dido (alas and woe for her!) are to go hunting together in the woodland when to-morrow's rising
35 sun goes forth and his rays unveil the world. On them, while the beaters run up and down, and the lawns are girt with toils, will I pour down a blackening rain-cloud mingled with hail, and startle all the sky in thunder. Their company will scatter for shelter in the dim darkness; Dido and the Trojan captain shall take refuge in the same cavern. I will be there, and if thy goodwill is assured me, I will unite them in wedlock, and make her
40 wholly his; here shall Hymen be present.' The Cytherean gave ready assent to her request, and laughed at the wily invention.

Meanwhile Dawn rises forth of ocean. A chosen company issue from the gates while the morning star is high; they pour forth with meshed nets, toils, broad-headed hunting spears, Massylian horsemen and sinewy sleuth-hounds. At her doorway the chief of
45 Carthage await their queen, who yet lingers in her chamber, and her horse stands splendid in gold and purple with clattering feet and jaws champing on the foamy bit. At last she comes forth amid a great thronging train, girt in a Sidonian mantle, broidered with needlework; her quiver is of gold, her tresses knotted into gold, a golden buckle

Gods conspire to create a scene: Dido and Aeneas will consummate their love in a cave.

clasps up her crimson gown. Therewithal the Phrygian train advances with joyous Iülus.
Himself first and foremost of all, Aeneas joins her company and unites his party to hers:
even as Apollo, when he leaves wintry Lycia and the streams of Xanthus to visit his
mother's Delos, and renews the dance, while Cretans and Dryopes and painted
5   Agathyrsians mingle clamorous about his altars: himself he treads the Cynthian ridges,
and plaits his flowing hair with soft heavy sprays and entwines it with gold; the arrows
rattle on his shoulder: as lightly as he went Aeneas; such glow and beauty is on his
princely face. When they are come to the mountain heights and pathless coverts, lo,
wild goats driven from the cliff-tops run down the ridge; in another quarter stags speed
10   over the open plain and gather their flying column in a cloud of dust as they leave the
hills. But the boy Ascanius is in the valleys, exultant on his fiery horse, and gallops past
one and another, praying that among the unwarlike herds a foaming boar may issue or
a tawny lion descend the hill.

Meanwhile the sky begins to thicken and roar aloud. A rain-cloud comes down mingled
15   with hail; the Tyrian train and the men of Troy, and the Dardanian boy of Venus' son
scatter in fear, and seek shelter far over the fields. Streams pour from the hills. Dido
and the Trojan captain take refuge in the same cavern. Primeval Earth and Juno the
bridesmaid give the sign; fires flash out high in air, witnessing the union, and Nymphs
cry aloud on the mountain-top. That day opened the gate of death and the springs of
20   ill. For now Dido recks not of eye or tongue, nor sets her heart on love in secret: she
calls it marriage, and with this name veils her fall.

Cave scene occurs as the gods planned it. Dido interprets this moment as a sacred marriage.

Straightway Rumour runs through the great cities of Libya,—Rumour, than whom none
other is more swift to mischief; she thrives on restlessness and gains strength by going:
at first small and timorous; soon she lifts herself on high and paces the ground with
25   head hidden among the clouds. Her, one saith, Mother Earth, when stung by wrath
against the gods, bore last sister to Coeus and Enceladus, fleet-footed and swift of wing,
ominous, awful, vast; for every feather on her body is a waking eye beneath, wonderful
to tell, and a tongue, and as many loud lips and straining ears. By night she flits between
sky and land, shrilling through the dusk, and droops not her lids in sweet slumber; in
30   daylight she sits on guard upon tall towers or the ridge of the house-roof, and makes
great cities afraid; obstinate in perverseness and forgery no less than messenger of truth.
She then exultingly filled the countries with manifold talk, and blazoned alike what was
done and undone: one Aeneas is come, born of Trojan blood; on him beautiful Dido
thinks no shame to fling herself; now they hold their winter, long-drawn through mutual
35   caresses, regardless of their realms and enthralled by passionate dishonour. This the
pestilent goddess spreads abroad in the mouths of men, and bends her course right on
to King Iarbas, and with her words fires his spirit and swells his wrath.

Rumors of Dido's alliance with Aeneas circulate in Dido's city. The queen risks charges of treason. Dido's father begs Jupiter to stop the love affair, and to reset the two lovers on their separate courses in life.

He, the seed of Ammon by a ravished Garamantian Nymph, had built to Jove in his
wide realms an hundred great temples, an hundred altars, and consecrated the wakeful
40   fire that keeps watch by night before the gods perpetually, where the soil is fat with
blood of beasts and the courts blossom with pied garlands. And he, distracted and on
fire at the bitter tidings, before his altars, amid the divine presences, often, it is said,
bowed in prayer to Jove with uplifted hands:

'Jupiter omnipotent, to whom from the broidered cushions of their banqueting halls the
45   Maurusian people now pour Lenaean offering, lookest thou on this? or do we shudder
vainly when our father hurls the thunderbolt, and do blind fires in the clouds and idle
rumblings appal our soul? The woman who, wandering in our coasts, planted a small
town on purchased ground, to whom we gave fields by the shore and laws of settlement,
she hath spurned our alliance and taken Aeneas for lord of her realm. And now that

Paris, with his effeminate crew, his chin and oozy hair swathed in the turban of Maeonia, takes and keeps her; since to thy temples we bear oblation, and hallow an empty name.'

In such words he pleaded, clasping the altars; the Lord omnipotent heard, and cast his eye on the royal city and the lovers forgetful of their fairer fame. Then he addresses this
5 charge to Mercury:

'Up and away, O son! call the breezes and slide down them on thy wings: accost the Dardanian captain who now loiters in Tyrian Carthage and casts not a look on destined cities; carry down my words through the fleet air. Not such an one did his mother most beautiful vouch him to us, nor for this twice rescue him from Grecian arms; but he was
10 to rule an Italy teeming with empire and loud with war, to transmit the line of Teucer's royal blood, and lay all the world beneath his law. If such glories kindle him in nowise, and he take no trouble for his own honour, does a father grudge his Ascanius the towers of Rome? with what device or in what hope loiters he among a hostile race, and casts not a glance on his Ausonian children and the fields of Lavinium? Let him set sail: this
15 is the sum: thereof be thou our messenger.'

He ended: his son made ready to obey his high command. And first he laces to his feet the shoes of gold that bear him high winging over seas or land as fleet as the gale; then takes the rod wherewith he calls wan souls forth of Orcus, or sends them again to the sad depth of hell, gives sleep and takes it away and unseals dead eyes; in whose strength
20 he courses the winds and swims across the tossing clouds. And now in flight he descries the peak and steep sides of toiling Atlas, whose crest sustains the sky; Atlas, whose pine-clad head is girt alway with black clouds and beaten by wind and rain; snow is shed over his shoulders for covering; rivers tumble over his aged chin; and his rough beard is stiff with ice. Here the Cyllenian, poised evenly on his wings, made a first stay; hence he shot
25 himself sheer to the water. Like a bird that flies low, skirting the sea about the craggy shores of its fishery, even thus the brood of Cyllene left his mother's father, and flew, cutting the winds between sky and land, along the sandy Libyan shore. So soon as his winged feet reached the settlement, he espies Aeneas founding towers and ordering new dwellings; his sword twinkled with yellow jasper, and a cloak hung from his shoulders
30 ablaze with Tyrian sea-purple, a gift that Dido had made costly and shot the warp with thin gold. Straightway he breaks in: 'Layest thou now the foundations of tall Carthage, and buildest up a fair city in dalliance? ah, forgetful of thine own kingdom and state! From bright Olympus I descend to thee at express command of heaven's sovereign, whose deity sways sky and earth; expressly he bids me carry this charge through the
35 fleet air: with what device or in what hope dost thou loiter idly on Libyan lands? if such glories kindle thee in nowise, yet cast an eye on growing Ascanius, on Iülus thine hope and heir, to whom the kingdom of Italy and the Roman land are due.' As these words left his lips the Cyllenian, yet speaking, quitted mortal sight and vanished into thin air away out of his eyes.

40 But Aeneas in truth gazed in dumb amazement, his hair thrilled up, and the accents faltered on his tongue. He burns to flee away and leave the pleasant land, aghast at the high warning and divine ordinance. Alas, what shall he do? how venture to smooth the tale to the frenzied queen? what prologue shall he find? and this way and that he rapidly throws his mind, and turns it on all hands in swift change of thought. In his perplexity
45 this seemed the better counsel; he calls Mnestheus and Sergestus, and brave Serestus, and bids them silently equip the fleet, gather their crews on shore, and order their armament, keeping the cause of the commotion hid; himself meanwhile, since Dido the gracious knows not nor looks for severance to so strong a love, will essay to approach

Jupiter answers the King's wishes. He sends Mercury to deliver his message to Aeneas: Leave Dido and resume your mission.

Mercury appears before Aeneas. His lecture to Aeneas emphasizes several Roman ideas and values that should be noted: Aeneas is free to ruin his own life, but is he free to ruin his son's life? How should we understand our duties to our family and to history? How important is our duty to fulfill our talents in life?

Aeneas instantly rallies to Mercury's call. His only concern is how to slip away without facing Dido's wrath.

her when she may be told most gently, and the way for it be fair. All at once gladly do as bidden, and obey his command.

But the Queen—who may delude a lover?—foreknew his devices, and at once caught the presaging stir. Safety's self was fear; to her likewise had evil Rumour borne the
5   maddening news that they equip the fleet and prepare for passage. Helpless at heart, she reels aflame with rage throughout the city, even as the startled Thyiad in her frenzied triennial orgies, when the holy vessels move forth and the cry of Bacchus re-echoes, and Cithaeron calls her with nightlong din. Thus at last she opens out upon Aeneas:

'And thou didst hope, traitor, to mask the crime, and slip away in silence from my land?
10 Our love holds thee not, nor the hand thou once gavest, nor the bitter death that is left for Dido's portion? Nay, under the wintry star thou labourest on thy fleet, and hastenest to launch into the deep amid northern gales; ah, cruel! Why, were thy quest not of alien fields and unknown dwellings, did thine ancient Troy remain, should Troy be sought in voyages over tossing seas? Fliest thou from me? me who by these tears and thine own
15 hand beseech thee, since naught else, alas! have I kept mine own—by our union and the marriage rites preparing; if I have done thee any grace, or aught of mine hath once been sweet in thy sight,—pity our sinking house, and if there yet be room for prayers, put off this purpose of thine. For thy sake Libyan tribes and Nomad kings are hostile; my Tyrians are estranged; for thy sake, thine, is mine honour perished, and the former
20 fame, my one title to the skies. How leavest thou me to die, O my guest? since to this the name of husband is dwindled down. For what do I wait? till Pygmalion overthrow his sister's city, or Gaetulian Iarbas lead me to captivity? At least if before thy flight a child of thine had been clasped in my arms,—if a tiny Aeneas were playing in my hall, whose face might yet image thine,—I would not think myself ensnared and deserted
25 utterly.'

She ended; he by counsel of Jove held his gaze unstirred, and kept his distress hard down in his heart. At last he briefly answers:

'Never, O Queen, will I deny that thy goodness hath gone high as thy words can swell the reckoning; nor will my memory of Elissa be ungracious while I remember myself,
30 and breath sways this body. Little will I say in this. I never hoped to slip away in stealthy flight; fancy not that; nor did I ever hold out the marriage torch or enter thus into alliance. Did fate allow me to guide my life by mine own government, and calm my sorrows as I would, my first duty were to the Trojan city and the dear remnant of my kindred; the high house of Priam should abide, and my hand had set up Troy towers
35 anew for a conquered people. But now for broad Italy hath Apollo of Grynos bidden me steer, for Italy the oracles of Lycia. Here is my desire; this is my native country. If thy Phoenician eyes are stayed on Carthage towers and thy Libyan city, what wrong is it, I pray, that we Trojans find our rest on Ausonian land? We too may seek a foreign realm unforbidden. In my sleep, often as the dank shades of night veil the earth, often
40 as the stars lift their fires, the troubled phantom of my father Anchises comes in warning and dread; my boy Ascanius, how I wrong one so dear in cheating him of an Hesperian kingdom and destined fields. Now even the gods' interpreter, sent straight from Jove— I call both to witness—hath borne down his commands through the fleet air. Myself in broad daylight I saw the deity passing within the walls, and these ears drank his
45 utterance. Cease to madden me and thyself alike with plaints. Not of my will do I follow Italy. . . .'

Long ere he ended she gazes on him askance, turning her eyes from side to side and perusing him with silent glances; then thus wrathfully speaks:

Dido learns of Aeneas' plan to leave. She unleashes her rage against him. Note how her speech reveals a contrast to Mercury's speech. She is Aeneas' enemy not just territorially, but philosophically as well.

Aeneas behaves like the good Stoic.

Aeneas rejects Dido's charges that he has betrayed her. He counters her Epicurean speech with the Stoic perspective. Note his argument.

Dido's wrath intensifies. Note her irrational argument -- the quintessential Epicurean.

'No goddess was thy mother, nor Dardanus founder of thy line, traitor! but rough Caucasus bore thee on his iron crags, and Hyrcanian tigresses gave thee suck. For why do I conceal it? For what further outrage do I wait? Hath our weeping cost him a sigh, or a lowered glance? Hath he broken into tears, or had pity on his lover? Where, where
5 shall I begin? Now neither doth Queen Juno nor our Saturnian lord regard us with righteous eyes. Nowhere is trust safe. Cast ashore and destitute I welcomed him, and madly gave him place and portion in my kingdom; I found him his lost fleet and drew his crews from death. Alas, the fire of madness speeds me on. Now prophetic Apollo, now oracles of Lycia, now the very gods' interpreter sent straight from Jove through
10 the air carries these rude commands! Truly that is work for the gods, that a care to vex their peace! I detain thee not, nor gainsay thy words: go, follow thine Italy down the wind; seek thy realm overseas. Yet midway my hope is, if righteous gods can do aught at all, thou wilt drain the cup of vengeance on the rocks, and re-echo calls on Dido's name. In murky fires I will follow far away, and when chill death hath severed body
15 from soul, my ghost will haunt thee in every region. Wretch, thou shalt repay! I will hear; and the rumour of it shall reach me deep in the under world.'

Even on these words she breaks off her speech unfinished, and, sick at heart, escapes out of the air and sweeps round and away out of sight, leaving him in fear and much hesitance, and with much on his mind to say. Her women catch her in their arms, and
20 carry her swooning to her marble chamber and lay her on her bed.

Note Aeneas' self-restraint. He wants to comfort Dido, but he fulfills his divine commands.

But good Aeneas, though he would fain soothe and comfort her grief, and talk away her distress, with many a sigh, and melted in soul by his great love, yet fulfils the divine commands and returns to his fleet. Then indeed the Teucrians set to work, and haul down their tall ships all along the shore. The hulls are oiled and afloat; they carry from
25 the woodland green boughs for oars and massy logs unhewn, in hot haste to go. . . . One might descry them shifting their quarters and pouring out of all the town: even as ants, mindful of winter, plunder a great heap of wheat and store it in their house; a black column advances on the plain as they carry home their spoil on a narrow track through the grass. Some shove and strain with their shoulders at big grains, some marshal the
30 ranks and chastise delay; all the path is aswarm with work. What then were thy thoughts, O Dido, as thou sawest it? What sighs didst thou utter, viewing from the fortress roof the broad beach aswarm, and seeing before thine eyes the whole sea stirred with their noisy din? Injurious Love, to what dost thou not compel mortal hearts! Again, she must needs break into tears, again essay entreaty, and bow her spirit down to love, not to
35 leave aught untried and go to death in vain.

Dido weeps as she watches Aeneas prepare to sail away. She plans more attempts to dissuade him.

Dido summons her sister to comfort her. Her slavish surrendering to her emotions strikes a sharp contrast to Aeneas' self-control.

'Anna, thou seest the bustle that fills the shore. They have gathered round from every quarter; already their canvas woos the breezes, and the merry sailors have garlanded the sterns. This great pain, my sister, I shall have strength to bear, as I have had strength to foresee. Yet this one thing, Anna, for love and pity's sake—for of thee alone was the
40 traitor fain, to thee even his secret thoughts were confided, alone thou knewest his moods and tender fits—go, my sister, and humbly accost the haughty stranger: I did not take the Grecian oath in Aulis to root out the race of Troy; I sent no fleet against her fortresses; neither have I disentombed his father Anchises' ashes and ghost, that he should refuse my words entrance to his stubborn ears. Whither does he run? let him
45 grant this grace—alas, the last!—to his lover, and await fair winds and an easy passage. No more do I pray for the old delusive marriage, nor that he give up fair Latium and abandon a kingdom. A breathing-space I ask, to give my madness rest and room, till my very fortune teach my grief submission. This last favour I implore: sister, be pitiful; grant this to me, and I will restore it in full measure when I die.'

So she pleaded, and so her sister carries and recarries the piteous tale of weeping. But by no weeping is he stirred, inflexible to all the words he hears. Fate withstands, and lays divine bars on unmoved mortal ears. Even as when the eddying blasts of northern Alpine winds are emulous to uproot the secular strength of a mighty oak, it wails on,
5 and the trunk quivers and the high foliage strews the ground; the tree clings fast on the rocks, and high as her top soars into heaven, so deep strike her roots to hell; even thus is the hero buffeted with changeful perpetual accents, and distress thrills his mighty breast, while his purpose stays unstirred, and tears fall in vain.

Then indeed, hapless and dismayed by doom, Dido prays for death, and is weary of
10 gazing on the arch of heaven. The more to make her fulfil her purpose and quit the light, she saw, when she laid her gifts on the altars alight with incense, awful to tell, the holy streams blacken, and the wine turn as it poured into ghastly blood. Of this sight she spoke to none—no, not to her sister. Likewise there was within the house a marble temple of her ancient lord, kept of her in marvellous honour, and fastened with snowy
15 fleeces and festal boughs. Forth of it she seemed to hear her husband's voice crying and calling when night was dim upon earth, and alone on the house-tops the screech-owl often made moan with funeral note and long-drawn sobbing cry. Therewithal many a warning of wizards of old terrifies her with appalling presage. In her sleep fierce Aeneas drives her wildly, and ever she seems being left by herself alone, ever going
20 uncompanioned on a weary way, and seeking her Tyrians in a solitary land: even as frantic Pentheus sees the arrayed Furies and a double sun, and Thebes shows herself twofold to his eyes: or Agamemnonian Orestes, renowned in tragedy, when his mother pursues him armed with torches and dark serpents, and the Fatal Sisters crouch avenging in the doorway.

25 So when, overcome by her pangs, she caught the madness and resolved to die, she works out secretly the time and fashion, and accosts her sorrowing sister with mien hiding her design and hope calm on her brow.

'I have found a way, mine own—wish me joy, sisterlike—to restore him to me or release me of my love for him. Hard by the ocean limit and the set of sun is the extreme
30 Aethiopian land, where ancient Atlas turns on his shoulders the starred burning axletree of heaven. Out of it hath been shown to me a priestess of Massylian race, warder of the temple of the Hesperides, even she who gave the dragon his food, and kept the holy boughs on the tree, sprinkling clammy honey and slumberous poppy-seed. She professes with her spells to relax the purposes of whom she will, but on others to bring
35 passion and pain; to stay the river-waters and turn the stars backward: she calls up ghosts by night; thou shalt see earth moaning under foot and mountain-ashes descending from the hills. I take heaven, sweet, to witness, and thee, mine own darling sister, I do not willingly arm myself with the arts of magic. Do thou secretly raise a pyre in the inner court, and let them lay on it the arms that the accursed one left hanging in our chamber,
40 and all the dress he wore, and the bridal bed where I fell. It is good to wipe out all the wretch's traces, and the priestess orders thus.' So speaks she, and is silent, while pallor overruns her face. Yet Anna deems not her sister veils death behind these strange rites, and grasps not her wild purpose, nor fears aught deeper than at Sychaeus' death. So she makes ready as bidden.

Dido's sister repeatedly carries to Aeneas messages of Dido's anguish, but Aeneas remains resolved to leave. Note the sharp contrast: Dido's hysteria vs. Aeneas' focus.

Dido plans her suicide while Aeneas sails away. Note the contrasting solutions to pain: Dido's suicide versus Aeneas' endurance.

Dido surrenders to her "madness" and summons her sister a final time – this time to prepare her death bed.

Dido gathers memorabilia that
Aeneas left her. She scatters
them around her death bed.
Her infatuation and madness
intensifies.

But the Queen, the pyre being built up of piled faggots and sawn ilex in the inmost of
her dwelling, hangs the room with chaplets and garlands it with funeral boughs: on the
pillow she lays the dress he wore, the sword he left, and an image of him, knowing what
was to come. Altars are reared around, and the priestess, with hair undone, thrice peals
5 from her lips the hundred gods of Erebus and Chaos, and the triform Hecate, the triple-
faced maidenhood of Diana. Likewise she had sprinkled pretended waters of Avernus'
spring, and rank herbs are sought mown by moonlight with brazen sickles, dark with
milky venom, and sought is the talisman torn from a horse's forehead at birth ere the
dam could snatch it. . . . Herself, the holy cake in her pure hands, hard by the altars,
10 with one foot unshod and garments flowing loose, she invokes the gods ere she die,
and the stars that know of doom; then prays to whatsoever deity looks in righteousness
and remembrance on lovers ill allied.

Night fell; weary creatures took quiet slumber all over earth, and woodland and wild
waters had sunk to rest; now the stars wheel midway on their gliding path, now all the
15 country is silent, and beasts and gay birds that haunt liquid levels of lake or thorny rustic
thicket lay couched asleep under the still night. But not so the distressed Phoenician,
nor does she ever sink asleep or take the night upon eyes or breast; her pain redoubles,
and her love swells to renewed madness, as she tosses on the strong tide of wrath. Even
so she begins, and thus revolves with her heart alone:

Dido relates her fallen status.
She sees that her people view
her as a traitor. She blames her
sister for encouraging her to
love Aeneas.

20 'See, what do I? Shall I again make trial of mine old wooers that will scorn me? and
stoop to sue for a Numidian marriage among those whom already over and over I have
disdained for husbands? Then shall I follow the Ilian fleets and the uttermost bidding
of the Teucrians? because it is good to think they were once raised up by my succour,
or the grace of mine old kindness is fresh in their remembrance? And how should they
25 let me, if I would? or take the odious woman on their haughty ships? art thou ignorant,
ah me, even in ruin, and knowest not yet the forsworn race of Laomedon? And then?
shall I accompany the triumphant sailors, a lonely fugitive? or plunge forth girt with all
my Tyrian train? so hardly severed from Sidon city, shall I again drive them seaward,
and bid them spread their sails to the tempest? Nay die thou, as thou deservest, and let
30 the steel end thy pain. With thee it began; overborne by my tears, thou, O my sister,
dost load me with this madness and agony, and layest me open to the enemy. I could
not spend a wild life without stain, far from a bridal chamber, and free from touch of
distress like this! O faith ill kept, that was plighted to Sychaeus' ashes!' Thus her heart
broke in long lamentation.

Mercury awakens Aeneas and
advises him to leave Carthage.
The god reprimands Aeneas a
second time for lingering when
he should be on his mission.
The motif of sleep versus
wakefulness is an important
one for the hero candidate in
western and eastern myths.

35 Now Aeneas was fixed to go, and now, with all set duly in order, was taking hasty sleep
on his high stern. To him as he slept the god appeared once again in the same fashion
of countenance, and thus seemed to renew his warning, in all points like to Mercury,
voice and hue and golden hair and limbs gracious in youth. 'Goddess-born, canst thou
sleep on in such danger? and seest not the coming perils that hem thee in, madman! nor
40 hearest the breezes blowing fair? She, fixed on death, is revolving craft and crime grimly
in her bosom, and swells the changing surge of wrath. Fliest thou not hence headlong,
while headlong flight is yet possible? Even now wilt thou see ocean weltering with
broken timbers, see the fierce glare of torches and the beach in a riot of flame, if dawn
break on thee yet dallying in this land. Up ho! linger no more! Woman is ever a fickle
45 and changing thing.' So spoke he, and melted in the black night.

Aeneas rallies his troops to
leave Carthage at once. He
advises them that it is the will
of the gods.

Then indeed Aeneas, startled by the sudden phantom, leaps out of slumber and bestirs
his crew. 'Haste and awake, O men, and sit down to the thwarts; shake out sail speedily.
A god sent from high heaven, lo! again spurs us to speed our flight and cut the twisted
cables. We follow thee, holy one of heaven, whoso thou art, and again joyfully obey thy

command. O be favourable; give gracious aid and bring fair sky and weather.' He spoke, and snatching his sword like lightning from the sheath, strikes at the hawser with the drawn steel. The same zeal catches all at once; rushing and tearing they quit the shore; the sea is hidden under their fleets; strongly they toss up the foam and sweep the blue
5 water.

And now Dawn broke, and, leaving the saffron bed of Tithonus, shed her radiance anew over the world; when the Queen saw from her watch-tower the first light whitening, and the fleet standing out under squared sail, and discerned shore and haven empty of all their oarsmen. Thrice and four times she struck her hand on her lovely
10 breast and rent her yellow hair: 'God!' she cries, 'shall he go? shall an alien make mock of our realm? Will they not issue in armed pursuit from all the city, and some launch ships from the dockyards? Go; bring fire in haste, serve weapons, swing out the oars! What do I talk? or where am I? what mad change is on my purpose? Alas, Dido! now thou dost feel thy wickedness; that had graced thee once, when thou gavest away thy
15 crown. Behold the faith and hand of him! who, they say, carries his household's ancestral gods about with him! who stooped his shoulders to a father outworn with age! Could I not have riven his body in sunder and strewn it on the waves? and slain with the sword his comrades and his dear Ascanius, and served him for the banquet at his father's table? But the chance of battle had been dubious. If it had! whom did I fear with my death
20 upon me? I should have borne firebrands into his camp and filled his decks with flame, blotted out father and son and race together, and flung myself atop of all. Sun, whose fires lighten all the works of the world, and thou, Juno, mediatress and witness of these my distresses, and Hecate, cried on by night in crossways of cities, and you, fatal avenging sisters and gods of dying Elissa, hear me now; bend your just deity to my woes,
25 and listen to our prayers. If it must needs be that the accursed one touch his haven and float up to land, if thus Jove's decrees demand, and this is the appointed term,—yet, distressed in war by an armed and gallant nation, driven homeless from his borders, rent from Iülus' embrace, let him sue for succour and see death on death untimely on his people; nor when he hath yielded him to the terms of a harsh peace, may he have
30 joy of his kingdom or the pleasant light; but let him fall before his day and without burial on a waste of sand. This I pray; this and my blood with it I pour for the last utterance. And you, O Tyrians, hunt his seed with your hatred for all ages to come; send this guerdon to our ashes. Let no kindness nor truce be between the nations. Arise out of our dust, O unnamed avenger, to pursue the Dardanian settlement with firebrand
35 and steel. Now, then, whensoever strength shall be given, I invoke the enmity of shore to shore, wave to water, sword to sword; let their battles go down to their children's children.'

So speaks she as she kept turning her mind round about, seeking how soonest to break away from the hateful light. Thereon she speaks briefly to Barce, nurse of Sychaeus; for
40 a heap of dusky ashes held her own, in her country of long ago:

'Sweet nurse, bring Anna my sister hither to me. Bid her haste and sprinkle river water over her body, and bring with her the beasts ordained for expiation: so let her come: and thou likewise veil thy brows with a pure chaplet. I would fulfil the rites of Stygian Jove that I have fitly ordered and begun, so to set the limit to my distresses and give
45 over to the flames the funeral pyre of the Dardanian.'

Dido watches from her palace window as Aeneas and his fleet set sail. Note her shifting emotions expressed in her speech: sadness, anger, and rage.

Dido calls on her sister to help her prepare her funeral pyre.

In a fit of madness, Dido runs inside and prepares to kill herself with Aeneas's sword.

So speaks she; the old woman went eagerly with quickened pace. But Dido, fluttered and fierce in her awful purpose, with bloodshot restless gaze, and spots on her quivering cheeks burning through the pallor of imminent death, bursts into the inner courts of the house, and mounts in madness the high funeral pyre, and unsheathes the sword of
5 Dardania, a gift asked for no use like this. Then after her eyes fell on the Ilian raiment and the bed she knew, dallying a little with her purpose through her tears, she sank on the pillow and spoke the last words of all:

Dido delivers her final speech as she dies.

'Dress he wore, sweet while doom and deity allowed! receive my spirit now, and release me from my distresses. I have lived and fulfilled Fortune's allotted course; and now
10 shall I go a queenly phantom under the earth. I have built a renowned city; I have seen my ramparts rise; by my brother's punishment I have avenged my husband of his enemy; happy, ah me! and over happy, had but the keels of Dardania never touched our shores!' She spoke; and burying her face in the pillow, 'Death it will be,' she cries, 'and unavenged; but death be it. Thus, thus is it good to pass into the dark. Let the pitiless
15 Dardanian's gaze drink in this fire out at sea, and my death be the omen he carries on his way.'

Dido's attendants lament her death. Note their expression of not only grief, but betrayal.

She ceased; and even as she spoke her people see her sunk on the steel, and blood reeking on the sword and spattered on her hands. A cry rises in the high halls; Rumour riots down the quaking city. The house resounds with lamentation and sobbing and
20 bitter crying of women; heaven echoes their loud wails; even as though all Carthage or ancient Tyre went down as the foe poured in, and the flames rolled furious over the roofs of house and temple. Swooning at the sound, her sister runs in a flutter of dismay, with torn face and smitten bosom, and darts through them all, and calls the dying woman by her name. 'Was it this, mine own? Was my summons a snare? Was it this thy
25 pyre, ah me, this thine altar fires meant? How shall I begin my desolate moan? Didst thou disdain a sister's company in death? Thou shouldst have called me to share thy doom; in the self-same hour, the self-same pang of steel had been our portion. Did these very hands build it, did my voice call on our father's gods, that with thee lying thus I should be away as one without pity? Thou hast destroyed thyself and me together,
30 O my sister, and the Sidonian lords and people, and this thy city. Give her wounds water: I will bathe them and catch on my lips the last breath that haply yet lingers.' So speaking she had climbed the high steps, and, wailing, clasped and caressed her half-lifeless sister in her bosom, and stanched the dark streams of blood with her gown. She, essaying to lift her heavy eyes, swoons back; the deep-driven wound gurgles in her
35 breast. Thrice she rose, and strained to lift herself on her elbow; thrice she rolled back on the pillow, and with wandering eyes sought the light of high heaven, and moaned as she found it.

The gods pity Dido and release her from her painful life. Note, however, the emphasis here on the fact that Dido's tragic suicide was HER doing, and not the work of the gods.

Then Juno omnipotent, pitying her long pain and difficult decease, sent Iris down from heaven to unloose the struggling life from the body where it clung. For since neither by
40 fate did she perish, nor as one who had earned her death, but woefully before her day, and fired by sudden madness, not yet had Proserpine taken her lock from the golden head, nor sentenced her to the Stygian under world. So Iris on dewy saffron pinions flits down through the sky athwart the sun in a trail of a thousand changing dyes, and stopping over her head: 'This hair, sacred to Dis, I take as bidden, and release thee from
45 that body of thine.' So speaks she, and cuts it with her hand. And therewith all the warmth ebbed forth from her, and the life passed away upon the winds.

BOOK SIXTH – THE VISION OF THE UNDERWORLD

So speaks he weeping, and gives his fleet the rein, and at last glides in to Euboïc Cumae's coast. They turn the prows seaward; the ships grounded fast on their anchors' teeth, and the curving ships line the beach. The warrior band leaps forth eagerly on the Hesperian shore; some seek the seeds of flame hidden in veins of flint, some scour the woods, the thick coverts of wild beasts, and find and shew the streams. But good Aeneas seeks the fortress where Apollo sits high enthroned, and the lone mystery of the awful Sibyl's cavern depth, over whose mind and soul the prophetic Delian breathes high inspiration and reveals futurity.

Now they draw nigh the groves of Trivia and the roof of gold. Daedalus, as the story runs, when in flight from Minos' realm he dared to spread his fleet wings to the sky, glided on his unwonted way towards the icy northern star, and at length lit gently on the Chalcidian fastness. Here, on the first land he retrod, he dedicated his winged oarage to thee, O Phoebus, in the vast temple he built. On the doors is Androgeus' death; thereby the children of Cecrops, bidden, ah me! to pay for yearly ransom seven souls of their sons; the urn stands there, and the lots are drawn. Right opposite the land of Gnosus rises from the sea; on it is the cruel love of the bull, the disguised stealth of Pasiphaë, and the mingled breed and double issue of the Minotaur, record of a shameful passion; on it the famous dwelling's laborious inextricable maze; but Daedalus, pitying the great love of the princess, himself unlocked the tangled treachery of the palace, guiding with the clue her lover's blind footsteps. Thou too hadst no slight part in the work he wrought, O Icarus, did grief allow. Twice had he essayed to portray thy fate in gold; twice the father's hands dropped down. Nay, their eyes would scan all the story in order, were not Achates already returned from his errand, and with him the priestess of Phoebus and Trivia, Deïphobe daughter of Glaucus, who thus accosts the king: 'Other than this are the sights the time demands: now were it well to sacrifice seven unbroken bullocks of the herd, as many fitly chosen sheep of two years old.' Thus speaks she to Aeneas; nor do they delay to do her sacred bidding; and the priestess calls the Teucrians into the lofty shrine.

A vast cavern is scooped in the side of the Euboïc cliff, whither lead an hundred wide passages by an hundred gates, whence peal forth as manifold the responses of the Sibyl. They had reached the threshold, when the maiden cries: *It is time to enquire thy fate: the god, lo! the god!* And even as she spoke thus in the gateway, suddenly countenance nor colour nor ranged tresses stayed the same; her wild heart heaves madly in her panting bosom; and she expands to sight, and her voice is more than mortal, now the god breathes on her in nearer deity. 'Lingerest thou to vow and pray,' she cries, 'Aeneas of Troy? lingerest thou? for not till then will the vast portals of the spellbound house swing open.' So spoke she, and sank to silence. A cold shiver ran through the Teucrians' iron frames, and the king pours heart-deep supplication:

'Phoebus, who hast ever pitied the sore travail of Troy, who didst guide the Dardanian shaft from Paris' hand full on the son of Aeacus, in thy leading have I pierced all these seas that skirt mighty lands, the Massylian nations far withdrawn, and the fields the Syrtes fringe; thus far let the fortune of Troy follow us. You too may now unforbidden spare the nation of Pergama, gods and goddesses to whomsoever Ilium and the great glory of Dardania did wrong. And thou, O prophetess most holy, foreknower of the future, grant (for no unearned realm does my destiny claim) a resting-place in Latium

En route to Italy, Aeneas visits the underworld where he encounters the dead. He meets his dead father, his drowned troops, and Dido who killed herself when Aeneas left her. Watch closely how Aeneas copes with each of these encounters.

At the threshold to the underworld, the gods reveal to Aeneas his destiny. Note again the insistence that Aeneas should embrace his mission and not "linger". Aeneas sees several dead figures from mythology and from his own life.

to the Teucrians, to their wandering gods and the storm-tossed deities of Troy. Then will I ordain to Phoebus and Trivia a temple of solid marble, and festal days in Phoebus' name. Thee likewise a mighty sanctuary awaits in our realm. For here will I place thine oracles and the secrets of destiny uttered to my people, and consecrate chosen men, O
5 gracious one. Only commit not thou thy verses to leaves, lest they fly disordered, the sport of rushing winds; thyself utter them, I beseech thee.' His lips made an end of utterance.

But the prophetess, not yet tame to Phoebus' hand, rages fiercely in the cavern, so she may shake the mighty godhead from her breast; so much the more does he tire her
10 maddened mouth and subdue her wild breast and shape her to his pressure. And now the hundred mighty portals of the house open of their own accord, and bring through the air the answer of the soothsayer:

'O past at length with the great perils of the sea! though heavier yet by land await thee, the Dardanians shall come to the realm of Lavinium; relieve thy heart of this care; but
15 not so shall they have joy of their coming. Wars, grim wars I discern, and Tiber afoam with streams of blood. A Simoïs shall not fail thee, a Xanthus, a Dorian camp; another Achilles is already found for Latium, he too goddess-born; nor shall Juno's presence ever leave the Teucrians; while thou in thy need, to what nations or what towns of Italy shalt thou not sue! Again is an alien bride the source of all that Teucrian woe, again a
20 foreign marriage-chamber. . . . Yield not thou to distresses, but all the bolder go forth to meet them, as thy fortune shall allow thee way. The path of rescue, little as thou deemest it, shall first open from a Grecian town.'

Aeneas asks to see his deceased father. In an effort to persuade the gods to help him, Aeneas reminds the gods of previous mythological figures that they helped to descend into the underworld and whom they then returned to the living.

In such words the Sibyl of Cumae chants from the shrine her perplexing terrors, echoing through the cavern truth wrapped in obscurity: so does Apollo clash the reins and ply
25 the goad in her maddened breast. So soon as the spasm ceased and the raving lips sank to silence, Aeneas the hero begins: 'No shape of toil, O maiden, rises strange or sudden on my sight; all this ere now have I guessed and inly rehearsed in spirit. One thing I pray; since here is the gate named of the infernal king, and the darkling marsh of Acheron's overflow, be it given me to go to my beloved father, to see him face to face;
30 teach thou the way, and open the consecrated portals. Him on these shoulders I rescued from encircling flames and a thousand pursuing weapons, and brought him safe from amid the enemy; he accompanied my way over all the seas, and bore with me all the threats of ocean and sky, in weakness, beyond his age's strength and due. Nay, he it was who besought and enjoined me to seek thy grace and draw nigh thy courts. Have pity,
35 I beseech thee, on son and father, O gracious one! for thou art all-powerful, nor in vain hath Hecate given thee rule in the groves of Avernus. If Orpheus could call up his wife's ghost in the strength of his Thracian lyre and the music of the strings,—if Pollux redeemed his brother by exchange of death, and passes and repasses so often,—why make mention of great Theseus, why of Alcides? I too am of Jove's sovereign race.'

40 In such words he pleaded and clasped the altars; when the soothsayer thus began to speak:

The gods tell Aeneas that they will help him, but he will face the same danger that previous figures faced: once he descends, he may not be able to ascend from the underworld.

'O sprung of gods' blood, child of Anchises of Troy, easy is the descent into hell; all night and day the gate of dark Dis stands open; but to recall thy steps and issue to upper air, this is the task and burden. Some few of gods' lineage have availed, such as Jupiter's
45 gracious favour or virtue's ardour hath upborne to heaven. Midway all is muffled in forest, and the black coils of Cocytus circle it round. Yet if thy soul is so passionate and so desirous twice to float across the Stygian lake, twice to see dark Tartarus, and thy pleasure is to plunge into the mad task, learn what must first be accomplished. Hidden

in a shady tree is a bough with leafage and pliant shoot all of gold, consecrate to nether Juno, wrapped in the depth of woodland and shut in by dim dusky vales. But to him only who first hath plucked the golden-tressed fruitage from the tree is it given to enter the hidden places of the earth. This hath beautiful Proserpine ordained to be borne to
5 her for her proper gift. The first torn away, a second fills the place in gold, and the spray burgeons with even such ore again. So let thine eyes trace it home, and thine hand pluck it duly when found; for lightly and unreluctant will it follow if thine is fate's summons; else will no strength of thine avail to conquer it nor hard steel to cut it away. Yet again, a friend of thine lies a lifeless corpse, alas! thou knowest it not, and defiles all the fleet
10 with death, while thou seekest our counsel and lingerest in our courts. First lay him in his resting-place and hide him in the tomb; lead thither black cattle; be this first thine expiation; so at last shalt thou behold the Stygian groves and the realm untrodden of the living.' She spoke, and her lips shut to silence.

Aeneas goes forth, and leaves the cavern with fixed eyes and sad countenance, his soul
15 revolving inly the unseen issues. By his side goes faithful Achates, and plants his footsteps in equal perplexity. Long they ran on in mutual change of talk; of what lifeless comrade spoke the soothsayer, of what body for burial? And even as they came, they see on the dry beach Misenus cut off by untimely death, Misenus the Aeolid, excelled of none other in stirring men with brazen breath and kindling battle with his trumpet-
20 note. He had been attendant on mighty Hector; in Hector's train he waged battle, renowned alike for bugle and spear: after victorious Achilles robbed him of life the valiant hero had joined Dardanian Aeneas' company, and followed no meaner leader. But now, while he makes his hollow shell echo over the seas, ah fool! and calls the gods to rival his blast, jealous Triton, if belief is due, had caught him among the rocks and
25 sunk him in the foaming waves. So all surrounded him with loud murmur and cries, good Aeneas the foremost. Then weeping they quickly hasten on the Sibyl's orders, and work hard to pile trees for the altar of burial, and heap it up into the sky. They move into the ancient forest, the deep coverts of game; pitch-pines fall flat, ilex rings to the stroke of axes, and ashen beams and oak are split in clefts with wedges; they roll in huge
30 mountain-ashes from the hills. Aeneas likewise is first in the work, and cheers on his crew and arms himself with their weapons. And alone with his sad heart he ponders it all, gazing on the endless forest, and utters this prayer: 'If but now that bough of gold would shew itself to us on the tree in this depth of woodland! since all the soothsayer's tale of thee, Misenus, was, alas! too truly spoken.' Scarcely had he said thus, when twin
35 doves haply came flying down the sky, and lit on the green sod right under his eyes. Then the kingly hero knows them for his mother's birds, and joyfully prays: 'Ah, be my guides, if way there be, and direct your aëry passage into the groves where the rich bough overshadows the fertile ground! and thou, O goddess mother, fail not our wavering fortune.' So spoke he and stayed his steps, marking what they signify, whither
40 they urge their way. Feeding and flying they advance at such distance as following eyes could keep them in view; then, when they came to Avernus' pestilent gorge, they tower swiftly, and sliding down through the liquid air, choose their seat and light side by side on a tree, through whose boughs shone out the contrasting flicker of gold. As in chill mid-winter the woodland is wont to blossom with the strange leafage of the mistletoe,
45 sown on an alien tree and wreathing the smooth stems with burgeoning saffron; so on the shadowy ilex seemed that leafy gold, so the foil tinkled in the light breeze. Immediately Aeneas seizes it and eagerly breaks off its resistance, and carries it beneath the Sibyl's roof.

And therewithal the Teucrians on the beach wept Misenus, and bore the last rites to the
50 thankless ashes. First they build up a vast pyre of resinous billets and sawn oak, whose sides they entwine with dark leaves and plant funereal cypresses in front, and adorn it

Aeneas weeps to see his crew. He acknowledges that they died because of his irresponsibility.

Aeneas memorializes his crew.

above with his shining armour. Some prepare warm water in cauldrons bubbling over the flames, and wash and anoint the chill body, and make their moan; then, their weeping done, lay his limbs on the pillow, and spread over it crimson raiment, the accustomed pall. Some uplift the heavy bier, a melancholy service, and with averted
5 faces in their ancestral fashion hold and thrust in the torch. Gifts of frankincense, food, and bowls of olive oil, are poured and piled upon the fire. After the embers sank in and the flame died away, they soaked with wine the remnant of thirsty ashes, and Corynaeus gathered the bones and shut them in an urn of brass; and he too thrice encircled his comrades with fresh water, and cleansed them with light spray sprinkled from a bough
10 of fruitful olive, and spoke the last words of all. But good Aeneas heaps a mighty mounded tomb over him, with his own armour and his oar and trumpet, beneath a skyey mountain that now is called Misenus after him, and keeps his name immortal from age to age.

This done, he hastens to fulfil the Sibyl's ordinance. A deep cave yawned dreary and
15 vast, shingle-strewn, sheltered by the black lake and the gloom of the forests; over it no flying things could wing their way unharmed, such a vapour streamed from the dark gorge and rose into the overarching sky. Here the priestess first arrays four black-bodied bullocks and pours wine upon their forehead; and plucking the topmost hairs from between the horns, lays them on the sacred fire for first-offering, calling aloud on
20 Hecate, mistress of heaven and hell. Others lay knives beneath, and catch the warm blood in cups. Aeneas himself smites with the sword a black-fleeced she-lamb to the mother of the Eumenides and her mighty sister, and a barren heifer, Proserpine, to thee. Then he uprears darkling altars to the Stygian king, and lays whole carcases of bulls upon the flames, pouring fat oil over the blazing entrails. And lo! about the first rays of
25 sunrise the ground moaned underfoot, and the woodland ridges began to stir, and dogs seemed to howl through the dusk as the goddess came. 'Apart, ah keep apart, O ye unsanctified!' cries the soothsayer; 'retire from all the grove; and thou, stride on and unsheath thy steel; now is need of courage, O Aeneas, now of strong resolve.' So much she spoke, and plunged madly into the cavern's opening; he with unflinching steps keeps
30 pace with his advancing guide.

Gods who are sovereign over souls! silent ghosts, and Chaos and Phlegethon, the wide dumb realm of night! as I have heard, so let me tell, and according to your will unfold things sunken deep under earth in gloom.

Aeneas goes further into the underworld. He reaches the river that the dead souls cross. Hundreds of dead figures clamor for Charon, the ferryman that transports dead souls.

They went darkling through the dusk beneath the solitary night, through the empty
35 dwellings and bodiless realm of Dis; even as one walks in the forest beneath the jealous light of a doubtful moon, when Jupiter shrouds the sky in shadow and black night blots out the world. Right in front of the doorway and in the entry of the jaws of hell Grief and avenging Cares have made their bed; there dwell wan Sicknesses and gloomy Eld, and Fear, and ill-counselling Hunger, and loathly Want, shapes terrible to see; and Death
40 and Travail, and thereby Sleep, Death's kinsman, and the Soul's guilty Joys, and death-dealing War full in the gateway, and the Furies in their iron cells, and mad Discord with bloodstained fillets enwreathing her serpent locks.

Midway an elm, shadowy and high, spreads her boughs and secular arms, where, one saith, idle Dreams dwell clustering, and cling under every leaf. And monstrous creatures
45 besides, many and diverse, keep covert at the gates, Centaurs and twy-shaped Scyllas, and the hundredfold Briareus, and the beast of Lerna hissing horribly, and the Chimaera armed with flame, Gorgons and Harpies, and the body of the triform shade. Here Aeneas snatches at his sword in a sudden flutter of terror, and turns the naked edge on them as they come; and did not his wise fellow-passenger remind him that these lives

flit thin and unessential in the hollow mask of body, he would rush on and vainly lash through phantoms with his steel.

Hence a road leads to Tartarus and Acheron's wave. Here the dreary pool swirls thick in muddy eddies and disgorges into Cocytus with its load of sand. Charon, the dread
5   ferryman, guards these flowing streams, ragged and awful, his chin covered with untrimmed masses of hoary hair, and his glassy eyes aflame; his soiled raiment hangs knotted from his shoulders. Himself he plies the pole and trims the sails of his vessel, the steel-blue galley with freight of dead; stricken now in years, but a god's old age is lusty and green. Hither all crowded, and rushed streaming to the bank, matrons and
10 men and high-hearted heroes dead and done with life, boys and unwedded girls, and children laid young on the bier before their parents' eyes, multitudinous as leaves fall dropping in the forests at autumn's earliest frost, or birds swarm landward from the deep gulf, when the chill of the year routs them overseas and drives them to sunny lands. They stood pleading for the first passage across, and stretched forth passionate
15 hands to the farther shore. But the grim sailor admits now one and now another, while some he pushes back far apart on the strand. Moved with marvel at the confused throng: 'Say, O maiden,' cries Aeneas, 'what means this flocking to the river? of what are the souls so fain? or what difference makes these retire from the banks, those go with sweeping oars over the leaden waterways?'

20 To him the long-lived priestess thus briefly returned: 'Seed of Anchises, most sure progeny of gods, thou seest the deep pools of Cocytus and the Stygian marsh, by whose divinity the gods fear to swear falsely. All this crowd thou discernest is helpless and unsepultured; Charon is the ferryman; they who ride on the wave found a tomb. Nor is it given to cross the awful banks and hoarse streams ere the dust hath found a resting-
25 place. An hundred years they wander here flitting about the shore; then at last they gain entrance, and revisit the pools so sorely desired.'

Anchises' son stood still, and ponderingly stayed his footsteps, pitying at heart their cruel lot. There he discerns, mournful and unhonoured dead, Leucaspis and Orontes, captains of the Lycian squadron, whom, as they sailed together from Troy over gusty
30 seas, the south wind overwhelmed and wrapped the waters round ship and men.

Lo, there went by Palinurus the steersman, who of late, while he watched the stars on their Libyan passage, had slipped from the stern and fallen amid the waves. To him, when he first knew the melancholy form in that depth of shade, he thus opens speech: 'What god, O Palinurus, reft thee from us and sank thee amid the seas? forth and tell.
35 For in this single answer Apollo deceived me, never found false before, when he prophesied thee safety on ocean and arrival on the Ausonian coasts. See, is this his promise-keeping?'

And he: 'Neither did Phoebus on his oracular seat delude thee, O prince, Anchises' son, nor did any god drown me in the sea. For while I clung to my appointed charge and
40 governed our course, I pulled the tiller with me in my fall, and the shock as I slipped wrenched it away. By the rough seas I swear, fear for myself never wrung me so sore as for thy ship, lest, the rudder lost and the pilot struck away, those gathering waves might master it. Three wintry nights in the water the blustering south drove me over the endless sea; scarcely on the fourth dawn I descried Italy as I rose on the climbing wave.
45 Little by little I swam shoreward; already I clung safe; but while, encumbered with my dripping raiment, I caught with crooked fingers at the jagged needles of mountain rock, the barbarous people attacked me in arms and ignorantly deemed me a prize. Now the wave holds me, and the winds toss me on the shore. By heaven's pleasant light and

Note the description of a dreadful Charon and a population of helpless dead souls, who are desperate to cross the river of death and rest in the region of the dead.

Note that the priestess refers to Aeneas as "seed of Anchises, most pure progeny of gods" – a deliberate reminder of Aeneas's debt to his father and to his divine ancestry.

Aeneas sees the members of his crew that drowned en route to Italy. Recall that they drowned because Aeneas, their captain, abandoned his duties. Watch for Aeneas's apology to them.

Aeneas asks Palinurus, his steersman, what god allowed for him to drown.

Palinurus tells Aeneas how he died a slow death: three days treading water in the wintery ocean, then captured and tortured by tribes on land. He asks Aeneas to help him cross into the realm of the dead, assuming that Aeneas is guided by a divinity.

breezes I beseech thee, by thy father, by Iülus thy rising hope, rescue me from these distresses, O unconquered one! Either do thou, for thou canst, cast earth over me and again seek the haven of Velia; or do thou, if in any wise that may be, if in any wise the goddess who bore thee shews a way,—for not without divine will do I deem thou wilt
5 float across these vast rivers and the Stygian pool,—lend me a pitying hand, and bear me over the waves in thy company, that at least in death I may find a quiet resting-place.'

Aeneas soothes Palinurus's distress by assuring him that he will memorialize his valor.

Thus he ended, and the soothsayer thus began: 'Whence, O Palinurus, this fierce longing of thine? Shalt thou without burial behold the Stygian waters and the awful river of the
10 Furies? Cease to hope prayers may bend the decrees of heaven. But take my words to thy memory, for comfort in thy woeful case: far and wide shall the bordering cities be driven by celestial portents to appease thy dust; they shall rear a tomb, and pay the tomb a yearly offering, and for evermore shall the place keep Palinurus' name.' The words soothed away his distress, and for a while drove grief away from his sorrowing heart;
15 he is glad in the land of his name.

A guard of the underworld asks Aeneas why they are traveling among the dead. Aeneas and his guide assure the guard that they mean no harm and that Aeneas is there to meet his dead father, Anchises. Aeneas's guide gives a golden bough to the boatman to persuade him to take Aeneas and his guide on board. Note: there is a long mythological tradition associated with the golden bough.

So they complete their journey's beginning, and draw nigh the river. Just then the waterman descried them from the Stygian wave advancing through the silent woodland and turning their feet towards the bank, and opens on them in these words of challenge: 'Whoso thou art who marchest in arms towards our river, forth and say, there as thou
20 art, why thou comest, and stay thine advance. This is the land of Shadows, of Sleep, and slumberous Night; no living body may the Stygian hull convey. Nor truly had I joy of taking Alcides on the lake for passenger, nor Theseus and Pirithoüs, born of gods though they were and unconquered in might. He laid fettering hand on the warder of Tartarus, and dragged him cowering from the throne of my lord the King; they essayed
25 to ravish our mistress from the bridal chamber of Dis.' Thereto the Amphrysian soothsayer made brief reply: 'No such plot is here; be not moved; nor do our weapons offer violence; the huge gatekeeper may bark on for ever in his cavern and affright the bloodless ghosts; Proserpine may keep her honour within her uncle's gates. Aeneas of Troy, renowned in goodness as in arms, goes down to meet his father in the deep shades
30 of Erebus. If the sight of such affection stirs thee in nowise, yet this bough' (she discovers the bough hidden in her raiment) 'thou must know.' Then his heaving breast allays its anger, and he says no more; but marvelling at the awful gift, the fated rod so long unseen, he steers in his dusky vessel and draws to shore. Next he routs out the souls that sate on the long benches, and clears the thwarts, while he takes mighty Aeneas
35 on board. The galley groaned under the weight in all her seams, and the marsh-water leaked fast in. At length prophetess and prince are landed unscathed on the ugly ooze and livid sedge.

Aeneas's guide tosses a drugged cake to the 3-headed dog that guards the entrance to the underworld. The dog falls into a drunken sleep and Aeneas quickly enters the realm of the dead.

This realm rings with the triple-throated baying of vast Cerberus, couched huge in the cavern opposite; to whom the prophetess, seeing the serpents already bristling up on
40 his neck, throws a cake made slumberous with honey and drugged grain. He, with threefold jaws gaping in ravenous hunger, catches it when thrown, and sinks to earth with monstrous body outstretched, and sprawling huge over all his den. The warder overwhelmed, Aeneas makes entrance, and quickly issues from the bank of the irremeable wave.

Immediately wailing voices are loud in their ears, the souls of babies crying on the doorway sill, whom, torn from the breast and portionless in life's sweetness, a dark day cut off and drowned in bitter death. Hard by them are those condemned to death on false accusation. Neither indeed are these dwellings assigned without lot and judgment;
5   Minos presides and shakes the urn; he summons a council of the silent people, and inquires of their lives and charges. Next in order have these mourners their place whose own innocent hands dealt them death, who flung away their souls in hatred of the day. How fain were they now in upper air to endure their poverty and sore travail! It may not be; the unlovely pool locks them in her gloomy wave, and Styx pours her ninefold
10   barrier between. And not far from here are shewn stretching on every side the Wailing Fields; so they call them by name. Here they whom pitiless love hath wasted in cruel decay hide among untrodden ways, shrouded in embosoming myrtle thickets; not death itself ends their distresses. In this region he discerns Phaedra and Procris and woeful Eriphyle, shewing on her the wounds of her merciless son, and Evadne and Pasiphaë;
15   Laodamia goes in their company, and she who was once Caeneus and a man, now woman, and again returned by fate into her shape of old. Among whom Dido the Phoenician, fresh from her death-wound, wandered in the vast forest; by her the Trojan hero stood, and knew the dim form through the darkness, even as the moon at the month's beginning to him who sees or thinks he sees her rising through the vapours; he
20   let tears fall, and spoke to her lovingly and sweet:

'Alas, Dido! so the news was true that reached me; thou didst perish, and the sword sealed thy doom! Ah me, was I cause of thy death? By the stars I swear, by the heavenly powers and all that is sacred beneath the earth, unwillingly, O queen, I left thy shore. But the gods, at whose orders now I pass through this shadowy place, this land of
25   mouldering overgrowth and deep night, the gods' commands drove me forth; nor could I deem my departure would bring thee pain so great as this. Stay thy footstep, and withdraw not from our gaze. From whom fliest thou? the last speech of thee fate ordains me is this.'

In such words and with starting tears Aeneas soothed the burning and fierce-eyed soul.
30   She turned away with looks fixed fast on the ground, stirred no more in countenance by the speech he essays than if she stood in iron flint or Marpesian stone. At length she started, and fled wrathfully into the shadowy woodland, where Sychaeus, her ancient husband, responds to her distresses and equals her affection. Yet Aeneas, dismayed by her cruel doom, follows her far on her way with pitying tears.

35   Thence he pursues his appointed path. And now they trod those utmost fields where the renowned in war have their haunt apart. Here Tydeus meets him; here Parthenopaeus, glorious in arms, and the pallid phantom of Adrastus; here the Dardanians long wept on earth and fallen in the war; sighing he discerns all their long array, Glaucus and Medon and Thersilochus, the three children of Antenor, and
40   Polyphoetes, Ceres' priest, and Idaeus yet charioted, yet grasping his arms. The souls throng round him to right and left; nor is one look enough; lingering delighted, they pace by his side and enquire wherefore he is come. But the princes of the Grecians and Agamemnon's armies, when they see him glittering in arms through the gloom, hurry terror-stricken away; some turn backward, as when of old they fled to the ships; some
45   raise their voice faintly, and gasp out a broken ineffectual cry.

And here he saw Deïphobus son of Priam, with face cruelly torn, face and both hands, and ears lopped from his mangled temples, and nostrils maimed by a shameful wound. Barely he knew the cowering form that hid its dreadful punishment; then he springs to accost it in familiar speech:

Aeneas surveys the dead souls around him, noting their different causes of death. Some were condemned to death unjustly; others took their own lives. Among the suicides, Dido comes into Aeneas's view – her death-wound still fresh. Aeneas weeps when he sees her.

Aeneas openly grieves at Dido's sight. Note the questions that Aeneas's speech raises regarding fate and free will; self-control versus self-absorption; stoicism versus epicureanism.

Dido rejects Aeneas. Aeneas weeps and follows her. What price has the hero had to pay in order to achieve his destiny? What Roman messages emerge?

Aeneas surveys Greek and Trojan warriors that fought for their countries. When Agamemnon's Greek troops see the Roman warrior, Aeneas, they retreat in fear. Aeneas sees the Trojan warrior, Deiphobus, who was tortured to death.

'Deïphobus mighty in arms, seed of Teucer's royal blood, whose wantonness of vengeance was so cruel? who was allowed to use thee thus? Rumour reached me that on that last night, outwearied with endless slaughter, thou hadst sunk on the heap of mingled carnage. Then mine own hand reared an empty tomb on the Rhoetean shore,

5 mine own voice thrice called aloud upon thy ghost. Thy name and armour keep the spot; thee, O my friend, I could not see nor lay in the native earth I left.'

Whereto the son of Priam: 'In nothing, O my friend, wert thou wanting; thou hast paid the full to Deïphobus and the dead man's shade. But me my fate and the Laconian woman's murderous guilt thus dragged down to doom; these are the records of her

10 leaving. For how we spent that last night in delusive gladness thou knowest, and must needs remember too well. When the fated horse leapt down on the steep towers of Troy, bearing armed infantry for the burden of its womb, she, in feigned procession, led round our Phrygian women with Bacchic cries; herself she upreared a mighty flame amid them, and called the Grecians out of the fortress height. Then was I fast in mine

15 ill-fated bridal chamber, deep asleep and outworn with my charge, and lay overwhelmed in slumber sweet and profound and most like to easeful death. Meanwhile that crown of wives removes all the arms from my dwelling, and slips out the faithful sword from beneath my head: she calls Menelaus into the house and flings wide the gateway: be sure she hoped her lover would magnify the gift, and so she might quench the fame of her

20 ill deeds of old. Why do I linger? They burst into the chamber, they and the Aeolid, counsellor of crime, in their company. Gods, recompense the Greeks even thus, if with righteous lips I call for vengeance! But come, tell in turn what hap hath brought thee hither yet alive. Comest thou driven on ocean wanderings, or by promptings from heaven? or what fortune keeps thee from rest, that thou shouldst draw nigh these sad

25 sunless dwellings, this disordered land?'

In this change of talk Dawn had already crossed heaven's mid axle on her rose-charioted way; and haply had they thus drawn out all the allotted time; but the Sibyl made brief warning speech to her companion: 'Night falls, Aeneas; we waste the hours in weeping. Here is the place where the road disparts; by this that runs to the right under great Dis'

30 city is our path to Elysium; but the leftward wreaks vengeance on the wicked and sends them to unrelenting hell.' But Deïphobus: 'Be not angered, mighty priestess; I will depart, I will refill my place and return into darkness. Go, glory of our people, go, enjoy a fairer fate than mine.' Thus much he spoke, and on the word turned away his footsteps.

35 Aeneas looks swiftly back, and sees beneath the cliff on the left hand a wide city, girt with a triple wall and encircled by a racing river of boiling flame, Tartarean Phlegethon, that echoes over its rolling rocks. In front is the gate, huge and pillared with solid adamant, that no warring force of men nor the very habitants of heaven may avail to overthrow; it stands up a tower of iron, and Tisiphone sitting girt in bloodstained pall

40 keeps sleepless watch at the entry by night and day. Hence moans are heard and fierce lashes resound, with the clank of iron and dragging chains. Aeneas stopped and hung dismayed at the tumult. 'What shapes of crime are here? declare, O maiden; or what the punishment that pursues them, and all this upsurging wail?' Then the soothsayer thus began to speak: 'Illustrious chief of Troy, no pure foot may tread these guilty courts;

45 but to me Hecate herself, when she gave me rule over the groves of Avernus, taught how the gods punish, and guided me through all her realm. Gnosian Rhadamanthus here holds unrelaxing sway, chastises secret crime revealed, and exacts confession, wheresoever in the upper world one vainly exultant in stolen guilt hath till the dusk of death kept clear from the evil he wrought. Straightway avenging Tisiphone, girt with

50 her scourge, tramples down the shivering sinners, menaces them with the grim snakes

Deiphobus relates to Aeneas the story of the Trojan Horse that the Greeks used to gain entry into their city of Troy and then destroy it.

Aeneas's guide urges him to not waste time weeping and to move on to seek his father in Elysium, the land of virtuous souls. Deiphobus sends Aeneas off as the "glory of our people" and returns to his place in Hades.

Aeneas sees dead souls suffering terrible punishments for their crimes against the gods, against the state, or against their cultural values. Note the Roman messages regarding patriotism, personal behavior, and piety.

in her left hand, and summons forth her sisters in merciless train. Then at last the sacred gates are flung open and grate on the jarring hinge. Markest thou what sentry is seated in the doorway? what shape guards the threshold? More grim within sits the monstrous Hydra with her fifty black yawning throats: and Tartarus' self gapes sheer and strikes
5 into the gloom through twice the space that one looks upward to Olympus and the skyey heaven. Here Earth's ancient children, the Titans' brood, hurled down by the thunderbolt, lie wallowing in the abyss. Here likewise I saw the twin Aloïds, enormous of frame, who essayed with violent hands to pluck down high heaven and thrust Jove from his upper realm. Likewise I saw Salmoneus in the cruel payment he gives for
10 mocking Jove's flame and Olympus' thunders. Borne by four horses and brandishing a torch, he rode in triumph midway through the populous city of Grecian Elis, and claimed for himself the worship of deity; madman! who would mimic the storm-cloud and the inimitable bolt with brass that rang under his trampling horse-hoofs. But the Lord omnipotent hurled his shaft through thickening clouds (no firebrand his nor
15 smoky glare of torches) and dashed him headlong in the fury of the whirlwind. Therewithal Tityos might be seen, fosterling of Earth the mother of all, whose body stretches over nine full acres, and a monstrous vulture with crooked beak eats away the imperishable liver and the entrails that breed in suffering, and plunges deep into the breast that gives it food and dwelling; nor is any rest given to the fibres that ever grow
20 anew. Why tell of the Lapithae, of Ixion and Pirithoüs? over whom a stone hangs just slipping and just as though it fell; or the high banqueting couches gleam golden-pillared, and the feast is spread in royal luxury before their faces; couched hard by, the eldest of the Furies wards the tables from their touch and rises with torch upreared and thunderous lips. Here are they who hated their brethren while life endured, or struck a
25 parent or entangled a client in wrong, or who brooded alone over found treasure and shared it not with their fellows, this the greatest multitude of all; and they who were slain for adultery, and who followed unrighteous arms, and feared not to betray their masters' plighted hand. Imprisoned they await their doom. Seek not to be told that doom, that fashion of fortune wherein they are sunk. Some roll a vast stone, or hang
30 outstretched on the spokes of wheels; hapless Theseus sits and shall sit for ever, and Phlegyas in his misery gives counsel to all and witnesses aloud through the gloom, *Learn by this warning to do justly and not to slight the gods.* This man sold his country for gold, and laid her under a tyrant's sway; he set up and pulled down laws at a price; this other forced his daughter's bridal chamber and a forbidden marriage; all dared some
35 monstrous wickedness, and had success in what they dared. Not had I an hundred tongues, an hundred mouths, and a voice of iron, could I sum up all the shapes of crime or name over all their punishments.'

Thus spoke Phoebus' long-lived priestess; then 'But come now,' she cries; 'haste on the way and perfect the service begun; let us go faster; I descry the ramparts cast in
40 Cyclopean furnaces, and in front the arched gateway where they bid us lay the gifts foreordained.' She ended, and advancing side by side along the shadowy ways, they pass over and draw nigh the gates. Aeneas makes entrance, and sprinkling his body with fresh water, plants the bough full in the gateway.

Now at length, this fully done, and the service of the goddess perfected, they came to
45 the happy place, the green pleasances and blissful seats of the Fortunate Woodlands. Here an ampler air clothes the meadows in lustrous sheen, and they know their own sun and a starlight of their own. Some exercise their limbs in tournament on the greensward, contend in games, and wrestle on the yellow sand. Some dance with beating footfall and lips that sing; with them is the Thracian priest in sweeping robe, and makes
50 music to their measures with the notes' sevenfold interval, the notes struck now with his fingers, now with his ivory rod. Here is Teucer's ancient brood, a generation

Aeneas enters Elysium, where virtuous dead souls like his father reside. Note the Roman message.

excellent in beauty, high-hearted heroes born in happier years, Ilus and Assaracus, and Dardanus, founder of Troy. Afar he marvels at the armour and chariots empty of their lords: their spears stand fixed in the ground, and their unyoked horses pasture at large over the plain: their life's delight in chariot and armour, their care in pasturing their sleek
5 horses, follows them in like wise low under earth. Others, lo! he beholds feasting on the sward to right and left, and singing in chorus the glad Paean-cry, within a scented laurel-grove whence Eridanus river surges upward full-volumed through the wood. Here is the band of them who bore wounds in fighting for their country, and they who were pure in priesthood while life endured, and the good poets whose speech abased not
10 Apollo; and they who made life beautiful by the arts of their invention, and who won by service a memory among men, the brows of all girt with the snow-white fillet. To their encircling throng the Sibyl spoke thus, and to Musaeus before them all; for he is midmost of all the multitude, and stands out head and shoulders among their upward gaze:

15 'Tell, O blissful souls, and thou, poet most gracious, what region, what place hath Anchises for his own? For his sake are we come, and have sailed across the wide rivers of Erebus.'

And to her the hero thus made brief reply: 'None hath a fixed dwelling; we live in the shady woodlands; soft-swelling banks and meadows fresh with streams are our
20 habitation. But you, if this be your heart's desire, scale this ridge, and I will even now set you on an easy pathway.' He spoke, and paced on before them, and from above shews the shining plains; thereafter they leave the mountain heights.

Aeneas meets his dead father, Anchises, who weeps and says that Aeneas might have forgotten his mission when he fell in love with Dido.

But lord Anchises, deep in the green valley, was musing in earnest survey over the imprisoned souls destined to the daylight above, and haply reviewing his beloved
25 children and all the tale of his people, them and their fates and fortunes, their works and ways. And he, when he saw Aeneas advancing to meet him over the greensward, stretched forth both hands eagerly, while tears rolled over his cheeks, and his lips parted in a cry: 'Art thou come at last, and hath thy love, O child of my desire, conquered the difficult road? Is it granted, O my son, to gaze on thy face and hear and answer in
30 familiar tones? Thus indeed I forecast in spirit, counting the days between; nor hath my care misled me. What lands, what space of seas hast thou traversed to reach me, through what surge of perils, O my son! How I dreaded the realm of Libya might work thee harm!'

And he: 'Thy melancholy phantom, thine, O my father, came before me often and often,
35 and drove me to steer to these portals. My fleet is anchored on the Tyrrhenian brine. Give thine hand to clasp, O my father, give it, and withdraw not from our embrace.'

Aeneas tries unsuccessfully to embrace his father. How did his father's phantom keep Aeneas on course?

So spoke he, his face wet with abundant weeping. Thrice there did he essay to fling his arms about his neck; thrice the phantom vainly grasped fled out of his hands even as light wind, and most like to fluttering sleep

Meanwhile Aeneas sees deep withdrawn in the covert of the vale a woodland and rustling forest thickets, and the river of Lethe that floats past their peaceful dwellings. Around it flitted nations and peoples innumerable; even as in the meadows when in clear summer weather bees settle on the variegated flowers and stream round the snow-
5   white lilies, all the plain is murmurous with their humming. Aeneas starts at the sudden view, and asks the reason he knows not; what are those spreading streams, or who are they whose vast train fills the banks? Then lord Anchises: 'Souls, for whom second bodies are destined and due, drink at the wave of the Lethean stream the heedless water of long forgetfulness. These of a truth have I long desired to tell and shew thee face to
10 face, and number all the generation of thy children, that so thou mayest the more rejoice with me in finding Italy.'—'O father, must we think that any souls travel hence into upper air, and return again to bodily fetters? why this their strange sad longing for the light?' 'I will tell,' rejoins Anchises, 'nor will I hold thee in suspense, my son.' And he unfolds all things in order one by one.

15 'First of all, heaven and earth and the liquid fields, the shining orb of the moon and the Titanian star, doth a spirit sustain inly, and a soul shed abroad in them sways all their members and mingles in the mighty frame. Thence is the generation of man and beast, the life of winged things, and the monstrous forms that ocean breeds under his glittering floor. Those seeds have fiery force and divine birth, so far as they are not clogged by
20 taint of the body and dulled by earthy frames and limbs ready to die. Hence is it they fear and desire, sorrow and rejoice; nor can they pierce the air while barred in the blind darkness of their prison-house. Nay, and when the last ray of life is gone, not yet, alas! does all their woe, nor do all the plagues of the body wholly leave them free; and needs must be that many a long ingrained evil should take root marvellously deep. Therefore
25 they are schooled in punishment, and pay all the forfeit of a lifelong ill; some are hung stretched to the viewless winds; some have the taint of guilt washed out beneath the dreary deep, or burned away in fire. We suffer, each a several ghost; thereafter we are sent to the broad spaces of Elysium, some few of us to possess the happy fields; till length of days completing time's circle takes out the ingrained soilure and leaves
30 untainted the ethereal sense and pure spiritual flame. All these before thee, when the wheel of a thousand years hath come fully round, a God summons in vast train to the river of Lethe, that so they may regain in forgetfulness the slopes of upper earth, and begin to desire to return again into the body.'

Anchises ceased, and leads his son and the Sibyl likewise amid the assembled
35 murmurous throng, and mounts a hillock whence he might scan all the long ranks and learn their countenances as they came.

'Now come, the glory hereafter to follow our Dardanian progeny, the posterity to abide in our Italian people, illustrious souls and inheritors of our name to be, these will I rehearse, and instruct thee of thy destinies. He yonder, seest thou? the warrior leaning
40 on his pointless spear, holds the nearest place allotted in our groves, and shall rise first into the air of heaven from the mingling blood of Italy, Silvius of Alban name, the child of thine age, whom late in thy length of days thy wife Lavinia shall nurture in the woodland, king and father of kings; from him in Alba the Long shall our house have dominion. He next him is Procas, glory of the Trojan race; and Capys and Numitor;
45 and he who shall renew thy name, Silvius Aeneas, eminent alike in goodness or in arms, if ever he shall receive his kingdom in Alba. Men of men! see what strength they display, and wear the civic oak shading their brows. They shall establish Nomentum and Gabii and Fidena city, they the Collatine hill-fortress, Pometii and the Fort of Inuus, Bola and Cora: these shall be names that are now nameless lands. Nay, Romulus likewise, seed of
50 Mavors, shall join his grandsire's company, from his mother Ilia's nurture and Assaracus'

Aeneas and his father enjoy a happy reunion. His father shows him the river Lethe, a river of forgetfulness, on the other side of which resides a population of spirits waiting to be born on earth. These spirits will be the happy descendants of Aeneas and founders of the new Roman Empire.

Aeneas's father prophesizes Rome's glory. Note that Virgil assigns divine lineage to his emperor Augustus.

blood. Seest thou how the twin plumes straighten on his crest, and his father's own emblazonment already marks him for upper air? Behold, O son! by his augury shall Rome the renowned fill earth with her empire and heaven with her pride, and gird about seven fortresses with her single wall, prosperous mother of men; even as our lady of
5 Berecyntus rides in her chariot turret-crowned through the Phrygian cities, glad in the gods she hath borne, clasping an hundred of her children's children, all habitants of heaven, all dwellers on the upper heights. Hither now bend thy twin-eyed gaze; behold this people, the Romans that are thine. Here is Caesar and all Iülus' posterity that shall arise under the mighty cope of heaven. Here is he, he of whose promise once and again
10 thou hearest, Caesar Augustus, a god's son, who shall again establish the ages of gold in Latium over the fields that once were Saturn's realm, and carry his empire afar to Garamant and Indian, to the land that lies beyond our stars, beyond the sun's yearlong ways, where Atlas the sky-bearer wheels on his shoulder the glittering star-spangled pole. Before his coming even now the kingdoms of the Caspian shudder at oracular
15 answers, and the Maeotic land and the mouths of sevenfold Nile flutter in alarm. Nor indeed did Alcides traverse such spaces of earth, though he pierced the brazen-footed deer, or though he stilled the Erymanthian woodlands and made Lerna tremble at his bow: nor he who sways his team with reins of vine, Liber the conqueror, when he drives his tigers from Nysa's lofty crest. And do we yet hesitate to give valour scope in deeds,
20 or shrink in fear from setting foot on Ausonian land? Ah, and who is he apart, marked out with sprays of olive, offering sacrifice? I know the locks and hoary chin of the king of Rome who shall establish the infant city in his laws, sent from little Cures' sterile land to the majesty of empire. To him Tullus shall next succeed, who shall break the peace of his country and stir to arms men rusted from war and armies now disused to
25 triumphs; and hard on him over-vaunting Ancus follows, even now too elate in popular breath. Wilt thou see also the Tarquin kings, and the haughty soul of Brutus the Avenger, and the fasces regained? He shall first receive a consul's power and the merciless axes, and when his children would stir fresh war, the father, for fair freedom's sake, shall summon them to doom. Unhappy! yet howsoever posterity shall take the
30 deed, love of country and limitless passion for honour shall prevail. Nay, behold apart the Decii and the Drusi, Torquatus with his cruel axe, and Camillus returning with the standards. Yonder souls likewise, whom thou discernest gleaming in equal arms, at one now, while shut in Night, ah me! what mutual war, what battle-lines and bloodshed shall they arouse, so they attain the light of the living! father-in-law descending from the
35 Alpine barriers and the fortress of the Dweller Alone, son-in-law facing him with the embattled East. Nay, O my children, harden not your hearts to such warfare, neither turn upon her own heart the mastering might of your country; and thou, be thou first to forgive, who drawest thy descent from heaven; cast down the weapons from thy hand, O blood of mine. . . . He shall drive his conquering chariot to the Capitoline
40 height triumphant over Corinth, glorious in Achaean slaughter. He shall uproot Argos and Agamemnonian Mycenae, and the Aeacid's own heir, the seed of Achilles mighty in arms, avenging his ancestors in Troy and Minerva's polluted temple. Who might leave thee, lordly Cato, or thee, Cossus, to silence? who the Gracchan family, or these two sons of the Scipios, a double thunderbolt of war, Libya's bale? and Fabricius potent in
45 poverty, or thee, Serranus, sowing in the furrow? Whither whirl you me all breathless, O Fabii? thou art he, the most mighty, the one man whose lingering retrieves our State. Others shall beat out the breathing bronze to softer lines, I believe it well; shall draw living lineaments from the marble; the cause shall be more eloquent on their lips; their pencil shall portray the pathways of heaven, and tell the stars in their arising: be thy
50 charge, O Roman, to rule the nations in thine empire; this shall be thine art, to lay down the law of peace, to be merciful to the conquered and beat the haughty down.'

Thus lord Anchises, and as they marvel, he so pursues: 'Look how Marcellus the conqueror marches glorious in the splendid spoils, towering high above them all! He

Note the promise of a Roman Empire that will rule the world by divine edict. This notion of world domination and imperialism that is divinely ordained will guide the rule of the emperor Augustus.

shall stay the Roman State, reeling beneath the invading shock, shall ride down Carthaginian and insurgent Gaul, and a third time hang up the captured armour before lord Quirinus.'

And at this Aeneas, for he saw going by his side one excellent in beauty and glittering
5 in arms, but his brow had little cheer, and his eyes looked down:

'Who, O my father, is he who thus attends him on his way? son, or other of his children's princely race? How his comrades murmur around him! how goodly of presence he is! but dark Night flutters round his head with melancholy shade.'

Then lord Anchises with welling tears began: 'O my son, ask not of the great sorrow of
10 thy people. Him shall fate but shew to earth, and suffer not to stay further. Too mighty, lords of heaven, did you deem the brood of Rome, had this your gift been abiding. What moaning of men shall arise from the Field of Mavors by the imperial city! what a funeral train shalt thou see, O Tiber, as thou flowest by the new-made grave! Neither shall the boyhood of any of Ilian race raise his Latin forefathers' hope so high; nor shall the land
15 of Romulus ever boast of any fosterling like this. Alas his goodness, alas his antique honour, and right hand invincible in war! none had faced him unscathed in armed shock, whether he met the foe on foot, or ran his spurs into the flanks of his foaming horse. Ah me, the pity of thee, O boy! if in any wise thou breakest the grim bar of fate, thou shalt be Marcellus. Give me lilies in full hands; let me strew bright blossoms, and these
20 gifts at least let me lavish on my descendant's soul, and do the unavailing service.'

Thus they wander up and down over the whole region of broad vaporous plains, and scan all the scene. And when Anchises had led his son over it, each point by each, and kindled his spirit with passion for the glories on their way, he tells him thereafter of the war he next must wage, and instructs him of the Laurentine peoples and the city of
25 Latinus, and in what wise each task may be turned aside or borne.

There are twin portals of Sleep, whereof the one is fabled of horn, and by it real shadows are given easy outlet; the other shining white of polished ivory, but false visions issue upward from the ghostly world. With these words then Anchises follows forth his son and the Sibyl together there, and dismisses them by the ivory gate. He pursues his way
30 to the ships and revisits his comrades; then bears on to Caieta's haven straight along the shore. The anchor is cast from the prow; the sterns are grounded on the beach.

Anchises advises Aeneas not to regard the deaths of warriors as tragedies. They memorialize these men with flowers. Anchises shows Aeneas future battles that he will have to win in Italy.

Anchises guides Aeneas to the threshold to earth. Aeneas exits the underworld through the ivory gate and reunites with his troops. Why Aeneas returns through "the gate of deluding lies" rather than through the gate of horn (real dreams to be fulfilled) remains unresolved by scholars. What seems certain is that this visit with his father has renewed Aeneas. How so?

BOOK TWELFTH – THE SLAYING OF TURNUS

Aeneas finally arrives in Italy, the place where he was destined *to found a second Troy*. However, first he must battle with the Latin tribe's armies and with their general, Turnus.

When Turnus sees the Latins broken and fainting in the thwart issue of war, his promise claimed for fulfilment, and men's eyes pointed on him, his own spirit rises in unappeasable flame.

And therewithal Aeneas, terrible in his mother's armour, kindles for warfare and awakes
5 into wrath, rejoicing that offer of treaty stays the war. Comforting his comrades and sorrowing Iülus' fear, he instructs them of destiny, and bids bear answer of assurance to King Latinus, and name the laws of peace.

Meanwhile the kings go forth; Latinus in mighty pomp rides in his four-horse chariot; twelve gilded rays go glittering round his brows, symbol of the Sun his ancestor; Turnus
10 moves behind a white pair, clenching in his hand two broad-headed spears. On this side lord Aeneas, fount of the Roman race, ablaze in star like shield and celestial arms, and close by Ascanius, second hope of mighty Rome, issue from the camp; and the priest, in spotless raiment, hath brought the young of a bristly sow and an unshorn sheep of two years old, and set his beasts by the blazing altars. They, turning their eyes towards
15 the sunrising, scatter salted corn from their hands and clip the beasts with steel over the temples, and pour cups on the altars.

Then Aeneas the good, with sword drawn, thus makes invocation:

Aeneas prays to the gods for help and promises to unite with the Latins rather than to brutally conquer them.

'Be the Sun now witness, and this Earth to my call, for whose sake I have borne to suffer so sore travail, and the Lord omnipotent, and thou his wife, at last, divine
20 daughter of Saturn, at last I pray more favorable; and thou, mighty Mavors, who wieldest all warfare in lordship beneath thy sway; and on the Springs and Rivers I call, and the Dread of high heaven, and the divinities of the blue seas: if haply victory fall to Turnus the Ausonian, the vanquished make covenant to withdraw to Evander's city; Iülus shall quit the soil; nor ever hereafter shall the Aeneadae return in arms to renew
25 warfare, or attack this realm with the sword. But if Victory grant battle to us and ours (as I think the rather, and so the rather may the gods seal their will), I will not bid Italy obey my Teucrians, nor do I claim the realm for mine; let both nations, unconquered, join treaty forever under equal law. Gods and worship shall be of my giving: my father Latinus shall bear the sword, and have a father's prescribed command. For me my
30 Teucrians shall establish a city, and Lavinia give the town her name.'

Turnus leads his troops against Aeneas and his Trojan army.

But long ere this the Rutulians deemed the battle unequal, and their hearts are stirred in changeful motion; and now the more, as they discern nigher that in ill-matched strength, heightened by Turnus, as advancing with noiseless pace he humbly worships at the altar with downcast eye, by his wasted cheeks and the pallor on his youthful frame.

35 The startled Italians watch, while all the birds together clamorously wheel round from flight, wonderful to see, and dim the sky with their pinions, and in thickening cloud urge their foe through air, till, conquered by their attack and his heavy prey, he yielded and dropped it from his talons into the river, and winged his way deep into the clouds.

One of Turnus's men strike Aeneas's troops with a spear, which incites warfare.

The spear flies on; where haply stood opposite in ninefold brotherhood all the beautiful
40 sons of one faithful Tyrrhene wife, borne of her to Gylippus the Arcadian, one of them, midway where the sewn belt rubs on the flank and the clasp bites the fastenings of the side, one of them, excellent in beauty and glittering in arms, it pierces clean through the ribs and stretches on the yellow sand. But of his banded brethren, their courage fired

by grief, some grasp and draw their swords, some snatch weapons to throw, and rush blindly forward.

The Laurentine columns rush forth against them; again from the other side Trojans and Agyllines and Arcadians in painted armour flood thickly in: so hath one passion seized
5 all to make decision by the sword. They pull the altars to pieces; through all the air goes a thick storm of weapons, and faster falls the iron rain.

But good Aeneas, his head bared, kept stretching his unarmed hand and calling loudly to his men: 'Whither run you? What is this strife that so spreads and swells? Ah, restrain your wrath! truce is already stricken, and all its laws ordained; mine alone is the right of
10 battle. Leave me alone, and my hand shall confirm the treaty; these rites already make Turnus mine.' Amid these accents, amid words like these, lo! a whistling arrow winged its way to him, sped from what hand or driven by what god, none knows, or what chance or deity brought such honor to the Rutulians; the renown of the high deed was buried, nor did any boast to have dealt Aeneas' wound.

Aeneas tries to restrain his troops, but fails. Aeneas himself is struck by an enemy arrow. Turnus is buoyed by this; later, the gods heal Aeneas.

15 Turnus, when he saw Aeneas retreating from the ranks and his captains in dismay, burns hot with sudden hope. At once he calls for his horses and armour, and with a bound leaps proudly into his chariot and handles the reins. He darts on, dealing many a brave man's body to death; many and one he rolls half-slain, or crushes whole files under his chariot, or seizes and showers spears on the fugitives.

Troops try to withdraw arrow head from Aeneas.

20 And while Turnus thus victoriously deals death over the plains, Mnestheus meantime and faithful Achates, and Ascanius by their side, set down Aeneas in the camp, dabbled with blood and leaning every other step on his long spear. He storms, and tries hard to pull out the dart where the reed had broken, and calls for the nearest way of remedy, to cut open the wound with broad blade, and tear apart the weapon's lurking-place, and
25 so send him back to battle. And now Iapix son of Iasus came, beloved beyond others of Phoebus, to whom once of old, smitten with sharp desire, Apollo gladly offered his own arts and gifts, augury and the lyre and swift arrows: he, to lengthen out the destiny of a parent given over to die, chose rather to know the potency of herbs and the practice of healing, and deal in a silent art unrenowned. Aeneas stood chafing bitterly, propped
30 on his vast spear, mourning Iülus and a great crowd of men around, unstirred by their tears.

At this, stirred deep by her son's cruel pain, Venus his mother plucked from Cretan Ida a stalk of dittamy with downy leaves and bright-tressed flowers, the plant not unknown to wild goats when winged arrows are fast in their body. This Venus bore down, her
35 shape girt in a dim halo; this she steeps with secret healing in the river-water poured out and sparkling abrim, and sprinkles life-giving juice of ambrosia and scented balm. With that water aged Iapix washed the wound, unwitting; and suddenly, lo! all the pain left his body, all the blood in the deep wound was stanched. And now following his hand the arrow fell out with no force, and strength returned afresh as of old. 'Hasten! arms
40 for him quickly! why stand you?' cries Iapix aloud, and begins to kindle their courage against the enemy; 'this comes not by human resource or schooling of art, nor does my hand save thee, Aeneas: a higher god is at work, and sends thee back to higher deeds.'

Venus, Aeneas's goddess-mother, withdraws arrow head from her son; heals him.

He, eager for battle, had already clasped on the greaves of gold right and left, and scorning delay, brandishes his spear. When the shield is adjusted by his side and the
45 corslet on his back, he clasps Ascanius in his armed embrace, and lightly kissing him through the helmet, cries: 'Learn of me, O boy, valour and toil indeed, fortune of others.

Aeneas rallies to battle, strengthened and inspired by gods.

Now mine hand shall give thee defence in war, and lead thee to great reward: do thou, when hereafter thine age ripens to fulness, keep this in remembrance, and as thou recallest the pattern of thy kindred, let thy spirit rise to thy father Aeneas, thine uncle Hector.'

5   These words uttered, he issued towering from the gates, brandishing his mighty spear: with him in serried column rush Antheus and Mnestheus, and all the throng streams forth of the camp.

The two enemy generals, Aeneas and Turnus, battle in search of one another. Aeneas is given divine guidance.

Aeneas and Turnus, dash amid the battle; now, now wrath surges within them, and unconquerable hearts are torn; now in all their might they rush upon wounds.

10   At this Aeneas' mother most beautiful inspired him to advance on the walls, directing his columns on the town and dismaying the Latins with sudden and swift disaster. As in search for Turnus he bent his glance this way and that round the separate ranks, he descries the city free from all this warfare, unpunished and unstirred.

Straightway he kindles at the view of a greater battle; he summons Mnestheus and 15 Sergestus and brave Serestus his captains, and mounts a hillock; there the rest of the Teucrian army gathers thickly, still grasping shield and spear. Standing on the high mound amid them, he speaks: 'Be there no delay to my words; Jupiter is with us; neither let any be slower to move that the design is sudden. This city to-day, the source of war, the royal seat of Latinus, unless they yield them to receive our yoke and obey their 20 conquerors, will I raze to ground, and lay her smoking roofs level with the dust. Must I wait forsooth till Turnus please to stoop to combat, and choose again to face his conqueror? This, O citizens, is the fountain-head and crown of the accursed war. Bring brands speedily, and reclaim the treaty in fire.'

Turnus recognizes he is the weaker warrior, but resolves to fight Aeneas with honor.

I am resolved to face Aeneas, resolved to bear what bitterness there is in death; nor 25 shalt thou longer see me shamed, sister of mine. Let me be mad, I pray thee, with this madness before the end.' He spoke, and leapt swiftly from his chariot to the field, and darting through weapons and through enemies, leaves his sorrowing sister, and bursts in rapid course amid their columns.

Aeneas swiftly vanquishes Turnus's troops and meets Turnus.

But lord Aeneas, hearing Turnus' name, abandons the walls, abandons the fortress 30 height, and in exultant joy flings aside all hindrance, breaks off all work, and clashes his armour terribly, vast as Athos, or as Eryx, or as the lord of Apennine when he roars with his tossing ilex woods and rears his snowy crest rejoicing into air. Now indeed Rutulians and Trojans and all Italy turned in emulous gaze, and they who held the high city, and they whose ram was battering the foundations of the wall, and unarmed their 35 shoulders. Latinus himself stands in amaze at the mighty men, born in distant quarters of the world, met and making decision with the sword. And they, in the empty level field that cleared for them, darted swiftly forward, and hurling their spears from far, close in battle shock with clangor of brazen shields. Earth utters a moan; the sword-strokes fall thick and fast, chance and valour joining in one.

40 Therewith Aeneas pursues, though ever and anon his knees, disabled by the arrow, hinder and stay his speed; and foot hard on foot presses hotly on his hurrying enemy: as when a hunter courses with a fleet barking hound some stag caught in a river-loop or girt by the crimson-feathered toils, and he, in terror of the snares and the high river-bank, darts back and forward in a thousand ways; but the keen Umbrian clings agape, 45 and just catches at him, and as though he caught him snaps his jaws while the baffled

teeth close on vacancy. Then indeed a cry goes up, and banks and pools answer round about, and all the sky echoes the din. He, even as he flies, chides all his Rutulians, calling each by name, and shrieks for the sword he knew.

But Aeneas denounces death and instant doom if one of them draw nigh, and doubles
5   their terror with threats of their city's destruction, and though wounded presses on. Five circles they cover at full speed, and unwind as many this way and that; for not light nor slight is the prize they seek, but Turnus' very lifeblood is at issue. Here there haply had stood a bitter-leaved wild olive, sacred to Faunus, a tree worshipped by mariners of old; on it, when rescued from the waves, they were wont to fix their gifts to the god of
10 Laurentum and hang their votive raiment; but the Teucrians, unregarding, had cleared away the sacred stem, that they might meet on unimpeded lists.

Here stood Aeneas' spear; hither borne by its own speed it was held fast stuck in the tough root. The Dardanian stooped over it, and would wrench away the steel, to follow with the weapon him whom he could not catch in running. Then indeed Turnus cries
15 in frantic terror: 'Faunus, have pity, I beseech thee! and thou, most gracious Earth, keep thy hold on the steel, as I ever have kept your worship, and the Aeneadae again have polluted it in war.' He spoke, and called the god to aid in vows that fell not fruitless. For all Aeneas' strength, his long struggling and delay over the tough stem availed not to unclose the hard grip of the wood. While he strains and pulls hard, the Daunian
20 goddess, changing once more into the charioteer Metiscus' likeness, runs forward and passes her brother his sword. But Venus, indignant that the Nymph might be so bold, drew nigh and wrenched away the spear where it stuck deep in the root. Erect in fresh courage and arms, he with his faithful sword, he towering fierce over his spear, they face one another panting in the battle shock.

25 Meanwhile the King of Heaven's omnipotence accosts Juno as she gazes on the battle   Gods discuss the battle from on
from a sunlit cloud. 'What yet shall be the end, O wife? what remains at the last? Heaven   high and determine its finale.
claims Aeneas as his country's god, thou thyself knowest and avowest to know, and fate lifts him to the stars. With what device or in what hope hangest thou chill in cloudland? Was it well that a deity should be sullied by a mortal's wound? or that the lost sword--
30 for what without thee could Juturna avail?--should be restored to Turnus and swell the force of the vanquished? Forbear now, I pray, and bend to our entreaties; let not the pain thus devour thee in silence, and distress so often flood back on me from thy sweet lips. The end is come. Thou hast had power to hunt the Trojans over land or wave, to kindle accursed war, to put the house in mourning, and plunge the bridal in grief: further
35 attempt I forbid thee.' Thus Jupiter began: thus the goddess, daughter of Saturn, returned with looks cast down:

'Even because this thy will, great Jupiter, is known to me for thine, have I left, though loth, Turnus alone on earth; nor else wouldst thou see me now, alone on this skyey seat, enduring good and bad; but girt in flame I were standing by their very lines, and dragging
40 the Teucrians into the deadly battle. I counselled Juturna, I confess it, to succour her hapless brother, and for his life's sake favoured a greater daring; yet not the arrow-shot, not the bending of the bow, I swear by the merciless well-head of the Stygian spring, the single ordained dread of the gods in heaven. And now I retire, and leave the battle in loathing. This thing I beseech thee, that is bound by no fatal law, for Latium and for
45 the majesty of thy kindred. When now they shall plight peace with prosperous marriages (be it so!), when now they shall join in laws and treaties, bid thou not the native Latins change their name of old, nor become Trojans and take the Teucrian name, or change their language, or alter their attire: let Latium be, let Alban kings endure through ages,

let Italian valour be potent in the race of Rome. Troy is fallen; let her and her name lie where they fell.'

Aeneas advances. Vanquishes Turnus.

But Aeneas presses on, brandishing his vast tree-like spear, and fiercely speaks thus: 'What more delay is there now? or why, Turnus, dost thou yet shrink away? Not in
5 speed of foot, in grim arms, hand to hand, must be the conflict. Transform thyself as thou wilt, and collect what strength of courage or skill is thine; pray that thou mayest wing thy flight to the stars on high, or that sheltering earth may shut thee in.'

Turnus fights; throws a rock; misses his mark.

The other, shaking his head: 'Thy fierce words dismay me not, insolent! the gods dismay me, and Jupiter's enmity.' And no more said, his eyes light on a vast stone, a stone
10 ancient and vast that haply lay upon the plain, set for a landmark to divide contested fields: scarcely might twelve chosen men lift it on their shoulders, of such frame as now earth brings to birth: then the hero caught it up with trembling hand and whirled it at the foe, rising higher and quickening his speed. But he knows not his own self running nor going nor lifting his hands or moving the mighty stone; his knees totter, his blood
15 freezes cold; the very stone he hurls, spinning through the empty void, neither wholly reached its distance nor carried its blow home. And as in sleep, when nightly rest weighs down our languorous eyes, we seem vainly to will to run eagerly on, and sink faint amidst our struggles; the tongue is powerless, the familiar strength fails the body, nor will words or utterance follow: so the disastrous goddess brings to naught all Turnus'
20 valour as he presses on.

Turnus loses his will to fight; Aeneas makes his mark.

His heart wavers in shifting emotion; he gazes on his Rutulians and on the city, and falters in terror, and shudders at the imminent spear; neither sees he whither he may escape nor how rush violently on the enemy, and nowhere his chariot or his sister at the reins. As he wavers Aeneas poises the deadly weapon, and, marking his chance,
25 hurls it in from afar with all his strength of body. Never with such a roar are stones hurled from some engine on ramparts, nor does the thunder burst in so loud a peal. Carrying grim death with it, the spear flies in fashion of some dark whirlwind, and opens the rim of the corslet and the utmost circles of the sevenfold shield. Right through the thigh it passes hurtling on; under the blow Turnus falls huge to earth with his leg
30 doubled under him.

Turnus appeals to Aeneas for pity and mercy.

The Rutulians start up with a groan, and all the hill echoes round about, and the width of high woodland returns their cry. Lifting up beseechingly his humbled eyes and suppliant hand: 'I have deserved it,' he says, 'nor do I ask for mercy; use thy fortune. If an unhappy parent's distress may at all touch thee, this I pray; even such a father was
35 Anchises to thee; pity Daunus' old age, and restore to my kindred which thou wilt, me or my body bereft of day. Thou art conqueror, and Ausonia hath seen me stretch conquered hands. Lavinia is thine in marriage; press not thy hatred farther.'

Aeneas wavers, then finds his cause to fulfill his mission.

Aeneas stood wrathful in arms, with rolling eyes, and lowered his hand; and now and now yet more the speech began to bend him to waver: when high on his shoulder
40 appeared the sword-belt with the shining bosses that he knew, the luckless belt of the boy Pallas, whom Turnus had struck down with mastering wound, and wore on his shoulders the fatal ornament. The other, as his eyes drank in the plundered record of his fierce grief, kindles to fury, and cries terrible in anger: 'Mayest thou, thou clad in the spoils of my dearest, escape mine hands? Pallas it is, Pallas who now strikes the sacrifice,
45 and exacts vengeance in thy guilty blood.' So saying, he fiercely plunges the steel full in his breast. But his limbs grow slack and chill, and the life with a moan flies indignantly into the dark.

The path to paradise begins in hell.

— *Dante Alighieri*

PART III: THE MIDDLE AGES

DIVINE COMEDY

BY DANTE ALIGHIERI

TRANSLATED FROM ITALIAN INTO ENGLISH BY THE REV. H. F. CARY, M.A.

Introduction by M. B. McLatchey

Dante spent 13 years composing the *Divine Comedy*, from 1308 until his death in 1321. Termed a "comedy" because of its happy ending, it is generally regarded as one of the greatest epic poems in the history of literature; it is also one of the most personal accounts of an individual's exploration of the tenets of medieval Christian theology and philosophy.

Fig. 12: Dante

The Comedy is comprised of three distinct books that chronicle the narrator's ascension and spiritual pilgrimage through the three realms of the dead – from the *Inferno* (Hell), to *Purgatorio* (Purgatory), and finally to *Paradiso* (Paradise). In the three excerpts presented here, we witness the evolution of the narrator's psychological and spiritual condition from a state of despair and exile from his God in the pits of Hell, to growing spiritual and intellectual clarity in Purgatory, and ultimate reconciliation with his God in Heaven.

As neat and mechanical as this journey might appear on the surface, there is nothing formulaic about it. From his outset in the gloomy woods of the Inferno, the narrator makes clear to us that his study of the sinners around him is a self-study as well. Particularly in Purgatory, where sinners might be saved after death, the narrator fraternizes with the lost souls among him in a manner that makes clear Dante understands them, since he has also sinned. It is also in Purgatory where the narrator examines the nature of God's divine justice, and where he constructs some of the most ingenious punishments for sins and crimes against society that the mind could imagine.

The questions that Dante examined in the *Divine Comedy* occupied the most common peasant and the most learned scholars and saints of the medieval period: How should I live my life on earth? Will I be saved after death? What is the nature of God? How just is divine justice?

CANTO I

In the midway of this our mortal life,
I found me in a gloomy wood, astray
Gone from the path direct: and e'en to tell
It were no easy task, how savage wild
5 That forest, how robust and rough its growth,
Which to remember only, my dismay
Renews, in bitterness not far from death.
Yet to discourse of what there good befell,
All else will I relate discover'd there.
10 How first I enter'd it I scarce can say,

Such sleepy dullness in that instant weigh'd
My senses down, when the true path I left,
But when a mountain's foot I reach'd, where clos'd
15 The valley, that had pierc'd my heart with dread,
I look'd aloft, and saw his shoulders broad
Already vested with that planet's beam,
Who leads all wanderers safe through every way.

20 Then was a little respite to the fear,
That in my heart's recesses deep had lain,
All of that night, so pitifully pass'd:
And as a man, with difficult short breath,
Forespent with toiling, 'scap'd from sea to shore,
25 Turns to the perilous wide waste, and stands
At gaze; e'en so my spirit, that yet fail'd
Struggling with terror, turn'd to view the straits,
That none hath pass'd and liv'd. My weary frame
After short pause recomforted, again
30 I journey'd on over that lonely steep,

The hinder foot still firmer. Scarce the ascent
Began, when, lo! a panther, nimble, light,
And cover'd with a speckled skin, appear'd,
35 Nor, when it saw me, vanish'd, rather strove
To check my onward going; that ofttimes
With purpose to retrace my steps I turn'd.

The hour was morning's prime, and on his way
40 Aloft the sun ascended with those stars,
That with him rose, when Love divine first mov'd
Those its fair works: so that with joyous hope
All things conspir'd to fill me, the gay skin
Of that swift animal, the matin dawn
45 And the sweet season. Soon that joy was chas'd,
And by new dread succeeded, when in view
A lion came, 'gainst me, as it appear'd,

Note the contrast between the "dark woods," that signifies the speaker's moral confusion versus the "right road" or the straight and narrow path of living one's life according to God's will. The narrator's literal journey will take him through the regions of Hell, Purgatory, and Heaven. But his spiritual journey will take him on a pilgrimage toward reconciliation with his God. The narrator finds himself in a "savage wild" setting, an uncivilized, morally corrupted place – a post-Edenic world.

Note the dull-witted, "sleepy" state of the narrator signifying an unenlightened state. Knowledge (God's scripture) and Wakefulness (God's grace) await him.

The "lonely steep" underscores the central idea in Christian theology that each one of us makes his or her own individual – or lonely -- pilgrimage toward salvation.

Three beasts present themselves: a panther, an intimidating lion, and an insatiably hungry she-wolf. Scholars disagree regarding the symbolism of these animals. Dante's tendencies to blend his mastery of spiritual texts and pagan mythology suggest that he at least intends to paint a picture of unbridled energies – in Christian terms, degrees of sin.

With his head held aloft and hunger-mad,
That e'en the air was fear-struck. A she-wolf
Was at his heels, who in her leanness seem'd
Full of all wants, and many a land hath made
5   Disconsolate ere now. She with such fear
O'erwhelmed me, at the sight of her appall'd,
That of the height all hope I lost. As one,
Who with his gain elated, sees the time
When all unwares is gone, he inwardly
10   Mourns with heart-griping anguish; such was I,
Haunted by that fell beast, never at peace,
Who coming o'er against me, by degrees
Impell'd me where the sun in silence rests.

15   While to the lower space with backward step
I fell, my ken discern'd the form one of one,
Whose voice seem'd faint through long disuse of speech.
When him in that great desert I espied,
"Have mercy on me!" cried I out aloud,
20   "Spirit! or living man! what e'er thou be!"

He answer'd: "Now not man, man once I was,
And born of Lombard parents, Mantuana both
By country, when the power of Julius yet
25   Was scarcely firm. At Rome my life was past
Beneath the mild Augustus, in the time
Of fabled deities and false. A bard
Was I, and made Anchises' upright son
The subject of my song, who came from Troy,
30   When the flames prey'd on Ilium's haughty towers.
But thou, say wherefore to such perils past
Return'st thou? wherefore not this pleasant mount
Ascendest, cause and source of all delight?"
"And art thou then that Virgil, that well-spring,
35   From which such copious floods of eloquence
Have issued?" I with front abash'd replied.
"Glory and light of all the tuneful train!
May it avail me that I long with zeal
Have sought thy volume, and with love immense
40   Have conn'd it o'er. My master thou and guide!
Thou he from whom alone I have deriv'd
That style, which for its beauty into fame
Exalts me. See the beast, from whom I fled.
O save me from her, thou illustrious sage!

45

"For every vein and pulse throughout my frame
She hath made tremble." He, soon as he saw
That I was weeping, answer'd, "Thou must needs
Another way pursue, if thou wouldst 'scape
50   From out that savage wilderness. This beast,
At whom thou criest, her way will suffer none
To pass, and no less hindrance makes than death:
So bad and so accursed in her kind,
That never sated is her ravenous will,

Enter the narrator's spiritual guide: the Roman poet, Virgil. Interestingly, Dante chooses a pagan to guide his lost soul in his ascent from Hell to Paradise. Note the accolades that the speaker grants to his guide, Virgil.

Virgil redirects the narrator-pilgrim onto a safer and more passable route toward Heaven.

Still after food more craving than before.
To many an animal in wedlock vile
She fastens, and shall yet to many more,
Until that greyhound come, who shall destroy
5 Her with sharp pain. He will not life support
By earth nor its base metals, but by love,
Wisdom, and virtue, and his land shall be
The land 'twixt either Feltro. In his might
Shall safety to Italia's plains arise,
10 For whose fair realm, Camilla, virgin pure,
Nisus, Euryalus, and Turnus fell.
He with incessant chase through every town
Shall worry, until he to hell at length
Restore her, thence by envy first let loose.
15 I for thy profit pond'ring now devise,
That thou mayst follow me, and I thy guide
Will lead thee hence through an eternal space,
Where thou shalt hear despairing shrieks, and see
Spirits of old tormented, who invoke
20 A second death; and those next view, who dwell
Content in fire, for that they hope to come,
Whene'er the time may be, among the blest,
Into whose regions if thou then desire
T' ascend, a spirit worthier then I
25 Must lead thee, in whose charge, when I depart,
Thou shalt be left: for that Almighty King,
Who reigns above, a rebel to his law,
Adjudges me, and therefore hath decreed,
That to his city none through me should come.
30 He in all parts hath sway; there rules, there holds
His citadel and throne. O happy those,
Whom there he chooses!" I to him in few:
"Bard! by that God, whom thou didst not adore,
I do beseech thee (that this ill and worse
35 I may escape) to lead me, where thou saidst,
That I Saint Peter's gate may view, and those
Who as thou tell'st, are in such dismal plight."

Onward he mov'd, I close his steps pursu'd.

This pilgrimage toward spiritual salvation will be inspired by three guiding principles: love, wisdom, and virtue – and not by fear or desperation. Note the emphasis on the pilgrim's good character rather than his fear of god's wrath.

Virgil promises to guide the narrator through the two regions of the after-life – Hell and Purgatory – where he will witness sinners suffering horrific punishments as testament to God's divine justice.

Virgil informs the narrator-pilgrim that he will not ascend to Paradise with him for two good reasons. First, technically speaking in Dante's religious scheme pagans will never be united with God in Heaven. Second, also in Dante's scheme, love must be the guiding force that leads one to his God; Virgil represents rational thinking and Stoic morality. For this reason, when entering Heaven, Dante's real-life love, Beatrice, will assume Virgil's role as guide.

The narrator-pilgrim enthusiastically follows Virgil's lead.

CANTO II

Now was the day departing, and the air,
Imbrown'd with shadows, from their toils releas'd
All animals on earth; and I alone
Prepar'd myself the conflict to sustain,
5 Both of sad pity, and that perilous road,
Which my unerring memory shall retrace.

O Muses! O high genius! now vouchsafe
Your aid! O mind! that all I saw hast kept
10 Safe in a written record, here thy worth
And eminent endowments come to proof.

The narrator-pilgrim asks
Virgil whether he thinks he can
be saved – a curious question
for a pagan condemned to a
region of Hell in his own after-
life.

I thus began: "Bard! thou who art my guide,
Consider well, if virtue be in me
15 Sufficient, ere to this high enterprise
Thou trust me. Thou hast told that Silvius' sire,
Yet cloth'd in corruptible flesh, among
Th' immortal tribes had entrance, and was there
Sensible present. Yet if heaven's great Lord,
20 Almighty foe to ill, such favour shew'd,
In contemplation of the high effect,
Both what and who from him should issue forth,
It seems in reason's judgment well deserv'd:
Sith he of Rome, and of Rome's empire wide,
25 In heaven's empyreal height was chosen sire:
Both which, if truth be spoken, were ordain'd
And 'stablish'd for the holy place, where sits
Who to great Peter's sacred chair succeeds.
He from this journey, in thy song renown'd,
30 Learn'd things, that to his victory gave rise
And to the papal robe. In after-times
The chosen vessel also travel'd there,
To bring us back assurance in that faith,
Which is the entrance to salvation's way.

What is the route to salvation?
Literally speaking, Virgil is the
perfect guide for the narrator;
he chartered a course through
the underworld for his own
mythic hero, Aeneas.
Symbolically speaking, this
question is every Christian
pilgrim's question, and this
will be the guiding question for
the narrator as he makes his
way through fantastic
landscapes.

35 But I, why should I there presume? or who
Permits it? not, Aeneas I nor Paul.
Myself I deem not worthy, and none else
Will deem me. I, if on this voyage then
I venture, fear it will in folly end.
40 Thou, who art wise, better my meaning know'st,
Than I can speak." As one, who unresolves
What he hath late resolv'd, and with new thoughts
Changes his purpose, from his first intent
Remov'd; e'en such was I on that dun coast,
45 Wasting in thought my enterprise, at first
So eagerly embrac'd. "If right thy words

The pilgrim must free himself
from anxiety and dread and
surrender to God's grace.

I scan," replied that shade magnanimous,
"Thy soul is by vile fear assail'd, which oft
So overcasts a man, that he recoils

From noblest resolution, like a beast
At some false semblance in the twilight gloom.
That from this terror thou mayst free thyself,
I will instruct thee why I came, and what
5 I heard in that same instant, when for thee
Grief touch'd me first. I was among the tribe,
Who rest suspended, when a dame, so blest
And lovely, I besought her to command,
Call'd me; her eyes were brighter than the star
10 Of day; and she with gentle voice and soft
Angelically tun'd her speech address'd:
"O courteous shade of Mantua! thou whose fame
Yet lives, and shall live long as nature lasts!
A friend, not of my fortune but myself,
15 On the wide desert in his road has met
Hindrance so great, that he through fear has turn'd.
Now much I dread lest he past help have stray'd,
And I be ris'n too late for his relief,
From what in heaven of him I heard. Speed now,
20 And by thy eloquent persuasive tongue,
And by all means for his deliverance meet,
Assist him. So to me will comfort spring.
I who now bid thee on this errand forth
Am Beatrice; from a place I come.
25

Revisited with joy. Love brought me thence,
Who prompts my speech. When in my Master's sight
I stand, thy praise to him I oft will tell."

30 She then was silent, and I thus began:
"O Lady! by whose influence alone,
Mankind excels whatever is contain'd
Within that heaven which hath the smallest orb,
So thy command delights me, that to obey,
35 If it were done already, would seem late.
No need hast thou farther to speak thy will;
Yet tell the reason, why thou art not loth
To leave that ample space, where to return
Thou burnest, for this centre here beneath."
40

She then: "Since thou so deeply wouldst inquire,
I will instruct thee briefly, why no dread
Hinders my entrance here. Those things alone
Are to be fear'd, whence evil may proceed,
45 None else, for none are terrible beside.
I am so fram'd by God, thanks to his grace!
That any suff'rance of your misery
Touches me not, nor flame of that fierce fire
Assails me. In high heaven a blessed dame
50 Besides, who mourns with such effectual grief
That hindrance, which I send thee to remove,
That God's stern judgment to her will inclines."
To Lucia calling, her she thus bespake:
"Now doth thy faithful servant need thy aid

Virgil informs the narrator that he came to save his soul upon the request of Beatrice, the narrator's childhood friend and love.

Virgil recounts Beatrice's request from her place in Heaven that Virgil guide her friend on earth toward a reunion with his God. Note two key concepts. First, the Christian concept of souls in Heaven that love mortals on earth – a powerful connection between the living and the dead. Second, note that Beatrice cannot physically leave her post in Heaven. The narrator must make his way toward God's love in Heaven. He must come by his own volition.

And I commend him to thee." At her word
Sped Lucia, of all cruelty the foe,
And coming to the place, where I abode
Seated with Rachel, her of ancient days,
5   She thus address'd me: "Thou true praise of God!
Beatrice! why is not thy succour lent
To him, who so much lov'd thee, as to leave
For thy sake all the multitude admires?
Dost thou not hear how pitiful his wail,
10 Nor mark the death, which in the torrent flood,
Swoln mightier than a sea, him struggling holds?"
Ne'er among men did any with such speed
Haste to their profit, flee from their annoy,
As when these words were spoken, I came here,
15 Down from my blessed seat, trusting the force
Of thy pure eloquence, which thee, and all
Who well have mark'd it, into honour brings."

"When she had ended, her bright beaming eyes
20 Tearful she turn'd aside; whereat I felt
Redoubled zeal to serve thee. As she will'd,
Thus am I come: I sav'd thee from the beast,
Who thy near way across the goodly mount
Prevented. What is this comes o'er thee then?
25 Why, why dost thou hang back? why in thy breast
Harbour vile fear? why hast not courage there
And noble daring? Since three maids so blest
Thy safety plan, e'en in the court of heaven;
And so much certain good my words forebode."
30

As florets, by the frosty air of night
Bent down and clos'd, when day has blanch'd their leaves,
Rise all unfolded on their spiry stems;
So was my fainting vigour new restor'd,
35 And to my heart such kindly courage ran,
That I as one undaunted soon replied:
"O full of pity she, who undertook
My succour! and thou kind who didst perform
So soon her true behest! With such desire
40 Thou hast dispos'd me to renew my voyage,
That my first purpose fully is resum'd.
Lead on: one only will is in us both.
Thou art my guide, my master thou, and lord."

45 So spake I; and when he had onward mov'd,
I enter'd on the deep and woody way.

CANTO III

Narrator and Virgil enter Hell

Through me you pass into the city of woe:
Through me you pass into eternal pain:
Through me among the people lost for aye.
5 Justice the founder of my fabric mov'd:
To rear me was the task of power divine,
Supremest wisdom, and primeval love.
Before me things create were none, save things
Eternal, and eternal I endure.
10 "All hope abandon ye who enter here."

Such characters in colour dim I mark'd
Over a portal's lofty arch inscrib'd:
Whereat I thus: "Master, these words import
15 Hard meaning." He as one prepar'd replied:
"Here thou must all distrust behind thee leave;
Here be vile fear extinguish'd. We are come
Where I have told thee we shall see the souls
To misery doom'd, who intellectual good
20 Have lost." And when his hand he had stretch'd forth
To mine, with pleasant looks, whence I was cheer'd,
Into that secret place he led me on.

Here sighs with lamentations and loud moans
25 Resounded through the air pierc'd by no star,
That e'en I wept at entering. Various tongues,
Horrible languages, outcries of woe,
Accents of anger, voices deep and hoarse,
With hands together smote that swell'd the sounds,
30 Made up a tumult, that for ever whirls
Round through that air with solid darkness stain'd,
Like to the sand that in the whirlwind flies.

Virgil and the narrator enter the outlying regions of Hell, the Ante-Inferno, where they witness a variety of creative punishments for sins. These scenes underscore the nature of God's Divine Justice – a kind of poetic justice, unlike revenge, where the punishment mirrors aspects of the crime against God.

Note gate's inscription.

Adulterous Love Punished: Francesca/Paulo

Then turning, I to them my speech address'd.
35 And thus began: "Francesca! your sad fate
Even to tears my grief and pity moves.
But tell me; in the time of your sweet sighs,
By what, and how love granted, that ye knew
Your yet uncertain wishes?" She replied:
40 "No greater grief than to remember days
Of joy, when mis'ry is at hand! That kens
Thy learn'd instructor. Yet so eagerly
If thou art bent to know the primal root,
From whence our love gat being, I will do,

This scene graphically captures God's measured hand in delivering his justice. Two adulterous lovers, whom Dante knew in his personal life, remain frozen for eternity in an unfulfilled embrace. The unquiet state of unfulfilled love will be their eternal punishment.

As one, who weeps and tells his tale. One day
For our delight we read of Lancelot,
How him love thrall'd. Alone we were, and no
Suspicion near us. Ofttimes by that reading
5 Our eyes were drawn together, and the hue
Fled from our alter'd cheek. But at one point
Alone we fell. When of that smile we read,
The wished smile, rapturously kiss'd
By one so deep in love, then he, who ne'er
10 From me shall separate, at once my lips
All trembling kiss'd. The book and writer both
Were love's purveyors. In its leaves that day
We read no more." While thus one spirit spake,
The other wail'd so sorely, that heartstruck
15 I through compassion fainting, seem'd not far
From death, and like a corpse fell to the ground

Tellers of False Prophesies punished

Observe the narrator's empathy
for the condemned sinners.

And now the verse proceeds to torments new,
Fit argument of this the twentieth strain
20 Of the first song, whose awful theme records
The spirits whelm'd in woe. Earnest I look'd
Into the depth, that open'd to my view,
Moisten'd with tears of anguish, and beheld
A tribe, that came along the hollow vale,
25 In silence weeping: such their step as walk
Quires chanting solemn litanies on earth.

As on them more direct mine eye descends,
Each wondrously seem'd to be revers'd
30 At the neck-bone, so that the countenance
Was from the reins averted: and because
None might before him look, they were compell'd
To' advance with backward gait. Thus one perhaps
Hath been by force of palsy clean transpos'd,
35 But I ne'er saw it nor believe it so.

Purgatorio

Thither we drew,
find there were some, who in the shady place
Behind the rock were standing, as a man
40 Thru' idleness might stand. Among them one,
Who seem'd to me much wearied, sat him down,
And with his arms did fold his knees about,
Holding his face between them downward bent.
"Sweet Sir!" I cry'd, "behold that man, who shows
45 Himself more idle, than if laziness
Were sister to him." Straight he turn'd to us,
And, o'er the thigh lifting his face, observ'd,
Then in these accents spake: "Up then, proceed

Thou valiant one." Straight who it was I knew;
Nor could the pain I felt (for want of breath
Still somewhat urg'd me) hinder my approach.
And when I came to him, he scarce his head
5 Uplifted, saying "Well hast thou discern'd,
How from the left the sun his chariot leads."

His lazy acts and broken words my lips
To laughter somewhat mov'd; when I began:
10 "Belacqua, now for thee I grieve no more.
But tell, why thou art seated upright there?
Waitest thou escort to conduct thee hence?
Or blame I only shine accustom'd ways?

Belacqua is generally regarded as a fictitious name for a musician-friend of Dante's. He had a reputation for extreme laziness. Here, he is condemned to wait for God's judgment in Purgatory as long as he waited in life to repent and return to God.

> **Paradiso: Dante encounters Beatrice, who takes over as his guide. Spiritual**
> 15 **love replaces reason**

Her eyes fast fix'd on the eternal wheels,
Beatrice stood unmov'd; and I with ken
Fix'd upon her, from upward gaze remov'd
At her aspect, such inwardly became
20 As Glaucus, when he tasted of the herb,
That made him peer among the ocean gods;
Words may not tell of that transhuman change:
And therefore let the example serve, though weak,
For those whom grace hath better proof in store
25

If I were only what thou didst create,
Then newly, Love! by whom the heav'n is rul'd,
Thou know'st, who by thy light didst bear me up.
Whenas the wheel which thou dost ever guide,
30 Desired Spirit! with its harmony
Temper'd of thee and measur'd, charm'd mine ear,
Then seem'd to me so much of heav'n to blaze
With the sun's flame, that rain or flood ne'er made
A lake so broad. The newness of the sound,
35 And that great light, inflam'd me with desire,
Keener than e'er was felt, to know their cause.

Whence she who saw me, clearly as myself,
To calm my troubled mind, before I ask'd,
40 Open'd her lips, and gracious thus began:
"With false imagination thou thyself
Mak'st dull, so that thou seest not the thing,
Which thou hadst seen, had that been shaken off.
Thou art not on the earth as thou believ'st;
45 For light'ning scap'd from its own proper place
Ne'er ran, as thou hast hither now return'd."

Although divested of my first-rais'd doubt,
By those brief words, accompanied with smiles,
50 Yet in new doubt was I entangled more,
And said: "Already satisfied, I rest

From admiration deep, but now admire
How I above those lighter bodies rise."

For the route to redemption,
Dante recommends human
love and the compassion men
learn through The Passion of
Christ.

Whence, after utt'rance of a piteous sigh,
She tow'rds me bent her eyes, with such a look,
5   As on her frenzied child a mother casts;
Then thus began: "Among themselves all things
Have order; and from hence the form, which makes
The universe resemble God. In this
The higher creatures see the printed steps
10   Of that eternal worth, which is the end
Whither the line is drawn. All natures lean,
In this their order, diversely, some more,
Some less approaching to their primal source.
Thus they to different havens are mov'd on
15   Through the vast sea of being, and each one
With instinct giv'n, that bears it in its course;
This to the lunar sphere directs the fire,
This prompts the hearts of mortal animals,
This the brute earth together knits, and binds.
20   Nor only creatures, void of intellect,
Are aim'd at by this bow; but even those,
That have intelligence and love, are pierc'd.
That Providence, who so well orders all,
With her own light makes ever calm the heaven,
25   In which the substance, that hath greatest speed,
Is turn'd: and thither now, as to our seat
Predestin'd, we are carried by the force
Of that strong cord, that never looses dart,
But at fair aim and glad. Yet is it true,
30   That as ofttimes but ill accords the form
To the design of art, through sluggishness
Of unreplying matter, so this course
Is sometimes quitted by the creature, who
Hath power, directed thus, to bend elsewhere;
35   As from a cloud the fire is seen to fall,
From its original impulse warp'd, to earth,
By vicious fondness. Thou no more admire
Thy soaring, (if I rightly deem,) than lapse
Of torrent downwards from a mountain's height.
40   There would in thee for wonder be more cause,
If, free of hind'rance, thou hadst fix'd thyself
Below, like fire unmoving on the earth."
So said, she turn'd toward the heav'n her face.

Dante experiences God's grace. In a flash of intuition, he understands the Mystery of the Trinity.

Yet this to what I saw
Is less than little. Oh eternal light!
5 Sole in thyself that dwellst; and of thyself
Sole understood, past, present, or to come!
Thou smiledst; on that circling, which in thee
Seem'd as reflected splendour, while I mus'd;
For I therein, methought, in its own hue
10 Beheld our image painted: steadfastly
I therefore por'd upon the view. As one
Who vers'd in geometric lore, would fain
Measure the circle; and, though pondering long
And deeply, that beginning, which he needs,
15 Finds not; e'en such was I, intent to scan
The novel wonder, and trace out the form,
How to the circle fitted, and therein
How plac'd: but the flight was not for my wing;
Had not a flash darted athwart my mind,
20 And in the spleen unfolded what it sought.

Here vigour fail'd the tow'ring fantasy:
But yet the will roll'd onward, like a wheel
In even motion, by the Love impell'd,
25 That moves the sun in heav'n and all the stars.

THE CANTERBURY TALES

BY GEOFFREY CHAUCER

Introduction by M. B. McLatchey

In Geoffrey Chaucer's *Canterbury Tales*, produced in the late 14th-century, the narrator joins a company of twenty-nine pilgrims in a tavern near London to set out on a holy pilgrimage to the shrine of the martyr Saint Thomas Becket in Canterbury, England. Here begins one of the sharpest critiques of organized religion in the Middle Ages. Among the pilgrims with whom the narrator travels – an assortment of church clerics, merchants, and members of both high and low social classes – *not one of them* seems fully aware of the spiritual value of the journey that they are on; in fact, *all of them*, church authorities especially, seem prime candidates for absolution and salvation.

Fig. 13: Geoffrey Chaucer

As a journey toward spiritual redemption, the holy pilgrimage defined the Middle Ages in western Europe. Church authorities recommended that at least once in their lives, parishioners should participate in one of the many opportunities to travel (on foot or horse, depending upon their social status) from their homes to a sacred destination – whether it be one of the grand cathedrals of the time or a local church holding a saint's relics. In Chaucer's time, cathedral spires and bell towers beckoned these pilgrims toward their holy destinations. In Chaucer's *Tales*, the tavern host suggests that the group of pilgrims walk and ride together and – as a way to shorten their trip – entertain one another with stories. He decides that each pilgrim will tell two stories on the way to Canterbury and two on the way back. Whomever he judges to be the best storyteller will receive a meal at Bailey's tavern, courtesy of the other pilgrims. What follows is a medley of tales – saucy, baudy, unorthodox, and rich with disclosure of the character of the tale's teller.

Of the twenty-four tales that Chaucer completed, *The Pardoner's Tale* presents one of his sharpest and most entertaining charges against the church of his day. The Pardoner engages in the practice of "indulgences" – a church-ordained concept of absolution of sins through payment to the church. The more money a pilgrim offers the Pardoner, the faster the tack to salvation he offers in return. However, when the Pardoner boasts about cheating his parishioners out of their savings and then tells a tale condemning greed, the irony is too compelling to miss. Presented below are excerpts from Chaucer's Prologue and the Pardoner's Prologue.

THE CANTERBURY TALES PROLOGUE

Here bygynneth the Book of the tales of Caunterbury

Whan that Aprille, with hise shoures soote,
The droghte of March hath perced to the roote
And bathed every veyne in swich licour,
Of which vertu engendred is the flour;
Whan Zephirus eek with his swete breeth

Here begins the Book of the Tales of Canterbury

When April with his showers sweet with fruit
The drought of March has pierced unto the root
And bathed each vein with liquor that has power
To generate therein and sire the flower;
When Zephyr also has, with his sweet breath,

Inspired hath in every holt and heeth
The tendre croppes, and the yonge sonne
Hath in the Ram his halfe cours yronne,
And smale foweles maken melodye,
That slepen al the nyght with open eye-
So priketh hem Nature in hir corages-
Thanne longen folk to goon on pilgrimages
And palmeres for to seken straunge strondes
To ferne halwes, kowthe in sondry londes;
And specially, from every shires ende
Of Engelond, to Caunturbury they wende,
The hooly blisful martir for the seke
That hem hath holpen, whan that they were seeke.
Bifil that in that seson, on a day,
In Southwerk at the Tabard as I lay,
Redy to wenden on my pilgrymage
To Caunterbury, with ful devout corage,
At nyght were come into that hostelrye
Wel nyne and twenty in a compaignye
Of sondry folk, by aventure yfalle
In felaweshipe, and pilgrimes were they alle,
That toward Caunterbury wolden ryde.

Quickened again, in every holt and heath,
The tender shoots and buds, and the young sun
Into the Ram one half his course has run,
And many little birds make melody
That sleep through all the night with open eye
(So Nature pricks them on to ramp and rage)-
Then do folk long to go on pilgrimage,
And palmers to go seeking out strange strands,
To distant shrines well known in sundry lands.
And specially from every shire's end
Of England they to Canterbury wend,
The holy blessed martyr there to seek
Who helped them when they lay so ill and weal
Befell that, in that season, on a day
In Southwark, at the Tabard, as I lay
Ready to start upon my pilgrimage
To Canterbury, full of devout homage,
There came at nightfall to that hostelry
Some nine and twenty in a company
Of sundry persons who had chanced to fall
In fellowship, and pilgrims were they all
That toward Canterbury town would ride.

THE PARDONER'S PROLOGUE

Lordynges-quod he-in chirches whan I preche,
I peyne me to han an hauteyn speche,
And rynge it out as round as gooth a belle,
For I kan al by rote that I telle.
My theme is alwey oon and evere was,
Radix malorum est Cupiditas.
First I pronounce whennes that I come,
And thanne my bulles shewe I, alle and some;
Oure lige lordes seel on my patente,
That shewe I first, my body to warente,
That no man be so boold, ne preest ne clerk,
Me to destourbe of Cristes hooly werk.
And after that thanne telle I forth my tales,
Bulles of popes and of cardynales,
Of patriarkes and bishopes I shewe,
And in Latyn I speke a wordes fewe,

Masters, quoth he, in churches, when I preach,
I am at pains that all shall hear my speech,
And ring it out as roundly as a bell,
For I know all by heart the thing I tell.
My theme is always one, and ever was:
'Radix malorum est cupiditas.'
First I announce the place whence I have come,
And then I show my pardons, all and some.
Our liege-lord's seal on my patent perfect,
I show that first, my safety to protect,
And then no man's so bold, no priest nor clerk,
As to disturb me in Christ's holy work;
And after that my tales I marshal all.
Indulgences of pope and cardinal,
Of patriarch and bishop, these I do
Show, and in Latin speak some words, a few,

To saffron with my predicacioun,
And for to stire hem to devocioun.
Thanne shewe I forth my longe cristal stones,
Yerammed ful of cloutes and of bones;
Relikes been they, as wenen they echoon.
Thanne have I in latoun a sholder-boon
Which that was of an hooly Jewes sheepe.
Goode men, I seye, taak of my wordes keepe:
If that this boon be wasshe in any welle,
If cow, or calf, or sheep, or oxe swelle,
That any worm hath ete, or worm ystonge,
Taak water of that welle, and wassh his tonge,
And it is hool anon;

To spice therewith a bit my sermoning
And stir men to devotion, marvelling.
Then show I forth my hollow crystal-stones,
Which are crammed full of rags, aye, and of bones;
Relics are these, as they think, every one.
Then I've in latten box a shoulder bone
Which came out of a holy Hebrew's sheep.
'Good men,' say I, 'my words in memory keep;
If this bone shall be washed in any well,
Then if a cow, calf, sheep, or ox should swell
That's eaten snake, or been by serpent stung,
Take water of that well and wash its tongue,
And 'twill be well anon;

EVERYMAN

BY ANONYMOUS

PUBLISHED IN LODON BY J. M. DENT & SONS LTD.
AND IN NEW YORK BY E. P. DUTTON & CO
FIRST ISSUE OF THIS EDITION 1909 REPRINTED 1910, 1912, 1914

Introduction by M. B. McLatchey

Everyman is a late 15th-century English morality play that was most likely performed for audiences throughout Britain, but whose author remains unknown. In the late Middle Ages, morality plays like *Everyman* often dramatized the fundamental choice that humans faced: to embrace a Godly life or to surrender to evil. Character development and plot complexity were not of interest to the producers of these plays. Instead, as in *Everyman*, concepts were personified in order to swiftly draw audiences to the moral lessons before them.

These moral lessons were important to the religious and secular authorities of the day; they codified cultural ideals in a time of great uncertainty. Indeed, if there was one thing that was certain for the people of the Middle Ages it was their own mortality. Even in the late Middle Ages, when the Black Death seemed to have run its course – a plague that killed one third of the population of Europe in the 14th century – immunizations were centuries away and the mortality rate for young people remained dubious. As a dark reminder of every man's brief journey from dust to dust and from baptism to final rites, local churches continued to be constructed alongside local cemeteries. For the church, this setting reminded parishioners of salvation in the *next* life, hence the importance of clearing their accounts for the ultimate day of judgment.

In *Everyman*, when the main character, named Everyman, is called to death, he can persuade none of his friends - Beauty, Family members, Worldly Goods - to go with him, except Good Deeds. The lesson is familiar to Middle Age audiences: when death calls us, we must be ready. However, to the Middle Age mind, as *Everyman* reveals to us, *readiness* is not easily acquired.

CHARACTERS

Everyman	Strength
God: Adonai	Discretion
Death	Five-Wits
Messenger	Beauty
Fellowship	Knowledge
Cousin	Confession
Kindred	Angel
Goods	Doctor
Good-Deeds	

Here beginneth a treatise how the high father of heaven sendeth death to summon every creature to come and give account of their lives in this world and is in manner of a moral play.

Messenger. I pray you all give your audience,
5 And hear this matter with reverence,
By figure a moral play--
The *Summoning of Everyman* called it is,
That of our lives and ending shows
How transitory we be all day.
10 This matter is wondrous precious,
But the intent of it is more gracious,
And sweet to bear away.
The story saith,--Man, in the beginning,
Look well, and take good heed to the ending,
15 Be you never so gay!
Ye think sin in the beginning full sweet,
Which in the end causeth thy soul to weep,
When the body lieth in clay.
Here shall you see how *Fellowship* and *Jollity*,
20 Both *Strength*, *Pleasure*, and *Beauty*,
Will fade from thee as flower in May.
For ye shall hear, how our heaven king
Calleth *Everyman* to a general reckoning:
Give audience, and hear what he doth say.

25 *God.* I perceive here in my majesty,
How that all creatures be to me unkind,
Living without dread in worldly prosperity:
Of ghostly sight the people be so blind,
Drowned in sin, they know me not for their God;
30 In worldly riches is all their mind,
They fear not my rightwiseness, the sharp rod;
My law that I shewed, when I for them died,
They forget clean, and shedding of my blood red;
I hanged between two, it cannot be denied;
35 To get them life I suffered to be dead;
I healed their feet, with thorns hurt was my head:
I could do no more than I did truly,
And now I see the people do clean forsake me.
They use the seven deadly sins damnable;
40 As pride, covetise, wrath, and lechery,
Now in the world be made commendable;
And thus they leave of angels the heavenly company;
Everyman liveth so after his own pleasure,
And yet of their life they be nothing sure:
45 I see the more that I them forbear
The worse they be from year to year;

All that liveth appaireth ⊥ fast,
Therefore I will in all the haste

Messenger summons audience to hear the play's themes: that life is short; that earthly pleasures fade away; and that we should spend our days preparing for eternal salvation and our final day of judgment.

Note God's two points: First, that he gave men free will. Second, that men have used their free will to abandon God.

Note the reference to the Passion of Christ: the persecution and crucifixion of the son of God. In Christian theology, this event signaled the ultimate salvation for man: the Christ figure conquers the finite nature of death through his resurrection and he conquers sin through his modeling of forgiveness and compassion.

Note the allusion to the *seven deadly sins*, a set of objectionable vices often referenced in medieval art and meant to remind Christians of their inherently fallen nature and of their tendency toward sin. These seven vices are traditionally identified as: *envy, greed, gluttony, lust, pride, sloth, and wrath.*

Have a reckoning of Everyman's person
For and I leave the people thus alone
In their life and wicked tempests,
Verily they will become much worse than beasts;

God keeps a ledger of our good
deeds.

5   For now one would by envy another up eat;
Charity they all do clean forget.
I hoped well that Everyman
In my glory should make his mansion,
And thereto I had them all elect;

God is sad to see men use their free
will to choose the material life over
the spiritual life. Note the image of
God as a just, but merciful, judge.

10 But now I see, like traitors deject,
They thank me not for the pleasure that I to them meant,
Nor yet for their being that I them have lent;
I proffered the people great multitude of mercy,
And few there be that asketh it heartily;
15 They be so cumbered with worldly riches,
That needs on them I must do justice,
On Everyman living without fear.
Where art thou, *Death*, thou mighty messenger?

Death. Almighty God, I am here at your will,
20 Your commandment to fulfil.

God. Go thou to *Everyman*,
And show him in my name
A pilgrimage he must on him take,
Which he in no wise may escape;

Note the motif of life as a pilgrimage,
a journey of moral significance.

25 And that he bring with him a sure reckoning
Without delay or any tarrying.

Death. Lord, I will in the world go run over all,
And cruelly outsearch both great and small;
Every man will I beset that liveth beastly
30 Out of God's laws, and dreadeth not folly:
He that loveth riches I will strike with my dart,
His sight to blind, and from heaven to depart,
Except that alms be his good friend,
In hell for to dwell, world without end.

Hell, Purgatory, and Heaven were not
merely concepts in the Middle Ages.
They were material places in a
universe whose organizing principle
was salvation through divine justice.

35 Lo, yonder I see *Everyman* walking;
Full little he thinketh on my coming;
His mind is on fleshly lusts and his treasure,
And great pain it shall cause him to endure
Before the Lord Heaven King.

God recommends that Christians live
every day as though it is their
judgment day.

40 *Everyman*, stand still; whither art thou going
Thus gaily? Hast thou thy Maker forget?

Everyman. Why askst thou?
Wouldest thou wete? [8]

Death. Yea, sir, I will show you;
45 In great haste I am sent to thee
From God out of his majesty.

Everyman. What, sent to me?

Death. Yea, certainly.
Though thou have forget him here,
He thinketh on thee in the heavenly sphere,
5   As, or we depart, thou shalt know.

Everyman. What desireth God of me?

Death. That shall I show thee;
A reckoning he will needs have
Without any longer respite.

10   *Everyman*. To give a reckoning longer leisure I crave;
This blind matter troubleth my wit.

Death. On thee thou must take a long journey:
Therefore thy book of count with thee thou bring;
For turn again thou can not by no way,
15   And look thou be sure of thy reckoning:
For before God thou shalt answer, and show
Thy many bad deeds and good but a few;
How thou hast spent thy life, and in what wise,
Before the chief lord of paradise.
20   Have ado that we were in that way,
For, wete thou well, thou shalt make none attournay. [2]

Everyman. Full unready I am such reckoning to give.
I know thee not: what messenger art thou?

Death. I am *Death*, that no man dreadeth.
25   For every man I rest and no man spareth;
For it is God's commandment
That all to me should be obedient.

Everyman. O *Death*, thou comest when I had thee least in mind;
In thy power it lieth me to save,
30   Yet of my good will I give thee, if ye will be kind,
Yea, a thousand pound shalt thou have,
And defer this matter till another day.

Death. *Everyman*, it may not be by no way;
I set not by gold, silver, nor riches,
35   Ne by pope, emperor, king, duke, ne princes.
For and I would receive gifts great,
All the world I might get;
But my custom is clean contrary.
I give thee no respite: come hence, and not tarry.

40   *Everyman*. Alas, shall I have no longer respite?
I may say *Death* giveth no warning:

Everyman tells Death he needs more time to prepare before he dies. What is the moral message here?

God is presented as an eternal judge, who takes account of our good deeds and bad deeds.

Eveyrman tries to bribe Death. However, note Death's indifference in his reply: death cannot be avoided by popes and princes. What is the moral idea here?

To think on thee, it maketh my heart sick,
For all unready is my book of reckoning.
But twelve year and I might have abiding,
My counting book I would make so clear,
5 That my reckoning I should not need to fear.
Wherefore, *Death*, I pray thee, for God's mercy,
Spare me till I be provided of remedy.

Death. Thee availeth not to cry, weep, and pray:
But haste thee lightly that you were gone the journey,
10 And prove thy friends if thou can.
For, wete thou well, the tide abideth no man,
And in the world each living creature
For *Adam's* sin must die of nature.

Everyman. *Death*, if I should this pilgrimage take,
15 And my reckoning surely make,
Show me, for saint *charity*,
Should I not come again shortly?

Death. No, *Everyman*; and thou be once there,
Thou mayst never more come here,
20 Trust me verily.

Everyman. O gracious God, in the high seat celestial,
Have mercy on me in this most need;
Shall I have no company from this vale terrestrial
Of mine acquaintance that way me to lead?

25 **Death.** Yea, if any be so hardy,
That would go with thee and bear thee company.
Hie thee that you were gone to God's magnificence,
Thy reckoning to give before his presence.
What, weenest thou thy life is given thee,
30 And thy worldly goods also?

Everyman. I had wend so, verily.

Death. Nay, nay; it was but lent thee;
For as soon as thou art go,
Another awhile shall have it, and then go therefro
35 Even as thou hast done.
Everyman, thou art mad; thou hast thy wits five,
And here on earth will not amend thy life,
For suddenly I do come.

Everyman. O wretched caitiff, whither shall I flee,
40 That I might scape this endless sorrow!
Now, gentle *Death*, spare me till to-morrow,
That I may amend me
With good advisement.

Everyman observes that death can come to us without warning – certainly an idea that was familiar to an audience of the Middle Ages. But, what is the point of this observation for Christians?

Death invites Everyman to prove that he has virtuous friends, but also reminds him of his mortal nature.

Everyman embarks upon a final pilgrimage toward salvation before death. Note his begging for God's mercy.

Note the emphasis throughout this play on the theme that life is "loaned" to humans. Most historians agree that it took over a century for Europe to begin to recover from the plague that killed 30 – 60 percent of its population in the 14th century. The aftermath of the Black Death generated a series of religious reforms and economic initiatives.

Death. Nay, thereto I will not consent,
Nor no man will I respite,
But to the heart suddenly I shall smite
Without any advisement.
5 And now out of thy sight I will me hie;
See thou make thee ready shortly,
For thou mayst say this is the day
That no man living may scape away.

Everyman. Alas, I may well weep with sighs deep;
10 Now have I no manner of company
To help me in my journey, and me to keep;
And also my writing is full unready.
How shall I do now for to excuse me?
I would to God I had never be gete! 10
15 To my soul a full great profit it had be;
For now I fear pains huge and great.
The time passeth; Lord, help that all wrought;
For though I mourn it availeth nought.
The day passeth, and is almost a-go;
20 I wot not well what for to do.
To whom were I best my complaint to make?
What, and I to *Fellowship* thereof spake,
And showed him of this sudden chance?
For in him is all mine affiance;
25 We have in the world so many a day
Be on good friends in sport and play.
I see him yonder, certainly;
I trust that he will bear me company;
Therefore to him will I speak to ease my sorrow.
30 Well met, good *Fellowship*, and good morrow!

Fellowship. *Everyman*, good morrow by this day.
Sir, why lookest thou so piteously?
If any thing be amiss, I pray thee, me say,
That I may help to remedy.

35 **Everyman.** Yea, good *Fellowship*, yea,
I am in great jeopardy.

Fellowship. My true friend, show to me your mind;
I will not forsake thee, unto my life's end,
In the way of good company.

40 **Everyman.** That was well spoken, and lovingly.

Fellowship. Sir, I must needs know your heaviness;
I have pity to see you in any distress;
If any have you wronged ye shall revenged be,
Though I on the ground be slain for thee,--
45 Though that I know before that I should die.

Note two key motifs in this exchange between Death and Everyman. First, that we cannot pick the hour when death will call on us, but we can pick the place/situation. Secondly, we go to our deaths alone. The record of our lives that we bring to our Judgment Days is ours alone.

Everyman. Verily, *Fellowship*, gramercy.

Fellowship. Tush! by thy thanks I set not a straw.
Show me your grief, and say no more.

Everyman. If I my heart should to you break,
5   And then you to turn your mind from me,
And would not me comfort, when you hear me speak,
Then should I ten times sorrier be.

Fellowship. Sir, I say as I will do in deed.

Everyman. Then be you a good friend at need:
10   I have found you true here before.

Fellowship. And so ye shall evermore;
or, in faith, and thou go to Hell,
I will not forsake thee by the way!

Everyman. Ye speak like a good friend; I believe you well;
15   I shall deserve it, and I may.

Fellowship. I speak of no deserving, by this day.
For he that will say and nothing do
Is not worthy with good company to go;
Therefore show me the grief of your mind,
20   As to your friend most loving and kind.

Everyman. I shall show you how it is;
Commanded I am to go a journey,
A long way, hard and dangerous,
And give a strait count without delay
25   Before the high judge Adonai. [11]
Wherefore I pray you, bear me company,
As ye have promised, in this journey.

Fellowship. That is matter indeed! Promise is duty,
But, and I should take such a voyage on me,
30   I know it well, it should be to my pain:
Also it make me afeard, certain.
But let us take counsel here as well as we can,
For your words would fear a strong man.

Everyman. Why, ye said, If I had need,
35   Ye would me never forsake, quick nor dead,
Though it were to hell truly.

Fellowship. So I said, certainly,
But such pleasures be set aside, thee sooth to say:
And also, if we took such a journey,
40   When should we come again?

Everyman tells his friends that death
is calling him. He asks them to
accompany him to the grave.

Everyman. Nay, never again till the day of doom.

Friends abandon Everyman.

Fellowship. In faith, then will not I come there!
Who hath you these tidings brought?

Everyman. Indeed, *Death* was with me here.

5 *Fellowship.* Now, by God that all hath bought,
If *Death* were the messenger,
For no man that is living to-day
I will not go that loath journey--
Not for the father that begat me!

10 *Everyman.* Ye promised other wise, pardie.

Friends join us for life's
sensual pleasures.

Fellowship. I wot well I say so truly;
And yet if thou wilt eat, and drink, and make good cheer,
Or haunt to women, the lusty company,
I would not forsake you, while the day is clear,
15 Trust me verily!

Everyman. Yea, thereto ye would be ready;
To go to mirth, solace, and play,
Your mind will sooner apply
Than to bear me company in my long journey.

20 *Fellowship.* Now, in good faith, I will not that way.
But and thou wilt murder, or any man kill,
In that I will help thee with a good will!

Everyman. O that is a simple advice indeed!
Gentle *fellow*, help me in my necessity;
25 We have loved long, and now I need,
And now, gentle *Fellowship*, remember me.

Fellowship. Whether ye have loved me or no,
By Saint John, I will not with thee go.

Everyman. Yet I pray thee, take the labour, and do so much for me
30 To bring me forward, for saint charity,
And comfort me till I come without the town.

Fellowship. Nay, and thou would give me a new gown,
I will not a foot with thee go;
But and you had tarried I would not have left thee so.
35 And as now, God speed thee in thy journey,
For from thee I will depart as fast as I may.

Everyman. Whither away, *Fellowship?* will you forsake me?

Fellowship. Yea, by my fay, to God I betake thee.

Everyman. Farewell, good *Fellowship*; for this my heart is sore;
Adieu for ever, I shall see thee no more.

Fellowship. In faith, *Everyman*, farewell now at the end;
5 For you I will remember that parting is mourning.

Everyman. Alack! shall we thus depart indeed?
Our Lady, help, without any more comfort,
Lo, *Fellowship* forsaketh me in my most need:
For help in this world whither shall I resort?
10 *Fellowship* herebefore with me would merry make;
And now little sorrow for me doth he take.
It is said, in prosperity men friends may find,
Which in adversity be full unkind.
Now whither for succour shall I flee,
15 Sith that *Fellowship* hath forsaken me?
To my kinsmen I will truly,
Praying them to help me in my necessity;
I believe that they will do so,
For kind will creep where it may not go.
20 I will go say, for yonder I see them go.
Where be ye now, my friends and kinsmen?

Kindred. Here be we now at your commandment.
Cousin, I pray you show us your intent
In any wise, and not spare.

25 **Cousin**. Yea, *Everyman*, and to us declare
If ye be disposed to go any whither,
For wete you well, we will live and die together.

Kindred. In wealth and woe we will with you hold,
For over his kin a man may be bold.

30 **Everyman**. Gramercy, my friends and kinsmen kind.
Now shall I show you the grief of my mind:
I was commanded by a messenger,
That is an high king's chief officer;
He bade me go a pilgrimage to my pain,
35 And I know well I shall never come again;
Also I must give a reckoning straight,
For I have a great enemy, that hath me in wait,
Which intendeth me for to hinder.

Kindred. What account is that which ye must render?
40 That would I know.

Friends mourn the death of
Everyman, but cannot accompany
him in his journey to his God. To this
extent, Everyman decides in his final
speech in this exchange, his friends
are "fair-weather friends".

Enter Everyman's immediate family
members and cousins. They vow to
accompany Everyman to his last day
on earth.

Everyman asks his family to accompany him to his grave and help him present his "account" of his life to his God of judgment.

Everyman. Of all my works I must show
How I have lived and my days spent;
Also of ill deeds, that I have used
In my time, sith life was me lent;

5 And of all virtues that I have refused.
Therefore I pray you go thither with me,
To help to make mine account, for saint *charity*.

Cousin. What, to go thither? Is that the matter?
Nay, *Everyman*, I had liefer fast bread and water
10 All this five year and more.

Everyman. Alas, that ever I was bore! [12]
For now shall I never be merry
If that you forsake me.

Kindred. Ah, sir; what, ye be a merry man!
15 Take good heart to you, and make no moan.
But one thing I warn you, by Saint Anne,
As for me, ye shall go alone.

Everyman. My *Cousin*, will you not with me go?

Note Everyman's cousin's excuse: I can't accompany you to your death, Everyman, because I have a cramp in my toe.

Cousin. No, by our Lady; I have the cramp in my toe.
20 Trust not to me, for, so God me speed,
I will deceive you in your most need,
Kindred. It availeth not us to tice.
Ye shall have my maid with all my heart;
She loveth to go to feasts, there to be nice,
25 And to dance, and abroad to start:
I will give her leave to help you in that journey,
If that you and she may agree.

Everyman. Now show me the very effect of your mind.
Will you go with me, or abide behind?

30 **Kindred.** Abide behind? yea, that I will and I may!
Therefore farewell until another day.

Everyman claims his family have deceived him and abandoned him. Where is the error in his thinking?

Everyman. How should I be merry or glad?
For fair promises to me make,
But when I have most need, they me forsake.
35 I am deceived; that maketh me sad.

Cousin. Cousin *Everyman*, farewell now,
For verily I will not go with you;
Also of mine own an unready reckoning
I have to account; therefore I make tarrying.
40 Now, God keep thee, for now I go.

Everyman. Ah, *Jesus*, is all come hereto?
Lo, fair words maketh fools feign;
They promise and nothing will do certain.
My kinsmen promised me faithfully
5 For to abide with me steadfastly,
And now fast away do they flee:
Even so *Fellowship* promised me.
What friend were best me of to provide?
I lose my time here longer to abide.
10 Yet in my mind a thing there is;--
All my life I have loved riches;
If that my good now help me might,
He would make my heart full light.
I will speak to him in this distress.--
15 Where art thou, my *Goods* and riches?

Goods. Who calleth me? *Everyman?* what haste thou hast!
I lie here in corners, trussed and piled so high,
And in chests I am locked so fast,
Also sacked in bags, thou mayst see with thine eye,
20 I cannot stir; in packs low I lie.
What would ye have, lightly me say.

Everyman. Come hither, *Good*, in all the haste thou may,
For of counsel I must desire thee.

Goods. Sir, and ye in the world have trouble or adversity,
25 That can I help you to remedy shortly.

Everyman. It is another disease that grieveth me;
In this world it is not, I tell thee so.
I am sent for another way to go,
To give a straight account general
30 Before the highest *Jupiter* of all;
And all my life I have had joy and pleasure in thee.
Therefore I pray thee go with me,
For, peradventure, thou mayst before God Almighty
My reckoning help to clean and purify;
35 For it is said ever among,
That money maketh all right that is wrong.

Everyman asks Goods, things of material value, to accompany him to his day of judgment. He maintains that money and possessions cure all ills in life.

Goods. Nay, *Everyman*, I sing another song,
I follow no man in such voyages;
For and I went with thee
40 Thou shouldst fare much the worse for me;
For because on me thou did set thy mind,
Thy reckoning I have made blotted and blind,
That thine account thou cannot make truly;
And that hast thou for the love of me.

Note this important speech from Goods. How have material goods both helped and hurt Everyman's journey toward salvation?

Everyman. That would grieve me full sore,
When I should come to that fearful answer.
Up, let us go thither together.

Goods makes the distinction between the transitory nature of material things and the eternal nature of the soul and of the life after death.

Goods. Nay, not so, I am too brittle, I may not endure;
5 I will follow no man one foot, be ye sure.

Everyman. Alas, I have thee loved, and had great pleasure
All my life-days on good and treasure.

Goods gives advice to Everyman regarding how to enjoy material things during one's life.

Goods. That is to thy damnation without lesing,
For my love is contrary to the love everlasting.
10 But if thou had me loved moderately during,
As, to the poor give part of me,
Then shouldst thou not in this dolour be,
Nor in this great sorrow and care.

Everyman. Lo, now was I deceived or I was ware,
15 And all I may wyte [13] my spending of time.

Goods. What, weenest thou that I am thine?

Everyman. I had wend so.

Goods claims that a preoccupation with material things will kill men's souls.

Goods. Nay, *Everyman,* I say no;
As for a while I was lent thee,
20 A season thou hast had me in prosperity;
My condition is man's soul to kill;
If I save one, a thousand I do spill;
Weenest thou that I will follow thee?
Nay, from this world, not verily.

25 **Everyman.** I had wend otherwise.

Goods. Therefore to thy soul *Good* is a thief;
For when thou art dead, this is my guise
Another to deceive in the same wise
As I have done thee, and all to his soul's reprief.

30 **Everyman.** O false *Good,* cursed thou be!
Thou traitor to God, that hast deceived me,
And caught me in thy snare.

Goods. Marry, thou brought thyself in care,
Whereof I am glad,
35 I must needs laugh, I cannot be sad.

Everyman. Ah, *Good,* thou hast had long my heartly love;
I gave thee that which should be the Lord's above.
But wilt thou not go with me in deed?
I pray thee truth to say.

Goods. No, so God me speed,
Therefore farewell, and have good day.

Everyman. O, to whom shall I make my moan
For to go with me in that heavy journey?
5 First *Fellowship* said he would with me gone;
His words were very pleasant and gay,
But afterward he left me alone.
Then spake I to my kinsmen all in despair,
And also they gave me words fair,
10 They lacked no fair speaking,
But all forsake me in the ending.
Then went I to my *Goods* that I loved best,
In hope to have comfort, but there had I least;
For my *Goods* sharply did me tell
15 That he bringeth many into hell.
Then of myself I was ashamed,
And so I am worthy to be blamed;
Thus may I well myself hate.
Of whom shall I now counsel take?
20 I think that I shall never speed
Till that I go to my *Good-Deed*,
But alas, she is so weak,
That she can neither go nor speak;
Yet will I venture on her now.--
25 My *Good-Deeds*, where be you?

Good-Deeds. Here I lie cold in the ground;
Thy sins hath me sore bound,
That I cannot stir.

Everyman. O, *Good-Deeds*, I stand in fear;
30 I must you pray of counsel,
For help now should come right well.

Goods-Deeds. *Everyman*, I have understanding
That ye be summoned account to make
Before *Messias*, of Jerusalem King;
35 And you do by me [14] that journey what [15] you will I take.

Everyman. Therefore I come to you, my moan to make;
I pray you, that ye will go with me.

Good-Deeds. I would full fain, but I cannot stand verily.

Everyman. Why, is there anything on you fall?

40 **Good-Deeds**. Yea, sir, I may thank you of all;
If ye had perfectly cheered me,
Your book of account now full ready had be.
Look, the books of your works and deeds eke;

Everyman summarizes the plot and identifies the central theme of the play. He admits his shame and accepts blame for his own actions. Note the suggestion of *Last Rites* and Everyman's wish for *Reconciliation*, two key concepts in Christian theology.

Everyman considers his good deeds in his life, which are very few. Because "Good-Deeds" (as an aspect of his life) has been long neglected, it is in poor condition – too weak to stand on its own for Everyman.

Oh, see how they lie under the feet,
To your soul's heaviness.

Everyman. Our Lord *Jesus*, help me!
For one letter here I can not see.

5   **Good-Deeds.** There is a blind reckoning in time of distress!

Everyman. *Good-Deeds*, I pray you, help me in this need,
Or else I am for ever damned indeed;
Therefore help me to make reckoning
Before the redeemer of all thing,
10 That king is, and was, and ever shall.

Good-Deeds. *Everyman*, I am sorry of your fall,
And fain would I help you, and I were able.

Everyman. *Good-Deeds*, your counsel I pray you give me.

Good-Deeds. That shall I do verily;
15 Though that on my feet I may not go,
I have a sister, that shall with you also,
Called *Knowledge*, which shall with you abide,
To help you to make that dreadful reckoning.

Knowledge. *Everyman*, I will go with thee, and be thy guide,
20 In thy most need to go by thy side.

Everyman. In good condition I am now in every thing,
And am wholly content with this good thing;
Thanked be God my Creator.

Good-Deeds. And when he hath brought thee there,
25 Where thou shalt heal thee of thy smart,
Then go you with your reckoning and your *Good-Deeds* together
For to make you joyful at heart
Before the blessed Trinity.

Everyman. My *Good-Deeds*, gramercy;
30 I am well content, certainly,
With your words sweet.

Knowledge. Now go we together lovingly,
To *Confession*, that cleansing river.

Everyman. For joy I weep; I would we were there;
35 But, I pray you, give me cognition
Where dwelleth that holy man, *Confession*.

Knowledge. In the house of salvation:
We shall find him in that place,

Good-Deeds introduces Everyman to his sister, Knowledge, who says that she can help him by taking him to Confession. Everyman weeps for joy. Note the definition of a Christian life: *Good Deeds* joined to Knowledge (an understanding of the scriptures) and *Grace* (God's mercy).

Note the reference to the trinity: the Holy Father (God), the Son (Christ), and the Holy Spirit (God's grace).

That shall us comfort by God's grace.
Lo, this is *Confession*; kneel down and ask mercy,
For he is in good conceit with God almighty.

Everyman. O glorious fountain that all uncleanness doth clarify,
5   Wash from me the spots of vices unclean,
That on me no sin may be seen;
I come with *Knowledge* for my redemption,
Repent with hearty and full contrition;
For I am commanded a pilgrimage to take,
10 And great accounts before God to make.
Now, I pray you, *Shrift*, mother of salvation,
Help my good deeds for my piteous exclamation.

Confession. I know your sorrow well, *Everyman*,
Because with *Knowledge* ye come to me,
15 I will you comfort as well as I can,
And a precious jewel I will give thee,
Called penance, wise voider of adversity;
Therewith shall your body chastised be,
With abstinence and perseverance in God's service:
20 Here shall you receive that scourge of me,
Which is penance strong, that ye must endure,
To remember thy Saviour was scourged for thee
With sharp scourges, and suffered it patiently;
So must thou, or thou scape that painful pilgrimage;
25 *Knowledge*, keep him in this voyage,
And by that time *Good-Deeds* will be with thee.
But in any wise, be sure of mercy,
For your time draweth fast, and ye will saved be;
Ask God mercy, and He will grant truly,
30 When with the scourge of penance man doth him bind,
The oil of forgiveness then shall he find.

Everyman. Thanked be God for his gracious work!
For now I will my penance begin;
This hath rejoiced and lighted my heart,
35 Though the knots be painful and hard within.

Knowledge. *Everyman*, look your penance that ye fulfil,
What pain that ever it to you be,
And *Knowledge* shall give you counsel at will,
How your accounts ye shall make clearly.

40 **Everyman**. O eternal God, O heavenly figure,
O way of rightwiseness, O goodly vision,
Which descended down in a virgin pure
Because he would *Everyman* redeem,
Which *Adam* forfeited by his disobedience:
45 O blessed Godhead, elect and high-divine,
Forgive my grievous offence;
Here I cry thee mercy in this presence.
O ghostly treasure, O ransomer and redeemer

Side notes:

Note that "Confession" (the sacrament of Reconciliation) is in the house of Salvation.

In this turning moment in the play, Everyman asks God for forgiveness for his sinful life and he asks the Virgin Mother Mary to intercede on his behalf.

Note the catechism of the Medieval Christian. *Confession* presents Everyman with a kind of "jewel" called *Penance* if he confesses his sins. *Penance* will be the good works and prayer that Everyman will undertake in order to *reconcile* his relationship with his God.

Everyman will be anointed and forgiven as long as he recognizes God as his master and judge.

In this key scene, Everyman confesses his sins. Note his reference to the Genesis story and his comment that God is man's "ransomer" and "redeemer". Lastly, note the God/man relationship here, wherein God is master and man is servant to the master.

Of all the world, hope and conductor,
Mirror of joy, and founder of mercy,
Which illumineth heaven and earth thereby,
Hear my clamorous complaint, though it late be;
5 Receive my prayers; unworthy in this heavy life,
Though I be, a sinner most abominable,
Yet let my name be written in *Moses'* table;
O *Mary*, pray to the Maker of all thing,
Me for to help at my ending,
10 And save me from the power of my enemy,
For *Death* assaileth me strongly;
And, Lady, that I may by means of thy prayer
Of your Son's glory to be partaker,
By the means of his passion I it crave,
15 I beseech you, help my soul to save.--
Knowledge, give me the scourge of penance;
My flesh therewith shall give a quittance:
I will now begin, if God give me grace.

Knowledge. *Everyman*, God give you time and space:
20 Thus I bequeath you in the hands of our Saviour,
Thus may you make your reckoning sure.

Everyman asks to be saved from Purgatory. Good-Deeds has regained strength and offers to assist Everyman. Note the change in posture for Everyman: he can now "go upright upon the ground" with his Good-Deeds.

Everyman. In the name of the Holy Trinity,
My body sore punished shall be:
Take this body for the sin of the flesh;
25 Also thou delightest to go gay and fresh,
And in the way of damnation thou did me bring;
Therefore suffer now strokes and punishing.
Now of penance I will wade the water clear,
To save me from purgatory, that sharp fire.

Good-Deeds informs Everyman that he is ready to die and meet his Maker.

30 **Good-Deeds.** I thank God, now I can walk and go;
And am delivered of my sickness and woe.
Therefore with *Everyman* I will go, and not spare;
His good works I will help him to declare.

Knowledge. Now, *Everyman*, be merry and glad;
35 Your *Good-Deeds* cometh now; ye may not be sad;
Now is your *Good-Deeds* whole and sound,
Going upright upon the ground.

Everyman. My heart is light, and shall be evermore;
Now will I smite faster than I did before.

40 **Good-Deeds.** *Everyman*, pilgrim, my special friend,
Blessed be thou without end;
For thee is prepared the eternal glory.
Ye have me made whole and sound,
Therefore I will bide by thee in every stound. [16]

Everyman. Welcome, my *Good-Deeds*; now I hear thy voice,
I weep for very sweetness of love.

Knowledge. Be no more sad, but ever rejoice,
God seeth thy living in his throne above;
5 Put on this garment to thy behove,
Which is wet with your tears,
Or else before God you may it miss,
When you to your journey's end come shall.

Knowledge outfits Everyman with the robe of contrition (sorrow for sins) signifying his repentance.

Everyman. Gentle *Knowledge*, what do you it call?

10 **Knowledge**. It is a garment of sorrow:
From pain it will you borrow;
Contrition it is,
That getteth forgiveness;
It pleaseth God passing well.

15 **Good-Deeds**. *Everyman*, will you wear it for your heal?

Everyman. Now blessed be *Jesu, Mary's* Son!
For now have I on true contrition.
And let us go now without tarrying;
Good-Deeds, have we clear our reckoning?

20 **Good-Deeds**. Yea, indeed I have it here.

Everyman. Then I trust we need not fear;
Now, friends, let us not part in twain.

Knowledge. Nay, *Everyman*, that will we not, certain.

Good-Deeds. Yet must thou lead with thee
25 Three persons of great might.

Everyman. Who should they be?

Good-Deeds. *Discretion* and *Strength* they hight,
And thy *Beauty* may not abide behind.

Good-Deeds asks Discretion, Strength, Beauty and the Five-Wits (the five senses) to accompany Everyman on his pilgrimage to his grave.

Knowledge. Also ye must call to mind
30 Your *Five-wits* as for your counsellors.

Good-Deeds. You must have them ready at all hours.

Everyman. How shall I get them hither?

Knowledge. You must call them all together,
And they will hear you incontinent.

Everyman. My friends, come hither and be present
Discretion, *Strength*, my *Five-wits*, and *Beauty*.

Beauty. Here at your will we be all ready.
What will ye that we should do?

5 **Good-Deeds**. That ye would with *Everyman* go,
And help him in his pilgrimage,
Advise you, will ye with him or not in that voyage?

Strength. We will bring him all thither,
To his help and comfort, ye may believe me.

10 **Discretion**. So will we go with him all together.

Everyman. Almighty God, loved thou be,
I give thee laud that I have hither brought
Strength, *Discretion*, *Beauty*, and *Five-wits*; lack I nought;
And my *Good-Deeds*, with *Knowledge* clear,
15 All be in my company at my will here;
I desire no more to my business.

Strength. And I, *Strength*, will by you stand in distress,
Though thou would in battle fight on the ground.

Five-wits. And though it were through the world round,
20 We will not depart for sweet nor sour.

Beauty. No more will I unto death's hour,
Whatsoever thereof befall.

Discretion. *Everyman*, advise you first of all;
Go with a good advisement and deliberation;
25 We all give you virtuous monition
That all shall be well.

Everyman. My friends, hearken what I will tell:
I pray God reward you in his heavenly sphere.
Now hearken, all that be here,
30 For I will make my testament
Here before you all present.
In alms half my good I will give with my hands twain
In the way of charity, with good intent,
And the other half still shall remain
35 In quiet to be returned there it ought to be.
This I do in despite of the fiend of hell
To go quite out of his peril
Ever after and this day.

Knowledge. *Everyman*, hearken what I say;
40 Go to priesthood, I you advise,

And receive of him in any wise
The holy sacrament and ointment together;
Then shortly see ye turn again hither;
We will all abide you here.

Knowledge advises Everyman that, before he dies, he must receive the last sacrament of the church: the Holy Eucharist and anointment with oil.

5 **Everyman.** Fain would I receive that holy body
And meekly to my ghostly father I will go.

Five-wits. *Everyman*, that is the best that ye can do:
God will you to salvation bring,
For priesthood exceedeth all other thing;
10 To us Holy Scripture they do teach,
And converteth man from sin heaven to reach;
God hath to them more power given,
Than to any angel that is in heaven;
With five words he may consecrate
15 God's body in flesh and blood to make,
And handleth his maker between his hands;
The priest bindeth and unbindeth all bands,
Both in earth and in heaven;
Thou ministers all the sacraments seven;
20 Though we kissed thy feet thou were worthy;
Thou art surgeon that cureth sin deadly:
No remedy we find under God
But all only priesthood.
Everyman, God gave priests that dignity,
25 And setteth them in his stead among us to be;
Thus be they above angels in degree.

Five-Wits delivers Everyman to his true savior, God, who offers his salvation. Note the Medieval acknowledgement of Heaven and Hell as real and tangible places.

Knowledge. If priests be good it is so surely;
But when Jesus hanged on the cross with great smart
There he gave, out of his blessed heart,
30 The same sacrament in great torment:
He sold them not to us, that Lord Omnipotent.
Therefore Saint Peter the apostle doth say
That Jesu's curse hath all they
Which God their Saviour do buy or sell,
35 Or they for any money do take or tell.
Sinful priests giveth the sinners example bad;
Their children sitteth by other men's fires, I have heard;
And some haunteth women's company,
With unclean life, as lusts of lechery
40 These be with sin made blind.

Five-wits. I trust to God no such may we find;
Therefore let us priesthood honour,
And follow their doctrine for our souls' succour;
We be their sheep, and they shepherds be
45 By whom we all be kept in surety.
Peace, for yonder I see *Everyman* come,
Which hath made true satisfaction.

Five-Wits presents a medieval Christian view of God as shepherd and the people as sheep.

Good-Deeds. Methinketh it is he indeed.

244 PART III: THE MIDDLE AGES

Everyman. Now Jesu be our alder speed. [17]
I have received the sacrament for my redemption,
And then mine extreme unction:
Blessed be all they that counselled me to take it!
5 And now, friends, let us go without longer respite;
I thank God that ye have tarried so long.
Now set each of you on this rod your hand,
And shortly follow me:
I go before, there I would be; God be our guide.

Note that after Everyman receives his sacraments, all but Good-Deeds refuse to go with him to his death.

10 **Strength.** *Everyman,* we will not from you go,
Till ye have gone this voyage long.

Discretion. I, *Discretion,* will bide by you also.

Knowledge. And though this pilgrimage be never so strong,
I will never part you fro:
15 *Everyman,* I will be as sure by thee
As ever I did by Judas Maccabee.

Everyman feels weak.

Everyman. Alas, I am so faint I may not stand,
My limbs under me do fold;
Friends, let us not turn again to this land,
20 Not for all the world's gold,
For into this cave must I creep
And turn to the earth and there to sleep.

Beauty bids good-bye to Everyman.

Beauty. What, into this grave? alas!

Everyman. Yea, there shall you consume more and less.

25 **Beauty.** And what, should I smother here?

Everyman. Yea, by my faith, and never more appear.
In this world live no more we shall,
But in heaven before the highest Lord of all.

Beauty. I cross out all this; adieu by Saint *John;*
30 I take my cap in my lap and am gone.

Everyman. What, *Beauty,* whither will ye?

Beauty. Peace, I am deaf; I look not behind me,
Not and thou would give me all the gold in thy chest.

Everyman. Alas, whereto may I trust?
35 *Beauty* goeth fast away hie;
She promised with me to live and die.

Strength. *Everyman,* I will thee also forsake and deny;
Thy game liketh me not at all.

Everyman. Why, then ye will forsake me all.
Sweet *Strength*, tarry a little space.

Strength. Nay, sir, by the rood of grace
I will hie me from thee fast,
5 Though thou weep till thy heart brast.

Everyman. Ye would ever bide by me, ye said.

Strength. Yea, I have you far enough conveyed;
Ye be old enough, I understand,
Your pilgrimage to take on hand;
10 I repent me that I hither came.

Everyman. *Strength*, you to displease I am to blame;
Will you break promise that is debt?

Strength. In faith, I care not;
Thou art but a fool to complain,
15 You spend your speech and waste your brain;
Go thrust thee into the ground.

Everyman. I had wend surer I should you have found.
He that trusteth in his *Strength*
She him deceiveth at the length.
20 Both *Strength* and *Beauty* forsaketh me,
Yet they promised me fair and lovingly.

Discretion. *Everyman*, I will after *Strength* be gone,
As for me I will leave you alone.

Everyman. Why, *Discretion*, will ye forsake me?

25 **Discretion.** Yea, in faith, I will go from thee,
For when *Strength* goeth before
I follow after evermore.

Everyman. Yet, I pray thee, for the love of the Trinity,
Look in my grave once piteously.

30 **Discretion.** Nay, so nigh will I not come.
Farewell, every one!

Everyman. O all thing faileth, save God alone;
Beauty, *Strength*, and *Discretion*;
For when *Death* bloweth his blast,
35 They all run from me full fast.

Five-wits. *Everyman*, my leave now of thee I take;
I will follow the other, for here I thee forsake.

Strength leaves Everyman. Everyman is decaying in bodily form. Note the motif of the transitory nature of material things (from dust to dust) and the eternal nature of the spiritual things (the soul).

Discretion leaves Everyman.

The five senses leave Everyman.

Everyman. Alas! then may I wail and weep,
For I took you for my best friend.

Five-wits. I will no longer thee keep;
Now farewell, and there an end.

5 **Everyman.** O Jesu, help, all hath forsaken me!

Good-Deeds agrees to enter the
afterlife with Everyman.

Good-Deeds. Nay, *Everyman*, I will bide with thee,
I will not forsake thee indeed;
Thou shalt find me a good friend at need.

Everyman. Gramercy, *Good-Deeds*; now may I true friends see;
10 They have forsaken me every one;
I loved them better than my *Good-Deeds* alone.
Knowledge, will ye forsake me also?

Knowledge. Yea, *Everyman*, when ye to death do go:
But not yet for no manner of danger.

15 **Everyman.** Gramercy, *Knowledge*, with all my heart.

Knowledge. Nay, yet I will not from hence depart,
Till I see where ye shall be come.

Everyman is ready for death.
His "accounts" are in order and
he now greets Death happily.

Everyman. Methinketh, alas, that I must be gone,
To make my reckoning and my debts pay,
20 For I see my time is nigh spent away.
Take example, all ye that this do hear or see,
How they that I loved best do forsake me,
Except my *Good-Deeds* that bideth truly.

Note the key theme in Good
Deed's speech: *all earthly
things is but vanity.*

Good-Deeds. All earthly things is but vanity:
25 *Beauty*, *Strength*, and *Discretion*, do man forsake,
Foolish friends and kinsmen, that fair spake,
All fleeth save *Good-Deeds*, and that am I.

Everyman. Have mercy on me, God most mighty;
And stand by me, thou Mother and Maid, holy *Mary*.

30 **Good-Deeds.** Fear not, I will speak for thee.

Everyman. Here I cry God mercy.

Good-Deeds. Short our end, and minish our pain;
Let us go and never come again.

Everyman enjoys his
redemption and his salvation.
Note the Latin: *Into thy hands
I commend my spirit.*

Everyman. Into thy hands, Lord, my soul I commend;
35 Receive it, Lord, that it be not lost;
As thou me boughtest, so me defend,

And save me from the fiend's boast,
That I may appear with that blessed host
That shall be saved at the day of doom.
In manus tuas--of might's most
5   For ever-- *commendo spiritum meum.*

Knowledge. Now hath he suffered that we all shall endure;
The *Good-Deeds* shall make all sure.
Now hath he made ending;
Methinketh that I hear angels sing
10   And make great joy and melody,
Where *Everyman's* soul received shall be.

Knowledge hears the angels sing.
The angels serve Everyman as
God's ambassadors and assist
Everyman as the soul leaves the
body.

Angel. Come, excellent elect spouse to Jesu:
Hereabove thou shalt go
Because of thy singular virtue:
15   Now the soul is taken the body fro;
Thy reckoning is crystal-clear.
Now shalt thou into the heavenly sphere,
Unto the which all ye shall come
That liveth well before the day of doom.

20   **Doctor**. This moral men may have in mind;
Ye hearers, take it of worth, old and young,
And forsake pride, for he deceiveth you in the end,
And remember *Beauty*, *Five-wits*, *Strength*, and *Discretion*,
They all at the last do *Everyman* forsake,
25   Save his *Good-Deeds*, there doth he take.
But beware, and they be small
Before God, he hath no help at all.
None excuse may be there for *Everyman*.
Alas, how shall he do then?
30   For after death amends may no man make,
For then mercy and pity do him forsake.
If his reckoning be not clear when he do come,
God will say-- *ite maledicti in ignem æternum.*
And he that hath his account whole and sound,
35   High in heaven he shall be crowned;
Unto which place God bring us all thither
That we may live body and soul together.
Thereto help the Trinity,
Amen, say ye, for saint *Charity*.

The Doctor's speech sums up
the lessons of the play and
reinforces its central Christian
idea that no man can escape
death, and thus he must live
every day preparing his
"accounts" for salvation. Note
the Latin inscription: "ite
maledicti in ignem aeternum"
meaning "Divine Law - Go,
Accursed, into Everlasting
Fire." Everlasting fire in the pit
of Hell will be the fate of those
whose accounts are not clear
when Death calls them.

40   **Thus endeth this morall play of *Everyman*.**

Those who cannot remember the past

are condemned to repeat it.

— *George Santayana, The Life of Reason*

PART IV: ADDITIONAL READINGS

ADDITIONAL READINGS

Introduction by M. B. McLatchey

Part IV features additional readings drawn from historical periods that reach beyond this text's historical survey from ancient times to the medieval age. As such, these more modern readings invite students to uncover links between ancient and modern ideas, and to discover the larger questions that have interested human beings not just during a particular historical period, but for generations. For each of the selected readings that follow, I have offered suggestions for research. However, as evidenced by their permanent place in history, these readings are rich with a variety of questions that are worth exploring.

READINGS INCLUDED IN THIS SECTION

The Emperor's New Clothes	Hans Christian Andersen
The Declaration of Independence	Thomas Jefferson
Federalist Paper No. 10	James Madison
Federalist Paper No. 47	James Madison
The Constitution of the United States of America	
The Bill of Rights	
Democracy in America	Alexis De Tocqueville
Ben Franklin Readings	Benjamin Franklin
A Vindication of the Rights of Woman	Mary Wollstonecraft

THE EMPEROR'S NEW CLOTHES

BY HANS CHRISTIAN ANDERSEN

Introduction by M. B. McLatchey

In this popular tale, several issues are explored that correspond to those found in Plato's *Republic*, particularly his *Allegory of the Cave*. The fundamental question that both literary works ask is, "What constitutes an enlightened life?" Questions regarding personal character are explored, as well as what it means to live a life of integrity. Like the cave dwellers in Plato's allegory, will the adults in *The Emperor's New Clothes* answer to the tyranny of the mob or will they answer to what they know in their souls and intellects is right?

EXCERPTED FROM ANDERSEN'S FAIRY TALES

Many years ago, there was an Emperor, who was so excessively fond of new clothes, that he spent all his money in dress. He did not trouble himself in the least about his soldiers; nor did he care to go either to the theatre or the chase, except for the opportunities then afforded him for displaying his new clothes. He had a different suit for each hour of the day; and as of any other king or emperor, one is accustomed to say, "he is sitting in council," it was always said of him, "The Emperor is sitting in his wardrobe."

Time passed merrily in the large town which was his capital; strangers arrived every day at the court. One day, two rogues, calling themselves weavers, made their appearance. They gave out that they knew how to weave stuffs of the most beautiful colors and elaborate patterns, the clothes manufactured from which should have the wonderful property of remaining invisible to everyone who was unfit for the office he held, or who was extraordinarily simple in character.

"These must, indeed, be splendid clothes!" thought the Emperor. "Had I such a suit, I might at once find out what men in my realms are unfit for their office, and also be able to distinguish the wise from the foolish! This stuff must be woven for me immediately." And he caused large sums of money to be given to both the weavers in order that they might begin their work directly.

So the two pretended weavers set up two looms, and affected to work very busily, though in reality they did nothing at all. They asked for the most delicate silk and the purest gold thread; put both into their own knapsacks; and then continued their pretended work at the empty looms until late at night.

"I should like to know how the weavers are getting on with my cloth," said the Emperor to himself, after some little time had elapsed; he was, however, rather embarrassed, when he remembered that a simpleton, or one unfit for his office, would be unable to see the manufacture. To be sure, he thought he had nothing to risk in his own person; but yet, he would prefer sending somebody else, to bring him intelligence about the weavers, and their work, before he troubled himself in the affair. All the people throughout the city had heard of the wonderful property the cloth was to possess; and all were anxious to learn how wise, or how ignorant, their neighbors might prove to be.

"I will send my faithful old minister to the weavers," said the Emperor at last, after some deliberation, "he will be best able to see how the cloth looks; for he is a man of sense, and no one can be more suitable for his office than he is."

So the faithful old minister went into the hall, where the knaves were working with all their might, at their empty looms. "What can be the meaning of this?" thought the old man, opening his eyes very wide. "I cannot discover the least bit of thread on the looms." However, he did not express his thoughts aloud.

The impostors requested him very courteously to be so good as to come nearer their looms; and then asked him whether the design pleased him, and whether the colors were not very beautiful; at the same time pointing to the empty frames. The poor old minister looked and looked, he could not discover anything on the looms, for a very good reason, viz: there was nothing there. "What!" thought he again. "Is it possible that I am a simpleton? I have never thought so myself; and no one must know it now if I am so. Can it be, that I am unfit for my office? No, that must not be said either. I will never confess that I could not see the stuff."

"Well, Sir Minister!" said one of the knaves, still pretending to work. "You do not say whether the stuff pleases you." "Oh, it is excellent!" replied the old minister, looking at the loom through his spectacles. "This pattern, and the colors, yes, I will tell the Emperor without delay, how very beautiful I think them."

"We shall be much obliged to you," said the impostors, and then they named the different colors and described the pattern of the pretended stuff. The old minister listened attentively to their words, in order that he might repeat them to the Emperor; and then the knaves asked for more silk and gold, saying that it was necessary to complete what they had begun. However, they put all that was given them into their knapsacks; and continued to work with as much apparent diligence as before at their empty looms.

The Emperor now sent another officer of his court to see how the men were getting on, and to ascertain whether the cloth would soon be ready. It was just the same with this gentleman as with the minister; he surveyed the looms on all sides, but could see nothing at all but the empty frames.

"Does not the stuff appear as beautiful to you, as it did to my lord the minister?" asked the impostors of the Emperor's second ambassador; at the same time making the same gestures as before, and talking of the design and colors which were not there.

"I certainly am not stupid!" thought the messenger. "It must be, that I am not fit for my good, profitable office! That is very odd; however, no one shall know anything about it." And accordingly he praised the stuff he could not see, and declared that he was delighted with both colors and patterns. "Indeed, please your Imperial Majesty," said he to his sovereign when he returned, "the cloth which the weavers are preparing is extraordinarily magnificent."

The whole city was talking of the splendid cloth which the Emperor had ordered to be woven at his own expense.

And now the Emperor himself wished to see the costly manufacture, while it was still in the loom. Accompanied by a select number of officers of the court, among whom were the two honest men who had already admired the cloth, he went to the crafty impostors, who, as soon as they were aware of the Emperor's approach, went on working more diligently than ever; although they still did not pass a single thread through the looms.

"Is not the work absolutely magnificent?" said the two officers of the crown, already mentioned. "If your Majesty will only be pleased to look at it! What a splendid design! What glorious colors!" and at the same time they pointed to the empty frames; for they imagined that everyone else could see this exquisite piece of workmanship.

"How is this?" said the Emperor to himself. "I can see nothing! This is indeed a terrible affair! Am I a simpleton, or am I unfit to be an Emperor? That would be the worst thing that could happen—Oh! the cloth is charming," said he, aloud. "It has my complete approbation." And he smiled most graciously, and looked closely at the empty looms; for on no account would he say that he could not see what two of the officers of his court had praised so much. All his retinue now strained their eyes, hoping to discover something on the looms, but they could see no more than the others; nevertheless, they all exclaimed, "Oh, how beautiful!" and advised his majesty to have some new clothes made from this splendid material, for the approaching procession. "Magnificent! Charming! Excellent!" resounded on all sides; and everyone was uncommonly gay. The Emperor shared in the general satisfaction; and presented the impostors with the riband of an order of knighthood, to be worn in their button-holes, and the title of "Gentlemen Weavers."

The rogues sat up the whole of the night before the day on which the procession was to take place, and had sixteen lights burning, so that everyone might see how anxious they were to finish the Emperor's new suit. They pretended to roll the cloth off the looms; cut the air with their scissors; and sewed with needles without any thread in them. "See!" cried they, at last. "The Emperor's new clothes are ready!"

And now the Emperor, with all the grandees of his court, came to the weavers; and the rogues raised their arms, as if in the act of holding something up, saying, "Here are your Majesty's trousers! Here is the scarf! Here is the mantle! The whole suit is as light as a cobweb; one might fancy one has nothing at all on, when dressed in it; that, however, is the great virtue of this delicate cloth."

"Yes indeed!" said all the courtiers, although not one of them could see anything of this exquisite manufacture.

"If your Imperial Majesty will be graciously pleased to take off your clothes, we will fit on the new suit, in front of the looking glass."

The Emperor was accordingly undressed, and the rogues pretended to array him in his new suit; the Emperor turning round, from side to side, before the looking glass.

"How splendid his Majesty looks in his new clothes, and how well they fit!" everyone cried out. "What a design! What colors! These are indeed royal robes!"

"The canopy which is to be borne over your Majesty, in the procession, is waiting," announced the chief master of the ceremonies.

"I am quite ready," answered the Emperor. "Do my new clothes fit well?" asked he, turning himself round again before the looking glass, in order that he might appear to be examining his handsome suit.

So now the Emperor walked under his high canopy in the midst of the procession, through the streets of his capital; and all the people standing by, and those at the windows, cried out, "Oh! How beautiful are our Emperor's new clothes! What a magnificent train there is to the mantle; and how gracefully the scarf hangs!" in short, no one would allow that he could not see these much-admired clothes; because, in doing so, he would have declared himself either a simpleton or unfit for his office. Certainly, none of the Emperor's various suits, had ever made so great an impression, as these invisible ones.

"But the Emperor has nothing at all on!" said a little child.

"Listen to the voice of innocence!" exclaimed his father; and what the child had said was whispered from one to another.

"But he has nothing at all on!" at last cried out all the people. The Emperor was vexed, for he knew that the people were right; but he thought the procession must go on now! And the lords of the bedchamber took greater pains than ever, to appear holding up a train, although, in reality, there was no train to hold.

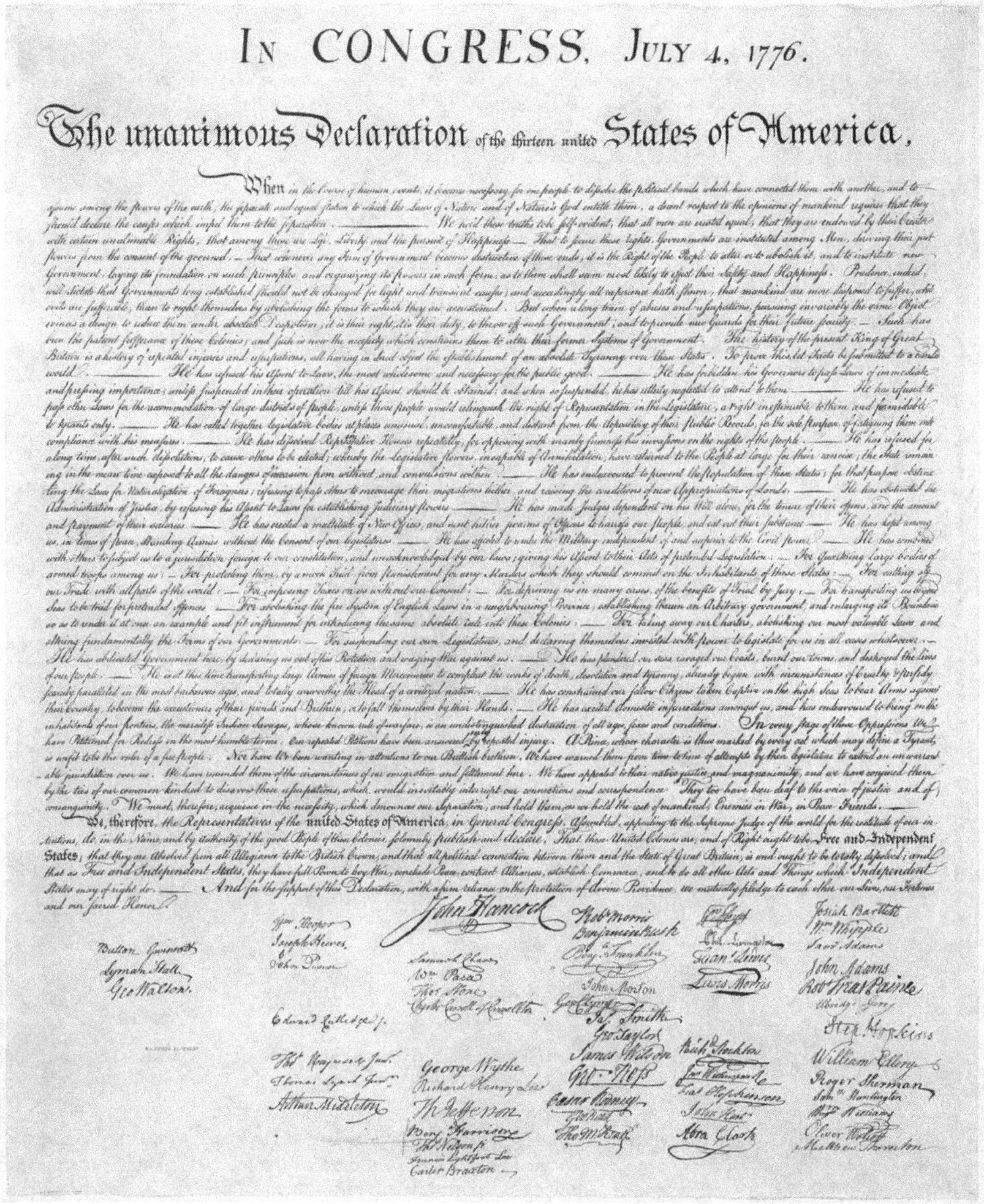

THE DECLARATION OF INDEPENDENCE OF THE UNITED STATES OF AMERICA

BY THOMAS JEFFERSON

Introduction by M. B. McLatchey

When Jefferson crafted the *Declaration of Independence*, he examined closely what the term *independence* meant to the founding brothers. In defining this term and in imagining the requisite elements for a free and fulfilled life, he drew heavily on Aristotle's *Ethics of Happiness*. In tracing Aristotle's influence on this seminal American document, we see the degree to which the founders sought to inherit Greek values and political ideals.

THE UNANIMOUS DECLARATION OF THE THIRTEEN UNITED STATES OF AMERICA

IN CONGRESS, JULY 4, 1776

When in the Course of human events, it becomes necessary for one people to dissolve the political bands which have connected them with another, and to assume, among the Powers of the earth, the separate and equal station to which the Laws of Nature and of Nature's God entitle them, a decent respect to the opinions of mankind requires that they should declare the causes which impel them to the separation.

We hold these truths to be self-evident, that all men are created equal, that they are endowed by their Creator with certain unalienable Rights, that among these are Life, Liberty, and the pursuit of Happiness. That to secure these rights, Governments are instituted among Men, deriving their just powers from the consent of the governed, That whenever any Form of Government becomes destructive of these ends, it is the Right of the People to alter or to abolish it, and to institute new Government, laying its foundation on such principles and organizing its powers in such form, as to them shall seem most likely to effect their Safety and Happiness. Prudence, indeed, will dictate that Governments long established should not be changed for light and transient causes; and accordingly all experience hath shown, that mankind are more disposed to suffer, while evils are sufferable, than to right themselves by abolishing the forms to which they are accustomed. But when a long train of abuses and usurpations, pursuing invariably the same Object evinces a design to reduce them under absolute Despotism, it is their right, it is their duty, to throw off such Government, and to provide new Guards for their future security. --Such has been the patient sufferance of these Colonies; and such is now the necessity which constrains them to alter their former Systems of Government. The history of the present King of Great Britain is a history of repeated injuries and usurpations, all having in direct object the establishment of an absolute Tyranny over these States. To prove this, let Facts be submitted to a candid world.

He has refused his Assent to Laws, the most wholesome and necessary for the public good.

He has forbidden his Governors to pass Laws of immediate and pressing importance, unless suspended in their operation till his Assent should be obtained; and when so suspended, he has utterly neglected to attend to them.

He has refused to pass other Laws for the accommodation of large districts of people, unless those people would relinquish the right of Representation in the Legislature, a right inestimable to them and formidable to tyrants only.

He has called together legislative bodies at places unusual, uncomfortable, and distant from the depository of their Public Records, for the sole purpose of fatiguing them into compliance with his measures.

He has dissolved Representative Houses repeatedly, for opposing with manly firmness his invasions on the rights of the people.

He has refused for a long time, after such dissolutions,to cause others to be elected; whereby the Legislative Powers, incapable of Annihilation, have returned to the People at large for their exercise; the State remaining in the mean time exposed to all the dangers of invasion from without, and convulsions within.

He has endeavoured to prevent the population of these States; for that purpose obstructing the Laws of Naturalization of Foreigners; refusing to pass others to encourage their migration hither, and raising the conditions of new Appropriations of Lands.

He has obstructed the Administration of Justice, by refusing his Assent to Laws for establishing Judiciary Powers.

He has made judges dependent on his Will alone, for the tenure of their offices, and the amount and payment of their salaries.

He has erected a multitude of New Offices, and sent hither swarms of Officers to harass our People, and eat out their substance.

He has kept among us, in times of peace, Standing Armies without the Consent of our legislatures.

He has affected to render the Military independent of and superior to the Civil Power.

He has combined with others to subject us to a jurisdiction foreign to our constitution, and unacknowledged by our laws; giving his Assent to their Acts of pretended legislation:

For quartering large bodies of armed troops among us:

For protecting them, by a mock Trial, from Punishment for any Murders which they should commit on the Inhabitants of these States:

For cutting off our Trade with all parts of the world:

For imposing taxes on us without our Consent:

For depriving us, in many cases, of the benefits of Trial by Jury:

For transporting us beyond Seas to be tried for pretended offences:

For abolishing the free System of English Laws in a neighbouring Province, establishing therein an Arbitrary government, and enlarging its Boundaries so as to render it at once an example and fit instrument for introducing the same absolute rule into these Colonies:

For taking away our Charters, abolishing our most valuable Laws, and altering fundamentally the Forms of our Governments:

For suspending our own Legislatures, and declaring themselves invested with Power to legislate for us in all cases whatsoever.

He has abdicated Government here, by declaring us out of his Protection and waging War against us.

He has plundered our seas, ravaged our Coasts, burnt our towns, and destroyed the lives of our people.

He is at this time transporting large armies of foreign mercenaries to compleat the works of death, desolation and tyranny, already begun with circumstances of Cruelty & perfidy scarcely paralleled in the most barbarous ages, and totally unworthy of the Head of a civilized nation.

He has constrained our fellow Citizens taken Captive on the high Seas to bear Arms against their Country, to become the executioners of their friends and Brethren, or to fall themselves by their Hands.

He has excited domestic insurrections amongst us, and has endeavoured to bring on the inhabitants of our frontiers, the merciless Indian Savages, whose known rule of warfare, is an undistinguished destruction of all ages, sexes and conditions.

In every stage of these Oppressions We have Petitioned for Redress in the most humble terms: Our repeated Petitions have been answered only by repeated injury. A Prince, whose character is thus marked by every act which may define a Tyrant, is unfit to be the ruler of a free People.

Nor have We been wanting in attention to our Brittish brethren. We have warned them from time to time of attempts by their legislature to extend an unwarrantable jurisdiction over us. We have reminded them of the circumstances of our emigration and settlement here. We have appealed to their native justice and magnanimity, and we have conjured them by the ties of our common kindred to disavow these usurpations, which would inevitably interrupt our connections and correspondence. They too have been deaf to the voice of justice and of consanguinity. We must, therefore, acquiesce in the necessity, which denounces our Separation, and hold them, as we hold the rest of mankind, Enemies in War, in Peace Friends.

We, therefore, the Representatives of the United States of America, in General Congress, Assembled, appealing to the Supreme Judge of the world for the rectitude of our intentions, do, in the Name, and by the Authority of the good People of these Colonies, solemnly publish and declare, That these United Colonies are, and of Right ought to be Free and Independent States; that they are Absolved from all Allegiance to the British Crown, and that all political connection between them and the State of Great Britain, is and ought to be totally dissolved; and that as Free and Independent States, they have full Power to levy War, conclude Peace, contract Alliances, establish Commerce, and to do all other Acts and Things which Independent States may of right do. And for the support of this Declaration, with a firm reliance on the Protection of Divine Providence, we mutually pledge to each other our Lives, our Fortunes and our sacred Honor.

FEDERALIST NO. 10

BY JAMES MADISON

Introduction by M. B. McLatchey

As an architect of America's republic, Madison struggled to understand and ultimately define the differences between free and tyrannical systems of government. Like the other founders, he studied classical history and the elements of a Greek democracy versus those of a Roman republic. In choosing the model of the Roman Republic for the *Constitution of the United States*, Madison identified the founders' priorities for the colonies: liberty, prosperity, and security.

Federalist Paper No.10 illuminates the necessity to protect individual freedom by limiting the power of special interests – a subject discussed frequently among Americans today.

THE UNION AS A SAFEGUARD AGAINST DOMESTIC FACTION AND INSURRECTION

FROM THE DAILY ADVERTISER. THURSDAY, NOVEMBER 22, 1787.

To the People of the State of New York:

Among the numerous advantages promised by a well constructed Union, none deserves to be more accurately developed than its tendency to break and control the violence of faction. The friend of popular governments never finds himself so much alarmed for their character and fate, as when he contemplates their propensity to this dangerous vice. He will not fail, therefore, to set a due value on any plan which, without violating the principles to which he is attached, provides a proper cure for it. The instability, injustice, and confusion introduced into the public councils, have, in truth, been the mortal diseases under which popular governments have everywhere perished; as they continue to be the favorite and fruitful topics from which the adversaries to liberty derive their most specious declamations. The valuable improvements made by the American constitutions on the popular models, both ancient and modern, cannot certainly be too much admired; but it would be an unwarrantable partiality, to contend that they have as effectually obviated the danger on this side, as was wished and expected. Complaints are everywhere heard from our most considerate and virtuous citizens, equally the friends of public and private faith, and of public and personal liberty, that our governments are too unstable, that the public good is disregarded in the conflicts of rival parties, and that measures are too often decided, not according to the rules of justice and the rights of the minor party, but by the superior force of an interested and overbearing majority. However anxiously we may wish that these complaints had no foundation, the evidence, of known facts will not permit us to deny that they are in some degree true. It will be found, indeed, on a candid review of our situation, that some of the distresses under which we labor have been erroneously charged on the operation of our governments; but it will be found, at the same time, that other causes will not alone account for many of our heaviest misfortunes; and, particularly, for that prevailing and increasing distrust of public engagements, and alarm for private rights, which are echoed from one end of the continent to the other. These must be chiefly, if not wholly, effects of the unsteadiness and injustice with which a factious spirit has tainted our public administrations.

By a faction, I understand a number of citizens, whether amounting to a majority or a minority of the whole, who are united and actuated by some common impulse of passion, or of interest, adversed to the rights of other citizens, or to the permanent and aggregate interests of the community.

There are two methods of curing the mischiefs of faction: the one, by removing its causes; the other, by controlling its effects.

There are again two methods of removing the causes of faction: the one, by destroying the liberty which is essential to its existence; the other, by giving to every citizen the same opinions, the same passions, and the same interests.

It could never be more truly said than of the first remedy, that it was worse than the disease. Liberty is to faction what air is to fire, an aliment without which it instantly expires. But it could not be less folly to abolish liberty, which is essential to political life, because it nourishes faction, than it would be to wish the annihilation of air, which is essential to animal life, because it imparts to fire its destructive agency.

The second expedient is as impracticable as the first would be unwise. As long as the reason of man continues fallible, and he is at liberty to exercise it, different opinions will be formed. As long as the connection subsists between his reason and his self-love, his opinions and his passions will have a reciprocal influence on each other; and the former will be objects to which the latter will attach themselves. The diversity in the faculties of men, from which the rights of property originate, is not less an insuperable obstacle to a uniformity of interests. The protection of these faculties is the first object of government. From the protection of different and unequal faculties of acquiring property, the possession of different degrees and kinds of property immediately results; and from the influence of these on the sentiments and views of the respective proprietors, ensues a division of the society into different interests and parties.

The latent causes of faction are thus sown in the nature of man; and we see them everywhere brought into different degrees of activity, according to the different circumstances of civil society. A zeal for different opinions concerning religion, concerning government, and many other points, as well of speculation as of practice; an attachment to different leaders ambitiously contending for pre-eminence and power; or to persons of other descriptions whose fortunes have been interesting to the human passions, have, in turn, divided mankind into parties, inflamed them with mutual animosity, and rendered them much more disposed to vex and oppress each other than to co-operate for their common good. So strong is this propensity of mankind to fall into mutual animosities, that where no substantial occasion presents itself, the most frivolous and fanciful distinctions have been sufficient to kindle their unfriendly passions and excite their most violent conflicts. But the most common and durable source of factions has been the various and unequal distribution of property. Those who hold and those who are without property have ever formed distinct interests in society. Those who are creditors, and those who are debtors, fall under a like discrimination. A landed interest, a manufacturing interest, a mercantile interest, a moneyed interest, with many lesser interests, grow up of necessity in civilized nations, and divide them into different classes, actuated by different sentiments and views. The regulation of these various and interfering interests forms the principal task of modern legislation, and involves the spirit of party and faction in the necessary and ordinary operations of the government.

No man is allowed to be a judge in his own cause, because his interest would certainly bias his judgment, and, not improbably, corrupt his integrity. With equal, nay with greater reason, a body of men are unfit to be both judges and parties at the same time; yet what are many of the most important acts of legislation, but so many judicial determinations, not indeed concerning the rights of single persons, but concerning the rights of large bodies of citizens? And what are the different classes of legislators but advocates and parties to the causes which they determine? Is a law proposed concerning private debts? It is a question to which the creditors are parties on one side and the debtors on the other. Justice ought to hold the balance between them. Yet the parties are, and must be, themselves the judges; and the most numerous party, or, in other words, the most powerful faction must be expected to prevail. Shall domestic manufactures be encouraged, and in what degree, by restrictions on foreign manufactures? are questions which would be differently decided by the landed and the manufacturing classes, and probably by neither with a sole regard to justice and the public good. The apportionment of taxes on the various descriptions of property is an act which seems to require the most exact impartiality; yet there is, perhaps, no legislative act in which greater opportunity and temptation are given to a predominant party to trample on the rules of justice. Every shilling with which they overburden the inferior number, is a shilling saved to their own pockets.

It is in vain to say that enlightened statesmen will be able to adjust these clashing interests, and render them all subservient to the public good. Enlightened statesmen will not always be at the helm. Nor, in many cases, can such an adjustment be made at all without taking into view indirect and remote considerations, which will rarely prevail over the immediate interest which one party may find in disregarding the rights of another or the good of the whole.

The inference to which we are brought is, that the CAUSES of faction cannot be removed, and that relief is only to be sought in the means of controlling its EFFECTS.

If a faction consists of less than a majority, relief is supplied by the republican principle, which enables the majority to defeat its sinister views by regular vote. It may clog the administration, it may convulse the society; but it will be unable to execute and mask its violence under the forms of the Constitution. When a majority is included in a faction, the form of popular government, on the other hand, enables it to sacrifice to its ruling passion or interest both the public good and the rights of other citizens. To secure the public good and private rights against the danger of such a faction, and at the same time to preserve the spirit and the form of popular government, is then the great object to which our inquiries are directed. Let me add that it is the great desideratum by which this form of government can be rescued from the opprobrium under which it has so long labored, and be recommended to the esteem and adoption of mankind.

By what means is this object attainable? Evidently by one of two only. Either the existence of the same passion or interest in a majority at the same time must be prevented, or the majority, having such coexistent passion or interest, must be rendered, by their number and local situation, unable to concert and carry into effect schemes of oppression. If the impulse and the opportunity be suffered to coincide, we well know that neither moral nor religious motives can be relied on as an adequate control. They are not found to be such on the injustice and violence of individuals, and lose their efficacy in proportion to the number combined together, that is, in proportion as their efficacy becomes needful.

From this view of the subject it may be concluded that a pure democracy, by which I mean a society consisting of a small number of citizens, who assemble and administer the government in person, can admit of no cure for the mischiefs of faction. A common passion or interest will, in almost every case, be felt by a majority of the whole; a communication and concert result from the form of government itself; and there is nothing to check the inducements to sacrifice the weaker party or an obnoxious individual. Hence it is that such democracies have ever been spectacles of turbulence and contention; have ever been found incompatible with personal security or the rights of property; and have in general been as short in their lives as they have been violent in their deaths. Theoretic politicians, who have patronized this species of government, have erroneously supposed that by reducing mankind to a perfect equality in their political rights, they would, at the same time, be perfectly equalized and assimilated in their possessions, their opinions, and their passions.

A republic, by which I mean a government in which the scheme of representation takes place, opens a different prospect, and promises the cure for which we are seeking. Let us examine the points in which it varies from pure democracy, and we shall comprehend both the nature of the cure and the efficacy which it must derive from the Union.

The two great points of difference between a democracy and a republic are: first, the delegation of the government, in the latter, to a small number of citizens elected by the rest; secondly, the greater number of citizens, and greater sphere of country, over which the latter may be extended.

The effect of the first difference is, on the one hand, to refine and enlarge the public views, by passing them through the medium of a chosen body of citizens, whose wisdom may best discern the true interest of their country, and whose patriotism and love of justice will be least likely to sacrifice it to temporary or partial considerations. Under such a regulation, it may well happen that the public voice, pronounced by the representatives of the people, will be more consonant to the public good than if pronounced by the people themselves, convened for the purpose. On the other hand, the effect may be inverted. Men of factious tempers, of local prejudices, or of sinister designs, may, by intrigue, by corruption, or by other means, first obtain the suffrages, and then betray the interests, of the people. The question resulting is, whether small or extensive republics are more favorable to the election of proper guardians of the public weal; and it is clearly decided in favor of the latter by two obvious considerations:

In the first place, it is to be remarked that, however small the republic may be, the representatives must be raised to a certain number, in order to guard against the cabals of a few; and that, however large it may be, they must be limited to a certain number, in order to guard against the confusion of a multitude. Hence, the number of representatives in the two cases not being in proportion to that of the two constituents, and being proportionally greater in the small republic, it follows that, if the proportion of fit characters be not less in the large than in the small republic, the former will present a greater option, and consequently a greater probability of a fit choice.

In the next place, as each representative will be chosen by a greater number of citizens in the large than in the small republic, it will be more difficult for unworthy candidates to practice with success the vicious arts by which elections are too often carried; and the suffrages of the people being more free, will be more likely to centre in men who possess the most attractive merit and the most diffusive and established characters.

It must be confessed that in this, as in most other cases, there is a mean, on both sides of which inconveniences will be found to lie. By enlarging too much the number of electors, you render the representatives too little acquainted with all their local circumstances and lesser interests; as by reducing it too much, you render him unduly attached to these, and too little fit to comprehend and pursue great and national objects. The federal Constitution forms a happy combination in this respect; the great and aggregate interests being referred to the national, the local and particular to the State legislatures.

The other point of difference is, the greater number of citizens and extent of territory which may be brought within the compass of republican than of democratic government; and it is this circumstance principally which renders factious combinations less to be dreaded in the former than in the latter. The smaller the society, the fewer probably will be the distinct parties and interests composing it; the fewer the distinct parties and interests, the more frequently will a majority be found of the same party; and the smaller the number of individuals composing a majority, and the smaller the compass within which they are placed, the more easily will they concert and execute their plans of oppression. Extend the sphere, and you take in a greater variety of parties and interests; you make it less probable that a majority of the whole will have a common motive to invade the rights of other citizens; or if such a common motive exists, it will be more difficult for all who feel it to discover their own strength, and to act in unison with each other. Besides other impediments, it may be remarked that, where there is a consciousness of unjust or dishonorable purposes, communication is always checked by distrust in proportion to the number whose concurrence is necessary.

Hence, it clearly appears, that the same advantage which a republic has over a democracy, in controlling the effects of faction, is enjoyed by a large over a small republic,—is enjoyed by the Union over the States composing it. Does the advantage consist in the substitution of representatives whose enlightened views and virtuous sentiments render them superior to local prejudices and schemes of injustice? It will not be denied that the representation of the Union will be most likely to possess these requisite endowments. Does it consist in the greater security afforded by a greater variety of parties, against the event of any one party being able to outnumber and oppress the rest? In an equal degree does the increased variety of parties comprised within the Union, increase this security. Does it, in fine, consist in the greater obstacles opposed to the concert and accomplishment of the secret wishes of an unjust and interested majority? Here, again, the extent of the Union gives it the most palpable advantage.

In the extent and proper structure of the Union, therefore, we behold a republican remedy for the diseases most incident to republican government. And according to the degree of pleasure and pride we feel in being republicans, ought to be our zeal in cherishing the spirit and supporting the character of Federalists.

PUBLIUS

FEDERALIST NO. 47

BY JAMES MADISON

Introduction by M. B. McLatchey

As an architect of America's republic, Madison struggled to understand and ultimately define the differences between free and tyrannical systems of government. Like the other founders, he studied classical history and the elements of a Greek democracy versus those of a Roman republic. In choosing the model of the Roman Republic for the *Constitution of the United States*, Madison identified the founders' priorities for the colonies: liberty, prosperity, and security.

Federalist Paper No. 47 argues for the model of a Roman Republic for the new republic of America based upon its two advantages: first, its distribution of power across three governing branches; second, its emphasis on wider representation of a diverse body of people.

THE PARTICULAR STRUCTURE OF THE NEW GOVERNMENT AND THE DISTRIBUTION OF POWER AMONG ITS DIFFERENT PARTS.

FOR THE INDEPENDENT JOURNAL. WEDNESDAY, JANUARY 30, 1788.

To the People of the State of New York:

Having reviewed the general form of the proposed government and the general mass of power allotted to it, I proceed to examine the particular structure of this government, and the distribution of this mass of power among its constituent parts.

One of the principal objections inculcated by the more respectable adversaries to the Constitution, is its supposed violation of the political maxim, that the legislative, executive, and judiciary departments ought to be separate and distinct. In the structure of the federal government, no regard, it is said, seems to have been paid to this essential precaution in favor of liberty. The several departments of power are distributed and blended in such a manner as at once to destroy all symmetry and beauty of form, and to expose some of the essential parts of the edifice to the danger of being crushed by the disproportionate weight of other parts.

No political truth is certainly of greater intrinsic value, or is stamped with the authority of more enlightened patrons of liberty, than that on which the objection is founded. The accumulation of all powers, legislative, executive, and judiciary, in the same hands, whether of one, a few, or many, and whether hereditary, self-appointed, or elective, may justly be pronounced the very definition of tyranny. Were the federal Constitution, therefore, really chargeable with the accumulation of power, or with a mixture of powers, having a dangerous tendency to such an accumulation, no further arguments would be necessary to inspire a universal reprobation of the system. I persuade myself, however, that it will be made apparent to every one, that the charge cannot be supported, and that the maxim on which it relies has been totally misconceived and misapplied. In order to form correct ideas on this important subject, it will be proper to investigate the sense in which the preservation of liberty requires that the three great departments of power should be separate and distinct.

The oracle who is always consulted and cited on this subject is the celebrated Montesquieu. If he be not the author of this invaluable precept in the science of politics, he has the merit at least of displaying and recommending it most effectually to the attention of mankind. Let us endeavor, in the first place, to ascertain his meaning on this point.

The British Constitution was to Montesquieu what Homer has been to the didactic writers on epic poetry. As the latter have considered the work of the immortal bard as the perfect model from which the principles and rules of the epic art were to be drawn, and by which all similar works were to be judged, so this great political critic appears to have viewed the Constitution of England as the standard, or to use his own expression, as the mirror of political liberty; and to have delivered, in the form of elementary truths, the several characteristic principles of that particular system. That we may be sure, then, not to mistake his meaning in this case, let us recur to the source from which the maxim was drawn.

On the slightest view of the British Constitution, we must perceive that the legislative, executive, and judiciary departments are by no means totally separate and distinct from each other. The executive magistrate forms an integral part of the legislative authority. He alone has the prerogative of making treaties with foreign sovereigns, which, when made, have, under certain limitations, the force of legislative acts. All the members of the judiciary department are appointed by him, can be removed by him on the address of the two Houses of Parliament, and form, when he pleases to consult them, one of his constitutional councils. One branch of the legislative department forms also a great constitutional council to the executive chief, as, on another hand, it is the sole depositary of judicial power in cases of impeachment, and is invested with the supreme appellate jurisdiction in all other cases. The judges, again, are so far connected with the legislative department as often to attend and participate in its deliberations, though not admitted to a legislative vote.

From these facts, by which Montesquieu was guided, it may clearly be inferred that, in saying "There can be no liberty where the legislative and executive powers are united in the same person, or body of magistrates," or, "if the power of judging be not separated from the legislative and executive powers," he did not mean that these departments ought to have no PARTIAL AGENCY in, or no CONTROL over, the acts of each other. His meaning, as his own words import, and still more conclusively as illustrated by the example in his eye, can amount to no more than this, that where the WHOLE power of one department is exercised by the same hands which possess the WHOLE power of another department, the fundamental principles of a free constitution are subverted. This would have been the case in the constitution examined by him, if the king, who is the sole executive magistrate, had possessed also the complete legislative power, or the supreme administration of justice; or if the entire legislative body had possessed the supreme judiciary, or the supreme executive authority. This, however, is not among the vices of that constitution. The magistrate in whom the whole executive power resides cannot of himself make a law, though he can put a negative on every law; nor administer justice in person, though he has the appointment of those who do administer it. The judges can exercise no executive prerogative, though they are shoots from the executive stock; nor any legislative function, though they may be advised with by the legislative councils. The entire legislature can perform no judiciary act, though by the joint act of two of its branches the judges may be removed from their offices, and though one of its branches is possessed of the judicial power in the last resort. The entire legislature, again, can exercise no executive prerogative, though one of its branches constitutes the supreme executive magistracy, and another, on the impeachment of a third, can try and condemn all the subordinate officers in the executive department.

The reasons on which Montesquieu grounds his maxim are a further demonstration of his meaning. "When the legislative and executive powers are united in the same person or body," says he, "there can be no liberty, because apprehensions may arise lest THE SAME monarch or senate should ENACT tyrannical laws to EXECUTE them in a tyrannical manner." Again: "Were the power of judging joined with the legislative, the life and liberty of the subject would be exposed to arbitrary control, for THE JUDGE would then be THE LEGISLATOR. Were it joined to the executive power, THE JUDGE might behave with all the violence of AN OPPRESSOR." Some of these reasons are more fully explained in other passages; but briefly stated as they are here, they sufficiently establish the meaning which we have put on this celebrated maxim of this celebrated author.

If we look into the constitutions of the several States, we find that, notwithstanding the emphatical and, in some instances, the unqualified terms in which this axiom has been laid down, there is not a single instance in which the several departments of power have been kept absolutely separate and distinct. New Hampshire, whose constitution was the last formed, seems to have been fully aware of the impossibility and inexpediency of avoiding any mixture whatever of these departments, and has qualified the doctrine by declaring "that the legislative, executive, and judiciary powers ought to be kept as separate from, and independent of, each other AS THE NATURE OF A FREE GOVERNMENT WILL ADMIT; OR AS IS CONSISTENT WITH THAT CHAIN OF CONNECTION THAT BINDS THE WHOLE FABRIC OF THE CONSTITUTION IN ONE INDISSOLUBLE BOND OF UNITY AND AMITY." Her constitution accordingly mixes these departments in several respects. The Senate, which is a branch of the legislative department, is also a judicial tribunal for the trial of impeachments. The President, who is the head of the executive department, is the presiding member also of the Senate; and, besides an equal vote in all cases, has a casting vote in case of a tie. The executive head is himself eventually elective every year by the legislative department, and his council is every year chosen by and from the members of the same department. Several of the officers of state are also appointed by the legislature. And the members of the judiciary department are appointed by the executive department.

The constitution of Massachusetts has observed a sufficient though less pointed caution, in expressing this fundamental article of liberty. It declares "that the legislative department shall never exercise the executive and judicial powers, or either of them; the executive shall never exercise the legislative and judicial powers, or either of them; the judicial shall never exercise the legislative and executive powers, or either of them." This declaration corresponds precisely with the doctrine of Montesquieu, as it has been explained, and is not in a single point violated by the plan of the convention. It goes no farther than to prohibit any one of the entire departments from exercising the powers of another department. In the very Constitution to which it is prefixed, a partial mixture of powers has been admitted. The executive magistrate has a qualified negative on the legislative body, and the Senate, which is a part of the legislature, is a court of impeachment for members both of the executive and judiciary departments. The members of the judiciary department, again, are appointable by the executive department, and removable by the same authority on the address of the two legislative branches. Lastly, a number of the officers of government are annually appointed by the legislative department. As the appointment to offices, particularly executive offices, is in its nature an executive function, the compilers of the Constitution have, in this last point at least, violated the rule established by themselves.

I pass over the constitutions of Rhode Island and Connecticut, because they were formed prior to the Revolution, and even before the principle under examination had become an object of political attention.

The constitution of New York contains no declaration on this subject; but appears very clearly to have been framed with an eye to the danger of improperly blending the different departments. It gives, nevertheless, to the executive magistrate, a partial control over the legislative department; and, what is more, gives a like control to the judiciary department; and even blends the executive and judiciary departments in the exercise of this control. In its council of appointment members of the legislature are associated with the executive authority, in the appointment of officers, both executive and judiciary. And its court for the trial of impeachments and correction of errors is to consist of one branch of the legislature and the principal members of the judiciary department.

The constitution of New Jersey has blended the different powers of government more than any of the preceding. The governor, who is the executive magistrate, is appointed by the legislature; is chancellor and ordinary, or surrogate of the State; is a member of the Supreme Court of Appeals, and president, with a casting vote, of one of the legislative branches. The same legislative branch acts again as executive council of the governor, and with him constitutes the Court of Appeals. The members of the judiciary department are appointed by the legislative department and removable by one branch of it, on the impeachment of the other.

According to the constitution of Pennsylvania, the president, who is the head of the executive department, is annually elected by a vote in which the legislative department predominates. In conjunction with an executive council, he appoints the members of the judiciary department, and forms a court of impeachment for trial of all officers, judiciary as well as executive. The judges of the Supreme Court and justices of the peace seem also to be removable by the legislature; and the executive power of pardoning in certain cases, to be referred to the same department. The members of the executive council are made EX-OFFICIO justices of peace throughout the State.

In Delaware, the chief executive magistrate is annually elected by the legislative department. The speakers of the two legislative branches are vice-presidents in the executive department. The executive chief, with six others, appointed, three by each of the legislative branches constitutes the Supreme Court of Appeals; he is joined with the legislative department in the appointment of the other judges. Throughout the States, it appears that the members of the legislature may at the same time be justices of the peace; in this State, the members of one branch of it are EX-OFFICIO justices of the peace; as are also the members of the executive council. The principal officers of the executive department are appointed by the legislative; and one branch of the latter forms a court of impeachments. All officers may be removed on address of the legislature.

Maryland has adopted the maxim in the most unqualified terms; declaring that the legislative, executive, and judicial powers of government ought to be forever separate and distinct from each other. Her constitution, notwithstanding, makes the executive magistrate appointable by the legislative department; and the members of the judiciary by the executive department.

The language of Virginia is still more pointed on this subject. Her constitution declares, "that the legislative, executive, and judiciary departments shall be separate and distinct; so that neither exercise the powers properly belonging to the other; nor shall any person exercise the powers of more than one of them at the same time, except that the justices of county courts shall be eligible to either House of Assembly." Yet we find not only this express exception, with respect to the members of the inferior courts, but that the chief magistrate, with his executive council, are appointable by the legislature; that two members of the latter are triennially displaced at the pleasure of the legislature; and that all the principal offices, both executive and judiciary, are filled by the same department. The executive prerogative of pardon, also, is in one case vested in the legislative department.

The constitution of North Carolina, which declares "that the legislative, executive, and supreme judicial powers of government ought to be forever separate and distinct from each other," refers, at the same time, to the legislative department, the appointment not only of the executive chief, but all the principal officers within both that and the judiciary department.

In South Carolina, the constitution makes the executive magistracy eligible by the legislative department. It gives to the latter, also, the appointment of the members of the judiciary department, including even justices of the peace and sheriffs; and the appointment of officers in the executive department, down to captains in the army and navy of the State.

In the constitution of Georgia, where it is declared "that the legislative, executive, and judiciary departments shall be separate and distinct, so that neither exercise the powers properly belonging to the other," we find that the executive department is to be filled by appointments of the legislature; and the executive prerogative of pardon to be finally exercised by the same authority. Even justices of the peace are to be appointed by the legislature.

In citing these cases, in which the legislative, executive, and judiciary departments have not been kept totally separate and distinct, I wish not to be regarded as an advocate for the particular organizations of the several State governments. I am fully aware that among the many excellent principles which they exemplify, they carry strong marks of the haste, and still stronger of the inexperience, under which they were framed. It is but too obvious that in some instances the fundamental principle under consideration has been violated by too great a mixture, and even an actual consolidation, of the different powers; and that in no instance has a competent provision been made for maintaining in practice the separation delineated on paper. What I have wished to evince is, that the charge brought against the proposed Constitution, of violating the sacred maxim of free government, is warranted neither by the real meaning annexed to that maxim by its author, nor by the sense in which it has hitherto been understood in America. This interesting subject will be resumed in the ensuing paper.

PUBLIUS

THE CONSTITUTION OF THE UNITED STATES

Introduction by M. B. McLatchey

We do well to remember that the individuals who crafted the Constitution of the United States were well acquainted with tyranny. At the close of the American Revolution in 1783, after eight years of military contests with British troops, the delegates that gathered for a Federal Convention in the summer of 1787 had one goal in mind: liberty. Drafted by a delegation of representatives from seven states -- some of the brightest minds in American history -- the Constitution of the United States codifies the principles that continue to guide our republic today. First among these principles were the requirement for an effective, but limited central government and the need for wide and equal representation among its citizens. The issues that weighed on the minds of these men were the same ones that American citizens, legislators, and justices debate today. What is the right relationship between a government and its people, or between a federal government and the states? In a republic that prizes equality among its citizens, how do we also protect individual liberties? How should power be distributed among the people of a just republic? What sustained these architects of the republic was the guidance they received in knowing that men before them had also struggled for their freedoms and examined these same questions: the poets Homer and Virgil; philosophers such as Socrates, Plato and Aristotle; and statesmen like Caesar and Cicero. The degree to which they absorbed the ideals and values of these ancient thinkers cannot be underestimated.

Preamble

We the People of the United States, in Order to form a more perfect Union, establish Justice, insure domestic Tranquility, provide for the common defence, promote the general Welfare, and secure the Blessings of Liberty to ourselves and our Posterity, do ordain and establish this Constitution for the United States of America.

Article. I.

Section. 1.
All legislative Powers herein granted shall be vested in a Congress of the United States, which shall consist of a Senate and House of Representatives.

Section. 2.
The House of Representatives shall be composed of Members chosen every second Year by the People of the several States, and the Electors in each State shall have the Qualifications requisite for Electors of the most numerous Branch of the State Legislature.

No Person shall be a Representative who shall not have attained to the Age of twenty five Years, and been seven Years a Citizen of the United States, and who shall not, when elected, be an Inhabitant of that State in which he shall be chosen.

Representatives and direct Taxes shall be apportioned among the several States which may be included within this Union, according to their respective Numbers, which shall be determined by adding to the whole Number of free Persons, including those bound to Service for a Term of Years, and excluding Indians not taxed, three fifths of all other Persons. The actual Enumeration shall be made within three Years after the first Meeting of the Congress of the United States, and within every subsequent Term of ten Years, in such Manner as they shall by Law direct. The Number of Representatives shall not exceed one for every thirty Thousand, but each State shall have at Least one Representative; and until such enumeration shall be made, the State of New Hampshire shall be entitled to chuse three, Massachusetts eight, Rhode-Island and Providence Plantations one, Connecticut five, New-York six, New Jersey four, Pennsylvania eight, Delaware one, Maryland six, Virginia ten, North Carolina five, South Carolina five, and Georgia three.

When vacancies happen in the Representation from any State, the Executive Authority thereof shall issue Writs of Election to fill such Vacancies.

The House of Representatives shall chuse their Speaker and other Officers; and shall have the sole Power of Impeachment.

Section. 3.

The Senate of the United States shall be composed of two Senators from each State, chosen by the Legislature thereof for six Years; and each Senator shall have one Vote.

Immediately after they shall be assembled in Consequence of the first Election, they shall be divided as equally as may be into three Classes. The Seats of the Senators of the first Class shall be vacated at the Expiration of the second Year, of the second Class at the Expiration of the fourth Year, and of the third Class at the Expiration of the sixth Year, so that one third may be chosen every second Year; and if Vacancies happen by Resignation, or otherwise, during the Recess of the Legislature of any State, the Executive thereof may make temporary Appointments until the next Meeting of the Legislature, which shall then fill such Vacancies.

No Person shall be a Senator who shall not have attained to the Age of thirty Years, and been nine Years a Citizen of the United States, and who shall not, when elected, be an Inhabitant of that State for which he shall be chosen.

The Vice President of the United States shall be President of the Senate, but shall have no Vote, unless they be equally divided.

The Senate shall chuse their other Officers, and also a President pro tempore, in the Absence of the Vice President, or when he shall exercise the Office of President of the United States.

The Senate shall have the sole Power to try all Impeachments. When sitting for that Purpose, they shall be on Oath or Affirmation. When the President of the United States is tried, the Chief Justice shall preside: And no Person shall be convicted without the Concurrence of two thirds of the Members present.

Judgment in Cases of Impeachment shall not extend further than to removal from Office, and disqualification to hold and enjoy any Office of honor, Trust or Profit under the United States: but the Party convicted shall nevertheless be liable and subject to Indictment, Trial, Judgment and Punishment, according to Law.

Section. 4.

The Times, Places and Manner of holding Elections for Senators and Representatives, shall be prescribed in each State by the Legislature thereof; but the Congress may at any time by Law make or alter such Regulations, except as to the Places of chusing Senators.

The Congress shall assemble at least once in every Year, and such Meeting shall be on the first Monday in December, unless they shall by Law appoint a different Day.

Section. 5.

Each House shall be the Judge of the Elections, Returns and Qualifications of its own Members, and a Majority of each shall constitute a Quorum to do Business; but a smaller Number may adjourn from day to day, and may be authorized to compel the Attendance of absent Members, in such Manner, and under such Penalties as each House may provide.

Each House may determine the Rules of its Proceedings, punish its Members for disorderly Behaviour, and, with the Concurrence of two thirds, expel a Member.

Each House shall keep a Journal of its Proceedings, and from time to time publish the same, excepting such Parts as may in their Judgment require Secrecy; and the Yeas and Nays of the Members of either House on any question shall, at the Desire of one fifth of those Present, be entered on the Journal.

Neither House, during the Session of Congress, shall, without the Consent of the other, adjourn for more than three days, nor to any other Place than that in which the two Houses shall be sitting.

Section. 6.

The Senators and Representatives shall receive a Compensation for their Services, to be ascertained by Law, and paid out of the Treasury of the United States. They shall in all Cases, except Treason, Felony and Breach of the Peace, be privileged from Arrest during their Attendance at the Session of their respective Houses, and in going to and returning from the same; and for any Speech or Debate in either House, they shall not be questioned in any other Place.

No Senator or Representative shall, during the Time for which he was elected, be appointed to any civil Office under the Authority of the United States, which shall have been created, or the Emoluments whereof shall have been encreased during such time; and no Person holding any Office under the United States, shall be a Member of either House during his Continuance in Office.

Section. 7.

All Bills for raising Revenue shall originate in the House of Representatives; but the Senate may propose or concur with Amendments as on other Bills.

Every Bill which shall have passed the House of Representatives and the Senate, shall, before it become a Law, be presented to the President of the United States: If he approve he shall sign it, but if not he shall return it, with his Objections to that House in which it shall have originated, who shall enter the Objections at large on their Journal, and proceed to reconsider it. If after such Reconsideration two thirds of that House shall agree to pass the Bill, it shall be sent, together with the Objections, to the other House, by which it shall likewise be reconsidered, and if approved by two thirds of that House, it shall become a Law. But in all such Cases the Votes of both Houses shall be determined by yeas and Nays, and the Names of the Persons voting for and against the Bill shall be entered on the Journal of each House respectively. If any Bill shall not be returned by the President within ten Days (Sundays excepted) after it shall have been presented to him, the Same shall be a Law, in like Manner as if he had signed it, unless the Congress by their Adjournment prevent its Return, in which Case it shall not be a Law.

Every Order, Resolution, or Vote to which the Concurrence of the Senate and House of Representatives may be necessary (except on a question of Adjournment) shall be presented to the President of the United States; and before the Same shall take Effect, shall be approved by him, or being disapproved by him, shall be repassed by two thirds of the Senate and House of Representatives, according to the Rules and Limitations prescribed in the Case of a Bill.

Section. 8.

The Congress shall have Power To lay and collect Taxes, Duties, Imposts and Excises, to pay the Debts and provide for the common Defence and general Welfare of the United States; but all Duties, Imposts and Excises shall be uniform throughout the United States;

To borrow Money on the credit of the United States;

To regulate Commerce with foreign Nations, and among the several States, and with the Indian Tribes;

To establish an uniform Rule of Naturalization, and uniform Laws on the subject of Bankruptcies throughout the United States;

To coin Money, regulate the Value thereof, and of foreign Coin, and fix the Standard of Weights and Measures;

To provide for the Punishment of counterfeiting the Securities and current Coin of the United States;

To establish Post Offices and post Roads;

To promote the Progress of Science and useful Arts, by securing for limited Times to Authors and Inventors the exclusive Right to their respective Writings and Discoveries;

To constitute Tribunals inferior to the supreme Court;

To define and punish Piracies and Felonies committed on the high Seas, and Offences against the Law of Nations;

To declare War, grant Letters of Marque and Reprisal, and make Rules concerning Captures on Land and Water;

To raise and support Armies, but no Appropriation of Money to that Use shall be for a longer Term than two Years;

To provide and maintain a Navy;

To make Rules for the Government and Regulation of the land and naval Forces;

To provide for calling forth the Militia to execute the Laws of the Union, suppress Insurrections and repel Invasions;

To provide for organizing, arming, and disciplining, the Militia, and for governing such Part of them as may be employed in the Service of the United States, reserving to the States respectively, the Appointment of the Officers, and the Authority of training the Militia according to the discipline prescribed by Congress;

To exercise exclusive Legislation in all Cases whatsoever, over such District (not exceeding ten Miles square) as may, by Cession of particular States, and the Acceptance of Congress, become the Seat of the Government of the United States, and to exercise like Authority over all Places purchased by the Consent of the Legislature of the State in which the Same shall be, for the Erection of Forts, Magazines, Arsenals, dock-Yards, and other needful Buildings;--And

To make all Laws which shall be necessary and proper for carrying into Execution the foregoing Powers, and all other Powers vested by this Constitution in the Government of the United States, or in any Department or Officer thereof.

Section. 9.
The Migration or Importation of such Persons as any of the States now existing shall think proper to admit, shall not be prohibited by the Congress prior to the Year one thousand eight hundred and eight, but a Tax or duty may be imposed on such Importation, not exceeding ten dollars for each Person.

The Privilege of the Writ of Habeas Corpus shall not be suspended, unless when in Cases of Rebellion or Invasion the public Safety may require it.

No Bill of Attainder or ex post facto Law shall be passed.

No Capitation, or other direct, Tax shall be laid, unless in Proportion to the Census or enumeration herein before directed to be taken.

No Tax or Duty shall be laid on Articles exported from any State.

No Preference shall be given by any Regulation of Commerce or Revenue to the Ports of one State over those of another; nor shall Vessels bound to, or from, one State, be obliged to enter, clear, or pay Duties in another.

No Money shall be drawn from the Treasury, but in Consequence of Appropriations made by Law; and a regular Statement and Account of the Receipts and Expenditures of all public Money shall be published from time to time.

No Title of Nobility shall be granted by the United States: And no Person holding any Office of Profit or Trust under them, shall, without the Consent of the Congress, accept of any present, Emolument, Office, or Title, of any kind whatever, from any King, Prince, or foreign State.

Section. 10.

No State shall enter into any Treaty, Alliance, or Confederation; grant Letters of Marque and Reprisal; coin Money; emit Bills of Credit; make any Thing but gold and silver Coin a Tender in Payment of Debts; pass any Bill of Attainder, ex post facto Law, or Law impairing the Obligation of Contracts, or grant any Title of Nobility.

No State shall, without the Consent of the Congress, lay any Imposts or Duties on Imports or Exports, except what may be absolutely necessary for executing it's inspection Laws: and the net Produce of all Duties and Imposts, laid by any State on Imports or Exports, shall be for the Use of the Treasury of the United States; and all such Laws shall be subject to the Revision and Controul of the Congress.

No State shall, without the Consent of Congress, lay any Duty of Tonnage, keep Troops, or Ships of War in time of Peace, enter into any Agreement or Compact with another State, or with a foreign Power, or engage in War, unless actually invaded, or in such imminent Danger as will not admit of delay.

Article. II.

Section. 1.

The executive Power shall be vested in a President of the United States of America. He shall hold his Office during the Term of four Years, and, together with the Vice President, chosen for the same Term, be elected, as follows:

Each State shall appoint, in such Manner as the Legislature thereof may direct, a Number of Electors, equal to the whole Number of Senators and Representatives to which the State may be entitled in the Congress: but no Senator or Representative, or Person holding an Office of Trust or Profit under the United States, shall be appointed an Elector.

The Electors shall meet in their respective States, and vote by Ballot for two Persons, of whom one at least shall not be an Inhabitant of the same State with themselves. And they shall make a List of all the Persons voted for, and of the Number of Votes for each; which List they shall sign and certify, and transmit sealed to the Seat of the Government of the United States, directed to the President of the Senate. The President of the Senate shall, in the Presence of the Senate and House of Representatives, open all the Certificates, and the Votes shall then be counted. The Person having the greatest Number of Votes shall be the President, if such Number be a Majority of the whole Number of Electors appointed; and if there be more than one who have such Majority, and have an equal Number of Votes, then the House of Representatives shall immediately chuse by Ballot one of them for President; and if no Person have a Majority, then from the five highest on the List the said House shall in like Manner chuse the President. But in chusing the President, the Votes shall be taken by States, the Representation from each State having one Vote; A quorum for this purpose shall consist of a Member or Members from two thirds of the States, and a Majority of all the States shall be necessary to a Choice. In every Case, after the Choice of the President, the Person having the greatest Number of Votes of the Electors shall be the Vice President. But if there should remain two or more who have equal Votes, the Senate shall chuse from them by Ballot the Vice President.

The Congress may determine the Time of chusing the Electors, and the Day on which they shall give their Votes; which Day shall be the same throughout the United States.

No Person except a natural born Citizen, or a Citizen of the United States, at the time of the Adoption of this Constitution, shall be eligible to the Office of President; neither shall any Person be eligible to that Office who shall not have attained to the Age of thirty five Years, and been fourteen Years a Resident within the United States.

In Case of the Removal of the President from Office, or of his Death, Resignation, or Inability to discharge the Powers and Duties of the said Office, the Same shall devolve on the Vice President, and the Congress may by Law provide for the Case of Removal, Death, Resignation or Inability, both of the President and Vice President, declaring what Officer shall then act as President, and such Officer shall act accordingly, until the Disability be removed, or a President shall be elected.

The President shall, at stated Times, receive for his Services, a Compensation, which shall neither be increased nor diminished during the Period for which he shall have been elected, and he shall not receive within that Period any other Emolument from the United States, or any of them.

Before he enter on the Execution of his Office, he shall take the following Oath or Affirmation:--"I do solemnly swear (or affirm) that I will faithfully execute the Office of President of the United States, and will to the best of my Ability, preserve, protect and defend the Constitution of the United States."

Section. 2.
The President shall be Commander in Chief of the Army and Navy of the United States, and of the Militia of the several States, when called into the actual Service of the United States; he may require the Opinion, in writing, of the principal Officer in each of the executive Departments, upon any Subject relating to the Duties of their respective Offices, and he shall have Power to grant Reprieves and Pardons for Offences against the United States, except in Cases of Impeachment.

He shall have Power, by and with the Advice and Consent of the Senate, to make Treaties, provided two thirds of the Senators present concur; and he shall nominate, and by and with the Advice and Consent of the Senate, shall appoint Ambassadors, other public Ministers and Consuls, Judges of the supreme Court, and all other Officers of the United States, whose Appointments are not herein otherwise provided for, and which shall be established by Law: but the Congress may by Law vest the Appointment of such inferior Officers, as they think proper, in the President alone, in the Courts of Law, or in the Heads of Departments.

The President shall have Power to fill up all Vacancies that may happen during the Recess of the Senate, by granting Commissions which shall expire at the End of their next Session.

Section. 3.
He shall from time to time give to the Congress Information of the State of the Union, and recommend to their Consideration such Measures as he shall judge necessary and expedient; he may, on extraordinary Occasions, convene both Houses, or either of them, and in Case of Disagreement between them, with Respect to the Time of Adjournment, he may adjourn them to such Time as he shall think proper; he shall receive Ambassadors and other public Ministers; he shall take Care that the Laws be faithfully executed, and shall Commission all the Officers of the United States.

Section. 4.
The President, Vice President and all civil Officers of the United States, shall be removed from Office on Impeachment for, and Conviction of, Treason, Bribery, or other high Crimes and Misdemeanors.

Article III.

Section. 1.
The judicial Power of the United States shall be vested in one supreme Court, and in such inferior Courts as the Congress may from time to time ordain and establish. The Judges, both of the supreme and inferior Courts, shall hold their Offices during good Behaviour, and shall, at stated Times, receive for their Services a Compensation, which shall not be diminished during their Continuance in Office.

Section. 2.
The judicial Power shall extend to all Cases, in Law and Equity, arising under this Constitution, the Laws of the United States, and Treaties made, or which shall be made, under their Authority;--to all Cases affecting Ambassadors, other public Ministers and Consuls;--to all Cases of admiralty and maritime Jurisdiction;--to Controversies to which the

United States shall be a Party;--to Controversies between two or more States;-- between a State and Citizens of another State,--between Citizens of different States,--between Citizens of the same State claiming Lands under Grants of different States, and between a State, or the Citizens thereof, and foreign States, Citizens or Subjects.

In all Cases affecting Ambassadors, other public Ministers and Consuls, and those in which a State shall be Party, the supreme Court shall have original Jurisdiction. In all the other Cases before mentioned, the supreme Court shall have appellate Jurisdiction, both as to Law and Fact, with such Exceptions, and under such Regulations as the Congress shall make.

The Trial of all Crimes, except in Cases of Impeachment, shall be by Jury; and such Trial shall be held in the State where the said Crimes shall have been committed; but when not committed within any State, the Trial shall be at such Place or Places as the Congress may by Law have directed.

Section. 3.

Treason against the United States, shall consist only in levying War against them, or in adhering to their Enemies, giving them Aid and Comfort. No Person shall be convicted of Treason unless on the Testimony of two Witnesses to the same overt Act, or on Confession in open Court.

The Congress shall have Power to declare the Punishment of Treason, but no Attainder of Treason shall work Corruption of Blood, or Forfeiture except during the Life of the Person attainted.

Article. IV.

Section. 1.

Full Faith and Credit shall be given in each State to the public Acts, Records, and judicial Proceedings of every other State. And the Congress may by general Laws prescribe the Manner in which such Acts, Records and Proceedings shall be proved, and the Effect thereof.

Section. 2.

The Citizens of each State shall be entitled to all Privileges and Immunities of Citizens in the several States.

A Person charged in any State with Treason, Felony, or other Crime, who shall flee from Justice, and be found in another State, shall on Demand of the executive Authority of the State from which he fled, be delivered up, to be removed to the State having Jurisdiction of the Crime.

No Person held to Service or Labour in one State, under the Laws thereof, escaping into another, shall, in Consequence of any Law or Regulation therein, be discharged from such Service or Labour, but shall be delivered up on Claim of the Party to whom such Service or Labour may be due.

Section. 3.

New States may be admitted by the Congress into this Union; but no new State shall be formed or erected within the Jurisdiction of any other State; nor any State be formed by the Junction of two or more States, or Parts of States, without the Consent of the Legislatures of the States concerned as well as of the Congress.

The Congress shall have Power to dispose of and make all needful Rules and Regulations respecting the Territory or other Property belonging to the United States; and nothing in this Constitution shall be so construed as to Prejudice any Claims of the United States, or of any particular State.

Section. 4.

The United States shall guarantee to every State in this Union a Republican Form of Government, and shall protect each of them against Invasion; and on Application of the Legislature, or of the Executive (when the Legislature cannot be convened), against domestic Violence.

Article. V.

The Congress, whenever two thirds of both Houses shall deem it necessary, shall propose Amendments to this Constitution, or, on the Application of the Legislatures of two thirds of the several States, shall call a Convention for proposing Amendments, which, in either Case, shall be valid to all Intents and Purposes, as Part of this Constitution, when ratified by the Legislatures of three fourths of the several States, or by Conventions in three fourths thereof, as the one or the other Mode of Ratification may be proposed by the Congress; Provided that no Amendment which may be made prior to the Year One thousand eight hundred and eight shall in any Manner affect the first and fourth Clauses in the Ninth Section of the first Article; and that no State, without its Consent, shall be deprived of its equal Suffrage in the Senate.

Article. VI.

All Debts contracted and Engagements entered into, before the Adoption of this Constitution, shall be as valid against the United States under this Constitution, as under the Confederation.

This Constitution, and the Laws of the United States which shall be made in Pursuance thereof; and all Treaties made, or which shall be made, under the Authority of the United States, shall be the supreme Law of the Land; and the Judges in every State shall be bound thereby, any Thing in the Constitution or Laws of any State to the Contrary notwithstanding.

The Senators and Representatives before mentioned, and the Members of the several State Legislatures, and all executive and judicial Officers, both of the United States and of the several States, shall be bound by Oath or Affirmation, to support this Constitution; but no religious Test shall ever be required as a Qualification to any Office or public Trust under the United States.

Article. VII.

The Ratification of the Conventions of nine States, shall be sufficient for the Establishment of this Constitution between the States so ratifying the Same.

The Word, "the," being interlined between the seventh and eighth Lines of the first Page, the Word "Thirty" being partly written on an Erazure in the fifteenth Line of the first Page, The Words "is tried" being interlined between the thirty second and thirty third Lines of the first Page and the Word "the" being interlined between the forty third and forty fourth Lines of the second Page.

Attest William Jackson Secretary

done in Convention by the Unanimous Consent of the States present the Seventeenth Day of September in the Year of our Lord one thousand seven hundred and Eighty seven and of the Independance of the United States of America the Twelfth In witness whereof We have hereunto subscribed our Names,

THE BILL OF RIGHTS

Introduction by M. B. McLatchey

The first ten amendments to the U.S. Constitution, known as the *Bill of Rights*, reflect the founders' fundamental interest in guarding the liberties of the individual against a strong, centralized government. In the drafting of the Constitution of the United States, a faction of the delegates in attendance – known as anti-Federalists and with Jefferson leading them – warned against the potential of replacing one tyrannical form of government with a new one. Their discomfort with the powers that the U.S. Constitution apparently granted to a central government generated a debate among the delegates that forced them to acknowledge their shared ideal of individual freedom. The Bill of Rights -- crafted in September of 1789 , two years after the U.S. Constitution – strikes the balance that they were looking for between a united America and an America that cherishes the liberty and rights of the individual.

CONGRESS OF THE UNITED STATES

begun and held at the City of New-York, on Wednesday the fourth of March, one thousand seven hundred and eighty nine.

THE Conventions of a number of the States, having at the time of their adopting the Constitution, expressed a desire, in order to prevent misconstruction or abuse of its powers, that further declaratory and restrictive clauses should be added: And as extending the ground of public confidence in the Government, will best ensure the beneficent ends of its institution.

RESOLVED by the Senate and House of Representatives of the United States of America, in Congress assembled, two thirds of both Houses concurring, that the following Articles be proposed to the Legislatures of the several States, as amendments to the Constitution of the United States, all, or any of which Articles, when ratified by three fourths of the said Legislatures, to be valid to all intents and purposes, as part of the said Constitution; viz.

ARTICLES in addition to, and Amendment of the Constitution of the United States of America, proposed by Congress, and ratified by the Legislatures of the several States, pursuant to the fifth Article of the original Constitution.

Amendment I

Congress shall make no law respecting an establishment of religion, or prohibiting the free exercise thereof; or abridging the freedom of speech, or of the press; or the right of the people peaceably to assemble, and to petition the Government for a redress of grievances.

Amendment II

A well regulated Militia, being necessary to the security of a free State, the right of the people to keep and bear Arms, shall not be infringed.

Amendment III

No Soldier shall, in time of peace be quartered in any house, without the consent of the Owner, nor in time of war, but in a manner to be prescribed by law.

Amendment IV

The right of the people to be secure in their persons, houses, papers, and effects, against unreasonable searches and seizures, shall not be violated, and no Warrants shall issue, but upon probable cause, supported by Oath or affirmation, and particularly describing the place to be searched, and the persons or things to be seized.

Amendment V

No person shall be held to answer for a capital, or otherwise infamous crime, unless on a presentment or indictment of a Grand Jury, except in cases arising in the land or naval forces, or in the Militia, when in actual service in time of War or public danger; nor shall any person be subject for the same offence to be twice put in jeopardy of life or limb; nor shall be compelled in any criminal case to be a witness against himself, nor be deprived of life, liberty, or property, without due process of law; nor shall private property be taken for public use, without just compensation.

Amendment VI

In all criminal prosecutions, the accused shall enjoy the right to a speedy and public trial, by an impartial jury of the State and district wherein the crime shall have been committed, which district shall have been previously ascertained by law, and to be informed of the nature and cause of the accusation; to be confronted with the witnesses against him; to have compulsory process for obtaining witnesses in his favor, and to have the Assistance of Counsel for his defence.

Amendment VII

In Suits at common law, where the value in controversy shall exceed twenty dollars, the right of trial by jury shall be preserved, and no fact tried by a jury, shall be otherwise re-examined in any Court of the United States, than according to the rules of the common law.

Amendment VIII

Excessive bail shall not be required, nor excessive fines imposed, nor cruel and unusual punishments inflicted.

Amendment IX

The enumeration in the Constitution, of certain rights, shall not be construed to deny or disparage others retained by the people.

Amendment X

The powers not delegated to the United States by the Constitution, nor prohibited by it to the States, are reserved to the States respectively, or to the people.

DEMOCRACY IN AMERICA

INFLUENCE OF DEMOCRACY ON PROGRESS OF OPINION IN THE UNITED STATES

BY ALEXIS DE TOCQUEVILLE, 1840

Introduction by M. B. McLatchey

To this day, Alexis de Tocqueville's observations regarding the nature of American democracy are prized for their candor and insightfulness. As a Frenchman looking in from the outside, de Tocqueville reports the peculiarities of the politics and social ideas of early Americans. In his essays, he wonders aloud about the "social contract" that Americans made with one another when they founded their New Republic. In particular, he asks if in the new republic of America it is possible to protect an individual's liberties in a culture that so prizes equality. In the readings that follow, de Tocqueville ponders this question and others so relevant to our interests today that it is as if he is reporting on current-day debates.

DE TOCQUEVILLE'S PREFACE TO THE SECOND PART

The Americans live in a democratic state of society, which has naturally suggested to them certain laws and a certain political character. This same state of society has, moreover, engendered amongst them a multitude of feelings and opinions which were unknown amongst the elder aristocratic communities of Europe: it has destroyed or modified all the relations which before existed, and established others of a novel kind. The—aspect of civil society has been no less affected by these changes than that of the political world. The former subject has been treated of in the work on the Democracy of America, which I published five years ago; to examine the latter is the object of the present book; but these two parts complete each other, and form one and the same work.

I must at once warn the reader against an error which would be extremely prejudicial to me. When he finds that I attribute so many different consequences to the principle of equality, he may thence infer that I consider that principle to be the sole cause of all that takes place in the present age: but this would be to impute to me a very narrow view. A multitude of opinions, feelings, and propensities are now in existence, which owe their origin to circumstances unconnected with or even contrary to the principle of equality. Thus if I were to select the United States as an example, I could easily prove that the nature of the country, the origin of its inhabitants, the religion of its founders, their acquired knowledge, and their former habits, have exercised, and still exercise, independently of democracy, a vast influence upon the thoughts and feelings of that people. Different causes, but no less distinct from the circumstance of the equality of conditions, might be traced in Europe, and would explain a great portion of the occurrences taking place amongst us.

I acknowledge the existence of all these different causes, and their power, but my subject does not lead me to treat of them. I have not undertaken to unfold the reason of all our inclinations and all our notions: my only object is to show in what respects the principle of equality has modified both the former and the latter.

Some readers may perhaps be astonished that—firmly persuaded as I am that the democratic revolution which we are witnessing is an irresistible fact against which it would be neither desirable nor wise to struggle—I should often have had occasion in this book to address language of such severity to those democratic communities which this revolution has brought into being. My answer is simply, that it is because I am not an adversary of democracy, that I have sought to speak of democracy in all sincerity.

Men will not accept truth at the hands of their enemies, and truth is seldom offered to them by their friends: for this reason I have spoken it. I was persuaded that many would take upon themselves to announce the new blessings which the principle of equality promises to mankind, but that few would dare to point out from afar the dangers with which it threatens them. To those perils therefore I have turned my chief attention, and believing that I had discovered them clearly, I have not had the cowardice to leave them untold.

I trust that my readers will find in this Second Part that impartiality which seems to have been remarked in the former work. Placed as I am in the midst of the conflicting opinions between which we are divided, I have endeavored to suppress within me for a time the favorable sympathies or the adverse emotions with which each of them inspires me. If those who read this book can find a single sentence intended to flatter any of the great parties which have agitated my country, or any of those petty factions which now harass and weaken it, let such readers raise their voices to accuse me.

The subject I have sought to embrace is immense, for it includes the greater part of the feelings and opinions to which the new state of society has given birth. Such a subject is doubtless above my strength, and in treating it I have not succeeded in satisfying myself. But, if I have not been able to reach the goal which I had in view, my readers will at least do me the justice to acknowledge that I have conceived and followed up my undertaking in a spirit not unworthy of success.

A. De T.

March, 1840

SECTION 2: INFLUENCE OF DEMOCRACY ON THE FEELINGS OF AMERICANS

Why Democratic Nations Show A More Ardent And Enduring Love Of Equality Than Of Liberty

The first and most intense passion which is engendered by the equality of conditions is, I need hardly say, the love of that same equality. My readers will therefore not be surprised that I speak of its before all others. Everybody has remarked that in our time, and especially in France, this passion for equality is every day gaining ground in the human heart. It has been said a hundred times that our contemporaries are far more ardently and tenaciously attached to equality than to freedom; but as I do not find that the causes of the fact have been sufficiently analyzed, I shall endeavor to point them out.

It is possible to imagine an extreme point at which freedom and equality would meet and be confounded together. Let us suppose that all the members of the community take a part in the government, and that each of them has an equal right to take a part in it. As none is different from his fellows, none can exercise a tyrannical power: men will be perfectly free, because they will all be entirely equal; and they will all be perfectly equal, because they will be entirely free. To this ideal state democratic nations tend. Such is the completest form that equality can assume upon earth; but there are a thousand others which, without being equally perfect, are not less cherished by those nations.

The principle of equality may be established in civil society, without prevailing in the political world. Equal rights may exist of indulging in the same pleasures, of entering the same professions, of frequenting the same places—in a word, of living in the same manner and seeking wealth by the same means, although all men do not take an equal share in the government. A kind of equality may even be established in the political world, though there should be no political freedom there. A man may be the equal of all his countrymen save one, who is the master of all without distinction, and who selects equally from among them all the agents of his power. Several other combinations might be easily imagined, by which very great equality would be united to institutions more or less free, or even to institutions wholly without freedom. Although men cannot become absolutely equal unless they be entirely free, and consequently equality, pushed to its furthest extent, may be confounded with freedom, yet there is good reason for distinguishing the one from the other. The taste which men have for liberty, and that which they feel for equality, are, in fact, two different things; and I am not afraid to add that, amongst democratic nations, they are two unequal things.

Upon close inspection, it will be seen that there is in every age some peculiar and preponderating fact with which all others are connected; this fact almost always gives birth to some pregnant idea or some ruling passion, which attracts to itself, and bears away in its course, all the feelings and opinions of the time: it is like a great stream, towards which each of the surrounding rivulets seems to flow. Freedom has appeared in the world at different times and under various forms; it has not been exclusively bound to any social condition, and it is not confined to democracies. Freedom cannot, therefore, form the distinguishing characteristic of democratic ages. The peculiar and preponderating fact which marks those ages as its own is the equality of conditions; the ruling passion of men in those periods is the love of this equality. Ask not what singular charm the men of democratic ages find in being equal, or what special reasons they may have for clinging so tenaciously to equality rather than to the other advantages which society holds out to them: equality is the distinguishing characteristic of the age they live in; that, of itself, is enough to explain that they prefer it to all the rest.

But independently of this reason there are several others, which will at all times habitually lead men to prefer equality to freedom. If a people could ever succeed in destroying, or even in diminishing, the equality which prevails in its own body, this could only be accomplished by long and laborious efforts. Its social condition must be modified, its laws abolished, its opinions superseded, its habits changed, its manners corrupted. But political liberty is more easily lost; to neglect to hold it fast is to allow it to escape. Men therefore not only cling to equality because it is dear to them; they also adhere to it because they think it will last forever.

That political freedom may compromise in its excesses the tranquillity, the property, the lives of individuals, is obvious to the narrowest and most unthinking minds. But, on the contrary, none but attentive and clear-sighted men perceive the perils with which equality threatens us, and they commonly avoid pointing them out. They know that the calamities they apprehend are remote, and flatter themselves that they will only fall upon future generations, for which the present generation takes but little thought. The evils which freedom sometimes brings with it are immediate; they are apparent to all, and all are more or less affected by them. The evils which extreme equality may produce are slowly disclosed; they creep gradually into the social frame; they are only seen at intervals, and at the moment at which they become most violent habit already causes them to be no longer felt. The advantages which freedom brings are only shown by length of time; and it is always easy to mistake the cause in which they originate. The advantages of equality are instantaneous, and they may constantly be traced from their source. Political liberty bestows exalted pleasures, from time to time, upon a certain number of citizens. Equality every day confers a number of small enjoyments on every man. The charms of equality are every instant felt, and are within the reach of all; the noblest hearts are not insensible to them, and the most vulgar souls exult in them. The passion which equality engenders must therefore be at once strong and general. Men cannot enjoy political liberty unpurchased by some sacrifices, and they never obtain it without great exertions. But the pleasures of equality are self-proffered: each of the petty incidents of life seems to occasion them, and in order to taste them nothing is required but to live.

Democratic nations are at all times fond of equality, but there are certain epochs at which the passion they entertain for it swells to the height of fury. This occurs at the moment when the old social system, long menaced, completes its own destruction after a last intestine struggle, and when the barriers of rank are at length thrown down. At such times men pounce upon equality as their booty, and they cling to it as to some precious treasure which they fear to lose. The passion for equality penetrates on every side into men's hearts, expands there, and fills them entirely. Tell them not that by this blind surrender of themselves to an exclusive passion they risk their dearest interests: they are deaf. Show them not freedom escaping from their grasp, whilst they are looking another way: they are blind—or rather, they can discern but one sole object to be desired in the universe.

What I have said is applicable to all democratic nations: what I am about to say concerns the French alone. Amongst most modern nations, and especially amongst all those of the Continent of Europe, the taste and the idea of freedom only began to exist and to extend themselves at the time when social conditions were tending to equality, and as a consequence of that very equality. Absolute kings were the most efficient levellers of ranks amongst their subjects. Amongst these nations equality preceded freedom: equality was therefore a fact of some standing when freedom was still a novelty: the one had already created customs, opinions, and laws belonging to it, when the other, alone and for the first time, came into actual existence. Thus the latter was still only an affair of opinion and of taste, whilst the former had already crept into the habits of the people, possessed itself of their manners, and given a particular turn to the smallest actions of their lives. Can it be wondered that the men of our own time prefer the one to the other?

I think that democratic communities have a natural taste for freedom: left to themselves, they will seek it, cherish it, and view any privation of it with regret. But for equality, their passion is ardent, insatiable, incessant, invincible: they call for equality in freedom; and if they cannot obtain that, they still call for equality in slavery. They will endure poverty, servitude, barbarism—but they will not endure aristocracy. This is true at all times, and especially true in our own. All men and all powers seeking to cope with this irresistible passion, will be overthrown and destroyed by it. In our age, freedom cannot be established without it, and despotism itself cannot reign without its support.

OF INDIVIDUALISM IN DEMOCRATIC COUNTRIES

I have shown how it is that in ages of equality every man seeks for his opinions within himself: I am now about to show how it is that, in the same ages, all his feelings are turned towards himself alone. Individualism *a is a novel expression, to which a novel idea has given birth. Our fathers were only acquainted with egotism. Egotism is a passionate and exaggerated love of self, which leads a man to connect everything with his own person, and to prefer himself to everything in the world. Individualism is a mature and calm feeling, which disposes each member of the community to sever himself from the mass of his fellow-creatures; and to draw apart with his family and his friends; so that, after he has thus formed a little circle of his own, he willingly leaves society at large to itself. Egotism originates in blind instinct: individualism proceeds from erroneous judgment more than from depraved feelings; it originates as much in the deficiencies of the mind as in the perversity of the heart. Egotism blights the germ of all virtue; individualism, at first, only saps the virtues of public life; but, in the long run, it attacks and destroys all others, and is at length absorbed in downright egotism. Egotism is a vice as old as the world, which does not belong to one form of society more than to another: individualism is of democratic origin, and it threatens to spread in the same ratio as the equality of conditions.

[I adopt the expression of the original, however strange it may seem to the English ear, partly because it illustrates the remark on the introduction of general terms into democratic language which was made in a preceding chapter, and partly because I know of no English word exactly equivalent to the expression. The chapter itself defines the meaning attached to it by the author. – Translator's Note.]

Amongst aristocratic nations, as families remain for centuries in the same condition, often on the same spot, all generations become as it were contemporaneous. A man almost always knows his forefathers, and respects them: he thinks he already sees his remote descendants, and he loves them. He willingly imposes duties on himself towards the former and the latter; and he will frequently sacrifice his personal gratifications to those who went before and to those who will come after him. Aristocratic institutions have, moreover, the effect of closely binding every man to several of his fellow-citizens. As the classes of an aristocratic people are strongly marked and permanent, each of them is regarded by its own members as a sort of lesser country, more tangible and more cherished than the country at large. As in aristocratic communities all the citizens occupy fixed positions, one above the other, the result is that each of them always sees a man above himself whose patronage is necessary to him, and below himself another man whose co-operation he may claim. Men living in aristocratic ages are therefore almost always closely attached to something placed out of their own sphere, and they are often disposed to forget themselves. It is true that in those ages the notion of human fellowship is faint, and that men seldom think of sacrificing themselves for mankind; but they often sacrifice themselves for other men. In democratic ages, on the contrary, when the duties of each individual to the race are much more clear, devoted service to any one man becomes more rare; the bond of human affection is extended, but it is relaxed.

Amongst democratic nations new families are constantly springing up, others are constantly falling away, and all that remain change their condition; the woof of time is every instant broken, and the track of generations effaced. Those who went before are soon forgotten; of those who will come after no one has any idea: the interest of man is confined to those in close propinquity to himself. As each class approximates to other classes, and intermingles with them, its members become indifferent and as strangers to one another. Aristocracy had made a chain of all the members of the community, from the peasant to the king: democracy breaks that chain, and severs every link of it. As social conditions become more equal, the number of persons increases who, although they are neither rich enough nor powerful enough to exercise any great influence over their fellow-creatures, have nevertheless acquired or retained sufficient education and fortune to satisfy their own wants. They owe nothing to any man, they expect nothing from any man; they acquire the habit of always considering themselves as standing alone, and they are apt to imagine that their whole destiny is in their own hands. Thus not only does democracy make every man forget his ancestors, but it hides his descendants, and separates his contemporaries from him; it throws him back forever upon himself alone, and threatens in the end to confine him entirely within the solitude of his own heart.

INDIVIDUALISM STRONGER AT THE CLOSE OF A DEMOCRATIC REVOLUTION THAN AT OTHER PERIODS

The period when the construction of democratic society upon the ruins of an aristocracy has just been completed, is especially that at which this separation of men from one another, and the egotism resulting from it, most forcibly strike the observation. Democratic communities not only contain a large number of independent citizens, but they are constantly filled with men who, having entered but yesterday upon their independent condition, are intoxicated with their new power. They entertain a presumptuous confidence in their strength, and as they do not suppose that they can henceforward ever have occasion to claim the assistance of their fellow-creatures, they do not scruple to show that they care for nobody but themselves.

An aristocracy seldom yields without a protracted struggle, in the course of which implacable animosities are kindled between the different classes of society. These passions survive the victory, and traces of them may be observed in the midst of the democratic confusion which ensues. Those members of the community who were at the top of the late gradations of rank cannot immediately forget their former greatness; they will long regard themselves as aliens in the midst of the newly composed society. They look upon all those whom this state of society has made their equals as oppressors, whose destiny can excite no sympathy; they have lost sight of their former equals, and feel no longer bound by a common interest to their fate: each of them, standing aloof, thinks that he is reduced to care for himself alone. Those, on the contrary, who were formerly at the foot of the social scale, and who have been brought up to the common level by a sudden revolution, cannot enjoy their newly acquired independence without secret uneasiness; and if they meet with some of their former superiors on the same footing as themselves, they stand aloof from them with an expression of triumph and of fear. It is, then, commonly at the outset of democratic society that citizens are most disposed to live apart. Democracy leads men not to draw near to their fellow-creatures; but democratic revolutions lead them to shun each other, and perpetuate in a state of equality the animosities which the state of inequality engendered. The great advantage of the Americans is that they have arrived at a state of democracy without having to endure a democratic revolution; and that they are born equal, instead of becoming so.

BEN FRANKLIN READINGS

Autobiography
The Way to Wealth
Constitutional Convention Address on Prayer

BY BEN FRANKLIN (1706 – 1790)

Introduction by M. B. McLatchey

Benjamin Franklin's 18th-century aphorisms read like a modern and uniquely American rendering of the ancients that he read and loved: *Socrates, Aristotle, and Cicero.* Against a tide of political discord, human folly, and national turmoil, Franklin fought for the very virtues that these ancient philosophers and statesmen died defending: *wisdom over wealth; truth over treaty-making; character over compromise; virtue over power.*

For Franklin, as for the ancients, a debt in one's character is always a more serious matter than any national debt. This is a theme whose defending he will make his life's work. It is also a call to arms that he amplifies in the following readings: an excerpt from his autobiography; an address he delivers to his peers at the Constitutional Convention in 1787; and excerpts from *"The Way to Wealth"* – his essay that was widely distributed and first published in 1758 as the untitled preface to *Poor Richard's Almanack.*

Many scholars have argued that Franklin's writings – particularly his essay *"The Way to Wealth"* – deserve to take their place, along with the *Declaration of Independence* and the *U.S. Constitution,* as one of the three foremost American texts of the eighteenth century. At a minimum, Franklin deserves our attention for his relentless campaign to reinterpret for a modern age the wisdom and virtue of the ancients. Franklin passes on this wisdom in expressions so familiar they have become part of the American psyche.

AUTOBIOGRAPHY

BY BEN FRANKLIN (Published 1791)

Writing the Autobiography in his 79th year, Franklin crafts his life story as a letter to his son, looking back to when, at age 22, he undertook "the bold and arduous project of arriving at moral perfection."

Before I enter upon my public appearance in business, it may be well to let you know the then state of my mind with regard to my principles and morals, that you may see how far those influenced the future events of my life. My parents had early given me religious impressions, and brought me through my childhood piously in the Dissenting way. But I was scarce fifteen, when, after doubting by turns of several points, as I found them disputed in the different books I read, I began to doubt of Revelation itself. Some books against Deism fell into my hands; they were said to be the substance of sermons preached at Boyle's Lectures. It happened that they wrought an effect on me quite contrary to what was intended by them; for the arguments of the Deists, which were quoted to be refuted, appeared to me much stronger than the refutations; in short, I soon became a thorough Deist. My arguments perverted some others, particularly Collins and Ralph; but, each of them having afterwards wronged me greatly without the least compunction, and recollecting Keith's conduct towards me (who was another freethinker), and my own towards Vernon and Miss Read, which at times gave me great trouble, I began to suspect that this doctrine, though it might be true, was not very useful. My London pamphlet, which had for its motto these lines of Dryden:

"Whatever is, is right. Though purblind man Sees but a part o' the chain, the nearest link: His eyes not carrying to the equal beam, That poises all above;" and from the attributes of God, his infinite wisdom, goodness and power, concluded that nothing could possibly be wrong in the world, and that vice and virtue were empty distinctions, no such things existing, appeared now not so clever a performance as I once thought it; and I doubted whether some error had not insinuated itself unperceived into my argument, so as to infect all that followed, as is common in metaphysical reasoning.

I grew convinced that truth, sincerity and integrity in dealings between man and man were of the utmost importance to the felicity of life; and I formed written resolutions, which still remain in my journal book, to practice them ever while I lived. Revelation had indeed no weight with me, as such; but I entertained an opinion that, though certain actions might not be bad because they were forbidden by it, or good because it commanded them, yet probably these actions might be forbidden because they were bad for us, or commanded because they were beneficial to us, in their own natures, all the circumstances of things considered. And this persuasion, with the kind hand of Providence, or some guardian angel, or accidental favorable circumstances and situations, or all together, preserved me, thro' this dangerous time of youth, and the hazardous situations I was sometimes in among strangers, remote from the eye and advice of my father, without any willful gross immorality or injustice, that might have been expected from my want of religion. I say willful, because the instances I have mentioned had something of necessity in them, from my youth, inexperience, and the knavery of others. I had therefore a tolerable character to begin the world with; I valued it properly, and determined to preserve it.

Continuation of the Account of my Life, begun at Passy, near Paris, 1784.

It is some time since I received the above letters, but I have been too busy till now to think of complying with the request they contain. It might, too, be much better done if I were at home among my papers, which would aid my memory, and help to ascertain dates; but my return being uncertain and having just now a little leisure, I will endeavor to recollect and write what I can; if I live to get home, it may there be corrected and improved.

Not having any copy here of what is already written, I know not whether an account is given of the means I used to establish the Philadelphia public library, which, from a small beginning, is now become so considerable, though I remember to have come down to near the time of that transaction (1730). I will therefore begin here with an account of it, which may be struck out if found to have been already given.

At the time I established myself in Pennsylvania, there was not a good bookseller's shop in any of the colonies to the southward of Boston. In New York and Philadelphia the printers were indeed stationers; they sold only paper, etc., almanacs, ballads, and a few common school-books. Those who loved reading were obliged to send for their books from England; the members of the Junto had each a few. We had left the alehouse, where we first met, and hired a room to hold our club in. I proposed that we should all of us bring our books to that room, where they would not only be ready to consult in our conferences, but become a common benefit, each of us being at liberty to borrow such as he wished to read at home. This was accordingly done, and for some time contented us.

Finding the advantage of this little collection, I proposed to render the benefit from books more common, by commencing a public subscription library. I drew a sketch of the plan and rules that would be necessary, and got a skillful conveyancer, Mr. Charles Brockden, to put the whole in form of articles of agreement to be subscribed, by which each subscriber engaged to pay a certain sum down for the first purchase of books, and an annual contribution for increasing them. So few were the readers at that time in Philadelphia, and the majority of us so poor, that I was not able, with great industry, to find more than fifty persons, mostly young tradesmen, willing to pay down for this purpose forty shillings each, and ten shillings per annum. On this little fund we began. The books were imported; the library wag opened one day in the week for lending to the subscribers, on their promissory notes to pay double the value if not duly returned. The institution soon manifested its utility, was imitated by other towns, and in other provinces. The libraries were augmented by donations; reading became fashionable; and our people, having no public amusements to divert their attention from study, became better acquainted with books, and in a few years were observed by strangers to be better instructed and more intelligent than people of the same rank generally are in other countries.

When we were about to sign the above-mentioned articles, which were to be binding upon us, our heirs, etc., for fifty years, Mr. Brockden, the scrivener, said to us, "You are young men, but it is scarcely probable that any of you will live to see the expiration of the term fixed in the instrument." A number of us, however, are yet living; but the instrument was after a few years rendered null by a charter that incorporated and gave perpetuity to the company.

The objections and reluctances I met with in soliciting the subscriptions, made me soon feel the impropriety of presenting one's self as the proposer of any useful project, which might be supposed to raise one's reputation in the smallest degree above that of one's neighbors, when one has need of their assistance to accomplish that project. I therefore put myself as much as I could out of sight, and stated it as a scheme of a number of friends, who had requested me to go about and propose it to such as they thought lovers of reading. In this way my affair went on more smoothly, and I ever after practiced it on such occasions; and, from my frequent successes, can heartily recommend it. The present little sacrifice of your vanity will afterwards be amply repaid. If it remains a while uncertain to whom the merit belongs, some one more vain than yourself will be encouraged to claim it, and then even envy will be disposed to do you justice by plucking those assumed feathers, and restoring them to their right owner.

This library afforded me the means of improvement by constant study, for which I set apart an hour or two each day, and thus repaired in some degree the loss of the learned education my father once intended for me. Reading was the only amusement I allowed myself. I spent no time in taverns, games, or frolics of any kind; and my industry in my business continued as indefatigable as it was necessary. I was indebted for my printing-house; I had a young family coming on to be educated, and I had to contend with for business two printers, who were established in the place before me. My circumstances, however, grew daily easier. My original habits of frugality continuing, and my father having, among his instructions to me when a boy, frequently repeated a proverb of Solomon, "Seest thou a man diligent in his calling, he shall stand before kings, he shall not stand before mean men," I from thence considered industry as a means of obtaining wealth and distinction, which encouraged me, though I did not think that I should ever literally stand before kings, which, however, has since happened; for I have stood before five, and even had the honor of sitting down with one, the King of Denmark, to dinner.

We have an English proverb that says, "He that would thrive, must ask his wife." It was lucky for me that I had one as much disposed to industry and frugality as myself. She assisted me cheerfully in my business, folding and stitching pamphlets, tending shop, purchasing old linen rags for the papermakers, etc., etc. We kept no idle servants, our table was plain and simple, our furniture of the cheapest. For instance, my breakfast was a long time bread and milk (no tea), and I ate it out of a two penny earthen porringer, with a pewter spoon. But mark how luxury will enter families, and make a progress, in spite of principle: being called one morning to breakfast, I found it in a China bowl, with a spoon of silver! They had been bought for me without my knowledge by my wife, and had cost her the enormous sum of three-and-twenty shillings, for which she had no other excuse or apology to make, but that she thought her husband deserved a silver spoon and China bowl as well as any of his neighbors. This was the first appearance of plate and China in our house, which afterward, in a course of years, as our wealth increased, augmented gradually to several hundred pounds in value.

I had been religiously educated as a Presbyterian; and though some of the dogmas of that persuasion, such as the eternal decrees of God, election, reprobation, etc., appeared to me unintelligible, others doubtful, and I early absented myself from the public assemblies of the sect, Sunday being my studying day, I never was without some religious principles. I never doubted, for instance, the existence of the Deity; that he made the world, and governed it by his Providence; that the most acceptable service of God was the doing good to man; that our souls are immortal; and that all crime will be punished, and virtue rewarded, either here or hereafter. These I esteemed the essentials of every religion; and, being to be found in all the religions we had in our country, I respected them all, though with different degrees of respect, as I found them more or less mixed with other articles, which, without any tendency to inspire, promote, or confirm morality, served principally to divide us, and make us unfriendly to one another. This respect to all, with an opinion that the worst had some good effects, induced me to avoid all discourse that might tend to lessen the good opinion another might have of his own religion; and as our province increased in people, and new places of worship were continually wanted, and generally erected by voluntary contributions, my mite for such purpose, whatever might be the sect, was never refused.

Though I seldom attended any public worship, I had still an opinion of its propriety, and of its utility when rightly conducted, and I regularly paid my annual subscription for the support of the only Presbyterian minister or meeting we had in Philadelphia. He used to visit me sometimes as a friend, and admonish me to attend his administrations, and I was now and then prevailed on to do so, once for five Sundays successively. Had he been in my opinion a good preacher, perhaps I might have continued, notwithstanding the occasion I had for the Sunday's leisure in my course of study; but his discourses were chiefly either polemic arguments, or explications of the peculiar doctrines of our sect, and were all to me very dry, uninteresting, and unedifying, since not a single moral principle was inculcated or enforced, their aim seeming to be rather to make us Presbyterians than good citizens.

At length he took for his text that verse of the fourth chapter of Philippians, "Finally, brethren, whatsoever things are true, honest, just, pure, lovely, or of good report, if there be any virtue, or any praise, think on these things." And I imagined, in a sermon on such a text, we could not miss of having some morality. But he confined himself to five points only, as meant by the apostle, viz.: 1. Keeping holy the Sabbath day. 2. Being diligent in reading the holy Scriptures. 3. Attending duly the public worship. 4. Partaking of the Sacrament. 5. Paying a due respect to God's ministers. These might be all good things; but, as they were not the kind of good things that I expected from that text, I despaired of ever meeting with them from any other, was disgusted, and attended his preaching no more. I had some years before composed a little Liturgy, or form of prayer, for my own private use (viz., in 1728), entitled, Articles of Belief and Acts of Religion. I returned to the use of this, and went no more to the public assemblies. My conduct might be blamable, but I leave it, without attempting further to excuse it; my present purpose being to relate facts, and not to make apologies for them.

It was about this time I conceived the bold and arduous project of arriving at moral perfection. I wished to live without committing any fault at any time; I would conquer all that either natural inclination, custom, or company might lead me into. As I knew, or thought I knew, what was right and wrong, I did not see why I might not always do the one and avoid the other. But I soon found I had undertaken a task of more difficulty than I bad imagined. While my care was employed in guarding against one fault, I was often surprised by another; habit took the advantage of inattention; inclination was sometimes too strong for reason. I concluded, at length, that the mere speculative conviction that it was our interest to be completely virtuous, was not sufficient to prevent our slipping; and that the contrary habits must be broken, and good ones acquired and established, before we can have any dependence on a steady, uniform rectitude of conduct. For this purpose I therefore contrived the following method.

In the various enumerations of the moral virtues I had met with in my reading, I found the catalogue more or less numerous, as different writers included more or fewer ideas under the same name. Temperance, for example, was by some confined to eating and drinking, while by others it was extended to mean the moderating every other pleasure, appetite, inclination, or passion, bodily or mental, even to our avarice and ambition. I proposed to myself, for the sake of clearness, to use rather more names, with fewer ideas annexed to each, than a few names with more ideas; and I included under thirteen names of virtues all that at that time occurred to me as necessary or desirable, and annexed to each a short precept, which fully expressed the extent I gave to its meaning.

These names of virtues, with their precepts, were:

TEMPERANCE.   Eat not to dullness; drink not to elevation.

SILENCE.   Speak not but what may benefit others or yourself; avoid trifling conversation.

ORDER.   Let all your things have their places; let each part of your business have its time.

RESOLUTION.   Resolve to perform what you ought; perform without fail what you resolve.

FRUGALITY.   Make no expense but to do good to others or yourself; i.e., waste nothing.

INDUSTRY.   Lose no time; be always employed in something useful; cut off all unnecessary actions.

SINCERITY.   Use no hurtful deceit; think innocently and justly, and, if you speak, speak accordingly.

JUSTICE.   Wrong none by doing injuries, or omitting the benefits that are your duty.

MODERATION.   Avoid extremes; forbear resenting injuries so much as you think they deserve.

CLEANLINESS.   Tolerate no uncleanliness in body, clothes, or habitation.

TRANQUILLITY.   Be not disturbed at trifles, or at accidents common or unavoidable.

CHASTITY.   Rarely use venery but for health or offspring, never to dullness, weakness, or the injury of your own or another's peace or reputation.

HUMILITY.   Imitate Jesus and Socrates.

My intention being to acquire the habitude of all these virtues, I judged it would be well not to distract my attention by attempting the whole at once, but to fix it on one of them at a time; and, when I should be master of that, then to proceed to another, and so on, till I should have gone through' the thirteen; and, as the previous acquisition of some might facilitate the acquisition of certain others, I arranged them with that view, as they stand above. Temperance first, as it tends to procure that coolness and clearness of head, which is so necessary where constant vigilance was to be kept up, and guard maintained against the unremitting attraction of ancient habits, and the force of perpetual temptations. This being acquired and established, Silence would be more easy; and my desire being to gain knowledge at the same time that I improved in virtue, and considering that in conversation it was obtained rather by the use of the ears than of the tongue, and therefore wishing to break a habit I was getting into of prattling, punning, and joking, which only made me acceptable to trifling company, I gave Silence the second place. This and the next, Order, I expected would allow me more time for attending to my project and my studies. Resolution, once become habitual, would keep me firm in my endeavors to obtain all the subsequent virtues; Frugality and Industry freeing me from my remaining debt, and producing affluence and independence, would make more easy the practice of Sincerity and Justice, etc., etc. Conceiving then, that, agreeably to the advice of Pythagoras in his Golden Verses, daily examination would be necessary, I contrived the following method for conducting that examination.

I made a little book, in which I allotted a page for each of the virtues. I ruled each page with red ink, so as to have seven columns, one for each day of the week, marking each column with a letter for the day. I crossed these columns with thirteen red lines, marking the beginning of each line with the first letter of one of the virtues, on which line, and in its proper column, I might mark, by a little black spot, every fault I found upon examination to have been committed respecting that virtue upon that day.

THE WAY TO WEALTH: INDUSTRY PLUS FRUGALITY

BY BEN FRANKLIN (Published 1758)

ON INDUSTRY, IDLENESS AND WASTE

- A word to the wise is enough, and many words won't fill a bushel.

- The taxes are indeed very heavy, and if those laid on by the government were the only ones we had to pay, we might more easily discharge them; but we have many others, and much more grievous to some of us. We are taxed twice as much by our idleness, three times as much by our pride, and four times as much by our folly, and from these taxes the commissioners cannot ease or deliver us by allowing an abatement.

- God helps them that help themselves.

- It would be thought a hard government that should tax its people one tenth part of their time, to be employed in its service. But idleness taxes many of us much more, if we reckon all that is spent in absolute sloth, or doing of nothing, with that which is spent in idle employments or amusements, that amount to nothing. Sloth, by bringing on diseases, absolutely shortens life. Sloth, like rust, consumes faster than labor wears, while the used key is always bright.

- But dost thou love life, then do not squander time, for that's the stuff life is made of.

- How much more than is necessary do we spend in sleep! forgetting that the sleeping fox catches no poultry, and that there will be sleeping enough in the grave.

- If time be of all things the most precious, wasting time must be the greatest prodigality.

- Lost time is never found again, and what we call time-enough, always proves little enough.

- He that rises late, must trot all day, and shall scarce overtake his business at night.

- Laziness travels so slowly, that poverty soon overtakes him.

- Drive thy business, let not that it drives thee.

- Early to bed, and early to rise, makes a man healthy, wealthy and wise.

- He that lives upon hope will die fasting.

- There are no gains, without pains.

- He that hath a calling hath an office of profit and honor; but then the trade must be worked at, and the calling well followed, or neither the estate, nor the office, will enable us to pay our taxes.

- If we are industrious we shall never starve.

- Industry pays debts, while despair increases them.

- God gives all things to industry.

- Work while it is called today, for you know not how much you may be hindered tomorrow.

- One today is worth two tomorrows.

- If you were a servant, would you not be ashamed that a good master should catch you idle? Are you then your own master, be ashamed to catch yourself idle.

- When there is so much to be done for yourself, your family, your country, and your gracious king, be up by peep of day.

- Have you somewhat to do tomorrow, do it today.

- It is true there is much to be done, and perhaps you are weak handed, but stick to it steadily, and you will see great effects, for constant dropping wears away stones, and by diligence and patience the mouse ate in two the cable; and little strokes fell great oaks.

- Employ thy time well if thou meanest to gain leisure.

- Since thou art not sure of a minute, throw not away an hour.

- Leisure is time for doing something useful; this leisure the diligent man will obtain, but the lazy man never.

- Trouble springs from idleness, and grievous toil from needless ease.

- Industry gives comfort, and plenty, and respect.

- Flee pleasures, and they'll follow you.

- With our industry, we must be steady, settled and careful, and oversee our own affairs with our own eyes, and not trust too much to others.

- Keep thy shop, and thy shop will keep thee.

- If you would have your business done, go; if not, send.

- He that by the plough would thrive, Himself must either hold or drive.

- The eye of a master will do more work than both his hands.

- Want of care does us more damage than want of knowledge.

- Not to oversee workmen is to leave them your purse open.

- Trusting too much to others' care is the ruin of many.

- In the affairs of this world men are saved not by faith, but by the want of it.

- A man's own care is profitable.

- Sometimes a little neglect may breed great mischief.

ON FRUGALITY

- You may think perhaps that a little tea, or a little punch now and then, diet a little more costly, clothes a little finer, and a little entertainment now and then, can be no great Matter; but remember what Poor Richard says, many a little makes a mickle, and farther, beware of little expenses; a small leak will sink a great ship.

- Fools make feasts, and wise men eat them.

- Buy what thou hast no need of, and ere long thou shalt sell thy necessaries.

- Wise men learn by others' harms, fools scarcely by their own.

- Many a one, for the sake of finery on the back, have gone with a hungry belly, and half starved their families.

- It is hard for an empty bag to stand upright.

- Creditors have better memories than debtors.

- Creditors are a superstitious sect, great observers of set days and times.

- The borrower is a slave to the lender.

- Rather go to bed supperless than rise in debt.

- We may give advice, but we cannot give conduct.

- They that won't be counseled, can't be helped.

CONSTITUTIONAL CONVENTION ADDRESS ON PRAYER

BY BEN FRANKLIN

Delivered Thursday, June 28, 1787, Philadelphia, PA

Mr. President:

The small progress we have made after 4 or five weeks close attendance & continual reasoning with each other -- our different sentiments on almost every question, several of the last producing as many noes as ayes, is methinks a melancholy proof of the imperfection of the Human Understanding. We indeed seem to feel our own wont of political wisdom, since we have been running about in search of it. We have gone back to ancient history for models of government, and examined the different forms of those Republics which having been formed with the seeds of their own dissolution now no longer exist. And we have viewed Modern States all round Europe, but find none of their Constitutions suitable to our circumstances.

In this situation of this Assembly groping as it were in the dark to find political truth, and scarce able to distinguish it when to us, how has it happened, Sir, that we have not hitherto once thought of humbly applying to the Father of lights to illuminate our understandings? In the beginning of the contest with G. Britain, when we were sensible of danger we had daily prayer in this room for the Divine Protection. -- Our prayers, Sir, were heard, and they were graciously answered. All of us who were engaged in the struggle must have observed frequent instances of a Superintending providence in our favor. To that kind providence we owe this happy opportunity of consulting in peace on the means of establishing our future national felicity. And have we now forgotten that powerful friend? Or do we imagine that we no longer need His assistance.

I have lived, Sir, a long time and the longer I live, the more convincing proofs I see of this truth -- that *God governs in the affairs of men.* And if a sparrow cannot fall to the ground without his notice, is it probable that an empire can rise without his aid? We have been assured, Sir, in the sacred writings that "except the Lord build they labor in vain that build it." I firmly believe this; and I also believe that without his concurring aid we shall succeed in this political building no better than the Builders of Babel: We shall be divided by our little partial local interests; our projects will be confounded, and we ourselves shall be become a reproach and a bye word down to future age. And what is worse, mankind may hereafter this unfortunate instance, despair of establishing Governments by Human Wisdom, and leave it to chance, war, and conquest.

I therefore beg leave to move -- that henceforth prayers imploring the assistance of Heaven, and its blessings on our deliberations, be held in this Assembly every morning before we proceed to business, and that one or more of the Clergy of this City be requested to officiate in that service.

A VINDICATION OF THE RIGHTS OF WOMAN

WITH STRICTURES ON POLITICAL AND MORAL SUBJECTS

BY MARY WOLLSTONECRAFT (1759 – 1797)

Introduction by M.B. McLatchey

In an age of revolutions, Mary Wollstonecraft was a revolutionary. In these excerpts taken from her book *A Vindication of the Rights of Woman* (1792), she rejects accepted notions that women are helpless adornments of a household and argues that a confined existence in the home is unnatural for women. Like caged animals, she purports, they begin to exercise the same tyrannical power over their children and servants that their husbands wield over them. The antidote for women and for society, Wollstonecraft claims, is educational reform, giving women access to the same educational opportunities as men. From her homeland of England, Wollstonecraft watched as monarchies tumbled around her. A vocal supporter of anti-Royalists in the French Revolution and an observer of the American Revolution across the channel, Wollstonecraft campaigned for the same core principles for women that the revolutionaries had sought for mankind: *life, liberty, and the pursuit of happiness.*

ON THE ROOTS OF INEQUALITY

In tracing the causes that in my opinion, have degraded woman, I have confined my observations to such as universally act upon the morals and manners of the whole sex, and to me it appears clear, that they all spring from want of understanding. Whether this arises from a physical or accidental weakness of faculties, time alone can determine; for I shall not lay any great stress upon the example of a few women (Sappho, Eloisa, Mrs. Macaulay, the Empress of Russia, Madame d'Eon, etc. These, and many more, may be reckoned exceptions; and, are not all heroes, as well as heroines, exceptions to general rules? I wish to see women neither heroines nor brutes; but reasonable creatures.) who, from having received a masculine education, have acquired courage and resolution; I only contend that the men who have been placed in similar situations have acquired a similar character, I speak of bodies of men, and that men of genius and talents have started out of a class, in which women have never yet been placed.

ON THE WELFARE OF SOCIETY

I come round to my old argument; if woman be allowed to have an immortal soul, she must have as the employment of life, an understanding to improve. And when, to render the present state more complete, though everything proves it to be but a fraction of a mighty sum, she is incited by present gratification to forget her grand destination. Nature is counteracted, or she was born only to procreate and rot. Or, granting brutes, of every description, a soul, though not a reasonable one, the exercise of instinct and sensibility may be the step, which they are to take, in this life, towards the attainment of reason in the next; so that through all eternity they will lag behind man, who, why we cannot tell, had the power given him of attaining reason in his first mode of existence.

When I treat of the peculiar duties of women, as I should treat of the peculiar duties of a citizen or father, it will be found that I do not mean to insinuate, that they should be taken out of their families, speaking of the majority. "He that hath wife and children," says Lord Bacon, "hath given hostages to fortune; for they are impediments to great enterprises, either of virtue or mischief. Certainly the best works, and of greatest merit for the public, have proceeded from the unmarried or childless men." I say the same of women. But, the welfare of society is not built on extraordinary exertions; and were it more reasonably organized, there would be still less need of great abilities, or heroic virtues. In the regulation of a family, in the education of children, understanding, in an unsophisticated sense, is particularly required: strength both of body and mind; yet the men who, by their writings, have most earnestly labored to domesticate women, have endeavored by arguments dictated by a gross appetite, that satiety had rendered fastidious, to weaken their bodies and cramp their minds. But, if even by these sinister methods they really PERSUADED women, by working on their feelings, to stay at home, and fulfil the duties of a mother and mistress of a family, I should cautiously oppose opinions that led women to right conduct, by prevailing on them to make the discharge of a duty the business of life, though reason were insulted. Yet, and I appeal to experience, if by neglecting the understanding they are as much, nay, more attached from these domestic duties, than they could be by the most serious intellectual pursuit, though it may be observed, that the mass of mankind will never vigorously pursue an intellectual object, I may be allowed to infer, that reason is absolutely necessary to enable a woman to perform any duty properly, and I must again repeat, that sensibility is not reason.

ON REARING CHILDREN

Mankind seems to agree, that children should be left under the management of women during their childhood. Now, from all the observation that I have been able to make, women of sensibility are the most unfit for this task, because they will infallibly, carried away by their feelings, spoil a child's temper. The management of the temper, the first and most important branch of education, requires the sober steady eye of reason; a plan of conduct equally distant from tyranny and indulgence; yet these are the extremes that people of sensibility alternately fall into; always shooting beyond the mark. I have followed this train of reasoning much further, till I have concluded, that a person of genius is the most improper person to be employed in education, public or private. Minds of this rare species see things too much in masses, and seldom, if ever, have a good temper. That habitual cheerfulness, termed good humor, is, perhaps, as seldom united with great mental powers, as with strong feelings. And those people who follow, with interest and admiration, the flights of genius; or, with cooler approbation suck in the instruction, which has been elaborately prepared for them by the profound thinker, ought not to be disgusted, if they find the former choleric, and the latter morose; because liveliness of fancy, and a tenacious comprehension of mind, are scarcely compatible with that pliant urbanity which leads a man, at least to bend to the opinions and prejudices of others, instead of roughly confronting them.

But, treating of education or manners, minds of a superior class are not to be considered, they may be left to chance; it is the multitude, with moderate abilities, who call for instruction, and catch the color of the atmosphere they breathe. This respectable concourse, I contend, men and women, should not have their sensations heightened in the hot-bed of luxurious indolence, at the expense of their understanding; for, unless there be a ballast of understanding, they will never become either virtuous or free: an aristocracy, founded on property, or sterling talents, will ever sweep before it, the alternately timid and ferocious slaves of feeling.

ON MARRIAGE AND LOVE

Most of the evils of life arise from a desire of present enjoyment that outruns itself. The obedience required of women in the marriage state, comes under this description; the mind, naturally weakened by depending on authority, never exerts its own powers, and the obedient wife is thus rendered a weak indolent mother. Or, supposing that this is not always the consequence, a future state of existence is scarcely taken into the reckoning when only negative virtues are cultivated. For in treating of morals, particularly when women are alluded to, writers have too often considered virtue in a very limited sense, and made the foundation of it SOLELY worldly utility; nay, a still more fragile base has been given to this stupendous fabric, and the wayward fluctuating feelings of men have been made the standard of virtue. Yes, virtue as well as religion, has been subjected to the decisions of taste.

It would almost provoke a smile of contempt, if the vain absurdities of man did not strike us on all sides, to observe, how eager men are to degrade the sex from whom they pretend to receive the chief pleasure of life; and I have frequently, with full conviction, retorted Pope's sarcasm on them; or, to speak explicitly, it has appeared to me applicable to the whole human race. A love of pleasure or sway seems to divide mankind, and the husband who lords it in his little harem, thinks only of his pleasure or his convenience. To such lengths, indeed, does an intemperate love of pleasure carry some prudent men, or worn out libertines, who marry to have a safe companion, that they seduce their own wives. Hymen banishes modesty, and chaste love takes its flight.

Love, considered as an animal appetite, cannot long feed on itself without expiring. And this extinction, in its own flame, may be termed the violent death of love. But the wife who has thus been rendered licentious, will probably endeavor to fill the void left by the loss of her husband's attentions; for she cannot contentedly become merely an upper servant after having been treated like a goddess. She is still handsome, and, instead of transferring her fondness to her children, she only dreams of enjoying the sunshine of life. Besides, there are many husbands so devoid of sense and parental affection, that during the first effervescence of voluptuous fondness, they refuse to let their wives suckle their children. They are only to dress and live to please them: and love, even innocent love, soon sinks into lasciviousness when the exercise of a duty is sacrificed to its indulgence.

Personal attachment is a very happy foundation for friendship; yet, when even two virtuous young people marry, it would, perhaps, be happy if some circumstance checked their passion; if the recollection of some prior attachment, or disappointed affection, made it on one side, at least, rather a match founded on esteem. In that case they would look beyond the present moment, and try to render the whole of life respectable, by forming a plan to regulate a friendship which only death ought to dissolve.

Friendship is a serious affection; the most sublime of all affections, because it is founded on principle, and cemented by time. The very reverse may be said of love. In a great degree, love and friendship cannot subsist in the same bosom; even when inspired by different objects they weaken or destroy each other, and for the same object can only be felt in succession. The vain fears and fond jealousies, the winds which fan the flame of love, when judiciously or artfully tempered, are both incompatible with the tender confidence and sincere respect of friendship.

The man who can be contented to live with a pretty useful companion without a mind, has lost in voluptuous gratifications a taste for more refined enjoyments; he has never felt the calm satisfaction that refreshes the parched heart, like the silent dew of heaven--of being beloved by one who could understand him. In the society of his wife he is still alone, unless when the man is sunk in the brute. "The charm of life," says a grave philosophical reasoner, is "sympathy; nothing pleases us more than to observe in other men a fellow-feeling with all the emotions of our own breast."

But, according to the tenor of reasoning by which women are kept from the tree of knowledge, the important years of youth, the usefulness of age, and the rational hopes of futurity, are all to be sacrificed, to render woman an object of desire for a short time.

ON THE DESTRUCTIVENESS OF FORMING UNNATURAL DISTINCTIONS BETWEEN MEN & WOMEN

I mean, therefore, to infer, that the society is not properly organized which does not compel men and women to discharge their respective duties, by making it the only way to acquire that countenance from their fellow creatures, which every human being wishes some way to attain. The respect, consequently, which is paid to wealth and mere personal charms, is a true north-east blast, that blights the tender blossoms of affection and virtue. Nature has wisely attached affections to duties, to sweeten toil, and to give that vigor to the exertions of reason which only the heart can give. But, the affection which is put on merely because it is the appropriated insignia of a certain character, when its duties are not fulfilled is one of the empty compliments which vice and folly are obliged to pay to virtue and the real nature of things.

To illustrate my opinion, I need only observe, that when a woman is admired for her beauty, and suffers herself to be so far intoxicated by the admiration she receives, as to neglect to discharge the indispensable duty of a mother, she sins against herself by neglecting to cultivate an affection that would equally tend to make her useful and happy. True happiness, I mean all the contentment, and virtuous satisfaction that can be snatched in this imperfect state, must arise from well regulated affections; and an affection includes a duty. Men are not aware of the misery they cause, and the vicious weakness they cherish, by only inciting women to render themselves pleasing; they do not consider, that they thus make natural and artificial duties clash, by sacrificing the comfort and respectability of a woman's life to voluptuous notions of beauty, when in nature they all harmonize.

Cold would be the heart of a husband, were he not rendered unnatural by early debauchery, who did not feel more delight at seeing his child suckled by its mother, than the most artful wanton tricks could ever raise; yet this natural way of cementing the matrimonial tie, and twisting esteem with fonder recollections, wealth leads women to spurn. To preserve their beauty, and wear the flowery crown of the day, that gives them a kind of right to reign for a short time over the sex, they neglect to stamp impressions on their husbands' hearts, that would be remembered with more tenderness when the snow on the head began to chill the bosom, than even their virgin charms. The maternal solicitude of a reasonable affectionate woman is very interesting, and the chastened dignity with which a mother returns the caresses that she and her child receive from a father who has been fulfilling the serious duties of his station, is not only a respectable, but a beautiful sight. So singular, indeed, are my feelings, and I have endeavored not to catch factitious ones, that after having been fatigued with the sight of insipid grandeur and the slavish ceremonies that with cumberous pomp supplied the place of domestic affections, I have turned to some other scene to relieve my eye, by resting it on the refreshing green everywhere scattered by nature. I have then viewed with pleasure a woman nursing her children, and discharging the duties of her station with, perhaps, merely a servant made to take off her hands the servile part of the household business. I have seen her prepare herself and children, with only the luxury of cleanliness, to receive her husband, who returning weary home in the evening, found smiling babes and a clean hearth. My heart has loitered in the midst of the group, and has even throbbed with sympathetic emotion, when the scraping of the well-known foot has raised a pleasing tumult.

ON NEED FOR WOMEN TO BECOME STRONGER PROTECTORS OF SELVES, THUS OF THE SOCIETY

The preposterous distinctions of rank, which render civilization a curse, by dividing the world between voluptuous tyrants, and cunning envious dependents, corrupt, almost equally, every class of people, because respectability is not attached to the discharge of the relative duties of life, but to the station, and when the duties are not fulfilled, the affections cannot gain sufficient strength to fortify the virtue of which they are the natural reward. Still there are some loop-holes out of which a man may creep, and dare to think and act for himself; but for a woman it is an herculean task, because she has difficulties peculiar to her sex to overcome, which require almost super-human powers.

A truly benevolent legislator always endeavors to make it the interest of each individual to be virtuous; and thus private virtue becoming the cement of public happiness, an orderly whole is consolidated by the tendency of all the parts towards a common center. But, the private or public virtue of women is very problematical; for Rousseau, and a numerous list of male writers, insist that she should all her life, be subjected to a severe restraint, that of propriety. Why subject her to propriety--blind propriety, if she be capable of acting from a nobler spring, if she be an heir of immortality? Is sugar always to be produced by vital blood? Is one half of the human species, like the poor African slaves, to be subject to prejudices that brutalize them, when principles would be a surer guard only to sweeten the cup of man? Is not this indirectly to deny women reason? for a gift is a mockery, if it be unfit for use.

Women are in common with men, rendered weak and luxurious by the relaxing pleasures which wealth procures; but added to this, they are made slaves to their persons, and must render them alluring, that man may lend them his reason to guide their tottering steps aright. Or should they be ambitious, they must govern their tyrants by sinister tricks, for without rights there cannot be any incumbent duties. The laws respecting woman, which I mean to discuss in a future part, make an absurd unit of a man and his wife; and then, by the easy transition of only considering him as responsible, she is reduced to a mere cypher.

The being who discharges the duties of its station, is independent; and, speaking of women at large, their first duty is to themselves as rational creatures, and the next, in point of importance, as citizens, is that, which includes so many, of a mother. The rank in life which dispenses with their fulfilling this duty, necessarily degrades them by making them mere dolls. Or, should they turn to something more important than merely fitting drapery upon a smooth block, their minds are only occupied by some soft platonic attachment; or, the actual management of an intrigue may keep their thoughts in motion; for when they neglect domestic duties, they have it not in their power to take the field and march and counter-march like soldiers, or wrangle in the senate to keep their faculties from rusting.